GW00726747

ISBN 978-0-266-59681-3
PIBN 10873059

THE LOEB CLASSICAL LIBRARY

EDITED BY

E. CAPPS, PH.D., LL.D.   T. E. PAGE, LITT.D.
W. H. D. ROUSE, LITT.D.

PETRONIUS
SENECA
APOCOLOCYNTOSIS

First Printed 1913
Reprinted 1916, 1922, 1925

PETRONIUS

WITH AN ENGLISH TRANSLATION BY

MICHAEL HESELTINE

SENECA
APOCOLOCYNTOSIS

WITH AN ENGLISH TRANSLATION BY

W. H. D. ROUSE, M.A. LITT. D.

LONDON: WILLIAM HEINEMANN LTD.
NEW YORK: G. P. PUTNAM'S SONS
MCMXXV

Printed in Great Britain by
Woods and Sons, Ltd., London N. 1

CONTENTS

INTRODUCTION

THE author of the *Satyricon* is identified by the large majority of scholars with Gaius Petronius,[1] the courtier of Nero. There is a long tradition in support of the identification, and the probability that it is correct appears especially strong in the light of Tacitus's account of the character and death of Gaius Petronius in the eighteenth and nineteenth chapters of the sixteenth book of the Annals. Mr. John Jackson has translated the passage as follows:

"Petronius deserves a word in retrospect. He was a man who passed his days in sleep, his nights in the ordinary duties and recreations of life: others had achieved greatness by the sweat of their brows—Petronius idled into fame. Unlike most who walk the road to ruin, he was never regarded as either debauchee or wastrel, but rather as the finished artist in extravagance. In both word and action, he displayed a freedom and a sort of self-abandonment which were welcomed as the indiscretions of an unsophisticated nature. Yet, in his proconsulship of Bithynia, and later as consul elect, he showed himself an energetic and capable administrator. Then came the revulsion: his genuine or affected vices won him admittance into the narrow circle of Nero's intimates, and he became the Arbiter of Elegance, whose sanction alone divested pleasure of vulgarity and luxury of grossness.

[1] He is called Titus Petronius by Plutarch (De Adulatore et Amico, 27).

"His success aroused the jealousy of Tigellinus against a possible rival—a professor of voluptuousness better equipped than himself. Playing on the emperor's lust for cruelty, to which all other lusts were secondary, he suborned a slave to turn informer, charged Petronius with his friendship for Scaevinus, deprived him of the opportunity of defence, and threw most of his household into prison.

"At that time, it happened, the court had migrated to Campania; and Petronius had reached Cumae, when his detention was ordered. He disdained to await the lingering issue of hopes and fears: still, he would not take a brusque farewell of life. An incision was made in his veins: they were bound up under his directions, and opened again, while he conversed with his friends—not on the gravest of themes, nor in the key of the dying hero. He listened to no disquisitions on the immortality of the soul or the dogmas of philosophy, but to frivolous song and playful verses. Some of his slaves tasted of his bounty, others of the whip. He sat down to dinner, and then drowsed a little; so that death, if compulsory, should at least be natural. Even in his will, he broke through the routine of suicide, and flattered neither Nero nor Tigellinus nor any other of the mighty: instead, he described the emperor's enormities; added a list of his catamites, his women, and his innovations in lasciviousness; then sealed the document, sent it to Nero, and broke his signet-ring to prevent it from being used to endanger others."

The reflection arises at once that, given the *Satyricon*, this kind of book postulates this kind of author. The loose tongue, the levity, and the love of style are common to both. If books betray their writers

INTRODUCTION

characteristics, Gaius Petronius, as seen by Tacitus, had the imagination and experience needed to depict the adventures of Encolpius.

There is a little evidence, still based on the primary assumption, more exact in its bearing. The *Satyricon* contains a detailed criticism of and a poem directed against the style of a writer who must be Lucan. Gaius Petronius was not the man to pass over the poet, epigrammatist, and courtier, in whose epoch and circle he himself shone. He may have deplored Lucan's poetic influence, but he could not neglect it, for Lucan was essentially the singer of his own day. No age was so favourable as that of Nero for the introduction into a supremely scandalous tale of a reasoned and appreciative review of the *Pharsalia,* the outstanding poem of the time.

The criticism of the schools of rhetoric in their effect upon education and language, and the general style of the book in reflective and descriptive passages, point more vagu l to a similar date of composition.

Gaius Petronius found in his work a form which allowed complete expression to the many sides of his active and uncontrolled intellect. Its loose construction is matched by its indifference to any but stylistic reforms; it draws no moral; it is solely and properly occupied in presenting an aspect of things seen by a loiterer at one particular corner of the world. What we possess of it is a fragment, or rather a series of excerpts from the fifteenth and sixteenth books, we know not how representative of the original whole.

Of this the best-known portion, the description of Trimalchio's dinner, was hidden from the modern world until the middle of the seventeenth century, and was first printed in 1664.[1]

It is as difficult to grasp any structural outline in the *Satyricon* as it is in *Tristram Shandy*. Both alternate with flashing rapidity between exhibitions of pedantry, attacks on pedants, and indecency, in which Sterne is the more successful because he is the less obvious.

But Petronius, so far as his plan was not entirely original, was following as model Varro's Menippean satires, and had before him the libel of Seneca on Claudius, the *Apocolocyntosis*. The traditional title of his work, *Satyricon*, is derived from the word *Satura, a medley*, and means that he was free to pass at will from subject to subject, and from prose to verse and back: it is his achievement that the threads of his story, broken as we hold them, yet show something of the colour and variety of life itself. We call his book a novel, and so pay him a compliment which he alone of Roman writers has earned.

Petronius's novel shares with life the quality of moving ceaselessly without knowing why. It differs from most existences in being very seldom dull. An anonymous writer of the eighteenth century, making Observations on the Greek and Roman Classics in a Series of Letters to a Young Nobleman,[2] is of the opinion that: "You will in no Writer, my dear Lord, meet with so much true delicacy of thought, in none with purer language." This judgment is

---

[1] See section on the text, *codex Traguriensis*.
[2] Published in London, 1753.

INTRODUCTION

meant for the age of Smollett and Fielding; but there is no question of the justice of the later remark: "You will be charmed with the ease, and you will be surprised with the variety of his characters."

These characters are one and all the product of a period in history when the primary aim of the ripest civilization in the world was money-making. It was this aim which drew Trimalchio from his unknown birthplace in Asia Minor to the glitter and luxury and unnatural passion of a South Italian town. He differs from the minor personages who crowd his dining-room only in the enormous success with which he has plied the arts of prostitution, seduction, flattery and fraud. The persons in whom the action of the novel centres, Encolpius, the mouthpiece of the author, Ascyltos, and Giton, are there by the kindness of Agamemnon, a parasite teacher of the rhetoric which ate swiftly into the heart of Latin language and thought. Giton lives by his charms, Ascyltos is hardly more than a foil to Encolpius, a quarrelsome and lecherous butt.

That part of the novel which deals with Trimalchio's dinner introduces a crowd of characters, and gives the most vivid picture extant in classical literature of the life of the small town. The pulsating energy of greed is felt in it everywhere. Men become millionaires with American rapidity, and enjoy that condition as hazardously in Cumae as in Wall Street. The shoulders of one who wallows in Trimalchio's cushions are still sore with carrying firewood for sale; another, perhaps the first undertaker who made a fortune out of extravagant funerals, a gourmet and spendthrift, sits there composing lies to baffle his hungry creditors. Trimalchio towers above them by

reason of his more stable fortunes and his colossal impudence. He can afford to delegate the conduct of his business, to grow a little negligent, even—for his accounts are six months in arrear—to care for the life of the spirit.

He believes, of course, in astrology; he sings excerpts out of tune from the last musical play, and takes phrases from the lips of the comic star whom Nero delights to honour. He has two[1] libraries, one of Greek, one of Latin books, and mythology courses through his brain in incorrigible confusion.

His fellow townsmen and guests, whom he insults, do not aspire to these heights. Dama, Seleucus, and Phileros are rich merely in the common coin of every-day talk, in the proverbial wisdom which seems to gather strength and brightness from being constantly exchanged. "A hot drink is as good as an over-coat"—"Flies have their virtues, we are nothing but bubbles"—"An old love pinches like a crab"—"It is easy when everything goes fair and square." In these phrases and their like Latin literature speaks to us for once in the tones we know in England through Justice Shallow or Joseph Poorgrass. Nearly all warm themselves with this fatuous talk of riches and drink and deaths, but one man, Ganymede, a shrewd Asiatic immigrant like Trimalchio himself, blows cold on their sentimentality with his searching talk of bread-prices in Cumae, rising pitilessly through drought and the operation of a ring of bakers in league with officials. He tells us in brilliant phrases of the starving poor, of the decay of religion, of lost pride in using good flour. Then Echion, an old-

[1] The MS. says three, and may be right; he is drunk when he boasts of them.

clothes dealer, overwhelms him with a flood of subur-
ban chatter about games, and children, and chickens,
and the material blessings of education. But Ganymede is the sole character in Petronius's novel who
brings to light the reverse side of Trimalchio's splendour. A system of local government which showers
honours upon vulgarity, and allows Trimalchio his
bath, his improved sanitation, his host of servants, his
house with so many doors that no guest may go in and
out by the same one, is invariably true to type in
leaving poor men to die in the streets. The very
existence of poverty becomes dim for Trimalchio, half
unreal, so that he can jest at Agamemnon for taking
as the theme of a set speech the eternal quarrel of
rich and poor.

Between rich and poor in Cumae the one link is
commerce in vice. Trimalchio finds Fortunata the
chorus-girl standing for sale in the open market, and
calls her up to be the partner of his sterile and un-
meaning prodigality. She has learnt all the painful
lessons of the slums; she will not grace Trimalchio's
table until dinner is over, and she has seen the plate
safely collected from his guests, and the broken meats
apportioned to his slaves; she knows the sting of
jealousy, and the solace of intoxication or tears; nor-
mally she rules him, as Petruchio ruled Katharine, with
loud assertion and tempest of words. The only other
woman present at the dinner, Scintilla, the wife of
Trimalchio's friend Habinnas, a monumental mason,
is more drunken and unseemly, and leaves behind her
a less sharp taste of character.

Trimalchio's dinner breaks up with a false alarm of
fire, and the infamous heroes of the story give Agamemnon the slip. Trimalchio vanishes, and with his loss

the story becomes fragmentary once more, and declines in interest almost as much as in decency. Its attraction lies in the verse and criticism put into the mouth of Eumolpus, a debased poet whom Encolpius meets in a picture gallery. With him the adventures of the trio continue. There is a lodging-house brawl, a voyage where they find themselves in the hands of old enemies, the ship's captain Lichas, whose wife Hedyle they appear to have led astray, and Tryphaena, a peripatetic courtesan who takes the Mediterranean coast for her province, and has some unexplained claim on Giton's affections. They settle these disputes only to be involved in a shipwreck and cast ashore at Croton, where they grow fat on their pretension to be men of fortune, and disappear from sight, Encolpius after a disgraceful series of vain encounters with a woman named Circe, and Eumolpus after a scene where he bequeaths his body to be eaten by his heirs.

Coherence almost fails long before the end: the episode in which Encolpius kills a goose, the sacred bird of Priapus, gives a hint, but no more, that the wrath of Priapus was the thread on which the whole *Satyricon* was strung. But the life of the later portions of the novel lies in the critical and poetical fragments scattered through it. These show Petronius at his best as a lord of language, a great critic, an intelligent enthusiast for the traditions of classical poetry and oratory. The love of style which was stronger in him even than his interest in manners doubly enriches his work. It brings ready to his pen the proverbs with their misleading hints of modernity,[1] the debased syntax and abuse of gender, which fell from common

[1] See especially c. 41 to 46, 57 to 59.

lips daily, but is reproduced here alone in its fullness;[1] and side by side with these mirrored vulgarisms the gravity of the attack on professional rhetoric with which the novel begins, and the weight of the teacher's defence, that the parent will have education set to a tune of his own calling; Eumolpus's brilliant exposition of the supremacy of the poet's task over that of the rhetorician or historian; the curious, violent, epic fragment by which he upholds his doctrine.

Petronius employed a pause in literary invention and production in assimilating and expressing a view upon the makers[2] of poems, prose, pictures, philosophies, and statues, who preceded him, and thereby deepened his interpretation of contemporary life. His cynicism, his continual backward look at the splendours and severities of earlier art and other morals, are the inevitable outcome of this self-education.

By far the most genuine and pathetic expressions of his weariness are the poems which one is glad to be able to attribute to him. The best of them speak of quiet country and seaside, of love deeper than desire and founded on the durable grace of mind as well as the loveliness of the flesh, of simplicity and escape from Court.[3]

[1] See e.g. the notes of Buecheler or Friedlaender on the verbs *apoculamus* (c. 62), *duxissem* (c. 57), *plovebat* (c. 44), *percolopabant* (c. 44), the nouns *agaga* (c. 69), *babaecalis* (c. 37), *bacalusias* (c. 41), *barcalae* (c. 67), *burdubasta* (c. 45), *gingilipho* (c. 73), and such expressions as *caelus hic* (c. 39), *malus Fatus* (c. 42), *olim oliorum* (c. 43), *nummorum nummos* (c. 37), and the Graecisms *saplutus* and *topanta* (c. 37).

[2] e.g. c. 1 to 5, 55, 83, 88, 118.

[3] See e.g. Poems 2, 8, 11, 13-15, and 22; of the love-poems, 25 and 26, but above all 16 and 27, which show (if they can be by him) a side of Petronius entirely hidden in the *Satyricon.*

INTRODUCTION

He knew the antidote to the fevered life which burnt him up. His book is befouled with obscenity, and, like obscenity itself, is ceasing by degrees to be part of a gentleman's education. But he will always be read as a critic; he tells admirable stories of were-wolves and faithless widows;[1] he is one of the very few novelists who can distil common talk to their purpose without destroying its flavour. The translator dulls his brilliance, and must leave whole pages in the decent obscurity of Latin: he is fortunate if he adds a few to those who know something of Petronius beyond his name and the worst of his reputation.

The thanks of the editors and the translator are due to Messrs. Weidmann of Berlin, who have generously placed at their disposal a copyright text of the *Satyricon*, the epoch-making work of the late Professor Buecheler.

Mr. H. E. Butler, Professor of Latin in the University of London, is responsible for the selection of critical notes from Buecheler's *editio maior*, the Introduction to and text of the poems, and the Bibliography: the translator is indebted to him and to the editors for invaluable assistance in attempting to meet the difficulties which a rendering of Petronius continnes to present.

MICHAEL HESELTINE.

---

[1] In c.61 through Niceros, in c. 63 through Trimalchio, and in c.111 through Eumolpus (the famous and cosmopolitan tale of the Widow of Ephesus).

THE TEXT OF PETRONIUS

The sources for the text of Petronius fall into three groups.

(1) The *codex Leidensis* (Qù1) written by Scaliger and the editions of the de Tournes (Tornaesius) 1575 and Pithou (Pithoeus) 1577. These are our authorities for the fuller collection of excerpts. This source is known as **L.**

(2) A number of MSS. of which *codex Bernensis* (357) of the 10th century is typical. This group is our authority for the abridged collection of excerpts and is known collectiv] as **O.**

(3) The *codex Traguriensis* (Paris 7989) of the 15th century, which, save for a very few brief excerpts in L and O, is our sole authority for the *cena Trimalchiɲnis.* This MS. was discovered in 1650 at Tran in Dalmatia. It is known as **H.**

The text was not put on a scientific basis till the appearance of Buecheler's *Editio maior* in 1862.

In the Apparatus Criticus the source of the most important corrections is stated, and followed by the reading given by Buecheler in his *editio minor* as the probable reading of the archetype or as the oldest reading available. The sources from which the different portions of the text are derived are indicated by the letters in the margin of the text.

THE TEXT OF PETRONIUS
SIGLA

L = codex Scaligeranus, and editions of Tornaesius and Pithoeus.

O = MSS. containing abridged excerpts of which cod. Bernensis may be regarded as typical.

H = codex Traguriensis, our sole source for the *Cena Trimalchionis*.

Note. A great number of minor corrections and alternative readings are, owing to the demands of space, omitted from the critical notes.

BIBLIOGRAPHY

Most important Editions: I. Previous to Discovery of *Cena Trimalchionis.*

1482 Editio Princeps.
  Scriptores Panegyrici Latini, containing (1) Pliny the younger's *Panegyricus.* (2) Ten other panegyrics by various authors on diverse emperors. (3) The *Agricola* of Tacitus. (4) *Petronii arbitri satyrici fragmenta: quae extant.* Printed by Antonius Zarotus at Milan; the date is approximate.

1565 The edition of Johannes Sambucus, who made use of an old MS. of his own, and added a certain amount not previously printed. Antwerp (Chr. Plantin).

1575 The edition of Jean de Tournes (Tornaesius) based (among other sources) on codex Cuiacianus, afterwards used by Scaliger. Lyons (J. Tornaesius).

1577 The edition of P. Pithon (Pithoeus) based on three MSS. now lost. Paris (M. Patissonius).

1583 The edition of Ian. Dousa with notes. Leyden (Io. Paetsius).

1610 The edition of Melchior Goldastus with notes. Frankfort (Io. Bringer for I.Th. Schoenwetter).

II. Subsequent to Discovery of *Cena Trimalchionis.*

i. Editions of *Cena.*

1664 *Petronii Fragmentum Traguriense.* Padua (P. Frambotti).

1664 ANEKΔOTON *ex Petronii Satirico,* with introduction and notes by Jo. Caius Telebomenus (Jacobus Mentelius). Paris (E. Martin).

BIBLIOGRAPHY

1665 *Petronii Fragmentum* with notes by Io. Scheffer. Upsala (Henr. Curio).

1666 *Petronii Fragmentum* ed. Th. Reinesius. Leipzig (Chr. Michael for Sigism. Coerner).

ii. Complete Editions.

1669 The edition of M. Hadrianides. Amsterdam (J. Blaeu).

1709 The edition of P. Burmann with copious notes. Utrecht (Guil. van de Water). This is the last complete commentary.

1862 The *editio maior* of F. Buecheler. Berlin (Weidmann).

1862 The *editio minor* of the same : 4th edition on which this text is based 1904 : 5th edition revised by W. Heraeus 1911.

iii. Modern Editions of *Cena*.

1891 *Cena Trimalchionis* with German notes and translations by L. Friedlaender. Leipzig (Hirzel). Second edition 1906.

1902 *Cena Trimalchionis* with English notes by W. E. Waters. Boston (B. H. Sanborn).

1905 *Cena Trimalchionis* with English notes and translation by W. D. Lowe. Cambridge (Deighton Bell).

1905 *Cena Trimalchionis* with English notes and translation by M. J. Ryan. London (Walter Scott Publishing Co.).

iv. The *Bellum Civile*.

1911 The *Bellum Civile* of Petronius, with English notes and translation by Florence T. Baldwin. New York (Columbia University Press).

BIBLIOGRAPHY

ENGLISH TRANSLATIONS

1694 The Satyr of Petronius by Mr. Burnaby. London (S. Briscoe).

1736 The Works of Petronius by Mr. Addison. London (J. Watts).

1854 and 1880 Petronius by W. K. Kelly. London (Bohn and G. Bell & Sons).

1898 Trimalchio's Dinner. H. T. Peck. New York (Dodd, Mead and Co.).

THE POEMS ATTRIBUTED TO PETRONIUS.
Poetae Latini Minores, vol. 4. Baehrens (Teubner Series).
Editio minor of Buecheler.

THE MSS. OF PETRONIUS.

1863 The MSS. of the Satyricon of Petronius Arbiter described and collated by Charles Beck. Cambridge MSS. (Riverside Press).
Editio maior of Buecheler.

CRITICISMS AND APPRECIATIONS OF PETRONIUS.

1856 The Age of Petronius by Charles Beck. Cambridge, Mass. (Metcalf).

1875 L'Opposition sous les Césars by Gaston Boissier (Un Roman de moeurs sous Néron). Paris (Hachette).

1892 Etude sur Pétrone by A. Collignon. Paris (Hachette).

1898 Studies in Frankness by C. Whibley (p. 27). London (Heinemann).

BIBLIOGRAPHY

1902 Pétrone by E. Thomas. Paris (Fontemoing).
1903 Roman Society from Nero to M. Aurelius by
    S. Dill (pp. 120-137). London (Macmillan).
1905 Life and Principate of the Emperor Nero by
    B. Henderson (pp. 291-4). London (Me-
    thuen).
1909 Post-Augustan Poetry by H. E. Butler (p. 125).
    Oxford (Clarendon Press).

BIBLIOGRAPHY.

1910 The Bibliography of Petronius by S. Gaselee
    London (East and Blades).[1]

FORGED FRAGMENTS.

In 1692, fragments, forged by a Frenchman named
Nodot, were printed in the edition published by
Leers, at Rotterdam.

In 1800 another forgery appeared. The author was
a Spaniard named Joseph Marchena. *Fragmentum
Petronii ex bibl. Sti. Gall. gallice vertit ac notis perpetuis
illustravit Lallemandus, S. Theologiae Doctor*, 1800.

---

[1] The present bibliography is based entirely on this erudite
bibliographical work.

xxii

TITUS PETRONIUS ARBITER

TITI PETRONI ARBITRI
SATYRICON

1 *LO* "Num alio genere furiarum declamatores inquietan-
tur, qui clamant: 'haec vulnera pro libertate publica
excepi; hunc oculum pro vobis impendi: date mihi ducem, qui me ducat ad liberos meos, nam succisi poplites
membra non sustinent'? Haec ipsa tolerabilia essent,
si ad eloquentiam ituris viam facerent. Nunc et rerum
tumore et sententiarum vanissimo strepitu hoc tantum
proficiunt, ut cum in forum venerint, putent se in alium
orbem terrarum delatos. Et ideo ego adulescentulos
existimo in scholis stultissimos fieri, quia nihil ex his,
quae in usu habemus, aut audiunt aut vident, sed pira-
tas cum catenis in litore stantes, sed tyrannos edicta scri-
bentes, quibus imperent filiis ut patrum suorum capita
praecidant, sed responsa in pestilentiam data, ut vir-
gines tres aut plures immolentur, sed mellitos verborum globulos et omnia dieta factaque quasi papavere et
sesamo sparsa. Qui inter haec nutriuntur, non magis
2 sapere possunt, quam bene olere, qui in culina habitant. Pace vestra liceat dixisse, primi omnium eloquentiam perdidistis. Levibus enim atque inanibus
sonis ludibria quaedam excitando effecistis, ut corpus
orationis enervaretur et caderet. Nondum iuvenes
declamationibus continebantur, cum Sophocles aut
Euripides invenerunt verba quibus deberent loqui.
Nondum umbraticus doctor ingenia deleverat, cum
Pindarus novemque lyrici Homericis versibus canere

2

THE SATYRICON OF
TITUS PETRONIUS ARBITER

"Are our rhetoricians tormented by a new tribe of 1
Furies when they cry: 'These sears I earned in the
struggle for popular rights; I sacrificed this eye for
you: where is a guiding hand to lead me to my children?
My knees are hamstrung, and cannot support my
body'? Though indeed even these speeches might
be endured if they smoothed the path of aspirants to
oratory. But as it is, the sole result of this bombastic
matter and these loud empty phrases is that a pupil
who steps into a court thinks that he has been
carried into another world. I believe that college
makes complete fools of our young men, because
they see and hear nothing of ordinary life there. It
is pirates standing in chains on the beach, tyrants pen
in band ordering sons to cut off their fathers' heads,
oracles in time of pestilence demanding the blood of
three virgins or more, honey-balls of phrases, every
word and act besprinkled with poppy-seed and sesame. 2
People who are fed on this diet can no more be sensible
than people who live in the kitchen can be savoury. With
your permission I must tell you the truth, that you
teachers more than anyone have been the ruin of true
eloquence. Your tripping, empty tones stimulate certain
absurd effects into being, with the result that the sub-
stance of your speech languishes and dies. In the age
when Sophocles or Euripides found the inevitable word
for their verse, young men were not yet being confined
to set speeches. When Pindar and the nine lyric poets
were too modest to use Homer's lines, no cloistered

timuerunt. Et ne poetas [quidem] ad testimonium citem, certe neque Platona neque Demosthenen ad hoc genus exercitationis accessisse video. `Grandis et ut ita dicam pudica oratio non est maculosa nec turgida, sed naturali pulchritudine exsurgit. Nuper ventosa istace et enormis loquacitas Athenas ex Asia commigravit animosque iuvenum ad magna surgentes veluti pestilenti quodam sidere afflavit, semelque corrupta regula eloquentia[1] stetit et obmutuit. Ad summam, quis postea[2] Thucydidis, quis Hyperidis ad famam processit? Ac ne carmen quidem sani coloris enituit, sed omnia quasi eodem cibo pasta non potuerunt usque ad senectutem canescere. Pictura quoque non alium exitum fecit, postquam Aegyptiorum audacia tam magnae artis compendiariam invenit."

3   Non est passus Agamemnon me diutius declamare in porticn, quam ipse in schola sudaverat, sed "Adulescens" inquit "quoniam sermonem habes non publici saporis et, quod rarissimum est, amas bonam mentem, non fraudabo te arte secreta. Nihil[3] nimirum in his exercitationibus doctores peccant, qui necesse habent cum insanientibus furere. Nam nisi dixerint quae adulescentuli probent, ut ait Cicero, 'soli in scholis relinquentur.' Sicut [ficti][4] adulatores cum cenas divitum captant, nihil prius meditantur quam id quod putant gratissi-

---

[1] regula eloquentia *Haasius:* eloquentiae regula.
[2] ad summam quis postea *Haasius:* qui postea ad summam.
[3] nihil *added by Buecheler.* [4] ficti *bracketed by Buecheler.*

4

pedant had yet ruined young men's brains. I need
not go to the poets for evidence. I certainly do not
find that Plato or Demosthenes took any course of
training of this kind. Great style, which, if I may say
so, is also modest style, is never blotchy and bloated.
It rises supreme by virtue of its natural beauty. Your
flatulent and formless flow of words is a modern immigrant from Asia to Athens. Its breath fell upon
the mind of ambitious youth like the influence of a
baleful planet, and when the old tradition was once
broken, eloquence halted and grew dumb. In a word,
who after this came to equal the splendour of Thney-
dides or Hyperides? Even poetry did not glow with
the colour of health, but the whole of art, nourished
on one universal diet, lacked the vigour to reach the
grey bairs of old age. The decadence in painting was
the same, as soon as Egyptian charlatans had found a
short cut to this high calling."

Agamemnon[1] would not allow me to stand declaim- 3
ing out in the colonnade longer than he had spent
sweating inside the school. "Your talk has an uncommon
flavour, young man," he said, "and what is most unusual,
you appreciate good sense. I will not therefore deceive
you by making a mystery of my art. The fact is that the
teachers are not to blame for these exhibitions. They
are in a madhouse, and they must gibber. Unless
they speak to the taste of their young masters they
will be left alone in the colleges, as Cicero remarks.[2]
Like the toadies [of Comedy] cadging after the rich
man's dinners, they think first about what is calculated

---

[1] A teacher of rhetoric. Encolpius and Ascyltus were invited
to Trimalchio's dinner as Agamemnon's pupils.
[2] See *Pro Caelio*, 17, 41.

mum auditoribus fore: nec enim aliter impetrabunt quod petunt, nisi quasdam insidias anribus fecerint: sic eloquentiae magister, nisi tanquam piscator eam imposuerit bamⱥ escam, quam scierit appetituros esse pisci-

4 eulos, sine spe praedae morabitur in scopulo. Quid ergo est? Parentes obiurgatione digni sunt, qui nolunt liberos suos severa lege proficere. Primum enim sic ut omnia, spes quoque suas ambitioni douant. Deinde cum ad vota properant, cruda adhuc studia in forum pellunt et eloquentiam, qua nihil esse maius confitentur, pueris induunt adhuc nascentibus. Quod si paterentur laborum gradus fieri, ut studiosi iuvenes lectione severa irrigarentur, ut sapientiae praeceptis animos componerent, ut verba atroci stilo effoderent, ut quod vellent imitari diu audirent, ut persuaderent[1] sibi nihil esse magnificum, quod pueris placeret: iam illa grandis oratio haberet maiestatis suae pondus. Nunc pueri in scholis ludunt, iuvenes ridentur in foro, et quod utroque turpins est, quod quisque perperam didicit, in senectute confiteri non vult. Sed ne me putes improbasse schedium Lucilianae humilitatis, quod sentio, et ipse carmine effingam:

5   Artis severac si quis ambit[2] effectus
      mentemque magnis applicat, prius mores
      frugalitatis lege poliat exacta.
      Nec curet alto regiam trucem vultu
      cliensve cenas impotentium captet,
      nec perditis addictus obruat vino

[1] ut persuaderent *added by Buecheler.*
[2] ambit *margin ed. of Tornaesius:* amat.

6

to please their audience. They will never gain their object unless they lay traps for the ear. A master of oratory is like a fisherman; he must put the particular bait on his book which he knows will tempt the little fish, or he may sit waiting on his rock with no hope of a catch. Then what is to be done? It is the **4** parents who should be attacked for refusing to allow their children to profit by stern discipline. To begin with they consecrate even their young hopefuls, like everything else, to ambition. Then if they are in a hurry for the fulfilment of their vows, they drive the unripe schoolboy into the law courts, and thrust eloquence, the noblest of callings, upon children who are still struggling into the world. If they would allow work to go on step by step, so that bookish boys were steeped in diligent reading, their minds formed by wise sayings, their pens relentless in tracking down the right word, their ears giving a long bearing to pieces they wished to imitate, and if they would convince themselves that what took a boy's fancy was never fine; then the grand old style of oratory would have its full force and splendour. As it is, the boy wastes his time at school, and the young man is a laughing-stock in the courts. Worse than that, they will not admit when they are old the errors they have once imbibed at school. But pray do not think that I impugn Lucilius's rhyme[1] about modesty. I will myself put my own views in a poem:

"If any man seeks for success in stern art and applies **5** his mind to great tasks, let him first perfect his character by the rigid law of frugality. Nor must he care for the lofty frown of the tyrant's palace, or scheme for suppers with prodigals like a client, or drown the fires of his wit with wine in the company

[1] The allusion is not known.

mentis calorem, neve plausor in scaenam[1]
sedeat redemptus histrionis ad rictus.[2]
Sed sive armigerae rident Tritonidis arces,
seu Lacedaemonio tellus habitata colono
Sirenumve domus, det primos versibus annos
Maeoniumque bibat felici pectore fontem.
Mox et Socratico plenus grege mittat habenas
liber et ingentis quatiat Demosthenis arma.
Hinc Romana manus circumfluat et modo Graio
exonerata sono mutet suffusa saporem.
Interdum subducta foro det pagina cursum
et furtiva[3] sonet celeri distincta meatu;
dein[4] epulas et bella truci memorata canore
grandiaque indomiti Ciceronis verba minetur.
His animum succinge bonis: sic flumine largo
plenus Pierio defundes pectore verba."

6   Dum hunc diligentius audio, non notavi mihi Ascylti
fugam. Et dum in hoc dictorum aestu in hortis incedo,
ingens scholasticorum turba in porticum venit, ut apparebat, ab extemporali declamatione nescio cuius, qui
Agamemnonis suasoriam exceperat. Dum ergo iuvenes
sententias rident ordinemque totius dictionis infamant,
opportune subduxi me et cursim Ascylton persequi
coepi. Sed nec viam diligenter tenebam [quia] nec
quod stabulum esset sciebam. Itaque quocunque ie-
ram, eodem revertebar, donec et cursu fatigatus et

---

[1] scenam *Heinsius:* scena.
[2] histrionis ad rictus *O. Ribbeck:* histrioni addictus.
[3] furtiva *Heinsius:* fortuna.
[4] dein *Pithoeus:* dent.

óf the wicked, or sit before the stage applauding an actor's grimaces for a price.

"But whether the fortress of armoured Tritonis smiles upon him, or the land where the Spartan farmer lives, or the home of the Sirens, let him give the years of youth to poetry, and let his fortunate soul drink of the Maeonian fount. Later, when he is full of the learning of the Socratic school, let him loose the reins, and shake the weapons of mighty Demosthenes like a free man. Then let the company of Roman writers pour about him, and, newly unburdened from the music of Greece, steep his soul and transform his taste. Meanwhile, let him withdraw from the courts and suffer his pages to run free, and in secret make ringing strains in swift rhythm; then let him proudly tell tales of feasts, and wars recorded in fierce chant, and lofty words such as undaunted Cicero uttered. Gird up thy soul for these noble ends; so shalt thou be fully inspired, and shalt pour out words in swelling torrent from a heart the Muses love."

I was listening to him so carefully that I did not 6 notice Ascyltos slipping away. I was pacing the gardens in the beat of our conversation, when a great crowd of students came out into the porch, apparently from some master whose extemporary harangue had followed Agamemnon's discourse.[1] So while the young men were laughing at his epigrams, and denouncing the tendency of his style as a whole, I took occasion to steal away and began hurriedly to look for Ascyltos. But I did not remember the road accurately, and I did not know where our lodgings were. So wherever I went, I kept coming back to

[1] A declamation on a given deliberative theme (*suasoria*), which the teacher delivered as an example to his pupils.

7 sudore iam madens accedo aniculam quandam, quae
agreste bolus vendebat, et "Rogo" inquam "mater,
numquid scis ubi ego habitem?" delectata est illa
urbanitate tam stulta et "Quidni sciam?" inquit, con-
surrexitque et coepit me praecedere. Divinam ego
putabam et . . .

Subinde ut in locum secretiorem venimus, centonem
anus urbana reiecit et "Hic" inquit "debes habitare."
Cum ego negarem me agnoscere domum, video quosdam inter titulos nudasque meretrices furtim spatian-
tes. Tarde, immo iam sero intellexi me in fornicem
esse deductum. Execratus itaque aniculae insidias
operui caput et per medium lupanar fugere coepi in
alteram partem, cum ecce in ipso aditu occurrit mihi
acque lassus ac moriens Ascyltos; putares ab eadem
anicula esse deductum. Itaque ut ridens eum consa-
8 lutavi, quid in loco tam deformi faceret quaesivi. Sudorem ille manibus detersit et "Si scires" inquit "quae
mihi acciderunt." "Quid novi" inquam "ego?" at
ille deficiens "cum errarem" inquit "per totam civitatem nec invenirem, quo loco stabulum reliquissem,
accessit ad me pater familiae et ducem se itineris
humanissime promisit. Per anfractus deinde obscu-
rissimos egressus in hunc locum me perduxit prolatoque
L peculio coepit rogare stuprum. | Iam pro cella mere-
LO trix assem exegerat, | iam ille mihi iniecerat manum,
et nisi valentior fuissem, dedissem poenas" . . .

L | Adeo ubique omnes mihi videbantur satureum
bibisse . . . iunctis viribus molestum contempsimus . . .
9 Quasi per caliginem vidi Gitona in crepidine semitae

10

the same spot, till I was tired out with walking, and dripping with sweat. At last I went up to an old **7** woman who was selling country vegetables and said, "Please, mother, do you happen to know where I live?" She was charmed with such a polite fool. "Of course I do," she said, and got up and began to lead the way. I thought her a prophetess . . . . , and when we had got into an obscure quarter the obliging old lady pushed back a patchwork curtain and said, "This should be your house." I was saying that I did not remember it, when I noticed some men and naked women walking cautiously about among placards of price. Too late, too late I realized that I had been taken into a bawdy-house. I cursed the cunning old woman, and covered my head, and began to run through the brothel to another part, when just at the entrance Ascyltos met me, as tired as I was, and half-dead. It looked as though the same old lady had brought him there. I hailed him with a laugh, and asked him what he was doing in such an unpleasant spot. He mopped himself with his hands **8** and said, "If you only knew what has happened to me." "What is it?" I said. "Well," he said, on the point of fainting, "I was wandering all over the town without finding where I had left my lodgings, when a respectable person came up to me and very kindly offered to direct me. He took me round a number of dark turnings and brought me out here, and then began to offer me money and solicit me. A woman got threepence out of me for a room, and he had already seized me. The worst would have happened if I had not been stronger than he." . . .

Every one in the place seemed to be drunk on aphrodisiacs . . . but our united forces defied our assailant. . . .

I dimly saw Giton standing on the kerb of the road **9**

stantem et in eundem locum me conieci. . . . . .
Cum quaererem numquid nobis in prandium frater
parasset, consedit puer super lectum et manantes lacrimas pollice extersit.[1]   Perturbatus ego habitu fratris,
quid accidisset, quaesivi.   Et ille tarde quidem et invitus, sed postquam precibus etiam iracundiam miscni,
"Tuus" inquit "iste frater seu comes paulo ante in
conductum accucurrit coepitque mihi velle pudorem
LO extorquere. | Cum ego proclamarem, gladium strinxit
et 'Si Lucretia es' inquit 'Tarquinium invenisti.'"
L | Quibus ego auditis intentavi in oculos Ascylti manus
et "Quid dicis" inquam "muliebris patientiae scortum, cuius ne spiritus quidem purus est?"   Inhorre-
scere se finxit Ascyltos, mox sublatis fortins manibus
longe maiore nisu clamavit: "Non taces" inquit "gladiator obscene, quem de . . . ruina harena dimisit?
Non taces, nocturne percussor, qui ne tum quidem, cum
fortiter faceres, cum pura muliere pugnasti, cuius
eadem ratione in viridario frater fui, qua nunc in
10 deversorio puer est?"   "Subduxisti te" inquam[2] "a
praeceptoris colloquio."   "Quid ego, homo stultissime,
facere dehui, cum fame morerer? An videlicet audirem
sententias, id est vitrea fracta et somniorum interpre-
tamenta?   Multo me turpior es tu hercule, qui ut foris
cenares, poetam laudasti."
Itaque ex turpissima lite in risum diffusi pacatius ad
reliqua secessimus. . . .
Rursus in memoriam revocatus iniuriae "Ascylte"
inquam "intellego nobis convenire non posse.   Itaque

[1] extersit *Pithoeus:* expressit.
[2] inquam *Pithoeus:* inquit.

12

in the dark, and hurried towards him. . . . I was asking my brother whether he had got ready anything for us to eat, when the boy sat down at the head of the bed, and began to cry and rub away the tears with his thumb. My brother's looks made me uneasy, and I asked what had happened. The boy was unwilling to tell, but I added threats to entreaties, and at last he said, "That brother or friend of yours ran into our lodgings a little while ago and began to offer me violence. I shouted out, and he drew his sword and said, 'If you are a Lucretia, you have found your Tarquin.'"

When I heard this I shook my fist in Ascyltos's face. "What have you to say?" I cried, "You dirty fellow whose very breath is unclean?" Ascyltos first pretended to be shocked, and then made a great show of fight, and roared out much more loudly: "Hold your tongue, you filthy prizefighter. You were kicked out of the ring in disgrace. Be quiet, Jack Stab-in-the-dark. You never could face a clean woman in your best days. I was the same kind of brother to you in the garden, as this boy is now in the lodgings."

"You sneaked away from the master's talk," I said. 10 "Well, you fool, what do you expect? I was perishing of hunger. Was I to go on listening to his views, all broken bottles and interpretation of dreams? By God, you are far worse than I am, flattering a poet to get asked out to dinner."

Then our sordid quarrelling ended in a shout of laughter, and we retired afterwards more peaceably for what remained to be done. . . .

But his insult came into my head again. "Ascyltos," I said, "I am sure we cannot agree. We will

13

communes sarcinulas partiamur ac paupertatem nostram privatis quaestibus temptemus expellere. Et tu litteras scis et ego. Ne quaestibus tuis obstem, aliud aliquid promittam; alioqui mille causae quotidie nos collident et per totam urbem rumoribus different." Non recusavit Ascyltos et "Hodie" inquit "quia tanquam scholastici ad cenam promisimus, non perdamus noctem. Cras autem, quia hoc libet, et habitationem mihi prospiciam et aliquem fratrem." "Tardum est" inquam "differre quod placet." . . .

Hanc tam praecipitem divisionem libido faciebat; iam dudum enim amoliri cupiebam custodem molestum, ut veterem cum Gitone meo rationem reducerem.[1] . . .

11 Postquam lustravi oculis totam urbem, in cellulam redii, osculisque tandem bona fide exactis alligo artissimis complexibus puerum fruorque votis usque ad invidiam felicibus. Nec adhuc quidem omnia erant facta, cum Ascyltos furtim se foribus admovit discussisque fortissime claustris invenit me cum fratre ludentem. Risu itaque plausuque cellulam implevit, opertum me amiculo evolvit et "Quid agebas" inquit "frater sanctissime, qui diverti contubernium[2] facis?" Nec se solum intra verba continuit, sed lorum de pera solvit et me coepit non perfunctorie verberare, adiectis etiam petulantibus dietis: "Sic dividere cum fratre nolito". . .

12 Veniebamus in forum deficiente iam die, in quo notavimus frequentiam rerum venalium, non quidem pretiosarum sed tamen quarum fidem male ambulantem obscuritas temporis facillime tegeret. Cum ergo et ipsi raptum latrocinio pallium detulissemus, uti occasione opportunissima coepimus atque in quodam angulo

[1] reducerem *Buecheler:* deducerem.
[2] qui diverti contubernium *Buecheler:* quid . i . verticontubernium.

14

divide our luggage, and try to defeat our poverty by our own earnings. You are a scholar, and so am I. Besides, I will promise not to stand in the way of your success. Otherwise twenty things a day will bring us into opposition, and spread scandal about us all over the town." Ascyltos acquiesced, and said, "But as we are engaged to supper to-night like a couple of students, do not let us waste the evening. I shall be pleased to look out for new lodgings and a new brother to-morrow?" "Waiting for one's pleasures is weary work," I replied. . . .

I went sight-seeing all over the town and then 11 came back to the little room. At last I could ask for kisses openly. I hugged the boy close in my arms and had my fill of a happiness that might be envied. All was not over when Ascyltos came sneaking up to the door, shook back the bars by force, and found me at play with my brother. He filled the room with laughter and applause, pulled me out of the cloak I had over me, and said, "What are you at, my pure-minded brother, you that would break up our partner-ship?" Not content with gibing, he pulled the strap off his bag, and began to give me a regular flogging, saying sarcastically as he did so: "Don't make this kind of bargain with your brother." . . .

It was already dusk when we came into the market. 12 We saw a quantity of things for sale, of no great value, though the twilight very easily cast a veil over their shaky reputations. So for our part we stole a cloak and carried it off, and seized the opportunity of displaying the extreme edge of it in one corner of

15

laciniam extremam concutere, si quem forte emptorem splendor vestis posset adducere. Nec diu moratus. rusticus quidam familiaris oculis meis cum muliercula comite propius accessit ac diligentius considerare pallium coepit. Invicem Ascyltos iniecit contemplationem super umeros rustici emptoris ac subito exanimatus conticuit. Ac ne ipse quidem sine aliquo motu hominem conspexi, nam videbatur ille mihi esse, qui tunicam in solitudine invenerat. Plane is ipse erat. Sed cum Ascyltos timeret fidem oculorum, ne quid temere faceret, prius tanquam emptor propius accessit detraxitque umeris laciniam et diligentius temptavit.[1] O
13 lusum fortunae mirabilem. Nam adhuc nec suturae[2] quidem attulerat rusticus curiosas manus, et[3] tanquam mendici spolium etiam fastidiose venditabat. Ascyltos postquam depositum esse inviolatum vidit et personam vendentis contemptam, seduxit me paululum a turba et "Scis," inquit "frater, rediisse ad nos thesaurum de quo querebar? Illa est tunicula adhuc, ut apparet, intactis aureis plena. Quid ergo facimus, aut quo iure rem nostram vindicamus?"

Exhilaratus ego non tantum quia praedam videbam, sed etiam quod fortuna me a turpissima suspicione dimiserat, negavi circuitu agendum, sed plane iure civili dimicandum, ut si nollent[4] alienam rem domino reddere, ad interdictum venirent.[5]

[1] tentavit *Burmann:* ternuit.
[2] suturae *Pithoeus:* futurae *and* furtivae.
[3] et *Buecheler:* sed.
[4] nollent *Buecheler:* nollet.
[5] venirent *Buecheler:* veniret. *After* veniret *the MSS. place the poem* quid faciant, *etc. (p.* 18): *it is transposed to its present position by Buecheler.*

16

the market, hoping that the bright colour might
attract a purchaser.   In a little while a countryman,
whom I knew by sight, came up with a girl, and
began to examine the cloak narrowly.   Ascyltos in
turn cast a glance at the shoulders of our country
customer,[1] and was suddenly struck dumb with astonishment. I could not look upon the man myself without a
stir, for he was the person, I thought, who had found
the shirt in the lonely spot where we lost it. He was
certainly the very man. But as Ascyltos was afraid to
trust his eyes for fear of doing something rash, he first
came up close as if he were a purchaser, and pulled the
shirt off the countryman's shoulders, and then felt it
carefully. By a wonderful stroke of luck the country- 13
man had never laid his meddling hands on the seam,
and he was offering the thing for sale with a conde-
scending air as a beggar's leavings.   When Ascyltos
saw that our savings were untouched, and what a poor
creature the seller was, he took me a little aside from
the crowd, and said, "Do you know, brother, the
treasure I was grumbling at losing has come back to us.
That is the shirt, and I believe it is still full of gold
pieces: they have never been touched. What shall we
do?   How shall we assert our legal rights?"
    I was delighted, not only because I saw a chance of
profit, but because fortune had relieved me of a very
disagreeable suspicion.   I was against any roundabout
methods.   I thought we should proceed openly by
civil process, and obtain a decision in the courts if
they refused to give up other people's property to
the rightful owners.

[1] The rustic was carrying a shirt (*tunica*) hung over his
shoulders.

14   Contra Ascyltos leges timebat et "Quis" aichat "hoc
loco nos novit, aut quis habebit dicentibus fidem?
Mihi plane placet emere, quamvis nostrum sit, quod
agnoscimus, et parvo aere recuperare potins thesaurum,
quam in ambiguam litem descendere:

LO | Quid faciant leges, ubi sola pecunia regnat,
    aut ubi paupertas vincere nulla potest?
  Ipsi qui Cynica traducunt tempora pera,[1]
    non nunquam nummis vendere vera solent.[2]
  Ergo iudicium nihil est nisi publica merces,
    atque eques in causa qui sedet, empta probat."

L | Sed praeter unum dipondium,[3] quo cicer lupinosque
destinaveramus mercari, nihil ad manum erat. Itaque
ne interim praeda discederet, vel minoris pallium ad-
dicere placuit et[4] pretium maioris compendii leviorem
facere[5] iacturam. Cum primum ergo explicuimus mer-
cem, mulier operto[6] capite, quae cum rustico steterat,
inspectis diligentius signis iniecit utramque laciniae
manum magnaque vociferatione "Latrones" [tenere][7]
clamavit. Contra nos perturbati, ne videremur nihil
agere, et ipsi scissam et sordidam tenere coepimus
tunicam atque eadem invidia proclamare, nostra esse
spolia quae illi possiderent. Sed nullo genere par erat
causa, [nam][8] et cociones[9] qui ad clamorem confluxe-
rant, nostram scilicet de more ridebant invidiam, quod
pro illa parte vindicabant pretiosissimam vestem, pro

[1] pera *Heinsius:* cera.
[2] vendere vera solent *cod. Vossianus* (verba *L*): verba
solent emere *other MSS.*
[3] dupondium sicel lupinosque quibus destinaveramus *MSS.:*
*corrected by Gronovius, Buecheler and an unknown scholar
mentioned by Boschius.*
[4] et *Buecheler:* ut.   [5] facere *Buecheler:* faceret.
[6] operto *Wouwer:* aperto.   [7] and [8] *bracketed by Buecheler.*
[9] cociones qui *Salmasius:* conciones quae.

But Ascyltos was afraid of the law: "Nobody knows 14 us in this place," he said, "and nobody will believe ·. what we say. I should certainly like to buy the thing, although it is ours and we know it. It is better to get back our savings cheaply than to embark upon the perils of a lawsuit:

"Of what avail are laws where money rules alone, and the poor suitor can never succeed? The very men who mock at the times by carrying the Cynic's scrip have sometimes been known to betray the truth for a price. So a lawsuit is nothing more than a public auction, and the knightly juror who sits listening to the case gives his vote as he is paid."

But we had nothing in hand except one sixpence,[1] with which we had meant to buy pease and lupines. And so for fear our prize should escape us, we decided to sell the cloak cheaper than we had intended, and so to incur a slight loss for a greater gain. We had just unrolled our piece, when a veiled woman, who was standing by the countryman, looked carefully at the marks, and then seized the cloak with both hands, shouting at the top of her voice, "Thieves!" We were terrified, but rather than do nothing, we began to tug at the dirty torn shirt, and cried out with equal bitterness that these people had taken some spoil that was ours. But the dispute was in no way even, and the dealers who were attracted by the noise of course laughed at our indignation, since one side was laying claim to an expensive cloak, the other to a set of rags

[1] Literally, a coin worth 2 asses.

hac pannuciam ne centonibus quidem bonis dignam.
15 Hinc Ascyltos bene risum discussit, qui silentio facto
"Videmus"[1] inquit "suam cuique rem esse carissimam;
reddant nobis tunicam nostram et pallium suum reci-
piant." Etsi rustico mulierique placebat permutatio,
advocati tamen iam poenae nocturni, qui volebant
pallium lucri facere, flagitabant uti apud se utraque
deponerentur ac postero die iudex querellam inspiceret.
Neque enim res tantum, quae viderentur in controversiam esse, sed longe aliud quaeri, quod in utraque
parte scilicet latrocinii suspicio haberetur. Iam se-
questri placebant, et nescio quis ex cocionibus, calvus,
tuberosissimae frontis, qui solebat aliquando etiam
causas agere, invaserat pallium exhibiturumque cra-
stino die affirmabat. Ceterum apparebat nihil aliud
quaeri nisi ut semel deposita vestis inter praedones
strangularetur et nos metu criminis non veniremus ad
constitutum.

Idem plane et nos volebamus. Itaque utriusque partis
votum casus adiuvit. Indignatus enim rusticus, quod
nos centonem exhibendum postularemus, misit in
faciem Ascylti tunicam et liberatos querella iussit
pallium deponere, quod solum litem faciebat . . . .

Et recuperato, ut putabamus, thesauro in deversorium
praecipites abimus praeclusisque foribus ridere acumen
non minus cocionum quam calumniantium coepimus,
quod nobis ingenti calliditate pecuniam reddidissent.

Nolo quod cupio, statim tenere,
nec victoria mi placet parata . . .

[1] videmus *Jungermann:* videamus.

which would not serve to make a decent patchwork. 15 Ascyltos now cleverly stopped their laughter by calling for silence and saying, "Well, you see, every one has an affection for his own things. If they will give us our shirt, they shall have their cloak." The country-man and the woman were satisfied with this exchange, but by this time some policemen had been called in to punish us; they wanted to make a profit out of the cloak, and tried to persuade us to leave the disputed property with them and let a judge look into our com-plaints the next day. They urged that besides the counter-claims to these garments, a far graver question arose, since each party must lie under suspicion of thiev-ing. It was suggested that trustees should be appointed, and one of the traders, a bald man with a spotty fore-head, who used sometimes to do law work, laid hands on the cloak and declared that he would produce it to-morrow. But clearly the object was that the cloak should be deposited with a pack of thieves and be seen no more, in the hope that we should not keep our appointment, for fear of being charged. ·

It was obvious that our wishes coincided with his, and chance came to support the wishes of both sides. The countryman lost his temper when we said his rags must be shown in public, threw the shirt in Ascyltos's face, and asked us, now that we had no grievance, to give up the cloak which had raised the whole quarrel....

We thought we had got back our savings. We hurried away to the inn and shut the door, and then had a laugh at the wits of our false accusers and at the dealers too, whose mighty sharpness had returned our money to us. "I never want to grasp what I desire at once, nor do easy victories delight me."

TITUS PETRONIUS ARBITER

16 LO | **Sed ut** primum beneficio Gitonis praeparata nos im-
plevimus cena, ostium non satis audaci st pitu exso-
nuit impulsum.

Cum et ipsi ergo pallidi rogaremus, quis esset,
"Aperi" inquit "iam scies." Dumque loquimur, sera
sua sponte delapsa cecidit reclusaeque subito fores
admiserunt intrantem. Mulier autem erat operto
capite, illa scilicet quae paulo ante cum rustico steterat, et "Me derisisse" inquit "vos putabatis? ego sum
ancilla Quartillae, cuius vos sacrum ante cryptam
turbastis. Ecce ipsa venit ad stabulum petitque ut
vobiscum loqui liceat. Nolite perturbari. Nec accusat
errorem vestrum nec punit, immo potins miratur, quis
deus iuvenes tam urbanos in suam regionem detulerit."

17 Tacentibus adhuc nobis et ad neutram partem adsen-
tationem flectentibus intravit ipsa, una comitata virgine, sedensque super torum meum diu flevit. Ac ne
tune quidem nos ullum adiecimus verbum, sed attoniti
expectavimus lacrimas ad ostentationem doloris paratas. Ut ergo tam ambitiosus detumuit[1] imber, retexit
superbum pallio caput et manibus inter se usque ad
articulorum strepitum constrictis "Quaenam est"
inquit "haec audacia, aut ubi fabulas etiam antecessura
sura latrocinia didicistis? misereor mediusfidius vestri;
neque enim impune quisquam quod non licuit, ad-
spexit. Utique nostra regio tam praesentibus plena
est numinibus, ut facilius possis deum quam hominem
invenire. Ac ne me putetis ultionis causa huc venisse,
aetate magis vestra commoveor quam iniuria mea.
Imprudentes enim, ut adhuc puṭo, admisistis inex-
piabile scelus. Ipsa quidem illa nocte vexata tam peri-

---

[1] detumuit *Buecheler:* detonuit.

22

Thanks to Giton, we found supper ready, and we 16
were making a hearty meal, when a timid knock
sounded at the door.

We turned pale and asked who it was. "Open the
door," said a voice, "and you will see." While we
were speaking, the bar slipped and fell of its own
accord, the door suddenly swung open, and let in our
visitor. It was the veiled woman who had stood with
the countryman a little while before. "Did you think
you had deceived me?" she said. "I am Quartilla's
maid. You intruded upon her devotions before her
secret chapel. Now she has come to your lodgings,
and begs for the favour of a word with you. Do not be
uneasy; she will not be angry, or punish you for a
mistake. On the contrary, she wonders how Heaven
conveyed such polite young men to her quarter."
We still said nothing, and showed no approval one 17
way or the other. Then Quartilla herself came in
with one girl by her, sat down on my bed, and cried for
a long while. We did not put in a word even then,
but sat waiting in amazement for the end of this
carefully arranged exhibition of grief. When this very
designing rain had ceased, she drew her proud head
out of her cloak and wrung her hands together till
the joints cracked. "You bold creatures," she said,
"where did you learn to outrival the robbers of ro-
mance? Heaven knows I pity you. A man cannot
look upon forbidden things and go free. Indeed the
gods walk abroad so commonly in our streets that it
is easier to meet a god than a man. Do not suppose
that I have come here to avenge myself. I am more
sorry for your tender years than for my own wrongs.
For I still believe that heedless youth has led you into
deadly sin. I lay tormenting myself that night and

culoso inhorrui frigore, ut tertianae etiam impetum
timeam. Et ideo medicinam somnio petii iussaque
sum vos perquirere atque impetum morbi monstrata
subtilitate lenire. Sed de remedio non tam valde
laboro; maior enim in praecordiis dolor saevit, qui me
usque ad necessitatem mortis deducit, ne scilicet
iuvenili impulsi licentia quod in sacello Priapi vidistis,
vulgetis deorumque consilia proferatis in populum.
Protendo igitur ad genua vestra supinas manus peto-
que et oro, ne nocturnas religiones iocum risumque
faciatis, neve traducere velitis tot annorum secreta,
quae vix mille homines noverunt."

18   Secundum hanc deprecationem lacrimas rursus
effudit gemitibusque largis concussa tota facie ac pectore torum meum pressit. Ego eodem tempore et
misericordia turbatus et metu, bonum animum habere
eam iussi et de utroque esse securam: nam neque
sacra quemquam vulgaturum, et si quod praeterea
aliud remedium ad tertianam deus illi monstrasset,
adiuvaturos nos divinam providentiam vel periculo
nostro. Hilarior post hanc pollicitationem facta mulier
basiavit me spissius, et ex lacrimis in risum mota
descendentes ab aure capillos meos leuta[1] manu
L duxit | et "Facio" inquit "indutias vobiscum, et a
LO constituta lite dimitto. Quod | si non adnuissetis de
hac medicina quam peto, iam parata erat in crastinum
turba, quae et iniuriam meam vindicaret et dignitatem :

---

[1] lenta *Bongarsius:* tentata.

shivering with such a dreadful chill that I even fear an attack of tertian ague. So I asked for a remedy in my dreams, and was told to find you out and allay the raging of my disease by the clever plan you would show me. But I am not so greatly concerned about a cure; deep in my heart burns a greater grief, which drags me down to inevitable death. I am afraid that youthful indiscretion will lead you to publish abroad what you saw in the chapel of Priapus, and reveal our holy rites to the mob. So I kneel with folded hands before you, and beg and pray you not to make a laughing-stock of our nocturnal worship, not to deride the immemorial mystery to which less than a thousand souls hold the key."

She finished her prayer, and again cried bitterly, 18 and buried her face and bosom in my bed, shaken all over with deep sobs. I was distracted with pity and terror together. I reassured her, telling her not to trouble herself about either point. No one would betray her devotions, and we would risk our lives to assist the will of Heaven, if the gods had showed her any further cure for her tertian ague. At this promise the woman grew more cheerful, kissed me again and again and gently stroked the long hair that fell about my ears, having passed from crying to laughter. "I will sign a peace with you," she said, "and withdraw the suit I have entered against you. But if you had not promised me the cure I want, there was a whole regiment ready for to-morrow to wipe out my wrongs and uphold my honour:

25

TITUS PETRONIUS ARBITER

Contemni turpe est, legem donare superbum;
  hoc amo, quod possum qua libet ire via.
Nam sane et sapiens contemptus iurgia nectit,
  et qui non iugulat, victor abire solet" . . . .
Complosis deinde manibus in tantum repente risum
effusa est, ut timeremus. Idem ex altera parte et
19 ancilla fecit, quae prior venerat, idem virguncula, quae
una intraverat. Omnia mimico risn exsonuerant, cum
interim nos, quae tam repentina esset mutatio animorum facta, ignoraremus ac modo nosmet ipsos modo
mulieres intueremur . . . .
L | "Ideo vetui hodie in hoc deversorio quemquam
mortalium admitti, ut remedium tertianae sine ulla
interpellatione a vobis acciperem." Ut haec dixit
Quartilla, Ascyltos quidem paulisper obstupuit, ego
autem frigidior bieme Gallica factus nullum potni
verbum emittere. Sed ne quid tristius expectarem,
comitatus faciebat. Tres enim erant mulierculae, si
quid vellent conari, infirmissimae, scilicet contra nos,
quibus si nihil aliud, virilis sexus esset. Et praecincti
certe altius eramus. Immo ego sic iam paria compo-
sueram, ut si depugnandum foret, ipse cum Quartilla
consisterem, Ascyltos cum ancilla, Giton cum virgine . . . .
Tune vero excidit omnis constantia attonitis, et
mors non dubia miserorum oculos coepit obducere . . . .
20 "Rogo" inquam "domina, si quid tristius paras,
celerius confice; neque enim tam magnum facinus
admisimus, ut debeamus torti perire" . . . .

26

"To be flouted is disgraceful, but to impose terms is glorious: I rejoice that I can follow what course I please. For surely even a wise man will take up a quarrel when he is flouted, while the man who sheds no blood commonly comes off victorious." . . .

Then she clapped her hands and suddenly burst out laughing so loud that we were frightened. The maid who had come in first did the same on one side of us, and also the little girl who had come in with Quartilla. The whole place rang with farcical laughter, 19 while we kept looking first at each other and then at the women, not understanding how they could have changed their tune so quickly. . . .

" I forbade any mortal man to enter this inn to-day, just so that I might get you to cure me of my tertian ague without interruptions." When Quartilla said this, Ascyltos was struck dumb for a moment, while I turned colder than a Swiss winter, and could not utter a syllable. But the presence of my friends saved me from my worst fears. They were three weak women, if they wanted to make any attack on us. We had at least our manhood in our favour, if nothing else. And certainly our dress was more fit for action. Indeed I had already matched our forces in pairs. If it came to a real fight, I was to face Quartilla, Ascyltos her maid, Giton the girl. . . .

But then all our resolution yielded to astonishment, and the darkness of certain death began to fall on our unhappy eyes. . . .

" If you have anything worse in store, madam," I 20 said, " be quick with it. We are not such desperate criminals that we deserve to die by torture." . . .

27

Ancilla quae Psyche vocabatur, lodiculam in pavimento diligenter extendit . . . .

Sollicitavit inguina mea mille iam mortibus frigida . . . .

Operuerat Ascyltos pallio caput, admonitus scilicet periculosum esse alienis intervenire secretis . . . .

Duas institas ancilla protulit de sinu alteraque pedes nostros alligavit, altera manus . . . .

Ascyltos iam deficiente fabularum contextu "Quid? ego"[1] inquit "non sum dignus qui biham?" Ancilla risu meo prodita complosit manus et "Apposui quidem . . . adulescens, solus tantum medicamentum ebibisti?" "Itane est?" inquit Quartilla "quicquid saturei fuit, Encolpius ebibit?" . . . .

Non indecenti risn latera commovit . . . .

LO | Ac ne Giton quidem ultimo risum tenuit, utique postquam virguncula cervicem eius invasit et non repugnanti puero innumerabilia oscula dedit . . . .

21 L | Volebamus miseri exclamare, sed nec in auxilio erat quisquam, et hinc Psyche acu comatoria cupienti mihi invocare Quiritum fidem malas pungebat, illinc puella penicillo, quod et ipsum satureo tinxerat, Ascylton opprimebat . . . .

Ultimo cinaedus supervenit myrtea subornatus gausapa cinguloque succinctus . . . .

Modo extortis nos clunibus cecidit, modo basiis olidissimis inquinavit, donec Quartilla balaenaceam tenens virgam alteque succincta iussit infelicibus dari missionem . . . .

[1] ego *Goldast:* ergo.

28

The maid, whose name was Psyche, carefully spread a blanket on the floor. Sollicitavit inguina mea mille iam mortibus frigida . . . . Ascyltos had buried his head in his cloak. I suppose he had warning that it is dangerous to pry into other people's secrets. . . .

The maid brought two straps out of her dress and tied our feet with one and our hands with the other. . . .

The thread of our talk was broken. "Come," said Ascyltos, "do not I deserve a drink?" The maid was given away by my laughter at this. She clapped her hands and said, "I put one by you, young man. Did you drink the whole of the medicine yourself?" "Did he really?" said Quartilla, "did Encolpius drink up the whole of our Ioving-cup?" Her sides shook with delightful laughter. . . . Even Giton had to laugh at last, I mean when the little girl took him by the neck and showered countless kisses on his unresisting lips. . . .

We wanted to cry out for pain, but there was no 21 one to come to the rescue, and when I tried to cry "Help, all honest citizens!" Psyche pricked my check with a hair-pin, while the girl threatened Ascyltos with a wet sponge which she had soaked in an aphrodisiac. . . .

At last there arrived a low fellow in a fine brown suit with a waistband. . . .

Modo extortis nos clunibus cecidit, modo basiis olidissimis inquinavit, donec Quartilla balaenaceam tenens virgam alteque succincta iussit infelicibus dari missionem . . . .

TITUS PETRONIUS ARBITER

Uterque nostrum religiosissimis iuravit verbis inter duos periturum esse tam horribile secretum . . . .

Intraverunt palaestritae complures et nos legitimo perfusos oleo refecerunt. Utcunque ergo lassitudine abiecta cenatoria repetimus et in proximam cellam ducti sumus, in qua tres lecti strati erant et reliquus lautitiarum apparatus splendidissime expositus. Iussi ergo discubuimus, et gustatione mirifica initiati vino etiam Falerno inundamur. Excepti etiam pluribus ferculis cum laberemur in somnum, "Itane est?" inquit Quartilla "etiam dormire vobis in mente est, cum sciatis Priapi genio pervigilium deberi?" . . .

22 Cum Ascyltos gravatus tot malis in somnum laberetur, illa quae iniuria depulsa fuerat ancilla totam faciem eius fuligine longa perfricuit et non sentientis labra umerosque sopitionibus[1] pinxit. Iam ego etiam tot malis fatigatus minimum veluti gustum hauseram somni; idem et tota intra forisque familia fecerat, atque alii circa pedes discumbentium sparsi iacebant, alii parietibus appliciti, quidam in ipso limine coniunctis manebant capitibus; lucernae quoque umore defectae tenue et extremum lumen spargebant: cum duo Syri expilaturi [lagoenam][2] triclinium intraverunt, dumque inter argentum avidins rixantur, diductam fregerunt lagoenam. Cecidit etiam mensa cum argento, et ancillae super torum marcentis excussum forte altius

---

[1] sopitionibus, *probably corrupt*: sopionibus *MSS. of Catullus* 37, 10: ropionibus *Hertz.*

[2] lagoenam *bracketed by Jahn.*

We both of us took a solemn oath that the dreadful secret should die with us. . . .

A number of attendants came in, rubbed us down with pure oil, and refreshed us.   Our fatigue vanished, we put on evening dress again, and were shown into the next room, where three couches were laid and a whole rich dinner-service was finely spread out.   We were asked to sit down, and after beginning with some wonderful hors d'oeuvres we swam in wine, and that too Falernian.   We followed this with more courses, and were dropping off to sleep, when Quartilla said, "Well, how can you think of going to sleep, when you know that is your duty to devote the whole night to the genius of Priapus?" . . .

Ascyltos was heavy-eyed with all his troubles, and 22 was falling asleep, when the maid who had been driven away so rud 1 rubbed his face over with soot, and coloured his lips and his neck with vermilion while he drowsed.   By this time I was tired out with adventures too, and had just taken the tiniest taste of sleep. All the servants, indoors and out, had done the same. Some lay anyhow by the feet of the guests, some leaned against the walls, some even stayed in the doorway with their heads together.   The oil in the lamps had run out, and they gave a thin dying light.   All at once two Syrians came in to rob the dining-room, and in quarrelling greedily over the plate pulled a large jug in two and broke it.   The table fell over with the plate, and a cup which happened to fly

poculum caput tetigit.[1]   Ad quem ictum exclamavit
illa pariterque et fures prodidit et partem ebriorum
excitavit.   Syri illi qui venerant ad praedam, postquam deprehensos se intellexerunt, pariter secundum
lectum conciderunt, ut putares hoc convenisse, et
stertere tanquam olim dormientes coeperunt.

Iam et tricliniarches experrectus lucernis occidenti-
bus oleum infuderat, et pueri detersis paulisper oculis
redierant ad ministerium, cum intrans cymbalistria et
23 concrepans aera omnes excitavit.   Refectum igitur est
convivium et rursus Quartilla ad bibendum revocavit.
Adiuvit hilaritatem comissantis cymbalistria. . . .

Intrat cinaedus, homo omnium insulsissimus et plane
illa domo dignus, qui ut infractis manibus congemuit,
eiusmodi carmina effudit

"Huc huc cito[2] convenite nunc, spatalocinaedi,
    Fede tendite, cursum addite, convolate planta
    Femoreque[3] facili, clune agili et manu procaces,
    Molles, veteres, Deliaci manu recisi."

Consumptis versibus suis immundissimo me basio conspuit.   Mox et super lectum venit atque omni vi
detexit recusantem.   Super inguina mea diu multumque frustra moluit.   Profluebant per frontem su-
24 dantis acaciae rivi, et inter rugas malarum tantum erat
cretae, ut putares detectum parietem nimbo laborare.
Non tenui ego diutius lacrimas, sed ad ultimam perductus tristitiam "Quaeso" inquam "domina, certe

---

[1] tetegit *Buecheler:* fregit.
[2] cito *added by Buecheler.*
[3] que *added by Buecheler.*

32

some distance hit the head of the maid, who was lolling over a seat. The knock made her scream, and this showed up the thieves and woke some of the drunken party. The Syrians who had come to steal dropped side by side on a sofa, when they realized that they were being noticed, with the most convincing naturalness, and began to suore like old-established sleepers.

By this time the butler had got up and refilled the flickering lamps. The boys rubbed their eyes for a few minutes, and then came back to wait. Then a girl with cymbals came in, and the crash of the brass aroused everybody. Our evening began afresh, and 23 Quartilla called us back again to our cups. The girl with the cymbals gave her fresh spirits for the revel. . . .

Intrat cinaedus, homo omnium insulsissimus et plane illa domo dignus, qui ut infractis manibus congemuit, eiusmodi carmina effudit:

"Huc huc cito[1] convenite nunc, spatalocinaedi,
Fede tendite, cursum addite, convolate planta
Femoreque[2] facili, clune agili et m_{anu} procaces,
Molles, veteres, Deliaci manu recisi."

Consumptis versibus suis immundissimo me basio conspuit. Mox et super lectum venit atque omni vi detexit recusantem. Super inguina mea diu multumque frustra moluit. Profluebant per frontem sudantis acaciae rivi, et inter rugas malarum tantum erat 24 cretae, ut putares detectum parietem nimbo laborare. Non tenui ego diutius lacrimas, sed ad ultimam, perductus tristitiam "Quaeso" inquam "domina, certe

[1] cito *added by Buecheler.*
[2] que *added by Buecheler.*

D   33

embasicoetan iusseras dari." Complosit illa tenerius
manus et "O" inquit "hominem acutum atque urba-
nitatis vernaculae[1] fontem. Quid? tu non intellexeras
cinaedum embasicoetan vocari?" Deinde ut contuber-
nali meo melius succederet, "Per fidem" inquam
"vestram, Ascyltos in hoc triclinio solus ferias agit?"
"Ita" inquit Quartilla "et Ascylto embasicoetas de-
tur." Ab hac voce equum cinaedus mutavit transitu-
que ad comitem meum facto clunibus eum basiisque
LO distrivit. | Stabat inter haec Giton et risu dissolvebat
ilia sua. Itaque conspicata eum Quartilla, cuius esset
puer, diligentissima sciscitatione quaesivit. Cum ego
fratrem meum esse dixissem, "Quare ergo" inquit "me
non basiavit?" Vocatumque ad se in osculum appli-
cuit. Mox manum etiam demisit in sinum et per-
trectato vasculo tam rudi "Haec" inquit "belle cras
in promulside libidinis nostrae militabit; hodie enim
post asellum diaria non sumo."

25 Cum haec diceret, ad aurem eius Psyche ridens
accessit, et cum dixisset nescio quid, "Ita, ita" inquit
Quartilla "bene admonuisti. Cur non, quia bellissima
occasio est, devirginatur Pannychis nostra?" Continuoque producta est puella satis bella et quae non
plus quam septem annos habere videbatur, [et] ea ipsa
quae primum cum Quartilla in cellam venerat nostram.
Plaudentibus ergo universis et postulantibus nuptias
[fecerunt][2] obstupui ego et nec Gitona, verecundissi-
mum puerum, sufficere huic petulantiae affirmavi, nec

[1] vernaculae *Scioppius:* vernulae.
[2] fecerunt *bracketed by Mommsen.*

34

embasicoetan iusseras dari." Complosit illa tenerius
manus et "O" inquit "hominem acutum atque urba-
nitatis vernaculae fontem. Quid? tu non intellexeras
cinaedum embasicoetan vocari?" Deinde ut contuber-
nali meo melius succederet, "Per fidem" inquam
"vestram, Ascyltos in hoc triclinio solus ferias agit?"
"Ita" inquit Quartilla "et Ascylto embasicoetas de-
tur." Ab hac voce equum cinaedus mutavit transitu-
que ad comitem meum facto clunibus eum basiisque
distrivit. | Stabat inter haec Giton et risu dissolvebat *LO*
ilia sua. Itaque conspicata eum Quartilla, cuius esset
puer, diligentissima sciscitatione quaesivit. Cum ego
fratrem meum esse dixissem, "Quare ergo" inquit "me
non basiavit?" Vocatumque ad se in osculum appli-
cuit. Mox manum etiam demisit in sinum et per-
trectato vasculo tam rudi "Haec" inquit "belle cras
in promulside libidinis nostrae militabit: hodie enim
post asellum diaria non sumo."

Cum haec diceret, ad aurem eius Psyche ridens 25
accessit, et cum dixisset nescio quid, "Ita, ita" inquit
Quartilla "bene admonuisti. Cur non, quia bellissima
occasio est, devirginatur Pannychis nostra?" Continuoque producta est puella satis bella et quae non
plus quam septem annos habere videbatur, [et] ea ipsa
quae primum cum Quartilla in cellam venerat nostram.
Plaudentibus ergo universis et postulantibus nuptias
[fecerunt] obstupui ego et nec Gitona, verecundissi-
mum puerum, sufficere buie petulantiae affirmavi, nec

puellam eius aetatis esse, ut muliebris patientiae legem posset accipere. "Ita" inquit Quartilla "minor
est ista quam ego fui, cum primum virum passa sum?
Iunonem meam iratam habeam, si unquam me meminerim virginem fuisse. Nam et infans cum paribus
inclinata[1] sum, et subinde procedentibus[2] annis maioribus me pueris applicui, donec ad hanc aetatem perveni. Hinc etiam puto proverbium natum illud, ut
dicatur posse tanrum tollere, qui vitulum sustulerit."
Igitur ne maiorem iniuriam in secreto frater acciperet,
26 consurrexi ad officium nuptiale. Iam Psyche puellae
caput involverat flammeo, iam embasicoetas praeferebat facem, iam ebriae mulieres longum agmen plaudentes fecerant thalamumque incesta exornaverant
veste, cum[3] Quartilla quoque iocantium libidine accensa et ipsa surrexit correptumque Gitona in cubiculum traxit.

Sine dubio non repugnaverat puer, ac ne puella
quidem tristis expaverat nuptiarum nomen. Itaque
cum inclusi iacerent, consedimus ante limen thalami,
et in primis Quartilla per rimam improbe diductam
applicuerat oculum curiosum lusumque puerilem libidinosa speculabatur diligentia. Me quoque ad idem
spectaculum lenta manu traxit, et quia considerantium
cohaeserant[4] vultus, quicquid a spectaculo vacabat,
commovebat obiter labra et me tanquam furtivis subinde osculis verberabat. . . .

[1] inclinata *Buecheler:* inquinata.
[2] procedentibus *Barmann on authority of "Old MS.":*
prodeuntibus.
[3] cum *Buecheler:* tum.
[4] cohaeserant *Buecheler:* haeserant.

puellam eius aetatis esse, ut muliebris patientiae legem posset accipere. "Ita" inquit Quartilla "minor est ista quam ego fui, cum primum virum passa sum? Iunonem meam iratam habeam, si unquam me meminerim virginem fuisse. Nam et infans cum paribus inclinata[1] sum, et subinde procedentibus[2] annis maioribus me pueris applicui, donec ad hanc aetatem perveni. Hinc etiam puto proverbium natum illud, ut dicatur posse taurum tollere, qui vitulum sustulerit." Igitur ne maiorem iniuriam in secreto frater acciperet, consurrexi ad officium nuptiale. Iam Psyche puellae 26 caput involverat flammeo, iam embasicoetas praeferebat facem, iam ebriae mulieres longum agmen plaudentes fecerant thalamumque incesta exornaverant veste, cum[3] Quartilla quoque iocantium libidine accensa et ipsa surrexit correptumque Gitona in cubiculum traxit.

Sine dubio non repugnaverat puer, ac ne puella quidem tristis expaverat nuptiarum nomen. Itaque cum inclusi iacerent, consedimus ante limen thalami, et in primis Quartilla per rimam improbe diductam applicuerat oculum curiosum lusumque puerilem libidinosa speculabatur diligentia. Me quoque ad idem spectaculum lenta manu traxit, et quia considerantium cohaeserant[4] vultus, quicquid a spectaculo vacabat, commovebat obiter labra et me tanquam furtivis subinde osculis verberabat. . . .

37

TITUS PETRONIUS ARBITER

L |Abiecti in lectis sine metu reliquam exegimus noctem. . . .

H | Venerat iam tertius dies, id est expectatio liberae cenae, sed tot vulneribus confossis fuga magis placebat, quam quies. Itaque cum maesti deliberaremus, quonam genere praesentem evitaremus procellam, unus servus Agamemnonis interpellavit trepidantes et "Quid? vos" inquit "nescitis, hodie apud quem fiat? Trimalchio, lautissimus homo, horologium in triclinio et bucinatorem habet subornatum, ut subinde seiat, quantum de vita perdiderit." Amicimur ergo diligenter obliti omnium malorum, et Gitona libentissime servile officium tuentem usque hoc iubemus in
27 balnea[1] sequi. Nos interim vestiti errare coepimus...
immo iocari magis et circulis [ludentem][2] accedere,
HL cum subito | videmus senem calvum, tunica vestitum russea, inter pueros capillatos ludentem pila. Nec tam pueri nos, quamquam erat operae pretium, ad spectaculum duxerant, quam ipse pater familiae, qui soleatus pila prasina exercebatur. Nec amplius eam repetebat quae terram contigerat, sed follem plenum habebat servus sufficiebatque ludentibus. Notavimus etiam res novas. Nam duo spadones in diversa parte circuli stabant, quorum alter matellam teuchat argenteam, alter numerabat pilas, non quidem eas quae inter manus lusu expellente vibrabant, sed eas quae in terram decidebant. Cum has ergo miraremur lautitias,
H | accurrit Menelaus et "Hic est" inquit "apud quem cubitum ponetis, et quidem [3] iam principium cenae videtis." Et iam non loquebatur Menelaus cum

[1] balnea *Jahn:* balneo.
[2] ludentem *bracketed by Buecheler.*
[3] quidem *Buecheler:* quid.

38

We threw ourselves into bed and spent the rest of the night without terrors. . . .

The third day had come. A good dinner was promised. But we were bruised and sore. Escape was better even than rest. We were making some melancholy plans for avoiding the coming storm, when one of Agamemnon's servants came up as we stood hesitating, and said, "Do you not know at whose house it is today? Trimalchio, a very rich man, who has a clock and a uniformed trumpeter in his dining-room, to keep telling him how much of his life is lost and gone." We forgot our troubles and hurried into our clothes, and told Giton, who till now had been waiting on us very willingly, to follow us to the baths. We began to take a stroll in evening dress to pass the time, or rather to joke and mix with the groups of players, when all at once we saw a bald old man in a reddish shirt playing at ball with some long-haired boys. It was not the boys that attracted our notice, though they deserved it, but the old gentleman, who was in his house-shoes, busily engaged with a green ball. He never picked it up if it touched the ground. A slave stood by with a bagful and supplied them to the players. We also observed a new feature in the game. Two eunuchs were standing at different points in the group. One held a silver jordan, one counted the balls, not as they flew from hand to band in the rigour of the game, but when they dropped to the ground. We were amazed at such a display, and then Menelaus[1] ran up and said, "This is the man who will give you places at his table: indeed what you see is the overture to his dinner." Menelaus had just finished when

27

[1] Agamemnon's assistant, who would take junior classes in rhetoric. He is called *antescholanus*, assistant tutor, in c. 81.

HL·| Trimalchio digitos concrepuit, ad quod signum matellam spado lndenti subiecit. Exonerata ille vesica aquam poposcit ad manus, digitosque paululum adspersos in capite pueri tersit.

28 ˉ Longum erat singula excipere. Itaque intravimus balneum, et sudore calfacti momento temporis ad frigidam eximus. Iam Trimalchio unguento perfusus tergebatur, non linteis, sed palliis ex lana mollissima factis. Tres interim iatraliptae in conspectu eius *H* Falernum potabant, | et cum plurimum rixantes effunderent, Trimalchio hoc suum propinasse dicebat.

HL| Hinc involutus coccina gausapa lecticae impositus est praecedentibus phaleratis cursoribus quattuor et chiramaxio, in quo deliciae eius vehebantur, puer vetulus, lippus, domino Trimalchione deformior. Cum ergo auferretur, ad caput eius symphoniacus cum minimis tibiis accessit et tanquam in aurem aliquid secreto diceret, toto itinere cantavit.

Sequimur nos admiratione iam saturi et cum *H* Agamemnone ad ianuam pervenimus, | in cuius poste libellus erat cum hac inscriptione fixus: "Quisquis servus sine dominico iussu foras exierit, accipiet plagas *HL* centum." | In aditu autem ipso stabat ostiarius prasinatus, cerasino succinctus cingulo, atque in lance argentea pisum purgabat. Super limen autem cavea 29 pendebat aurea, in qua pica varia intrantes salutabat. Ceterum ego dum omnia stupeo, paene resupinatus crura mea fregi. Ad sinistram enim intrantibus non longe ab ostiarii cella canis ingens, catena vinctus, in pariete erat pictus superque quadrata littera scriptum "Cave canem." Et collegae quidem mei riserunt, ego autem collecto spiritu non destiti totum parietem persequi. Erat autem venalicium *cum* titulis pictum,

40

Trimalchio cracked his fingers. One eunuch came up at this signal and held the jordan for him as he played. He relieved himself and called for a basin, dipped in his hands and wiped them on a boy's head.

I cannot linger over details. We went into the bath. 28 We stayed till we ran with sweat, and then at once passed through into the cold water. Trimalchio was now anointed all over and rubbed down, not with towels, but with blankets of the softest wool. Three masseurs sat there drinking Falernian wine under his eyes. They quarrelled and spilt a quantity. Trimalchio said they were drinking his health. Then he was rolled up in a scarlet woollen coat and put in a litter. Four runners decked with medals went before him, and a band-cart on which his favourite rode. This was a wrinkled blear-eyed boy uglier than his master Trimalchio. As he was being driven off, a musician with a tiny pair of pipes arrived, and played the whole way as though he were whispering secrets in his ear.

We followed, lost in wonder, and came with Agamemnon to the door. A notice was fastened on the doorpost: "NO SLAVE TO GO OUT OF DOORS EXCEPT BY THE MASTER'S ORDERS. PENALTY, ONE HUNDRED STRIPES." Just at the entrance stood a porter in green clothes, with a cherry-coloured belt, shelling peas in a silver dish. A golden cage hung in the doorway, and a spotted magpie in it greeted visitors. I was gazing 29 at all this, when I nearly fell backwards and broke my leg. For on the left hand as you went in, not far from the porter's office, a great dog on a chain was painted on the wall, and over him was written in large letters "BEWARE OF THE DOG." My friends laughed at me, but I plucked up courage and went on to examine the whole wall. It had a picture of a slave-market

41

et ipse Trimalchio capillatus caduceum tenebat Minervaque ducente Romam intrabat. Hinc quemadmodum ratiocinari didicisset, denique dispensator factus esset, omnia diligenter curiosus pictor cum inscriptione reddiderat. In deficiente vero iam porticn levatum mento in tribunal excelsum Mercurius rapiebat. Praesto erat Fortuna cornu abundanti copiosa et tres Parcae aurea pensa torquentes. Notavi etiam in porticn gregem cursorum cum magistro se exercentem. Praeterca grande armarium in angulo vidi, in cuius aedicula erant Lares argentei positi Venerisque signum marmoreum et pyxis aurea non pusilla, in quo barbam ipsius conditam esse dicebant.

Interrogare ergo atriensem coepi, quas in medio *H* picturas haberent. "Iliada et Odyssian" inquit | "ac Laenatis gladiatorium munus." Non licebat multaciam[1] considerare . . . .

HL 30 Nos | iam ad triclinium perveneramus, in cuius parte prima procurator rationes accipiebat. Et quod praecipuc miratus sum, in postibus triclinii fasces erant cum securibus fixi, quorum unam partem quasi embolum navis aeneum finiebat, in quo erat scriptum: "C.

---

[1] multaciam *corrupt: Buecheler suggests* multa iam.

on it, with the persons' names. Trimalchio was there
with long hair, holding a Mercury's staff.[1] Minerva
had him by the band and was leading him into Rome.
Then the painstaking artist had given a faithful picture
of his whole career with explanations: how he had
learned to keep accounts, and how at last he had been
made steward. At the point where the wall-space
gave out, Mercury had taken him by the chin, and was
whirling him up to his high official throne. Fortune stood by with her flowing horn of plenty, and
the three Fates spinning their golden threads. I also
observed a company of runners practising in the
gallery under a trainer, and in a corner I saw a large
cupboard containing a tiny shrine, wherein were silver
house-gods, and a marble image of Venus, and a large
golden box, where they told me Trimalchio's first
heard was laid up.   .

I began to ask the porter what pictures they had
in the ball. "The Iliad and the Odyssey," he said,
"and the gladiator's show given by Laenas." I could
not take them all in at once. . . . . .

We now went through to the dining-room. At the 30
entrance the steward sat receiving accounts. I was
particularly astonished to see rods and axes fixed on
the door posts of the dining-room, and one part of
them finished off with a kind of ship's beak,
inscribed:

[1] Mercury, as the god of business, was Trimalchio's patron.
It was Mercury who secured Trimalchio's selection to be a
Sevir Augustalis, an official responsible for duly carrying out
the worship of the Emperor. One of the privileges of the
Sevirs was to sit on a throne.

TITUS PETRONIUS ARBITER

·Pompeio Trimalchioni, seviro Augustali, Cinnamus dispensator." Sub eodem titulo et lucerna bilychnis de camera pendebat, et duac tabulae in utroque poste defixae, quarum altera, si bene memini. hoc habebat inscriptum: "III. et pridie kalendas Ianuarias C. noster foras cenat," altera lunae cursum stellarumque septem imagines pietas; et qui dies boni quique incommodi essent, distinguente bulla notabantur.

H | His repleti voluptatibus cum conaremur in triclinium intrare, exclamavit unus ex pueris, qui super hoc officium erat positus, "Dextro pede.' Sine dubio paulisper trepidavimus, ne contra praeceptum aliquis *HL* nostrum limen transiret. | Ceterum ut pariter movimus dextros gressus, servus nobis despoliatus procubuit ad pedes ac rogare coepit, ut se poenae eriperemus: nec magnum esse peccatum suum, propter quod periclitaretur; subducta enim sibi vestimenta dispensatoris in balneo, quae vix fuissent decem sestertiorum. Rettulimus ergo dextros pedes dispensatoremque in atrio[1] aureos numerantem deprecati sumus, ut servo remitteret poenam. Superbus ille sustulit vultum et "Non tam iactura me movet" inquit "quam negligentia nequissimi servi. Vestimenta mea cubitoria perdidit, quae mihi natali meo cliens quidam donaverat, Tyria sine dubio, sed iam semel lota. Quid ergo est? Dono vobis eum."

31   Obligati tam grandi beneficio cum intrassemus tri-

---

[1] in atrio *Buecheler:* in precario.

SATYRICON

"PRESENTED BY CINNAMUS THE STEWARD TO CAIUS POM-
PEIUS TRIMALCHIO, PRIEST OF THE COLLEGE OF AUGUSTUS."[1]
Under this inscription a double lamp hung from the
ceiling, and two calendars were fixed on either doorpost, one having this entry, if I remember right: "Our
master C. is out to supper on December the 30th and
31st," the other being painted with the moon in her
course, and the likenesses of the seven stars. Lucky
and unlucky days were marked too with distinctive
knobs.

Fed full of these delights, we tried to get into the
dining-room, when one of the slaves, who was entrusted with this duty, cried, "Right foot first!" For
a moment we were naturally nervous, for fear any of
us had broken the rule in crossing the threshold.
But just as we were all taking a step with the right
foot together, a slave stripped for flogging fell at our
feet, and began to implore us to save him from punishment. It was no great sin which had put him in such
peril; he had lost the steward's clothes in the bath,
and the whole lot were scarc 1 worth ten sesterces.
So we drew back our right feet, and begged the
steward, who sat counting gold pieces in the ball, to
let the slave off. He looked up haughtily, and said,
"It is not the loss I mind so much as the villain's
carelessness. He lost my dinner dress, which one of
my clients gave me on my birthday. It was Tyrian
dve, of course, but it had been washed once already.
Well, well, I make you a present of the fellow."

We were obliged by his august kindness, and when 31

---

[1] Rods and axes were the symbols of office of lictors, the
attendants on Roman magistrates, and the Sevirs had the
right to be attended by lictors. See c. 65.

45

clinium, occurrit nobis ille idem servus, pro quo rogaveramus, et stupentibus spississima basia impegit gratias agens humanitati nostrae. "Ad summam, statim scietis" ait "cm̄ dederitis beneficium. Vinum dominicum ministratoris gratia est" . . .

Tandem ergo discubuimus pueris Alexandrinis aquam in manus nivatam infundentibus aliisque insequentibus ad pedes ac paronychia cum ingenti subtilitate tollentibus. Ac ne in hoc quidem tam molesto tacebant officio, sed obiter cantabant. Ego experiri volui, an tota familia cantaret, itaque potionem po-posei. Paratissimus puer non minus me acido cantico excepit, et quisquis aliquid rogatus erat ut daret . . . pantomimi chorum, non patris familiae triclinium crederes. Allata est tamen gustatio valde lauta; nam iam omnes discubuerant praeter ipsum Trimalchionem, cui locus novo more primus servabatur. Ceterum in promulsidari asellus erat Corinthius cum bisaccio positus, qui habebat olivas in altera parte albas, in altera nigras. Tegebant asellum duac lances, in quarum marginibus nomen Trimalchionis inscriptum erat et argenti pondus. Ponticuli etiam ferruminati sustinebant glires melle ac papavere sparsos. Fuerunt et tomacula super craticulam argenteam ferventia posita, et infra craticulam Syriaca pruna cum granis Punici mali.

32 In his eramus lautitiis, cum ipse Trimalchio ad symphoniam allatus est positusque inter cervicalia minutissima expressit imprudentibus risum. Pallio enim coccineo adrasum excluserat caput circaque oneratas veste cervices laticlaviam immiserat mappam

we were in the dining-room, the slave for whom we had pleaded ran up, and to our astonishment rained kisses on us, and thanked us for our mercy. "One word," he said, "you will know in a minute who owes you a debt of gratitude: 'The master's wine is in the butler's gift.'" . . . .

At last then we sat down, and boys from Alexandria poured water cooled with snow over our hands. Others followed and knelt down at our feet, and proceeded with great skill to pare our hangnails. Even this unpleasant duty did not silence them, but they kept singing at their work. I wanted to find out whether the whole household could sing, so I asked for a drink. A ready slave repeated my order in a chant not less shrill. They all did the same if they were asked to hand anything. It was more like an actor's dance than a gentleman's dining-room. But some rich and tasty whets for the appetite were brought on; for every one had now sat down except Trimalchio, who had the first place kept for him in the new style. A donkey in Corinthian bronze stood on the side-board, with panniers holding olives, white in one side, black in the other. Two dishes hid the donkey; Trimalchio's name and their weight in silver was engraved on their edges. There were also dormice rolled in honey and poppy-seed, and supported on little bridges soldered to the plate. Then there were hot sausages laid on a silver grill, and under the grill damsons and seeds of pomegranate.

While we were engaged with these delicacies, Tri- **32** malchio was conducted in to the sound of music, propped on the tiniest of pillows. A laugh escaped the unwary. His head was shaven and peered out of a scarlet cloak, and over the heavy clothes on his neck he had put on a

47

fimbriis hinc atque illinc pendentibus. Habebat etiam
in minimo digito sinistrae manus anulum grandem
subauratum, extremo vero articulo digiti sequentis
minorem, ut mihi videbatur, totum aureum, sed plane
ferreis veluti stellis ferruminatum. Et ne has tantum
ostenderet divitias, dextrum nudavit lacertum armilla
aurea cultum et eboreo circulo lamina splendente
33 conexo. Ut deinde pinna argentea dentes perfodit,
"Amici" inquit "nondum mihi suave erat in triclinium
venire, sed ne diutius absentivos morae vobis essem,
omnem voluptatem mihi negavi. Permittetis tamen
finiri lusum." Sequebatur puer cum tabula terebin-
thina et crystallinis tesseris, notavique rem omnium
delicatissimam. Pro calculis enim albis ac nigris
aureos argenteosque habebat denarios. Interim dum
ille omnium textorum dieta inter lusum consumit,
gustantibus adhuc nobis repositorium allatum est cum
corbe, in quo gallina erat lignea patentibus in orhem
alis, quales esse solent quae incubant ova. Accessere
continuo duo servi et symphonia strepente scrutari
palcam coeperunt erutaque subinde pavonina ova
divisere convivis. Convertit ad hanc scaenam Trimalchio vultum et "Amici" ait "pavonis ova gallinae iussi
supponi. Et mehercules timeo ne iam concepti sint;
temptemus tamen, si adhuc sorbilia sunt." Accipi-
mus nos cochlearia non minus selibras pendentia ova-
que ex farina pingui figurata pertundimus. Ego
quidem paene proieci partem meam, nam videbatur
mihi iam in pullum coisse. Deinde ut audivi veterem
convivam: "Hic nescio quid boni debet esse," perse-

48

napkin with a broad stripe and fringes hanging from it all round. On the little finger of his left hand he had an enormous gilt ring, and on the top joint of the next finger a smaller ring which appeared to me to be entirely gold, but was really set all round with iron cut out in little stars. Not content with this display of wealth, he bared his right arm, where a golden bracelet shone, and an ivory bangle clasped with a plate of bright metal. Then he said, as he picked his teeth with a 33 silver quill, "It was not convenient for me to come to dinner yet, my friends, but I gave up all my own pleasure; I did not like to stay away any longer and keep you waiting. But you will not mind if I finish my game?" A boy followed him with a table of terebinth wood and crystal pieces, and I noticed the prettiest thing possible. Instead of black and white counters they used gold and silver coins. Trimalchio kept passing every kind of remark as he played, and we were still busy with the hors d'œuvres, when a tray was brought in with a basket on it, in which there was a hen made of wood, spreading out her wings as they do when they are sitting. The music grew loud: two slaves at once came up and began to hunt in the straw. Peahen's eggs were pulled out and handed to the guests. Trimalchio turned his head to look, and said, "I gave orders, my friends, that peahen's eggs should be put under a common hen. And upon my oath I am afraid they are hard-set by now. But we will try whether they are still fresh enough to suck.' We took our spoons, half-a-pound in weight at least, and hammered at the eggs, which were balls of fine meal. I was on the point of throwing away my portion. I thought a peachick had already formed. But hearing a practised diner say, "What treasure have we here?"

cutus putamen manu pinguissimam ficedulam inveni piperato vitello circumdatam.

34 Iam Trimalchio eadem omnia lusu intermisso poposcerat feceratque potestatem clara voce, si quis nostrum iterum vellet mulsum sumere, cum subito signum symphonia datur et gustatoria pariter a choro cantante rapiuntur. Ceterum inter tumultum cum forte paropsis excidisset et puer iacentem sustulisset, animadvertit Trimalchio colaphisque obiurgari puerum ac proicere rursus paropsidem iussit. Insecutus est lecticarius[1] argentumque inter reliqua purgamenta *H* scopis coepit everrere. | Subinde intraverunt duo Aethiopes capillati cum pusillis utribus, quales solent esse qui harenam in amphitheatro spargunt, vinumque dedere in manus; aquam enim nemo porrexit.

HL | Laudatus propter elegantias dominus "Aequum" inquit "Mars amat. Itaque iussi[2] suam cuique mensam assignari. Obiter et putidissimi[3] servi minorem nobis aestum frequentia sua facient."

Statim allatae sunt amphorae vitreae diligenter gypsatae, quarum in cervicibus pittacia erant affixa cum hoc titulo: "Falernum Opimianum annorum centum." Dum titulos perlegimus, complosit Trimalchio manus et "Eheu" inquit "ergo diutius vivit |
H vinum quam homuncio. Quare tengomenas[4] faciamus.
HL vita | vinum est. Verum Opimianum praesto. Heri

[1] supellecticarius *Dousa*.
[2] iussi *Burmann :* iussit *MSS.*
[3] putidissimi Heinsius : pudissimi *or* p̄dissimi.
[4] tengomenas *Buecheler :* tangomenas.

I poked through the shell with my finger, and found a fat becafico rolled up in spiced yolk of egg.

Trimalchio had now stopped his game, and 34 asked for all the same dishes, and in a loud voice invited any of us, who wished, to take a second glass of mead. Suddenly the music gave the sign, and the light dishes were swept away by a troop of singing servants. An entrée-dish happened to fall in the rush, and a boy picked it up from the ground. Trimalchio saw him, and directed that he should be punished by a box on the ear, and made to throw down the dish again. A chairman followed and began to sweep out the silver with a broom among the other rubbish. Then two long-haired Ethiopians with little wine-skins, just like the men who scatter sand in an amphitheatre, came in and gave us wine to wash our hands in, for no one offered us water.

We complimented our host on his arrangements. "Mars loves a fair field," said he, "and so I gave orders that every one should have a separate table. In that way these filthy slaves will not make us so hot by crowding past us."

Just then some glass jars carefully fastened with gypsum were brought on, with labels tied to their necks, inscribed, "Falernian of Opimius's vintage, 100 years in bottle."[1] As we were poring over the labels Trimalchio clapped his hands and cried, "Ah me, so wine lives longer than miserable man. So let us be merry.[2] Wine is life. I put on real wine of

[1] Opimius was consul in 121 B.C.
[2] The meaning of the word *tengomenas* is uncertain. Attempts have been made to connect it with the Greek τέγγειν, "to wet," because Alcaeus says τέγγε πνεύμονας οἴνῳ, "wet the lungs with wine."

non tam bonum posui, et multo honestiores cenabant."
Potantibus ergo nobis et accuratissime lautitias mi-
rantibus larvam argenteam attulit servus sic aptatam,
ut articuli eius vertebraeque luxatae in omnem partem
flecterentur.   Hanc cum super mensam semel iterumque abiecisset, et catenatio mobilis aliquot figuras ex-
primeret, Trimalchio adiecit:

"Eheu nos miseros, quam totus homuncio nil est.

Sic erimus cuncti, postquam nos auferet Orcus.

Ergo vivamus, dum licet esse bene."

35   Laudationem ferculum est insecutum plane non pro
expectatione magnum; novitas tamen omnium convertit oculos.   Rotundum enim repositorium duodecim
habebat signa in orbe disposita, super quae proprium
convenientemque materiae structor imposuerat cibum:
super arietem cicer arietinum, super tanrum bubulae
frustum, super geminos testiculos ac rienes, super can-
crum coronam, super leonem ficum Africanam, super
virginem steriliculam, super libram stateram in cuius
H altera parte scriblita erat, in altera placenta, | super
HL scorpionem pisciculum marinum, | super sagittarium
oclopetam, super capricornum locustam marinam,
super aquarium anserem, super pisces duos mullos.
In medio autem caespes cum herbis excisus favum
sustinebat.   Circumferebat Aegyptius puer clibano
argenteo panem. . . .
Atque ipse etiam taeterrima voce de laserpiciario

SATYRICON

Opimius's year. I produced some inferior stuff yesterday, and there was a much finer set of people to dinner." As we drank and admired each luxury in detail, a slave brought in a silver skeleton, made so that its limbs and spine could be moved and bent in every direction. He put it down once or twice on the table so that the supple joints showed several attitudes, and Trimalchio said appropriately: "Alas for us poor mortals, all that poor man is is nothing. So we shall all be, after the world below takes us away. Let us live then while it goes well with us."

After we had praised this outburst a dish followed, 35 not at all of the size we expected; but its novelty drew every eye to it There was a round plate with the twelve signs of the Zodiac set in order, and on each one the artist had laid some food fit and proper to the symbol; over the Ram ram's-head pease, a piece of beef on the Bull, kidneys over the Twins, over the Crab a crown, an African fig over the Lion, a barren sow's paunch over Virgo, over Libra a pair of scales with a muffin on one side and a cake on the other, over Scorpio a small sea-fish, over Sagittarius a bull's-eye,[1] over Capricornus a lobster, over Aquarius a goose, over Pisces two mullets. In the middle lay a honeycomb on a sod of turf with the green grass on it. An Egyptian boy took bread round in a silver chafing-dish. . . .

Trimalchio himself too ground out a tune from the

[1] The meaning is uncertain. The word is probably derived from *oculus*, "an eye," and *petere*, "to seek." See Lewis and Short s.v. *ocliferius*.

mimo canticum extorsit. Nos ut tristiores ad tam
36 viles accessimus cibos, "Suadeo" inquit Trimalchio
"cenemus; hoc est ius cenae." Haec ut dixit, ad
symphoniam quattuor tripudiantes procurrerunt su-
perioremque partem repositorii abstulerunt. Quo
facto videmus infra [scilicet in altero ferculo] altilia
et sumina leporemque in medio pinnis subornatum,
ut Pegasus videretur. Notavimus etiam circa angulos
repositorii Marsyas quattuor, ex quorum utriculis
garum piperatum currebat super pisces, qui tanquam
in euripo natabant. Damus omnes plausum a familia
inceptum et res electissimas ridentes aggredimur.
Non minus et Trimalchio eiusmodi methodio laetus
"Carpe" inquit. Processit statim scissor et ad symphoniam gesticulatus ita laceravit obsonium, ut putares
essedarium hydraule cantante pugnare. Ingerebat nihilo minus Trimalchio lentissima voce: "Carpe, Carpe."
Ego suspicatus ad aliquam urbanitatem totiens itera-
tam vocem pertinere, non erubui eum qui supra me
accumbebat, hoc ipsum interrogare. At ille, qui
saepius eiusmodi ludos spectaverat, "Vides illum"
inquit "qui obsonium carpit: Carpus vocatur. Itaque
quotiescunque dicit 'Carpe,' eodem verbo et vocat
et imperat."

37 Non potni amplius quicquam gustare, sed conversus
ad eum, ut quam plurima exciperem, longe accersere
fabulas coepi sciscitarique, quae esset mulier illa, quae
huc atque illuc discurreret. "Uxor" inquit "Trimalchionis, Fortunata appellatur, quae nummos modio

musical comedy "Assafoetida" in a most hideous voice. We came to such an evil entertainment rather depressed. "Now," said Trimalchio, "let us have 36 dinner. This is sauce for the dinner." As he spoke, four dancers ran up in time with the music and took off the top part of the dish. Then we saw in the well of it fat fowls and sow's bellies, and in the middle a hare got up with wings to look like Pegasus. Four figures of Marsyas at the corners of the dish also caught the eye; they let a spiced sauce run from their wine-skins over the fishes, which swam about in a kind of tide-race. We all took up the clapping which the slaves started, and attacked these delicacies with hearty laughter. Trimalchio was delighted with the trick he had played us, and said, "Now, Carver." The man came up at once, and making flourishes in time with the music pulled the dish to pieces; you would have said that a gladiator in a chariot was fighting to the accompaniment of a water-organ. Still Trimalchio kept on in a soft voice, "Oh, Carver, Carver." I thought this word over and over again must be part of a joke, and I made bold to ask the man who sat next me this very question. He had seen performances of this kind more often. "You see the fellow who is carving his way through the meat? Well, his name is Carver. So whenever Trimalchio says the word, you have his name, and he has his orders." [1]

I was now unable to eat any more, so I turned to 37 my neighbour to get as much news as possible. I began to seek for far-fetched stories, and to inquire who the woman was who kept running about everywhere. "She is Trimalchio's wife Fortunata," he said,

[1] Trimalchio's pun on his servant's name is expressed in Lowe's translation by "Carver, carve 'er."

metitur. Et modo, modo quid fuit? Ignoscet mihi
genius tuus, noluisses de manu illins panem accipere.
Nunc, nec quid nec quare, in caelum abiit et Trimalchionis topanta[1] est. Ad summam, mero meridie si
H dixerit illi tenebras esse, credet. | Ipse nescit quid
habeat, adeo saplutus[2] est; sed haec lupatria providet
omnia et ubi non putes. Est sicca, sobria, honorum
consiliorum [tantum auri vides], est tamen malae lin-
guae, pica pulvinaris. Quem amat, amat; quem non
amat, non amat. Ipse Trimalchio fundos habet, qua
milvi volant, nummorum nummos. Argentum in
ostiarii illius cella plus iacet, quam quisquam in for-
tunis habet. Familia vero babae babac,[3] non mehercules puto decumam partem esse quae dominum suum
38 noverit. Ad summam, quemvis ex istis babaecalis in
rutae folium coniciet. Nec est quod putes illum quicquam emere. Omnia domi nascuntur: lana, credrae,
piper, lacte gallinaceum si quaesieris, invenies. Ad

[1] Topanta *is colloquial for the Greek* τὰ πάντα "*all.*"

[2] Saplutus *is the Greek* ζάπλουτος "*very rich.*"

[3] Babae babae *is an exclamation of surprise. So* babaecalis
*in the next sentence is a person always agape with wonder,
a lout.*

"and she counts her money by the bushel. And what was she a little while ago? You will pardon me if I say that you would not have taken a piece of bread from her hand. Now without why or wherefore she is queen of Heaven, and Trimalchio's all in all. In fact, if she tells him that it is dark at high noon, he will believe it. He is so enormously rich that he does not know himself what he has; but this lynx-eyed woman has a plan for everything, even where you would not think it. She is temperate, sober, and prudent, but she has a nasty tongue, and henpecks him on his own sofa.[1] Whom she likes, she likes; whom she dislikes, she dislikes. Trimalchio has estates wherever a kite can fly in a day, is millionaire of millionaires. There is more plate lying in his steward's room than other people have in their whole fortunes. And his slaves! My word! I really don't believe that one out of ten of them knows his master by sight. Why, he can knock any of these young louts into a nettle-bed[2] if he chooses. 38 You must not suppose either that he buys anything. Everything is home-grown: wool, citrons, pepper; you can have cock's milk for the asking. Why, his wool

[1] The phrase means literally "a magpie belonging to a sofa," and clearly refers to domestic tyranny.

[2] *In rutae folium coniciet.* Literally "will throw into a rue-leaf." *Rutae folium* is said by Friedländer to be a proverbial expression for a small space. He refers to Martial XI, 31. The phrase occurs again in c. 58.

summam, parum illi bona lana nascebatur; arietes a
Tarento emit, et eos culavit in gregem. Mel Atticum
ut domi nasceretur, apes ab Athenis iussit afferri;
obiter et vernaculae quae sunt, meliusculae a Graeculis fient. Ecce intra hos dies scripsit, ut illi ex
India semen boletorum mitteretur. Nam mulam
quidem nullam habet, quae non ex onagro nata sit.
Vides tot culcitras: nulla non aut conchyliatum aut
coccineum tomentum habet. Tanta est animi beati-
tudo. Reliquos autem collibertos eius cave contem-
nas. Valde sucossi sunt. Vides illum qui in imo
imus recumbit: hodie sua octingenta possidet. De
nihilo crevit. Modo solebat collo suo ligna portare.
Sed quomodo dicunt—ego nihil scio, sed audivi—
quom[1] Incuboni pilleum rapuisset, [et] thesaurum invenit. Ego nemini invideo, si quid[2] deus dedit. Est
tamen sub alapa et non vult sibi male. Itaque proxime
casam[3] hoc titulo proscripsit: 'C. Pompeius Diogenes
ex kalendis Iuliis cenaculum locat; ipse enim domum
emit.' Quid ille qui libertini loco iacet, quam bene
se habuit. Non impropero illi. Sestertium suum
vidit decies, sed male vacillavit. Non puto illum

---

[1] quom *Buecheler:* quomodo.
[2] quid *Buecheler:* quo.
[3] casam *Buccheler:* cum.

was not growing of fine enough quality. He bought
rams from Tarentum and sent them into his flocks
with a smack behind. He had bees brought from
Athens to give him Attic honey on the premises; the
Roman-born bees incidentally will be improved by the
Greeks. Within the last few days, I may say, he has
written for a cargo of mushroom spawn from India.
And he has not got a single mule which is not the
child of a wild ass. You see all the cushions here:
every one has purple or scarlet stuffing. So high is
his felicity. But do not look down on the other freedmen who are his friends. They are very juicy people.
That one you see lying at the bottom of the end sofa
has his eight hundred thousand. He was quite a
nobody. A little time ago he was carrying loads of
wood on his back. People do say—I know nothing,
but I have heard—that he pulled off a goblin's cap
and found a fairy board.[1] If God makes presents I
am jealous of nobody. Still, he shows the marks of
his master's fingers,[2] and has a fine opinion of himself.
So he has just put up a notice on his bovel: 'This
attic, the property of Caius Pompeius Diogenes, to
let from the 1st of July, the owner having purchased
a house.' That person there too who is lying in
the freedman's place[3] is well pleased with himself.
I do not blame him. He had his million in his hands,
but he has had a bad shaking. I believe he cannot call

[1] *Incubo* was a goblin who guarded hid treasure. If one
stole his cap, he was compelled to reveal the treasure.
[2] On setting a slave free the master gave him a slap as a
symbol of his former power over him.
[3] Apparently a recognized place at table was assigned to a
freedman invited to dine with free men. Its position is not
known.

capillos liberos habere, nec mehercules sua culpa;
ipso enim homo melior non est; sed liberti scelerati,
qui omnia ad se fecerunt. Scito autem: sociorum
olla male fervet, et ubi semel res inclinata est, amici
de medio. Et quam honestam negotiationem exercuit,
quod illum sic vides. Libitinarius fuit. Solebat sic
cenare, quomodo rex: apros gausapatos, opera pistoria,
avis, cocos, pistores. Plus vini sub mensa effunde-
batur, quam aliquis in cella habet. Phantasia, non
homo. Inclinatis quoque rebus suis, cum timeret ne
creditores illum conturbare existimarent, hoc titulo
auctionem proscripsit: "C. Iulius Proculus auctionem
faciet rerum supervacuarum."

39 Interpellavit tam dulces fabulas Trimalchio; nam
iam sublatum erat ferculum, hilaresque convivae vino
sermonibusque publicatis operam coeperant dare. Is
ergo reclinatus in cubitum "Hoc vinum" inquit "vos
oportet suave faciatis. Pisces natare oportet. Rogo,
me putatis illa cena esse contentum, quam in theca
repositorii videratis? 'Sic notus Vlixes?' quid ergo
est? Oportet etiam inter cenandum philologiam nosse.
Patrono meo ossa bene quiescant, qui me hominem
inter homines voluit esse. Nam mihi nihil novi potest
afferri, sicut ille fericulus iam[1] habuit praxim. Caelus
hic, in quo duodecim dii habitant, in totidem se figuras
convertit, et modo fit aries. Itaque quisquis nascitur
illo signo, multa pecora habet, multum lanae, caput

---

[1] fericulus iam *Buecheler:* fericulusta meL

his hair his own. No fault of his I am sure; there is no better fellow alive; but it is the damned freedmen who have pocketed everything. You know how it is: the company's pot goes off the boil, and the moment business takes a bad turn your friends desert you. You see him in this state: and what a fine trade he drove! He was an undertaker. He used to dine like a prince: boars cooked in a cloth, •wonderful sweet things, game, chefs and confectioners! There used to be more wine spilt under the table than many a man has in his cellars. He was a fairy prince, not a mortal. When his business was failing, and he was afraid his creditors might guess that he was going bankrupt, he advertised a sale in this fashion: "Caius Julius Proculus will offer for sale some articles for which he has no further use."

Trimalchio interrupted these delightful tales; the 39 meat had now been removed, and the cheerful company began to turn their attention to the wine, and to general conversation. He lay back on his couch and said: "Now you must make this wine go down pleasantly. A fish must have something to swim in. But I say, did you suppose I would put up with the dinner you saw on the top part of that round dish— "Is this the old Ulysses whom ye knew?"[1]—well, well, one must not forget one's culture even at dinner. God rest the bones of my patron; he wanted me to be a man among men. No one can bring me anything new, as that last dish proved. The firmament where the twelve gods inhabit turns into as many figures, and at one time becomes a ram. So anyone who is born under that sign has plenty of flocks and wool,

---

[1] See Virgil, *Æneid*, II, 44.

praeterea durum, frontem expudoratam, cornum acutum. Plurimi hoc signo scholastici nascuntur et arietilh."[1] Laudamus urbanitatem mathematici; itaque adiecit: "deinde totus caelus taurulus fit. Itaque tunc calcitrosi nascuntur et bubulci et qui se ipsi pascunt. In geminis autem nascuntur bigae et boves et colei et qui utrosque parietes linunt. In cancro ego natus sum. Ideo multis pedibus sto, et in mari et in terra multa possideo; nam cancer et hoc et illoc quadrat. Et ideo iam dudum nihil super illum posui, ne genesim meam premerem. In leone cataphagae nascuntur et imperiosi; in virgine mulieres et fugitivi et compediti; in libra laniones et unguentarii et quicunque aliquid expediunt; in scorpione venenarii et percussores; in sagittario strabones, qui holera spectant, lardum tollunt; in capricorno aerumnosi, quibus prae mala sua cornua nascuntur; in aquario copones et cucurbitae; in piscibus obsonatores et rhetores. Sic orbis vertitur tanquam mola, et semper aliquid mali facit, ut homines aut nascantur aut pereant. Quod autem in medio caespitem videtis et supra caespitem favum, nihil sine ratione facio. terra mater est in medio quasi ovum corrotundata, et omnia bona in se habet tanquam favus."

40 "Sophos" universi clamamus et sublatis manibus ad cameram iuramus Hipparchum Aratumque com-

---

[1] arietilli *Heinsius:* arieti illi.

a hard head and a brazen forehead and sharp horns. Very many pedants and young rams are born under this sign." We applauded the elegance of his astrology, and so he went on: "Then the whole sky changes into a young bull. So men who are free with their heels are born now, and oxherds and people who have to find their own food. Under the Twins tandems are born, and oxen, and debauchees, and those who sit on both sides of the fence.[1] I was born under the Crab. So I have many legs to stand on, and many possessions by sea and land; for either one or the other suits your crab. And that was why just now I put nothing on top of the Crab, for fear of weighing down the house of my birth. Under the Lion gluttons and masterful men are born; under Virgo women, and runaway slaves, and chained gangs; under Libra butchers, and perfumers, and generally people who put things to rights; poisoners and assassins under Scorpio; under Sagittarius cross-eyed men, who take the bacon while they look at the vegetables; under Capricornus the poor folk whose troubles make horns sprout on them; under Aquarius inn-keepers and men with water on the brain; under Pisces chefs and rhetoricians. So the world turns like a mill, and always brings some evil to pass, causing the birth of men or their death. You saw the green turf in the middle of the dish, and the honeycomb on the turf; I do nothing without a reason. Mother Earth lies in the world's midst rounded like an egg, and in her all blessings are contained as in a honeycomb."

"Bravo!" we all cried, swearing with our hands 40 lifted to the ceiling that Hipparchus and Aratus

[1] Literally "those who bedaub walls on both sides," i.e. those who "hedge" in fight or friendship.

parandos illi homines non fuisse, donec advenerunt ministri ac toralia praeposuerunt toris, in quibus retia erant picta subsessoresque cum venabulis et totus venationis apparatus. Necdum sciebamus, quo mitteremus suspiciones nostras, cum extra triclinium clamor sublatus est ingens, et ecce canes Laconici etiam circa mensam discurrere coeperunt. Secutum est hos repositorium, in quo positus erat primae magnitudinis aper, et quidem pilleatus, e cuius dentibus sportellae dependebant duac palmulis textae, altera caryotis altera thebaicis repleta. Circa autem minores porcelli ex coptoplacentis facti, quasi uberibus imminerent, scrofam esse positam significabant. Et hi quidem apophoreti fuerunt. Ceterum ad scindendum aprum non ille Carpus accessit, qui altilia laceraverat, sed barbatus ingens, fasciis cruralibus alligatus et alicula subornatus polymita, strictoque venatorio cultro latus apri vehementer percussit, ex cuius plaga turdi evolaverunt. Parati aucupes cum harundinibus fuerunt et eos circa triclinium volitantes momento exceperunt. Inde cum suum cuique iussisset referri Trimalchio, adiecit: "Etiam videte, quam porcus ille silvaticus lotam[1] comederit glandem." Statim pueri ad sportellas accesserunt, quae pendebant e dentibus, thebaicasque et caryotas ad numerum divisere cenantibus.

41   Interim ego, qui privatum habebam secessum, in multas cogitationes deductus sum, quare aper pilleatus intrasset. Postquam itaque omnis bacalusias consumpsi,

---

[1] lotam *Muncker:* totam.

were not to be compared with him, until the servants came and spread over the couches coverlets painted with nets, and men lying in wait with hunting spears, and all the instruments of the chase. We were still wondering where to turn our expectations, when a great shout was raised outside the dining-room, and in came some Spartan hounds too, and began running round the table. A tray was brought in after them with a wild boar of the largest size upon it, wearing a cap of freedom, with two little baskets woven of palm-twigs hanging from his tusks, one full of dry dates and the other of fresh. Round it lay sucking-pigs made of simnel cake with their mouths to the teats, thereby showing that we had a sow before us. These sucking-pigs were for the guests to take away. Carver, who had mangled the fowls, did not come to divide the boar, but a big bearded man with bands wound round his legs, and a spangled hunting-coat of damasked silk, who drew a hunting-knife and plunged it hard into the boar's side. A number of thrushes flew out at the blow. As they fluttered round the dining-room there were fowlers ready with limed twigs who caught them in a moment. Trimalchio ordered everybody to be given his own portion, and added: "Now you see what fine acorns the woodland boar has been eating." Then boys came and took the baskets which hung from her jaws and distributed fresh and dry dates to the guests.

Meantime I had got a quiet corner to myself, and had **41** gone off on a long train of speculation,—why the pig had come in with a cap of freedom on. After turning the problem over every way[1] I ventured to put the

----

[1] *Bacalusias* may be derived from *baceolus* (Gk βάκηλος) a blockhead, and *ludere*, hence meaning perhaps "every kind of foolish explanation of the riddle."

duravi interrogare illum interpretem meum, quod[1] me torqueret. At ille: "Plane etiam hoc servus tuns indicare potest; non enim aenigma est, sed res aperta. Hic aper, cum heri summa cena eum[2] vindicasset, a convivis dimissus est; itaque hodie tanquam libertus in convivium revertitur." Damnavi ego stuporem meum et nihil amplius interrogavi, ne viderer nunquam inter honestos cenasse.

Dum haec loquimur, puer speciosus, vitibus hederisque redimitus, modo Bromium, interdum Lyaeum Euhiumque confessus, calathisco uvas circumtulit et poemata domini sui acutissima voce traduxit. Ad quem sonum conversus Trimalchio "Dionyse" inquit "liber esto." Puer detraxit pilleum apro capitique suo imposuit. Tum Trimalchio rursus adiecit: "Non negabitis me" inquit "habere Liberum patrem." Laudavimus dictum Trimalchionis et circumeuntem puerum sane perbasiamus.

Ab hoc ferculo Trimalchio ad lasanum surrexit. Nos libertatem sine tyranno nacti coepimus invitare convivarum sermones. Dama[3] itaque primus cum pataracina poposcisset, "Dici" inquit "nihil est. Dum versas te, nox fit. Itaque nihil est melius, quam de cubiculo recta in triclinium ire. Et mundum frigus habuimus. Vix me balneus calfecit. Tamen calda potio vestiarius est. Staminatas duxi, et plane matus sum. Vinns mihi in cerebrum abiit."

[1] quod *Buecheler:* quid.
[2] cena eum *Buecheler:* cenam.
[3] Damas *Heinsius:* clamat.

question which was troubling me to my old informant.
"Your humble servant can explain that too;" he said,
"there is no riddle, the thing is quite plain. Yesterday
when this animal appeared as *pièce de résistance* at
dinner, the guests dismissed him; and so to-day he
comes back to dinner as a freedman." I cursed
my dullness and asked no more questions, for fear of
showing that I had never dined among decent people.

As we were speaking, a beautiful boy with vine-
leaves and ivy in his hair brought round grapes in a
little basket, impersonating Bacchus in ecstasy, Bacchus
full of wine, Bacchus dreaming, and rendering his
master's verses in a most shrill voice. Trimalchio turned
round at the noise and said, "Dionysus, rise and be
free." The boy took the cap of freedom off the boar,
and put it on his head. Then Trimalchio went on:
"I am sure you will agree that the god of liberation
is my father."[1] We applauded Trimalchio's phrase, and
kissed the boy heartily as he went round.

After this dish Trimalchio got up and retired.
With the tyrant away we had our freedom, and we
began to draw the conversation of our neighbours.
Dama began after calling for bumpers: "Day is
nothing. Night is on you before you can turn round.
Then there is no better plan than going straight out
of bed to dinner. It is precious cold. I could scarc l
get warm in a bath. But a hot drink is as good as an
overcoat. I have taken some deep drinks[2] and I am
quite soaked. The wine has gone to my head."

[1] The name of the god Liber was fancifully derived from
the fact that wine frees men from cares. Trimalchio, who
confers freedom upon slaves, therefore takes him as his
patron or father.

[2] *Staminatas* means a draught of unmixed wine. The word
is variously derived from the Greek σταμνος or the Latin *stamen*.

42 . Excepit Seleucus fabulae partem et "Ego" inquit "non cotidie lavor; baliscns enim fullo est, aqua dentes habet, et cor nostrum cotidie liquescit. Sed cum mulsi pultarium obduxi, frigori laecasin dico. Nec sane lavare potui; fui enim hodie in funus. Homo bellus, tam bonus Chrysanthus animam ebulliit. Modo, modo me appellavit. Videor mihi cum illo loqui. Heu, eheu. Utres inflati ambulamus. Minoris quam muscae sumus, muscae tamen aliquam virtutem habent, nos non pluris sumus quam bullae. Et quid si non abstinax fuisset. Quinque dies aquam in os suum non coniecit, non micam panis. Tamen abiit ad plures. Medici illum perdiderunt, immo magis malus fatus; medicus enim nihil aliud est quam animi consolatio. Tamen bene elatus est, vitali lecto, stragulis bonis. Planctus est optime—manu misit aliquot—etiam si maligne illum ploravit uxor. Quid si non illam optime accepisset. Sed mulier quae mulier milvinum genus. Neminem nihil boni facere oportet; acque est enim ac si in puteum conicias. Sed antiquus amor cancer est."

43 Molestus fuit, Philerosque proclamavit: "Vivorum meminerimus. Ille habet, quod sibi debebatur: honeste vixit, honeste obiit. Quid habet quod queratur? Ab asse crevit et paratus fuit quadrantem de stercore mordicus tollere. Itaque crevit, quicquid crevit, tanquam favus. Puto mehercules illum reliquisse

Seleucus took up the tale and said : "I do not wash 42
every day; the bathman pulls you to pieces like a
fuller, the water bites, and the heart of man melts
away daily.   But when I have put down some draughts
of mead I let the cold go to the devil.[1]   Besides,
I could not wash ; I was at a funeral to-day.   A fine
fellow, the excellent Chrysanthus, has breathed his
last.   It was but the other day he greeted me.   I feel
as if I were speaking with him now.   Dear, dear, how
we bladders of wind strut about.   We are meaner
than flies; flies have their virtues, we are nothing but
bubbles.   And what would have happened if he had
not tried the fasting cure?   No water touched his
lips for five days, not a morsel of bread.   Yet he went
over to the majority.   The doctors killed him—no, it
was his unhappy destiny ; a doctor is nothing but a sop
to conscience.   Still, he was carried out in fine style on
a bier covered with a good pall.   The mourning was
very good too—he had freed a number of slaves—even
though his own wife was very grudging over her tears.
I daresay he did not treat her particularly kindly.   But
women one and all are a set of vultures.   It is no use
doing anyone a kindness; it is all the same as if you
put your kindness in a well.   But an old love pinches
like a crab."

He was a bore, and Phileros shouted out: "Oh, let 43
us remember the living.   He has got his deserts; he
lived decently and died decently.   What has he got to
grumble at?   He started with twopence, and he was
always ready to pick a halfpenny out of the dirt
with his teeth.   So he grew and grew like a honeycomb. Upon my word, I believe he left a clear hundred

[1] *Laecasin* is from the Greek λειχάζειν, Latin *fellare*, sensu
obsceno.

‸olida centum, et omnia in nummis habuit. De re tamen ego verum dicam, qui lingnam caninam comedi : durae buccae fuit, linguosus, discordia, non homo. Frater eius fortis fuit, amicus amico, manu plena, uncta[1] mensa. Et inter initia malam parram pilavit, sed recorrexit costas illius prima vindemia : vendidit enim vinum, quanti[2] ipse voluit. Et quod illins mentum sustulit, hereditatem accepit, ex qua plus involavit, quam illi relictum est. Et ille stips, dum fratri suo irascitur, nescio cui terrae filio patrimonium elegavit. Longe fugit, quisquis suos fugit. Habuit autem oricula-
HL rios[3] servos, qui illum pessum dederunt. | Nunquam
L autem recte faciet, qui cito credit, | utique homo negotians. Tamen verum quod frunitus est, quam diu vixit, ...[4] cui datum est, non cui destinatum. Plane Fortunae filius, in manu illins plumbum aurum fiebat. Facile est autem, ubi omnia quadrata currunt. Et quot putas illum annos secum tulisse? Septuaginta et supra. Sed corneolus fuit, aetatem bene ferebat, niger tanquam corvus. Noveram hominem olim olio-rum et adhuc salax erat. Non mehercules illum puto in domo canem reliquisse. Immo etiam pullarius[5] erat, omnis minervae homo. Nec improbo, hoc solum enim secum tulit."

44 Haec Phileros dixit, illa Ganymedes: "narratis quod nec ad caelum nec ad terram pertinet, cum interim nemo curat, quid annona mordet. Non me-

[1] plena uncta *Heinsius :* uncta plena.
[2] quanti *Scheffer :* quantum.
[3] oricularios *Reinesius :* oracularios.
[4] *Some words such as* bene vixit *have clearly dropped out.*
[5] pullarius *Burmann :* peullarius

thousand, and all in hard cash. Still, I have eaten the dog's tongue, I must speak the truth. He had a rough mouth, and talked continually, and was more of a discord than a man. His brother was a fine fellow, stood by his friends, open-banded and kept a good table. To begin with, he caught a Tartar:[1] but his first vintage set him on his feet: he used to get any price he asked for his wine. And what made him hold up his head was that he came into an estate out of which he got more than had been left to him. And that blockhead, in a fit of passion with his brother, left the family property away to some nobody or other. He that flies from his own family has far to travel. But he had some eaves-dropping slaves who did for him. A man who is always ready to believe what is told him will never do well, especially a business man. Still no doubt he enjoyed himself every day of his life. Blessed is he who gets the gift, not he for whom it is meant. He was a real Fortune's darling, lead turned gold in his hands. Yes, it is easy when everything goes fair and square. And how many years do you think he had on his shoulders? Seventy and more. But he was a tough old thing, carried his age well, as black as a crow. I had known him world without end, and he was still merry. I really do not think he spared a single creature in his house. No, he was still a gay one, ready for anything. Well, I do not blame him: it is only his past pleasures he can take with him."

So said Phileros, but Ganymede broke in: "You go 44 talking about things which are neither in heaven nor earth, and none of you care all the time how the price of food pinches. I swear I cannot get hold

[1] Literally "he plucked a bad magpie." The magpie was considered a bird of ill omen: Horace, *Odes* iii, 27.

hercules hodie buccam panis invenire potni. Et quomodo siccitas perseverat. Iam annum esuritio fuit.
Aediles male eveniat, qui cum pistoribus colludunt
'Serva me, servabo te.' Itaque populus minutus
laborat; nam isti maiores maxillae semper Saturnalia
agunt. O si haberemus illos leones, quos ego hic inveni,
cum primum ex Asia veni. Illud erat vivere. Simila
si siligine inferior esset,[1] laruas sic istos percolopabant, ut illis Iupiter iratus esset. [Sed] memini Safi-
nium: tune habitabat ad arcum veterem, me puero,
piper, non homo. Is quacunque ibat, terram adurebat.
Sed rectus, sed certus, amicus amico, cum quo audacter posses in tenebris micare. In curia autem quomodo
singulos [vel] pilabat [tractabat], nec schemas loquebatur sed derectum.[2] Cum ageret porro in foro, sic illius
vox crescebat tanquam tuba. Nec sudavit unquam
nec expuit, puto eum[3] nescio quid Asiadis habuisse.
Et quam benignus resalutare, nomina omnium reddere,
tanquam unus de nobis. Itaque illo tempore annona pro luto erat. Asse panem quem emisses, non
potuisses cum altera devorare. Nunc oculum bublum
vidi maiorem. Heu heu, quotidie peius. Haec colonia
retroversus crescit tanquam coda vituli. Sed quare nos[4]
habemus aedilem trium cauniarum, qui sibi mavult
assem quam vitam nostram? Itaque domi gaudet, plus
in die nummorum accipit, quam alter patrimonium

[1] Simila si siligine inferior esset *Buecheler:* similia sicilia
interiores et.
[2] derectum *Reiske:* dilectum.
[3] eum *Tilebomenus:* enim.
[4] nos *Tilebomenus:* non.

of ? mouthful of bread to-day. And how the drought
goes on. There has been a famine for a whole year
now. Damn the magistrates, who play 'Scratch my
back, and I'll scratch yours,' in league with the bakers.
So the little people come off badly; for the jaws of
the upper classes are always keeping carnival. I do wish
we had the bucks I found here when I first came out of
Asia. That was life. If the flour was any but the finest,
they beat those vampires into a jelly, until they put the
fear of God into them. I remember Safinius: he used
to live then by the old arch when I was a boy. He
was more of a mustard-pot than a man: used to
scorch the ground wherever he trod. Still he was
straight; you could trust him, a true friend: you
would not be afraid to play at morra[1] with him in the
dark. How he used to dress them down in the senate-
house, every one of them, never using roundabout
phrases, making a straightforward attack. And when he
was pleading in the courts, his voice used to swell like
a trumpet. ·Never any sweating or spitting: I imagine
he had a touch of the Asiatic style. And how kindly
he returned one's greeting, calling every one by name
quite like one of ourselves. So at that time food was
dirt-cheap. You could buy a larger loaf for twopence
than you and your better half together could get
through. One secs a bun bigger now. Lord, things are
worse every day. This town goes downhill like the calf's
tail. But why do we put up with a magistrate not worth
three pepper-corns, who cares more about putting twopence in his purse than keeping us alive? He sits
grinning at home, and pockets more money a day than

[1] In the game Morra one party held up a number of fingers
and the other had to guess what the number was. A man
who could play it in the dark would be a miracle.

habet. Iam scio, unde acceperit denarios mille aureos. Sed si nos colcos haberemus, non tantum sibi placeret. Nunc populus est domi leones, foras vulpes. Quod ad me attinet, iam pannos meos comedi, et si perseverat haec annona, casulas meas vendam. Quid enim futurum est, si nec dii nec homines huius coloniae miserentur? Ita meos fruniscar, ut ego puto omnia *HL* illa a diibus[1] fieri. | Nemo enim caelum caelum putat, nemo ieiunium servat, nemo Iovem pili facit, sed *H* omnes opertis oculis bona sua computant. | Antea stolatae ibant nudis pedibus in clivum, passis capillis, mentibus puris, et Iovem aquam exorabant. Itaque statim urceatim plovebat: aut tune aut nunquam: et omnes redibant udi[2] tanquam mures. Itaque dii pedes lanatos habent, quia nos religiosi non sumus. Agri iacent"—

45 "Oro te" inquit Echion centonarius "melius loquere. 'Modo sic, modo sic' inquit rusticus; varium porcum *HL* perdiderat. | Quod hodie non est, cras erit: sic vita *H* truditur. | Non mehercules patria melior dici potest, si homines haberet. Sed laborat hoc tempore, nec haec sola. Non debemus delicati esse, ubique medius caelus est. Tu si aliubi fueris, dices hic porcos coctos ambulare. Et ecce habituri sumus munus excellente in triduo die festa; familia non lanisticia, sed plurimi liberti. Et Titus noster magnum animum habet et est caldicerebrius: aut hoc aut illud crit, quid[3] utique.

---

[1] a diibus *Buecheler:* aedilibus.
[2] redibant *Jacobs:* ridebant   udi *Triller:* ut dii.
[3] quid *Heinsius:* quod.

other people have for a fortune. I happen to know where he came by a thousand in gold. If we had any spunk in us he would not be so pleased with himself. Nowadays people are lions in their own houses, and foxes out of doors. I have already eaten my rags, and if these prices keep up, I shall have to sell my cottages. Whatever is to happen if neither the gods nor man will take pity on this town? As I hope to have joy of my children, I believe all these things come from Heaven. For no one now believes that the gods are gods. There is no fasting done, no one cares a button for religion: they all shut their eyes and count their own goods. In old days the mothers in their best robes used to climb the hill with bare feet and loose hair, pure in spirit, and pray Jupiter to send rain. Then it used promptly to rain by the bucket: it was now or never: and they all came home, wet as drowned rats. As it is, the gods are gouty in the feet because we are sceptics. So our fields lie baking—"

"Oh, don't be so gloomy," said Echion, the old 45 clothes dealer. "'There's ups and there's downs,' as the country bumpkin said when he lost his spotted pig. What is not to-day, will be to-morrow: so we trudge through life. I engage you could not name a better country to call one's own, if only the men in it had sense. It has its troubles now like others. We must not be too particular when there is a sky above us all. If you were anywhere else, you would say that roast pork walked in the streets here. Just think, we are soon to be given a superb spectacle lasting three days; not simply a troupe of professional gladiators, but a large number of them freedmen. And our good Titus has a big imagination and is hot-blooded: it will be one thing or another, something real anyway. I know him

75

Nam illi domesticus sum, non est miscix. Ferrum optimum daturus est, sine fuga, carnarium in medio, ut amphitheater videat. Et habet unde: relictum est illi sestertium tricenties, decessit illins pater male. Ut quadringenta impendat, non sentiet patrimonium illins, et sempiterno nominabitur. Iam Manios aliquot habet et mulierem essedariam et dispensatorem Glyconis, qui deprehensus est, cum dominam suam delectaretur. Videbis populi rixam inter zelotypos et amasiunculos. Glyco autem, sestertiarius homo, dispensatorem ad bestias dedit. Hoc est se ipsum traducere. Quid servus peccavit, qui coactus est facere? Magis illa matella digna fuit quam taurus iactaret. Sed qui asinum non potest, stratum caedit. Quid autem Glyco putabat Hermogenis filicem unqnam bonum exitum facturam? Ille milvo volanti poterat ungues resecare; colubra restem non parit. Glyco, Glyco dedit suas; itaque quamdiu vixerit, habchit stigmam, nec illam nisi Orcus delebit. Sed sibi quisque peccat. Sed subolfacio, quod nobis epulum daturus est Mammaea, binos denarios mihi et meis. Quod si hoc fecerit, eripiat Norbano totum favorem. Scias oportet plenis velis hunc vinciturum. Et revera, quid ille nobis boni fecit? Dedit gladiatores sestertiarios iam decrepitos, quos si sufflasses, cecidissent; iam meliores bestiarios vidi. Occidit de lucerna equites,

very well, and he is all against half-measures. He
will give you the finest blades, no running away, but-
chery done in the middle, where the whole audience
can see it. And he has the wherewithal; he came
into thirty million when his father came to grief. If
he spends four hundred thousand, his estate will never
feel it, and his name will live for ever. He has already
collected some clowns, and a woman to fight from
a chariot, and Glyco's steward, who was caught
amusing Glyco's wife. You will see the crowd quarrel,
jealous husbands against gallants. A twopenny halfpenny fellow like Glyco goes throwing his steward
to the beasts. He only gives himself away. It is not
the slave's fault; he had to do as he was told. That
filthy wife of his rather deserved to be tossed by
the bull. But a man who cannot beat his donkey,
beats the saddle. How did Glyco suppose that a
sprig of Hermogenes's sowing would ever come to a
good end? He was one for paring the claws of a kite
on the wing, and you do not gather figs from thistles.[1]
Glyco? why, Glyco has given away his own flesh
and blood. He will be branded as long as he lives,
and nothing but death will wipe it out. But a man
must have his faults. My nose prophesies a good
meal from Mammaea, twopence each for me and mine.
If he does, he will put Norbanus[2] quite in the shade.
You know he will beat him hands down. After all,
what has Norbanus ever done for us? He produced
some decayed twopenny-halfpenny gladiators, who
would have fallen flat if you breathed on them; I have
seen better ruffians turned in to fight the wild beasts.
He shed the blood of some mounted infantry that might

[1] Literally "a viper does not bring forth a rope."
[2] A prosperous lawyer; see c. 46.

putares eos gallos gallinaceos; alter burdubasta, alter loripes, tertiarius mortuus pro mortuo, qui habebat[1] nervia praecisa. Unus alicuius flaturae fuit Thraex, qui et ipse ad dictata pugnavit. Ad summam, omnes postea sccti sunt; adeo de magna turba 'adhibete' acceperant, plane fugae merae. 'Munus tamen' inquit 'tibi dedi': et ego tibi plodo. Computa, et tibi plus do quam accepi. Manus manum lavat. Videris mihi, Agamemnon, dicere: 'Quid iste argutat molestus?' quia tu, qui potes loquere, non loquis.[2] Non es nostrae fasciae, et ideo pauperorum verba derides. Scimus te prae litteras fatuum esse. Quid ergo est? aliqna die te persuadeam, ut ad villam venias et videas casulas nostras? Inveniemus quod manducemus, pullum, ova: belle erit, etiam si omnia hoc anno tempestas dispare pallavit: inveniemus ergo unde saturi fiamus. Et iam tibi discipulus crescit cicaro meus. Iam quattuor partis dicit; si vixerit, habebis ad latus servulum. Nam quicquid illi vacat, caput de tabula non tollit. Ingeniosus est et bono filo, etiam si in aves morbosus est. Ego illi iam tres cardeles occidi, et dixi quod mustella comedit. Invenit tamen alias nenias, et libentissime pingit. Ceterum iam Graeculis calcem impingit et Latinas coepit non male appetere, etiam si magister eius sibi placens fit[3] nec uno loco consistit, sed venit,

46

---

[1] habebat *Buecheler:* habet.
[2] loquis *Burmann:* loqui.
[3] fit *Buecheler:* sit.

have come off a lamp; dunghill cocks you would have called them: one a spavined mule, the other bandy-legged, and the holder of the bye, just one corpse instead of another, and hamstrung. One man, a Thracian, had some stuffing, but he too fought according to the rule of the schools. In short, they were all flogged afterwards. How the great crowd roared at them, 'Lay it on'! They were mere runaways, to be sure. 'Still,' says Norbanus, 'I did give you a treat.' Yes, and I clap my hands at you. Reckon it up, and I give you more than I got. One good turn deserves another. Now, Agamemnon, you look as if you 46 were saying, 'What is this bore chattering for?' Only because you have the gift of tongues and do not speak. You do not come off our shelf, and so you make fun of the way we poor men talk. We know you are mad with much learning. But I tell you what; can I persuade you to come down to my place some day and see my little property? We shall find something to eat, a chicken and eggs: it will be delightful, even though the weather this year has made everything grow at the wrong time: we shall find something to fill ourselves up with. My little boy is growing into a follower of yours already. He can do simple division now; if he lives, you will have a little servant at your heels. Whenever he has any spare time, he never lifts his nose from the slate. He is clever, and comes of a good stock, even though he is too fond of birds. I killed three of his goldfinches just lately, and said a weasel had eaten them. But he has found some other hobby, and has taken to painting with great pleasure. He has made a hole in his Greek now, and begins to relish Latin finely, even though his master is conceited and will not stick to one thing at a time. The boy comes

dem litteras, sed non vult laborare. Est et alter non quidem doctus, sed curiosus, qui plus docet quam seit. Itaque feriatis diebus solet domum venire, et quicquid dederis, contentus est. Emi ergo nunc puero aliquot libra rubricata, quia volo illum ad domusionem aliquid de iure gustare. Habet haec res panem. Nam litteris satis inquinatus est. Quod si resilierit, destinavi illum artificii docere, aut tonstreinum[1] aut praeconem aut certe causidicum, quod illi auferre non possit nisi Orcus. Ideo illi cotidie clamo: 'Primigeni, crede mihi, quicquid diseis, tibi diseis. Vides Phileronem causidicum: si non didicisset, hodie famem a lahris non abigeret. Modo, modo collo suo circumferebat onera venalia, nunc etiam adversus Norbanum se extendit. Litterae thesaurum est, et artificium nunquam moritur.'"

47 Eiusmodi fabulae vibrabant, cum Trimalchio intravit et detersa fronte unguento manus lavit spatioque minimo interposito "Ignoscite mihi" inquit "amici, multis iam diebus venter mihi non respondit. Nec medici se inveniunt. Profuit mihi tamen malicorium[2] et taeda ex aceto. Spero tamen, iam veterem[3] pudorem sibi imponet. Alioquin circa stomachum mihi sonat, putes tanrum. Itaque si quis vestrum voluerit sua re [causa][4] facere, non est quod illum pudeatur. Nemo nostrum solide natus est. Ego nullum puto tam magnum tormentum esse quam continere. Hoc so-

---

[1] tonstrinum *Scheffer:* constreinum.
[2] malicorium *Scheffer:* maleicorum.
[3] veterem *Heinsius:* ventrem.
[4] causa *bracketed by Scheffer.*

asking me to give him some writing to do, though he does not want to work. I have another boy who is no scholar, but very inquiring, and can teach you more than he knows himself. So on holidays he generally comes home, and is quite pleased whatever you give him. I bought the child some books with red-letter headings in them a little time ago. I want him to have a smack of law in order to manage the property. Law has bread and butter in it. He has dipped quite deep enough into literature. If he is restless, I mean to have him learn a trade, a barber or an auctioneer, or at least a barrister, something that he can carry to the grave with him. So I drum it into him every day: 'Mark my words, Primigenius, whatever you learn, you learn for your own good. Look at Phileros, the barrister: if he had not worked, he would not be keeping the wolf from the door to-day. It is not so long since he used to carry things round on his back and sell them, and now he makes a brave show even against Norbanus. Yes, education is a treasure, and culture never dies.'"

Gossip of this kind was in the air, when Trimalchio 47 came in mopping his brow, and washed his hands in scent. After a short pause, he said, "You will excuse me, gentlemen? My bowels have not been working for several days. All the doctors are puzzled. Still, I found pomegranate rind useful, and pinewood boiled in vinegar. I hope now my stomach will learn to observe its old decencies. Besides, I have such rumblings inside me you would think there was a bull there. So if any of you gentlemen wishes to retire there is no need to be shy about it. We were none of us born quite solid. I cannot imagine any torture like holding oneself in. The one thing Jupiter himself cannot forbid

lum vetare ne Iovis potest. Rides, Fortunata, quae soles me nocte desomnem facere? Nec tamen in triclinio ullum vetuo[1] facere quod se iuvet, et medici vetant continere. Vel si quid plus venit, omnia foras parata sunt: aqua, lasani et cetera minutalia. Credite mihi, anathymiasis in cerebrum it et in toto corpore fluctum facit. Multos scio sic periisse, dum nolunt sibi verum dicere." Gratias agimus liberalitati indulgentiaeque eius, et subinde castigamus crebris potiunculis risum. Nec adhuc sciebamus nos in medio lautitiarum, quod[2] aiunt, clivo laborare. Nam cum mundatis ad symphoniam mensis tres albi sues in triclinium adducti sunt capistris et tintinnabulis culti, quorum unum bimum nomenculator esse dicebat, alterum trimum, tertium vero iam sexennem,[3] ego putabam petauristarios intrasse et porcos, sicut in circulis mos est, portenta aliqna facturos; sed Trimalchio expectatione discussa "Quem" inquit "ex eis vultis in cenam statim fieri? gallum enim gallinaceum, penthiacum et eiusmodi nenias rustici faciunt: mei coci etiam vitulos aeno coctos solent facere." Continuoque cocum vocari iussit, et non expectata electione nostra maximum natu iussit occidi, et clara voce: "Ex quota decuria es?" Cum ille se ex quadragesima respondisset, "Empticius an" inquit "domi natus?" "Neutrum" inquit cocus "sed testamento Pansae tibi relictus sum." "Vide ergo" ait "ut diligenter ponas;

[1] vetuo *Buecheler:* vetui.
[2] quod *Heinsius:* quo.
[3] sexennem *Wehl:* senem.

is that we should have relief. Why do you laugh, Fortunata; it is you who are always keeping me awake all night. Of course, as far as I am concerned, anyone may relieve himself in the dining-room. The doctors forbid retention. But if the matter is serious, everything is ready outside: water, towels, and all the other little comforts. Take my word for it, vapours go to the brain and make a disturbance throughout the body. I know many people have died this way, by refusing to admit the truth to themselves." We thanked him for his generosity and kindness, and then tried to suppress our laughter by drinking hard and fast. We did not yet realize that we had only got halfway through the delicacies, and still had an uphill task before us, as they say. The tables were cleared to the sound of music, and three white pigs, adorned with muzzles and bells, were led into the dining-room. One was two years old, the keeper said, the second three, and the other as much as six. I thought some ropewalkers had come in, and that the pigs would perform some wonderful tricks, as they do for crowds in the streets. Trimalchio ended our suspense by saying, "Now, which of them would you like turned into a dinner this minute? Any country hand can turn out a fowl or a Pentheus[1] hash, or trifles of that kind. My cooks are quite used to serving whole calves done in a cauldron." Then he told them to fetch a cook at once, and without waiting for our opinion ordered the eldest pig to be killed, and said in a loud voice, "Which division of the household do you belong to?" The man said he came from the fortieth. "Were you purchased or born on the estate?" "Neither; I was left to you under Pansa's will." "Well then," said

[1] Pentheus, king of Thebes, was torn in pieces by the Bacchae.

si non, te iubebo in decuriam viatorum conici." Et
48 cocum quidem potentiae admonitum in culinam obsonium duxit, Trimalchio autem mihi ad nos vultu
respexit et "Vinum" inquit "si non placet, mutabo;
vos illud oportet bonum faciatis. Deorum beneficio non emo, sed nunc quicquid ad salivam facit, in
suburbano nascitur eo, quod ego adhuc non novi.
Dicitur confine esse Tarraciniensibus et Tarentinis.
Nunc coniungere agellis Siciliam volo, ut cum Africam
libuerit ire, per meos fines navigem. Sed narra tu mihi,
Agamemnon, quam controversiam hodie declamasti?
Ego etiam[1] si causas non ago, in domusionem[2] tamen
litteras didici. Et ne me putes studia fastiditum,
II[3] bybliothecas habeo, unam Graecam, alteram Lati-
nam. Dic ergo, si me amas, peristasim declamationis
tuae." Cum dixisset Agamemnon: "Pauper et dives
inimici erant," ait Trimalchio "Quid est pauper?"
"Urbane" inquit Agamemnon et nescio quam controversiam exposuit. Statim Trimalchio "Hoc" inquit
"si factum est, controversia non est; si factum non
est, nihil est." Haec aliaque cum effusissimis prose-
queremur laudationibus, "Rogo" inquit "Agamemnon
mihi carissime, numquid duodecim aerumnas Herculis
tenes, aut de Vlixe fabulam, quemadmodum illi Cyclops pollicem forcipe[4] extorsit? Solebam haec ego
puer apud Homerum legere. Nam Sibyllam quidem
Cumis ego ipse oculis meis vidi in ampulla pendere,

[1] etiam *Wehl:* autem.
[2] domusionem *Wehl:* divisione.
[3] II *Tilebomenus:* tres.
[4] forcipe *Buecheler:* poricino.

84

Trimalchio, "mind you serve this carefully, or I will have you degraded to the messengers' division." So the cook was reminded of his master's power, and the 48 dish that was to be carried him off to the kitchen. Trimalchio turned to us with a mild expression and said, "I will change the wine if you do not like it. You will have to give it its virtues. Under God's providence, I do not have to buy it. Anything here which makes your months water is grown on a country estate of mine which I know nothing about as yet. I believe it is on the boundary of Terracina and Tarentum. Just now I want to join up all Sicily with properties of mine, so that if I take a fancy to go to Africa I shall travel through my own land. But do tell me, Agamemnon, what declamation[1] did you deliver in school to-day? Of course, I do not practise in court myself, but I learned literature for domestic purposes. And do not imagine that I despise learning. I have got two libraries, one Greek and one Latin. So give me an outline of your speech, if you love me." Then Agamemnon said: "A poor man and a rich man were once at enmity." "But what is a poor man?" Trimalchio replied. "Very clever," said Agamemnon, and went on expounding some problem or other. Trimalchio at once retorted: "If the thing really happened, there is no problem; if it never happened, it is all nonsense." We followed up this and other sallies with the most extravagant admiration. "Tell me, dear Agamemnon," said Trimalchio, "do you know anything of the twelve labours of Hercules, or the story of Ulysses and how the Cyclops twisted his thumb with the tongs? I used to read these things in Homer when I was a boy. Yes, and I myself with my own

[1] *Controversia* is a declamation on a controversial theme.

85

et cum illi pueri dicerent: Σίβυλλα, τί θέλεις; respondebat illa: ἀποθανεῖν θέλω."

19   Nondum efflaverat omnia, cum repositorium cum sue ingenti mensam occupavit. Mirari nos celeritatem coepimus et iurare, ne gallum quidem gallinaceum tam cito percoqui potuisse, tanto quidem magis, quod longe maior nobis porcus videbatur esse, quam paulo ante aper fuerat. Deinde magis magisque Trimalchio intuens eum "Quid? quid?" inquit "porcus hic non est exinteratus? Non mehercules est. Voca, voca cocum in medio." Cum constitisset ad mensam cocus tristis et diceret se oblitum esse exinterare, "quid? oblitus?" Trimalchio exclamat "Putes illum piper et cuminum non coniecisse. Despolia." Non fit mora, despoliatur cocus atque inter duos tortores maestus consistit. Deprecari tamen omnes coeperunt et dicere: "Solet fieri; rogamus, mittas; postea si fecerit, nemo nostrum pro illo rogabit." Ego, crudelissimae severitatis, non potni me tenere, sed inclinatus ad aurem Agamemnonis "plane" inquam "hic debet servus esse nequissimus; aliquis oblivisceretur porcum exinterare? Non mehercules illi ignoscerem, si piscem praeterisset." At non Trimalchio, qui relaxato in hilaritatem vultu "Ergo" inquit "quia tam malae memoriae es, palam nobis illum exintera." Recepta cocus tunica cultrum arripuit porcique ventrem hinc atque illinc timida manu secuit. Nec mora,

eyes saw the Sibyl hanging in a cage; and when the boys cried at her: 'Sibyl, Sibyl, what do you want?' 'I would that I were dead,' she used to answer."[1]

He had still more talk to puff out, when the table 49 was filled by a dish holding an enormous pig. We began to express astonishment at such speed, and took our oath that not even a fowl could have been properly cooked in the time, especially as the pig seemed to us to be much bigger than the boar had been a little while earlier. Trimalchio looked at it more and more closely and then said, "What, what, has not this pig been gutted? I swear it has not. The cook, send the cook up here to us." The poor cook came and stood by the table and said that he had forgotten to gut it. "What? Forgotten?" shouted Trimalchio. "You would think the fellow had only forgotten to season it with pepper and cummin. Off with his shirt!" In a moment the cook was stripped and stood dolefully between two executioners. Then we all began to beg him off and say: "These things will happen; do let him go; if he does it again none of us will say a word for him." I was as stiff and stern as could be; I could not restrain myself, but leaned over and said in Agamemnon's ear: "This must be a most wretched servant; how could anyone forget to gut a pig? On my oath I would not forgive him if he had let a fish go like that." But Trimalchio's face softened into smiles. "Well," he said, "if your memory is so bad, clean him here in front of us." The cook put on his shirt, seized a knife, and carved the pig's belly in various places with a shaking hand. At once the

[1] Sibyls were said to live to a great age; their mummies continued to be exhibited after their death. A confusion with the myth of Tithonus, who was turned into a grasshopper.

ex plagis ponderis inclinatione crescentibus tomacʋ.ᴅ cum botulis effusa sunt.

50 Flansum post hoc automatum familia dedit et "Gaio feliciter" conclamavit. Nec non cocus potione hono-ratus est et argentea corona, poculumque in lance accepit Corinthia. Quam cum Agamemnon propius consideraret, ait Trimalchio: "Solus sum qui vera Co-rinthea habeam." Expectabam, ut pro reliqua inso-lentia diceret sibi vasa Corintho afferri. Sed ille melius: "Et forsitan" inquit "quaeris, quare solus Corinthea vera possideam: quia scilicet aerarius, a quo emo, Corinthus vocatur. Quid est autem Corintheum, nisi quis Corinthum habet? Et ne me putetis nesapium esse, valde bene scio, unde primum Corinthea nata sint. Cum Ilium captum est, Hannibal, homo vafer et magnus stelio,[1] omnes statuas aeneas et aureas et argenteas in unum rogum congessit et eas incendit; factae sunt in unum aera miscellanea. Ita ex hac massa fabri sustulerunt et fecerunt catilla et paropsides et statuncula. Sic Corinthea nata sunt, ex omnibus in unum, nec hoc nec illud. Ignoscetis mihi, quod dixero: ego malo mihi vitrea, certe non olunt.[2] Quod
51 si non frangerentur, mallem mihi quam aurum; nunc autem vilia sunt. Fuit tamen faber qui fecit phialam vitream, quae non frangebatur. Admissus ergo Cae-sarem est cum suo munere, deinde fecit reporrigere Caesarem[3] et illam in pavimentum proiecit. Caesar non pote valdius quam expavit. At ille sustulit phialam

[1] stelio *Heinsius:* scelio.
[2] non olunt *Buecheler:* nolunt.
[3] Caesarem *Scheffer:* Caesari.

slits widened under the pressure from within, and sausages and black puddings tumbled out.

At this the slaves burst into spontaneous applause 50 and shouted, "God bless Gaius!" The cook too was rewarded with a drink and a silver crown, and was handed the cup on a Corinthian dish. Agamemnon began to peer at the dish rather closely, and Trimalchio said, "I am the sole owner of genuine Corinthian plate." I thought he would declare with his usual effrontery that he had cups imported direct from Corinth. But he went one better: "You may perhaps inquire," said he, "how I come to be alone in having genuine Corinthian stuff: the obvious reason is that the name of the dealer I buy it from is Corinthus. But what is real Corinthian, unless a man has Corinthus at his back? Do not imagine that I am an ignoramus. I know perfectly well how Corinthian plate was first brought into the world. At the fall of Ilium, Hannibal, a trickster and a great knave, collected all the sculptures, bronze, gold, and silver, into a single pile, and set light to them. They all melted into one amalgam of bronze. The workmen took bits out of this lump and made plates and entrée dishes and statuettes. That is how Corinthian metal was born, from all sorts lumped together, neither one kind nor the other. You will forgive me if I say that personally I prefer glass; glass at least does not smell. If it were not so breakable I should prefer it to gold; as it is, it is so cheap. But there was once a workman who 51 made a glass cup that was unbreakable. So he was given an audience of the Emperor with his invention; he made Caesar give it back to him and then threw it on the floor. Caesar was as frightened as could be. But the man picked up his cup from the ground: it

89

de terra; collisa erat tamquam vasum aeneum; deinde martiolum de sinu protulit et phialam otio belle correxit. Hoc facto putabat se solium[1] Iovis tenere, utique postquam Caesar[2] illi dixit: 'Numquid alius seit hanc condituram vitreorum?' vide modo. Postquam negavit, iussit illum Caesar decollari: quia enim, si scitum esset, aurum pro luto haberemus. In argento
52 plane studiosus sum. Habeo scyphos urnales plus minus C: quemadmodum Cassandra occidit filios suos, et pueri mortui iacent sic ut vivere[3] putes. Habeo capides[4] M, quas reliquit patrono meo Mummius,[5] ubi Daedalus Niobam in equum Troianum includit. Nam Hermerotis pugnas et Petraitis in poculis habeo, omnia ponderosa; meum enim intelligere nulla pecunia vendo."

Haec dum refert, puer calicem proiecit. Ad quem respiciens Trimalchio "Cito" inquit "te ipsum caede, quia nugax es." Statim puer demisso labro orare. At ille "Quid me" inquit "rogas? Tanquam ego tibi molestus sim. Suadeo, a te impetres, ne sis nugax." Tandem ergo exoratus a nobis missionem dedit puero. Ille dimissus circa mensam percucurrit . . .

et "Aquam foras, vinum intro" clamavit . . . excipimus urbanitatem iocantis, et ante omnes Agamemnon, qui sciebat, quibus meritis revocaretur ad

---

[1] solium *Heinsius:* coleum.
[2] Caesar *added by Buecheler.*
[3] sic ut vivere *Heinsius:* siculi vere.
[4] capides M *Buecheler:* capidem.
[5] patrono meo Mummius *Buecheler:* patronorum meus.

was dinted like a bronze bowl; then he took a little hammer out of his pocket and made the cup quite sound again without any trouble. After doing this he thought he had himself seated on the throne of Jupiter, especially when Caesar said to him: 'Does anyone else know how to blow glass like this?' Just see what happened. He said not, and then Caesar had him beheaded. Why? Because if his invention were generally known we should treat gold like dirt. Myself I have a great passion for silver. I own about 52 a hundred four-gallon cups engraved with Cassandra killing her children, and they lying there dead in the most lifelike way. I have a thousand jugs which Mummius[1] left to my patron, and on them you see Daedalus shutting Niobe into the Trojan horse. And I have got the fights between Hermeros and Petraites[2] on my cups, and every cup is a heavy one; for I do not sell my connoisseurship for any money."

As he was speaking, a boy dropped a cup. Trimalchio looked at him and said, "Quick, off with your own head, since you are so stupid." The boy's lip fell and he began to petition. "Why do you ask me?" said Trimalchio, "as if I should be hard on you! I advise you to prevail upon yourself not to be stupid." In the end we induced him to let the boy off. As soon as he was forgiven the boy ran round the table. . . .

Then Trimalchio shouted, "Out with water! In with wine!" . . . We took up the joke, especially Agamemnon, who knew how to earn a second invitation

---

[1] The name is suggested by the previous references to Corinth. L. Mummius Achaicus captured and sacked Corinth in 146 B.C.

[2] Celebrated gladiators of the period. Trimalchio in c. 71 orders the fights of Petraites to be depicted on his tomb.

cenam. Ceterum laudatus Trimalchio hilarius bibit
et iam ebrio proximus "Nemo" inquit "vestrum rogat
Fortunatam meam, ut saltet? Credite mihi: cordacem
nemo melius ducit."

Atque ipse erectis supra frontem manibus Syrum
histrionem exhibebat concinente tota familia: μάδεια
περιμάδεια. Et prodisset in medium, nisi Fortunata
ad aurem accessisset; [et] credo, dixerit non decere
gravitatem eius tam humiles ineptias. Nihil autem
tam inaequale erat; nam modo Fortunatam verebatur,
modo ad naturam suam revertebatur.[1]

53 Et plane interpellavit saltationis libidinem actuarius, qui tanquam urbis acta recitavit: "VII. kalendas
sextiles: in praedio Cumano, quod est Trimalchionis,
nati sunt pueri xxx, puellae xl; sublata in horreum
ex area tritici millia modium quingenta; boves domiti
quingenti. Eodem die: Mithridates servus in crucem
actus est, quia Gai nostri genio male dixerat. Eodem
die: in arcam relatum est, quod collocari non potuit,
sestertium centies. Eodem die: incendium factum
est in hortis Pompeianis, ortum ex aedibus Nastae
vilici." ."Quid?" inquit Trimalchio "quando mihi
Pompeiani horti empti sunt?" "Anno priore" inquit
actuarius "et ideo in rationem nondum venerunt."
Excanduit Trimalchio et "Quicunque" inquit "mihi
fundi empti fuerint, nisi intra sextum mensem sciero,

[1] fortunatam suam revertebatur modo ad naturam *MSS.,*
corrected by Heinsius and Buecheler.

to dinner. Trimalchio warmed to his drinking under our flattery, and was almost drunk when he said: "None of you ask dear Fortunata to dance. I tell you no one can dance the cancan better." He then lifted his hands above his head and gave us the actor Syrus, while all the slaves sang in chorus:

Madeia!
Perimadeia![1]

And Trimalchio would have come out into the middle of the room if Fortunata had not whispered in his ear. I suppose she told him that such low fooling was beneath his dignity. But never was anything so variable; at one moment he was afraid of Fortunata, and then he would return to his natural self.

But a clerk quite interrupted his passion for the 53 dance by reading as though from the gazette: "July the 26th. Thirty boys and forty girls were born on Trimalchio's estate at Cumae. Five hundred thousand pecks of wheat were taken up from the threshing-floor into the barn. Five hundred oxen were broken in. On the same date: the slave Mithridates was led to crucifixion for having damned the soul of our lord Gaius. On the same date: ten million sesterces which could not be invested were returned to the reserve. On the same day: there was a fire in our gardens at Pompeii, which broke out in the house of Nasta the bailiff." "Stop," said Trimalchio, "When did I buy any gardens at Pompeii?" "Last year," said the clerk, "so that they are not entered in your accounts yet." Trimalchio glowed with passion, and said, "I will not have any property which is bought in my name entered in my accounts

[1] The meaning of these words is uncertain.

in rationes meas inferri vetno." Iam etiam edicta aedilium recitabantur et saltuariorum testamenta, quibus Trimalchio cum elogio exheredabatur; iam nomina vilicorum et repudiata a circitore liberta in balneatoris contubernio deprehensa et atriensis Baias relegatus; iam reus factus dispensator et iudicium inter cubicularios actnm.

Petauristarii autem tandem venerunt. Baro insulsissimus cum scalis constitit puerumque iussit per gradus et in summa parte odaria saltare, circulos deinde ardentes transilire[1] et dentibus amphoram sustinere. Mirabatur haec solus Trimalchio dicebatque ingratum artificium esse. Ceterum duo esse in rebus humanis, quae libentissime spectaret, petauristarios et cornicines;[2] reliqua [animalia][3] acroamata tricas meras esse. "Nam et comoedos" inquit "emeram, sed malui illos Atellaniam[4] facere, et choraulen meum iussi Latine cantare."

54 Cum maxime haec dicente Gaio puer[5] . . . . Trimalchionis delapsus est. Conclamavit familia, nec minus convivae, non propter hominem tam putidum, cuius et cervices fractas libenter vidissent, sed propter malum exitum cenae, ne necesse haberent alienum mortuum plorare. Ipse Trimalchio cum graviter ingemuisset superque brachium tanquam laesum incubuisset, concurrere medici, et inter primos Fortunata crinibus passis cum scypho, miseramque se atque infe-

---

[1] transilire *Heinsius:* transire.
[2] cornicines *Heinsius:* cornices.
[3] animalia *bracketed by Buecheler.*
[4] Atellaniam *Buecheler:* atellam.
[5] *Some words such as* in brachium *have clearly fallen out.*

unless I hear of it within six months." We now had a further recitation of police notices, and some foresters' wills, in which Trimalchio was cut out in a codicil; then the names of bailiffs, and of a freed-woman who had been caught with a bathman and divorced by her husband, a night watchman; the name of a porter who had been banished to Baiae; the name of a steward who was being prosecuted, and details of an action between some valets.

But at last the acrobats came in. A very dull fool stood there with a ladder and made a boy dance from rung to rung and on the very top to the music of popular airs, and then made him hop through burning hoops, and pick up a wine jar with his teeth. No one was excited by this but Trimalchio, who kept saying that it was a thankless profession. There were only two things in the world that he could watch with real pleasure, acrobats and trumpeters; all other shows were silly nonsense. "Why," said he, "I once bought a Greek comedy company, but I preferred them to do Atellane plays,[1] and I told my flute-player to have Latin songs."

Just as Trimalchio was speaking the boy slipped 54 and fell [against his arm]. The slaves raised a cry, and so did the guests, not over a disgusting creature whose neck they would have been glad to see broken, but because it would have been a gloomy finish to the dinner to have to shed tears over the death of a perfect stranger. Trimalchio groaned aloud, and nursed his arm as if it was hurt. Doctors rushed up, and among the first Fortunata, with her hair down, and a cup in her hand, calling out what a poor unhappy

[1] Native Latin comedy as opposed to *comoedia palliata*, which was translated or adapted from the Greek.

licem proclamavit. Nam puer quidem, qui ceciderat, circumibat iam dudum pedes nostros et missionem rogabat. Pessime mihi erat, ne his precibus per ridiculum[1] aliquid catastropha quaereretur. Nec enim adhuc exciderat cocus ille, qui oblitus fuerat porcum exinterare. Itaque totum circumspicere triclinium coepi, ne per parietem automatum aliquod exiret, utique postquam servus verberari coepit, qui brachium domini contusum alba potins quam conchyliata involverat lana. Nec longe aberravit suspicio mea; in vicem enim poenae[2] venit decretum Trimalchionis, quo puerum iussit liberum esse, ne quis posset dicere, tantum virum esse a servo vulneratum.[3]

55 *HLO/H* | Comprobamus nos factum | et quam in praecipiti
   HLO res humanae essent, | vario sermone garrimus. |
     H "Ita" inquit Trimalchio "non oportet hunc casum
       sine inscriptione transire" statimque codicillos poposcit et non diu cogitatione distorta haec recitavit:
   HL | "Quod non expectes, ex transverso fit . . . .[4]
       —et supra nos Fortuna negotia curat.
   H | quare da nobis vina Falerna, puer."
  HLO   ab hoc epigrammate | coepit poetarum esse mentio
       diuque summa carminis penes Mopsum Thracem memorata est donec Trimalchio "Rogo" inquit "magister, quid putas inter Ciceronem et Publilium interesse? Ego alterum puto disertiorem fuisse, alterum honestiorem. Quid enim his melius dici potest?

[1] per ridiculum *Buecheler:* periculo.
[2] poenae *Hadrianides:* cenae.
[3] vulneratum *Scheffer:* liberatum.
[4] *Heinsius would supply* ubique, nostra, *to fill the gap between* fit *and* et.

woman she was. The creature who had fallen down was crawling round at our feet by this time, and begging for mercy. I was very much afraid that his petition was leading up to some comic surprise. The cook who had forgotten to gut the pig had not yet faded from my recollection. So I began looking all round the dining-room, in case any clockwork toy should jump out of the wall, especially after they had begun to beat a servant for dressing the bruise on his master's arm with white wool instead of purple. And my suspicions were not far out. Instead of punishment there came Trimalchio's decree that he should be made a free man, for fear anyone might be able to say that our hero had been wounded by a slave.

We applauded his action, and made small talk in different phrases about the uncertainty of man's affairs. "Ah," said Trimalchio, "then we should not let this occasion slip without a record." And he called at once for paper, and after very brief reflection declaimed these halting verses: 55

"What men do not look for turns about and comes to pass. And high over us Fortune directs our affairs. Wherefore, slave, hand us Falernian wine."

A discussion of poetry arose out of this epigram, and for a long time it was maintained that Mopsus of Thrace held the crown of song in his hand, until Trimalchio said, "Now, I ask you as a scholar, how would you compare Cicero and Publilius?[1] In my opinion the first has more eloquence, the second more beauty. For what could be better written than these lines?

[1] Publilius is Publilius Syrus, a famous writer of farce. It is not certain whether the verses which follow are actually by him or not.

"'Luxuriae rictu Martis marcent moenia.
Tuo palato clausus pavo pascitur[1]
plumato amictus aureo Babylonico,
gallina tibi Numidica, tibi gallus spado;
ciconia etiam, grata peregrina hospita
pietaticultrix gracilipes crotalistria,
avis exul hiemis, titulus tepidi temporis,
nequitiae nidum in caccabo fecit modo.[2]
Quo margarita cara tibi, hacam Indicam?[3]
An ut matrona ornata phaleris pelagiis
tollat pedes indomita in strato extraneo?
Zmaragdum ad quam rem viridem, pretio-
  sum vitrum?
Quo Carchedonios optas ignes lapideos,
nisi ut scintillet probitas e carbunculis?[4]
Aequum est induere nuptam ventum textilem,
palam prostare nudam in nebula linea?'

56 *H* | "Quod autem" inquit "putamus secundum litteras difficillimum esse artificium? Ego puto medicum et nummularium: medicus, qui seit quid homunciones intra praecordia sua habeant et quando febris veniat, etiam si illos odi pessime, quod mihi iubent saepe anatinam parari; nummularius, qui per argentum aes videt. Nam mutae bestiac laboriosissimae boves et oves: boves, quorum beneficio panem manducamus; oves, quod lana illac nos gloriosos faciunt. Et facinus indignum, aliquis ovillam est et tunicam habet. Apes enim ego divinas bestias puto, quae mel vomunt, etiam *HL* si dicuntur illud a Iove afferre; | ideo autem pungunt, quia ubicunque dulce est, ibi et acidum invenies."

[1] pascitur *Scaliger:* nascitur.   [2] modo *Jacobs:* meo.
[3] tibi, hacam Indicam. *Heinsius:* tribaca Indica
[4] e *cod. Bernensis:* est *other MSS.* carbunculis *Buecheler:* carbunculus—os *or*—as.

SATYRICON

" 'The high walls of Mars crumble beneath the gaping jaws of luxury. To please thy palate the peacock in his Babylonian vesture of gilded feathers is prisoned and fed, for thee the guinea-fowl, and for thee the capon. Even our beloved foreign guest the stork, type of parental love, with thin legs and sounding rattle, the bird exiled by winter, the harbinger of the warm weather, has now built a nest in thine abhorred cooking-pot. What are pearls of price, the fruits of India, to thee? For thy wife to be adorned with sea-spoils when she lies unchecked on a strange man's bed? For what end dost thou require the green emerald, the precious crystal, or the fire that lies in the jewels of Carthage, save that honesty should shine forth from amid the carbuncles? Thy bride might as well clothe herself with a garment of the wind as stand forth publicly naked under her clouds of muslin.'

"And now," said he, "what do we think is the 56 hardest profession after writing? I think a doctor's or a money-changer's. The doctor's, because he knows what poor men have in their insides, and when a fever will come—though I detest them specially, because they so often order me to live on duck. The money-changer's, because he secs the copper under the silver. Just so among the dumb animals, oxen and sheep are the hardest workers: the oxen, because thanks to the oxen we have bread to eat; the sheep, because their wool clothes us in splendour. It is a gross outrage when people eat lamb and wear shirts. Yes, and I hold the bees to be the most divine insects. They vomit honey, although people do say they bring it from Jupiter: and they have stings, because wherever you have a sweet thing there you will find something bitter too."

TITUS PETRONIUS ARBITER

H | Iam etiam philosophos de negotio deiciebat, cum pittacia in scypho circumferri coeperunt, puerque super hoc positus officium apophoreta recitavit. "Argentum sceleratum": allata est perna, super quam acetabula erant posita. "Cervical": offla collaris allata est. "Serisapia et contumelia": xerophagi ex sapa[1] datae sunt et contus cum malo. "Porri et persica": flagellum et cultrum accepit; "passeres et muscarium": uvam passam et mel Atticum. "Cenatoria et forensia": offlam et tabulas accepit. "Canale et pedale": lepus et solea est allata. "Muraena et littera": murem cum rana alligata fascemque betae accepit.[2] Diu risimus: sexcenta huiusmodi fuerunt, quae iam exciderunt memoriae meae.

57   Ceterum Ascyltos, intemperantis licentiae, cum omnia sublatis manibus eluderet et usque ad lacrimas rideret, unus ex conlibertis Trimalchionis excanduit, is ipse qui supra me discumbebat, et "Quid rides" inquit "vervex? An tibi non placent lautitiae domini mei? Tu enim beatior es et convivare melius soles. Ita tutelam huius loci habeam propitiam, ut ego si secundum illum discumberem, iam illi balatum duxis-

[1] xerophagi ex sapa *Friedlaender:* aecrophagie saele.
[2] accepit *added by Buecheler.*

100

He was just throwing the philosophers out of work, when tickets were carried round in a cup, and a boy who was entrusted with this duty read aloud the names of the presents for the guests.[1] "Tainted metal"; a ham was brought in with a vinegar bottle on top of it. "Something soft for the neck"; a scrap of neck-end was put on. "Repenting at leisure and obstinate badness"; we were given biscuits made with must, and a thick stick with an apple. "Leeks and peaches"; he took a scourge and a dagger. "Sparrows and fly-paper"; he picked up some dried grapes and a honey-pot. "Evening-dress and outdoor clothes"; he handled a piece of meat and some note-books. "Canal and foot-measure"; a bare and a slipper were introduced. "The muræna and a letter"; he took a mouse and a frog tied together, and a bundle of beetroot. We laughed loud and long: there were any number of these jokes, which have now escaped my memory.

Ascyltos let himself go completely, threw up his **57** hands and made fun of everything, and laughed till he cried. This annoyed one of Trimalchio's fellow-freedmen, the man who was sitting next above me. "What are you laughing at, sheep's head?" he said. "Are our host's good things not good enough for you? I suppose you are richer and used to better living? As I hope to have the spirits of this place on my side, if I had been sitting next him I should have put a stopper on his bleating by now. A nice young

[1] *Apophoreta* are presents for guests to carry away. It was customary to hand tickets to them on which riddles concealing the names of the presents were written. Trimalchio's jokes depend upon allusions to likenesses between the words in the riddle and the name of the present, and are therefore impossible to render in English.

sem. Bellum pomum, qui rideatur alios; larifuga nescio quis, nocturnus, qui non valet lotium suum. Ad summam, si circumminxero illum, nesciet qua fugiat. Non mehercules solco cito fervere, sed in molle carne vermes nascuntur. Ridet. Quid habet quod rideat? Numquid pater fetum emit lamna? Eques Romanus es: et ego regis filius. 'Quare ergo servivisti?' Quia ipse me dedi in servitutem et malui civis Romanus esse quam tributarius. Et nunc spero me sic vivere, ut nemini iocus sim. Homo inter homines sum, capite aperto ambulo; assem aerarium nemini debeo; constitutum habui nunquam; nemo mihi in foro dixit 'redde quod debes.' Glebulas emi, lamellulas paravi; viginti ventres paseo et canem; contubernalem meam redemi, ne quis in sinu illius manus tergeret; mille denarios pro capite solvi; sevir gratis factus sum; spero, sic moriar, ut mortuus non erubescam. Tu autem tam laboriosus es, ut post te non respicias? In alio peduclum vides, in te ricinum non vides. Tibi soli ridiclei videmur; ecce magister tuns, homo maior natus: placemus illi. Tu lacticulosus, nec mu nec ma argutas, vasus fictilis, immo lorus in aqua, lentior, non melior. Tu beatior es: bis prande, bis cena. Ego fidem meam malo quam thesanros. Ad summam, quisquam me bis poposcit? Annis quadraginta servivi; nemo tamen sciit, utrum servus essem an liber. Et puer capillatus in hanc coloniam veni; adhuc basilica non erat facta. Dedi

102

shaver to laugh at other people! Some vagabond fly by-night not worth his salt. In fact, when I've done with him he won't know where to take refuge. Upon my word, I am not easily annoyed as a rule, but in rotten flesh worms will breed. He laughs. What has he got to laugh about? Did his father pay solid gold for him when he was a baby? A Roman knight, are you? Well, I am a king's son. 'Then why have you been a slave?' Because I went into service to please myself, and preferred being a Roman citizen to going on paying taxes as a provincial. And now I hope I live such a life that no one can jeer at me. I am a man among men; I walk about bare-beaded; I owe nobody a brass farthing; I have never been in the Courts; no one has ever said to me in public, 'Pay me what you owe me.' I have bought a few acres and collected a little capital; I have to feed twenty bellies and a dog: I ransomed my fellow slave to preserve her from indignities; I paid a thousand silver pennies for my own freedom; I was made a priest of Augustus and excused the fees; I hope to die so that I need not blush in my grave. But are you so full of business that you have no time to look behind you? You can see the lice on others, but not the bugs on yourself. No one finds us comic but you: there is your schoolmaster, older and wiser than you: he likes us. You are a child just weaned, you cannot squeak out mu or ma, you are a clay-pot, a wash-leather in water, softer, not superior. If you are richer, then have two breakfasts and two dinners a day. I prefer my reputation to any riches. One word more. Who ever had to speak to me twice? I was a slave for forty years, and nobody knew whether I was a slave or free. I was a boy with long curls when I came to this place; they had not built the town-hall then.

103

tamen operam, ut domino satis facerem, homini maiiesto[1] et dignitosso, cuius pluris erat unguis, quam tu
totus es. Et habebam in domo, qui mihi pedem op-
ponerent hac illac; tamen—genio illius gratias—
enatavi. Haec sunt vera athla; nam [in] ingenuum
nasci tam facile est quam 'accede istoc.' Quid nunc
stupes tanquam hircus in ervilia?"

58 Post hoc dictum Giton, qui ad pedes stabat, risum
iam diu compressum etiam indecenter effudit. Quod
cum animadvertisset adversarius Ascylti, flexit convicium in puerum et "Tu autem" inquit "etiam tu
rides, caepa cirrata?[2] Io Saturnalia, rogo, mensis
december est? Quando vicesimam numerasti? Nescit[3]
quid faciat, crucis offla, corvorum cibaria. Curabo,
iam tibi Iovis iratus sit, et isti qui tibi non imperat.
Ita satur pane fiam, ut ego istud conliberto meo dono;
alioquin iam tibi depraesentiarum reddidissem. Bene
nos habemus, at isti nugae,[4] qui tibi non imperant.
Plane qualis dominus, talis et servus. Vix me tenco, nec[5]
sum natura caldicerebrius, sed[6] cum coepi, matrem
meam dupundii non facio. Recte, videbo te in publicum, mus, immo terrae tuber: nec sursum nec deorsum
non cresco, nisi dominum tuum in rutae folium non
conieci, nec tibi parsero, licet mehercules Iovem

[1] maiiesto *Buecheler following Muncker:* mali isto.
[2] cirrata *Reinesius:* pirrata.
[3] nescit *supplied by Buecheler.*
[4] nugae *Buecheler:* geuge.
[5] nec *Jahn:* et.
[6] caldicerebrius *Jahn:* caldus cicer eius: sed *added by Buecheler.*

But I tried to please my master, a fine dignified gentleman whose little finger was worth more than your whole body. And there were people in the house who put out a foot to trip me up here and there. But still—God bless my master!—I struggled through. These are real victories: being born free is as easy as saying, 'Come here.' But why do you stare at me now like a goat in a field of vetch?"

At this remark Giton, who was standing by my feet, burst out with an unseemly laugh, which he had now been holding in for a long while. Ascyltos's enemy noticed him, and turned his abuse on to the boy. "What," he said, "are you laughing too, you curly-headed onion? A merry Saturnalia indeed: what, have we December here? When did you pay five per cent on your freedom? He doesn't know what to do, the gallows-bird, the crows'-meat. I will call down the wrath of Jupiter at once on you and the fellow who cannot keep you in order. As sure as I get my bellyfull, I would have given you what you deserve now on the spot, but for my respect for my fellow-freedman. We are getting on splendidly, but those fellows are fools, who don't keep you in hand. Yes, like master, like man. I can scarce hold myself in, and I am not naturally hot-tempered, but when I once begin I do not care twopence for my own mother. Depend upon it, I shall meet you somewhere in public, you rat, you puff-ball. I will not grow an inch up or down until I have put your master's head in a nettle-bed,[1] and I shall have no mercy on you, I can tell you, however much you may call upon Jupiter

[1] Cf. note, p. 57.

Olympium clames. Curabo, longe tibi sit comula ista besalis et dominus dupunduarius. Recte, venies sub dentem: aut ego non me novi, aut non deridebis, licet barbam auream habeas. Athana tibi irata sit, curabo, et qui te primus deurode[1] fecit.

"Non didici geometrias, critica et alogias nenias, sed lapidarias litteras scio, partes centum dico ad aes, ad pondus, ad nummum. Ad summam, si quid vis, ego et tu sponsiunculam: exi, defero lamnam.[2] Iam scies patrem tuum mercedes perdidisse, quamvis et rhetoricam scis.[3] Ecce

'Qui de nobis[4] longe venio, late venio? solve me.' Dicam tibi, qui de nobis currit et de loco non movetur; qui de nobis crescit et minor fit. Curris, stupes, satagis, tanquam mus in matella. Ergo aut tace aut meliorem noli molestare, qui te natum non putat; nisi si me iudicas anulos buxeos curare, quos amicae tuae involasti. Occuponem propitium. Eamus in forum et pecunias mutuemur: iam scies hoc ferrum

---

[1] δεῦρο δὴ *Buecheler:* deurode.
[2] lamnam *Heinsius:* lăna.
[3] scis *Reiske:* scio.
[4] qui de nobis *Buecheler:* quidem vobis.

in Olympus. Those pretty eight-inch curls and that twopenny master of yours will be no use to you. Depend upon it, you will come under the harrow; if I know my own name you will not laugh any more, though you may have a gold beard like a god. I will bring down the wrath of Athena on you and the man who first made a minion of you.[1]

"No, I never learned geometry, and criticism, and suchlike nonsense.[2] But I know my tall letters, and I can do any sum into pounds, shillings, and pence. In fact, if you like, you and I will have a little bet. Come on, I put down the metal. Now I will show you that your father wasted the fees, even though you are a scholar in rhetoric. Look here:

'What part of us am I? I come far, I come wide.
    Now find me.'

I can tell you what part of us runs and does not move from its place; what grows out of us and grows smaller.[3] Ah! you run about and look scared and hustled, like a mouse in a pot. So keep your mouth shut, or do not worry your betters who are unaware of your existence; unless you think I have any respect for the boxwood rings you stole from your young woman. May the God of grab be on my side![4] Let us go on 'Change and borrow money: then you will see that my iron ring commands credit. My word, a

[1] *Deurode* is a transliteration of the Greek δεῦρο δή "come hither," used of a person trained to be obsequious.
[2] Lit. folly and nursery rhymes.
[3] The answer to these riddles according to Buecheler is "the foot, the eye, and the hair."
[4] *Occupo* is a goblin who helps people in business, like the Lares mentioned in c. 60.

fidem habere. Vah, bella res est volpis uda. Ita lucrum faciam et ita bene moriar aut populus per exitum meum iuret, nisi te ubique toga perversa fuero persecutus. Bella res et iste, qui te haec docet, mufrius, non magister. Nos[1] didicimus, dicebat enim magister: 'Sunt vestra salva? recta domum; cave, circumspicias; cave, maiorem maledicas. Aut numera mapalia: nemo dupondii evadit.' Ego, quod me sic vides, propter artificium meum diis gratias ago."

59 Coeperat Ascyltos respondere convicio, sed Trimalchio delectatus colliberti eloquentia "Agite" inquit "scordalias de medio. Suaviter sit potius, et tu, Hermeros, parce adulescentulo. Sanguen illi fervet,

HL tu melior esto. | Semper in hac re qui vincitur, vin-

H cit. | Et tu cum esses capo, cocococo, atque cor non habebas. Simus ergo, quod melius est, a primitiis hilares et Homeristas spectemus." Intravit factio statim hastisque senta concrepuit. Ipse Trimalchio in pulvino consedit, et cum Homeristae Graecis versibus colloquerentur, ut insolenter solent, ille canora voce Latine legebat librum. Mox silentio facto "scitis" inquit "quam fabulam agant? Diomedes et Ganymedes duo fratres fuerunt. Horum soror erat Helena. Agamemnon illam rapuit et Dianae cervam subiecit. Ita nunc Homeros dicit, quemadmodum

---

[1] nos *added by Jacobs, who read* nos magis.

108

draggled fox is a fine creature! I hope I may never get rich and make a good end, and have the people swearing by my death, if I do not put on the black cap[1] and hunt you down everywhere. It was a fine fellow who taught you to behave like this, too; a chattering ape, not a master. We had some real schooling, for the master used to say, 'Are all your belongings safe? Go straight home, and don't stop to look round you; and mind you do not abuse your elders. Count up all the wastrels, if you like; not one of them is worth twopence in the end.' Yes, I thank God for education; it made me what I am."

Ascyltos was preparing a retort to his abuse, but 59 Trimalchio was delighted with his fellow-freedman's readiness, and said, "Come now, stop all this wrangling. It is nicer to go on pleasantly, please do not be hard on the young man, Hermeros. Young blood is hot in him; you must be indulgent. A man who admits defeat in this kind of quarrel is always the winner. And you, too, when you were a young cockerel cried Cock-a-doodle-doo! and hadn't any sense in your head. So let us do better, and start the fun over again, and have a look at these reciters of Homer." A troop came in at once and clashed spear on shield. Trimalchio sat up on his cushion, and when the reciters talked to each other in Greek verse, as their conceited way is, he intoned Latin from a book. Soon there was silence, and then he said, "You know the story they are doing? Diomede and Ganymede were two brothers. Helen was their sister. Agamemnon carried her off and took in Diana by sacrificing a deer to her instead. So Homer is now telling

[1] *Toga perversa:* a magistrate wore his toga reversed when he had to pronounce a capital sentence.

inter se pugnent Troiani et Parentini. Vicit scilicet et Iphigeniam, filiam suam, Achilli dedit uxorem. Ob eam rem Aiax insanit et statim argumentum explicabit." Haec ut dixit Trimalchio, clamorem Homeristae sustulerunt, interque familiam discurrentem vitulus in lance donaria[1] elixus allatus est, et quidem galeatus. Secutus est Aiax strictoque gladio, tanquam insaniret, concidit, ac modo versa modo supina gesticulatus mucrone frusta collegit mirantibusque vitulum partitus est.

60   Nec diu mirari licuit tam elegantes strophas; nam repente lacunaria sonare coeperunt totumque triclinium intremuit. Consternatus ego exsurrexi et timui, ne per tectum petauristarius aliquis descenderet. Nec minus reliqui convivae mirantes erexere vultus, expectantes quid novi de caelo nuntiaretur. Ecce autem diductis lacunaribus subito circulus ingens, de cupa videlicet grandi excussus, demittitur, cuius per totum orhem coronae aureae cum alabastris unguenti pendebant. Dum haec apophoreta iubemur sumere, respiciens ad mensam . . .
iam illio repositorium cum placentis aliquot erat positum, quod medium Priapus a pistore factus teuchat, gremioque satis amplo omnis generis poma et uvas sustinebat more vulgato. Avidins ad pompam manus porreximus, et repente nova ludorum remissio hilaritatem hic refecit. Omnes enim placentae omniaque poma etiam minima vexatione contacta coeperunt effundere crocum, et usque ad os[2] molestus umor ac-

[1] donaria *Buecheler:* dunaria.
[2] os *Buecheler:* nos.

the tale of the war between Troy and Parentium.[1] Of course he won and married his daughter Iphigenia to Achilles. That drove Ajax mad, and he will show you the story in a minute." As he spoke the heroes raised a shout, and the slaves stood back to let a boiled calf on a presentation dish be brought in. There was a helmet on its head. Ajax followed and attacked it with his sword drawn as if he were mad; and after making passes with the edge and the flat he collected slices on the point, and divided the calf among the astonished company.

We were not given long to admire these elegant 60 *tours de force*; suddenly there came a noise from the ceiling, and the whole dining-room trembled. I rose from my place in a panic: I was afraid some acrobat would come down through the roof. All the other guests too looked up astonished, wondering what the new portent from heaven was announced. The whole ceiling parted asunder, and an enormous hoop, apparently knocked out of a giant cask, was let down. All round it were hung golden crowns and alabaster boxes of perfumes. We were asked to take these presents for ourselves, when I looked back at the table....

A dish with some cakes on it had now been put there, a Priapus made by the confectioner standing in the middle, holding up every kind of fruit and grapes in his wide apron in the conventional style. We reached greedily after his treasures, and a sudden fresh turn of humour renewed our merriment. All the cakes ánd all the fruits, however lightly they were touched, began to spurt out saffron, and the nasty juice flew

[1]Parentium is a town in Istria; Trimalchio has no reason but ignorance for selecting it as the enemy of Troy.

111

cidere. Rati ergo sacrum esse fericulum tam religioso apparatu perfusum, consurreximus altius et "Augusto, patri patriae, feliciter" diximus. Quibusdam tamen etiam post hanc venerationem poma rapientibus et ipsi[1] mappas implevimus, ego praecipue, qui nullo satis amplo munere putabam me onerare Gitonis sinum.

Inter haec tres pueri candidas succincti tunicas intraverunt, quorum duo Lares bullatos super mensam posuerunt, unus pateram vini circumferens "dii propitii" clamabat.

Aichat autem unum Cerdonem, alterum Felicionem, tertium Lucrionem[2] vocari. Nos etiam veram imaginem ipsius Trimalchionis, cum iam omnes basiarent, erubuimus praeterire.

61 Postquam ergo omnes bonam mentem bonamque valitudinem sibi optarunt, Trimalchio ad Nicerotem respexit et "solebas" inquit "suavius esse in convictu; nescio quid nunc taces nec muttis. Oro te, sic felicem me videas, narra illud quod tibi usu venit." Niceros delectatus affabilitate amici "omne me" inquit "lucrum transeat, nisi iam dudum gaudimonio dissilio, quod te talem video. Itaque hilaria mera sint, etsi timeo istos scholasticos, ne me rideant. Viderint: narrabo tamen: quid enim mihi aufert, qui ridet? Satins est rideri quam derideri." "Haec ubi dicta dedit," talem fabulam exorsus est:

"Cum adhuc servirem, habitabamus in vico angusto; nunc Gavillae domus est. Ibi, quomodo dii volunt, amare coepi uxorem Terentii coponis: noveratis Me-

---

[1] ipsi *Heinsius:* ipsas.
[2] Lucrionem *Reinesius:* lucronem.

even into our months. We thought it must be a sacred dish that was anointed with such holy appointments, and we all stood straight up and cried, "The gods bless Augustus, the father of his country." But as some people even after this solemnity snatched at the fruit, we filled our napkins too, myself especially, for I thought that I could never fill Giton's lap with a large enough present. Meanwhile three boys came in with their white tunics well tucked up, and two of them put images of the Lares with lockets round their necks on the table, while one carried round a bowl of wine and cried, "God be gracious unto us."

Trimalchio said that one of the images was called Gain, another Luck, and the third Profit. And as everybody else kissed Trimalchio's true portrait we were ashamed to pass it by.

So after they had all wished themselves good sense 61 and good health, Trimalchio looked at Niceros and said, "You used to be better company at a dinner; I do not know why you are dumb now, and do not utter a sound. Do please, to make me happy, tell us of your adventure." Niceros was delighted by his friend's amiability and said, "May I never turn another penny if I am not ready to burst with joy at seeing you in such a good humour. Well, it shall be pure fun then, though I am afraid your clever friends will laugh at me. Still, let them; I will tell my story; what harm does a man's laugh do me? Being laughed at is more satisfactory than being sneered at." So spake the hero,[1] and began the following story:

"While I was still a slave, we were living in a narrow street; the house now belongs to Gavilla. There it was God's will that I should fall in love with

[1] See Virgil. *Æneid* II, 790.

lissam Tarentinam, pulcherrimum · bacciballum. Sed
ego non mehercules corporaliter illam[1] aut propter
res venerias curavi, sed magis quod benemoria[2] fuit.
Si quid ab illa petii, nunquam mihi negatum; fecit
assem, semissem habui; quicquid habui, in illius sinum
demandavi, nec unquam fefellitus sum. Huius contubernalis ad villam supremum diem obiit. Itaque
per scutum per ocream egi aginavi, quemadmodum ad
illam pervenirem: scitis autem, in angustiis amici
62 apparent. Forte dominus Capuam exierat ad scruta
scita expedienda. Nactus ego occasionem persuadeo
hospitem nostrum, ut mecum ad quintum miliarium
veniat. Erat autem miles, fortis tanquam Orcus.
Apoculamus nos circa gallicinia, luna lucebat tanquam
meridie. Venimus intra monimenta: homo meus
coepit ad stelas facere, sedeo[3] ego cantabundus et
stelas numero. Deinde ut respexi ad comitem, ille
exuit se et omnia vestimenta secundum viam posuit.
Mihi anima[4] in naso esse, stabam tanquam mortuus.
At ille circumminxit vestimenta sua, et subito lupus
factus est. Nolite me iocari putare; ut mentiar,
nullius patrimonium tanti facio. Sed, quod coeperam
dicere, postquam lupus factus est, ululare coepit et in
silvas fugit. Ego primitus nesciebam ubi essem,
deinde accessi, ut vestimenta eius tollerem: illa autem
lapidea facta sunt. Qui mori timore nisi ego? Gladium
tamen strinxi et in tota via[5] umbras eccidi, donec ad

[1] illam *Buecheler:* autem.
[2] benemoria *Orelli:* bene moriar.
[3] sedco *Scheffer:* sed.
[4] anima *Muncker:* in animo.
[5] in tota via *Scheffer:* matavita tau.

the wife of Terentius the inn-keeper; you remember her, Melissa of Tarentum, a pretty round thing. But I swear it was no base passion; I did not care about her in that way, but rather because she had a beautiful nature. If I asked her for anything it was never refused me; if she made twopence I had a penny; whatever I had I put into her pocket, and I was never taken in. Now one day her husband died on the estate.[1] So I buckled on my shield and greaves, and schemed how to come at her: and as you know, one's friends turn up in tight places. My master happened to have gone to Capua to look after some silly business[2] or other. I seized my opportunity, and 62 persuaded a guest in our house to come with me as far as the fifth milestone. He was a soldier, and as brave as Hell. So we trotted off about cock-crow; the moon shone like high noon. We got among the tombstones[3]: my man went aside to look at the epitaphs, I sat down with my heart full of song and began to count the graves. Then when I looked round at my friend, he stripped himself and put all his clothes by the roadside. My heart was in my mouth, but I stood like a dead man. He made a ring of water round his clothes and suddenly turned into a wolf. Please do not think I am joking; I would not lie about this for any fortune in the world. But as I was saying, after he had turned into a wolf, he began to howl, and ran off into the woods. At first I hardly knew where I was, then I went up to take his clothes; but they had all turned into stone. No one could be nearer dead with terror than I was. But I drew my sword and went slaying shadows all the way till I

[1] Terentius was a slave managing the tavern for his master.
[2] Lit., elegant trash. [3] They would be by the roadside.

villam amicae meae pervenirem. Ut larua[1] intravi,
paene animam ebullivi, sudor mihi per bifurcum vola-
bat, oculi mortui, vix unquam refectus sum. Melissa
mea mirari coepit, quod tam sero ambularem, et 'Si
ante' inquit 'venisses, saltem nobis adiutasses; lupus
enim villam intravit et omnia pecora perculit, tanquam
lanius sanguinem illis misit. Nec tamen derisit, etiam
si fugit; servus enim noster lancea collum eius traiecit.' Haec ut audivi, operire oculos amplius non
potni, sed luce clara Gai nostri domum fugi tanquam
copo compilatus, et postquam veni in illum locum, in
quo lapidea vestimenta erant facta, nihil inveni nisi
sanguinem. Ut vero domum veni, iacebat miles meus
in lecto tanquam bovis, et collum illius medicus curabat. Intellexi illum versipellem esse, nec postea
cum illo panem gustare potni, non si me occidisses.
Viderint alii quid de hoc exopinissent; ego si mentior,
genios vestros iratos habeam."

63   Attonitis admiratione universis "Salvo" inquit "tuo
sermone" Trimalchio "si qua fides est, ut mihi pili
inhorruerunt, quia scio Niceronem nihil nugarum nar-
rare: immo certus est et minime linguosus. Nam et
ipse vobis rem horribilem narrabo: asinus in tegulis.
Cum adhuc capillatus essem, nam a puero vitam Chiam
gessi, ipsimi nostri[2] delicatus decessit, mehercules
margaritum, zacritus[3] et omnium numerum. Cum
ergo illum mater misella plangeret et nos tum plures
in tristimonio essemus, subito strigae stridere[4] coepe-

---

[1] ut larua *Buecheler;* in larvam.
[2] ipsimi nostri *Buecheler;* ipim mostri.
[3] zacritus *Roensch;* caccitus. *A Latin rendering of the
Greek* διάκριτος, *excellent. Cf. notes on c.* 37.
[4] stridere *added by Jacobs.*

116

came to my love's house. I went in like a corpse, and nearly gave up the ghost, the sweat ran down my legs, my eyes were dull, I could hardly be revived. My dear Melissa was surprised at my being out so late, and said, 'If you had come earlier you might at least have helped us; a wolf got into the house and worried all our sheep, and let their blood like a butcher. But he did not make fools of us, even though he got off; for our slave made a hole in his neck with a spear.' When I heard this, I could not keep my eyes shut any longer, but at break of day I rushed back to my master Gaius's house like a defrauded publican, and when I came to the place where the clothes were turned into stone, I found nothing but a pool of blood. But when I reached home, my soldier was lying in bed like an ox, with a doctor looking after his neck. I realized that he was a werewolf, and I never could sit down to a meal with him afterwards, not if you had killed me first. Other people may think what they like about this; but may all your guardian angels punish me if I am lying."

We were all dumb with astonishment, but Trimal- 63 chio said, "I pick no holes in your story; by the soul of truth, how my hair stood on end! For I know that Niceros never talks nonsense: he is very dependable, and not at all a chatterbox. Now I want to tell you a tale of horror myself: but I'm a donkey on the tiles compared with him. While I still had hair down my back, for I lived delicat ₁ [1] from my youth up, my master's favourite died. Oh! he was a pearl, one in a thousand, and a mirror of perfection! So while his poor mother was bewailing him, and several of us were

[1] Literally "a Chian life," i.e. luxurious and vicious. Thucydides calls the Chians shameless.

117

runt; putares canem leporem persequi. Habel:umus tune hominem Cappadocem, longum, valde audaculum et qui valebat: poterat bovem[1] iratum tollere. Hic audacter stricto gladio extra ostium procucurrit, involuta sinistra manu curiose, et mulierem tanquam hoc loco —salvum sit, quod tango—mediam traiecit. Audimus gemitum, et—plane non mentiar—ipsas non vidimus. Baro autem noster introversus se proiecit in lectum, et corpus totum lividum habebat quasi flagellis caesus, quia scilicet illum tetigerat mala manus. Nos eluso ostio redimus iterum ad officium, sed dum mater amplexaret corpus filii sui, tangit et videt manuciolum de stramentis factum. Non cor habebat, non intestina, non quicquam: scilicet iam puerum strigae involaverant et supposuerant stramenticium vavatonem. Rogo vos, oportet credatis, sunt mulieres plussciae, sunt nocturnae, et quod sursum est, deorsum faciunt. Ceterum baro ille longus post hoc factum nunquam coloris sui fuit, immo post paucos dies phreneticus periit."

64 Miramur nos et pariter credimus, osculatique mensam rogamus nocturnas, ut suis se teneant, dum redimus a cena.

Et sane iam lucernae mihi plures videbantur ardere totumque triclinium esse mutatum, cum Trimalchio "tibi dico" inquit "Plocame, nihil narras? Nihil nos delectaris? Et solebas suavius esse, canturire belle deverbia, adicere melicam. Heu heu, abistis dulcis caricae." "Iam" inquit ille "quadrigae mcae decu-

---

[1] bovem *Reiske:* Jovem.

sharing her sorrow, suddenly the witches began to screech; you would have thought there was a dog pursuing a bare. We had a Cappadocian in the house at the time, a tall fellow, mighty brave and a man of muscle; he could lift an angry bull off the ground. He rushed boldly out of doors with a naked sword, having carefully wrapped up his left band, and ran the woman through the middle, just about here—may the spot my finger is on be safe! We heard a groan, but to tell the honest truth we did not see the witches themselves. But our big fellow came back and threw himself on a bed: and his whole body was blue as if he had been flogged, of course because the witch's hand had touched him. We shut the door and returned to our observances, but when the mother put her arms round the body of her son, she felt it and saw that it was a little bundle of straw. It had no heart, no inside or anything: of course the witches had carried off the boy and put a straw changeling in his place. Ah! yes, I would beg you to believe there are wise women, and night-riders, who can turn the whole world upside down. Well, the tall slave never came back to his proper colour after this affair, and died raving mad in a few days."

We were full of wonder and faith, and we kissed 64 the table and prayed the Night-riders to stay at home as we returned from dinner.

By this time, I own, the lamps were multiplying before my eyes, and the whole dining-room was altering; then Trimalchio said, "Come you, Plocamus, have you got no story? Will you not entertain us? You used to be more pleasant company, and recite blank verse very prettily, and put in songs too. Dear, dear, all the sweet green figs are fallen!" "Ah, yes," the man replied, "my galloping days are over since I

currerunt, ex quo podagricus factus sum. Alioquin cum essem adulescentulus, cantando paene tisicus factus sum. Quid saltare? Quid deverbia? Quid tonstrinum? Quando parem babui nisi unum Apelletem?" Appositaque ad os manu nescio quid taetrum exsibilavit, quod postea Graecum esse affirmabat.

Nec non Trimalchio ipse cum tubicines esset imitatus, ad delicias suas respexit, quem Croesum appellabat. Puer autem lippus, sordidissimis dentibus, catellam nigram atque indecenter pinguem prasina involvebat fascia panemque semissem ponebat super torum atque [hac] nausea recusantem saginabat. Quo admonitus officii Trimalchio Scylacem iussit adduci "praesidium domus familiaeque." Nec mora, ingentis formae adductus est canis catena vinctus, admonitusque ostiarii calce, ut cubaret, ante mensam se posuit. Tum Trimalchio iactans candidum panem "nemo" inquit "in domo mea me plus amat." Indignatus puer, quod Scylacem tam effuse laudaret, catellam in terram deposuit hortatusque est, ut ad rixam properaret. Scylax, canino scilicet usus ingenio, taeterrimo latratu triclinium implevit Margaritamque Croesi paene laceravit. Nec intra rixam tumultus constitit, sed candelabrum etiam super mensam eversum et vasa omnia crystallina comminuit et oleo ferventi aliquot convivas respersit. Trimalchio ne videretur iactura motus, basiavit puerum ac iussit super dorsum ascendere suum. Non moratus ille usus est equo manuque plena scapulas eius subinde verberavit, interque risum proclamavit:

120

was taken with the gout. In the days when I was a young fellow I nearly got consumption with singing. How I could dance and recite and imitate the talk in a barber's shop! Was there ever my equal, except the one and only Apelles?" And he put his band to his mouth and whistled out some offensive stuff I did not catch: he declared afterwards it was Greek.

Then Trimalchio, after imitating a man with a trumpet, looked round for his favourite, whom he called Croesus. The creature had blear eyes and very bad teeth, and was tying up an unnaturally obese black puppy in a green handkerchief, and then putting a broken piece of bread on a chair, and cramming it down the throat of the dog, who did not want it and was sick. This reminded Trimalchio of his duties, and he ordered them to bring in Scylax, "the guardian of the house and the slaves." An enormous dog on a chain was at once led in, and on receiving a kick from the porter as a bint to lie down, he curled up in front of the table. Then Trimalchio threw him a bit of white bread and said, "No one in the house loves me better than Scylax." The favourite took offence at his lavish praise of the dog, and put down the puppy, and encouraged him to attack Scylax. Scylax, after the manner of dogs, filled the dining-room with a most hideous barking, and nearly tore Croesus's little Pearl to pieces. And the uproar did not end with a dog-fight, for a lamp upset over the table, and broke all the glass to pieces, and sprinkled some of the guests with hot oil. Trimalchio did not want to seem hurt at his loss, so he kissed his favourite, and told him to jump on his back. He mounted his borse at once and went on smacking Trimalchio's shoulders with his open

"Bucca, bucca, quot sunt hic?" repressus ergo ali-
quamdiu Trimalchio camellam grandem iussit misceri
. . . potiones dividi omnibus servis, qui ad pedes sede-
bant, adiecta exceptione: "Si quis" inquit "noluerit
accipere, caput illi perfunde. Interdiu severa, nunc
hilaria."

65   Hanc humanitatem insecutae sunt matteae, quarum
etiam recordatio me, si qua est dicenti fides, offendit.
Singulae enim gallinae altiles pro turdis circumlatae
sunt et ova anserina pilleata, quae ut comessemus,
ambitiosissime a nobis Trimalchio petiit dicens exossa-
tas esse gallinas. Inter haec triclinii valvas lictor
percussit, amictusque veste alba cum ingenti frequentia comissator intravit. Ego maiestate conterritus
praetorem putabam venisse. Itaque temptavi assur-
gere et nudos pedes in terram deferre. Risit hanc
trepidationem Agamemnon et "Contine te" inquit
"homo stultissime. Habinnas sevir est idemque lapi-
darius, qui videtur[1] monumenta optime facere."

Recreatus hoc sermone reposui cubitum, Habin-
namque intrantem cum admiratione ingenti spectabam.
Ille autem iam ebrius uxoris suae umeris imposuerat
manus, oneratusque aliquot coronis et unguento per
frontem in oculos fluente praetorio loco se posuit con-

---

[1] videtur *Scheffer:* videretur.

hand, saying, "How many are we, blind man's cheek?"[1]
After some time Trimalchio calmed himself, and ordered a great bowl of wine to be mixed, and drinks
to be served round to all the slaves, who were sitting
at our feet, adding this provision: "If anyone refuses
to take it, pour it over his head; business in the daytime and pleasure at night."

After this display of kindness, some savouries were 65
brought in, the memory of which, as sure as I tell you
this story, still makes me shudder. For instead of a
thrush a fat chicken was brought round to each of us,
and goose-eggs in caps, which Trimalchio kept
asking us to eat with the utmost insistence, saying
that they were chickens without the bones. Meanwhile a priest's attendant[2] knocked at the dining-
room door, and a man dressed in white for some
festivity came in with a number of others. I was
frightened by his solemn looks, and thought the
mayor had arrived. So I tried to get up and plant
my bare feet on the ground. Agamemnon laughed
at my anxiety and said, "Control yourself, you silly
fool! It is Habinnas of the priests' college, a monumental mason with a reputation for making first-class
tombstones." I was relieved by this news, and
lay down in my place again, and watched Habinnas'
entrance with great astonishment. He was quite
drunk, and had put his hands on his wife's shoulders;
he had several wreaths on, and ointment was running
down his forehead into his eyes. He sat down in the

---

[1] *Bucca* was a child's game (Hoodman Blind in English)
where one child was blindfolded and the others touched him
on the cheek, and asked him how many fingers, or how many
children, had touched him.

[2] The attendant on a Sevir Augusti. See note, p. 43.

tinuoque vinum et caldam poposcit. Delectatus hac Trimalchio hilaritate et ipse capaciorem poposcit scyphum quaesivitque, quomodo acceptus esset. "Omnia" inquit "habuimus praeter te; oculi enim mei hic erant. Et mehercules bene fuit. Scissa lautum novendiale servo suo misello faciebat, quem mortuum manu miserat. Et puto, cum vicensimariis magnam mantissam habet; quinquaginta enim millibus aestimant mortuum. Sed tamen suaviter fuit, 66 etiam si coacti sumus dimidias potiones super ossucula eius effundere." "Tamen" inquit Trimalchio "quid habuistis in cena?" "Dicam" inquit "si potuero; nam tam bonae memoriae sum, ut frequenter nomen meum obliviscar. Habuimus tamen in primo porcum poculo coronatum et circa saviunculum[1] et gizeria optime facta et certe betam et panem autopyrum de suo sibi, quem ego malo quam candidum; et vires facit, et cum mea re [causa][2] facio, non ploro. Sequens ferculum fuit scriblita frigida et super mel caldum infusum excellente Hispanum. Itaque de scriblita quidem non minimum edi, de melle me usque tetigi. Circa cicer et lupinum, calvae arbitratu et mala singula. Ego tamen duo sustuli et ecce in mappa alligata habeo; nam si aliquid muneris meo vernulae non tulero, habebo convicium. Bene me admonet domina mea. In prospectu habuimus ursinae frustum, de quo cum imprudens Scintilla gustasset, pacue intestina sua vomu-

[1] saviunculum *Hildebrand:* saucunculum.
[2] causa *bracketed by Buecheler.*

chief magistrate's place,[1] and at once called for wine
and hot water. Trimalchio was delighted at his good
humour, and demanded a larger cup for himself, and
asked him how he had been received. "We had
everything there except you," was the reply, "for my
eyes were here with you. Yes, it was really splendid.
Scissa was having a funeral feast on the ninth day for
her poor dear slave, whom she set free on his death-
bed. And I believe she will have an enormous sum
to pay the tax-collector, for they reckon that the
dead man was worth fifty thousand.[2] But anyhow
it was a pleasant affair, even if we did have to pour
half our drinks over his lamented bones." "Ah," 66
said Trimalchio, "but what did you have for dinner?"
"I will tell you if I can," he said, "but my memory
is in such a fine way that I often forget my own name.
Well, first we had a pig crowned with a wine-cup, gar-
nished with honey cakes, and liver very well done,
and beetroot of course, and pure wholemeal bread,
which I prefer to white myself; it puts strength into
you, and is good for the bowels. The next dish was
a cold tart, with excellent Spanish wine poured over
warm honey. Indeed I ate a lot of the tart, and
gave myself such a soaking of honey. Pease and
lupines were handed, a choice of nuts and an apple
each. I took two myself, and I have got them here
tied up in my napkin: for if I do not bring some
present back for my pet slave-boy there will be
trouble. Oh! yes, my wife reminds me. There was
a piece of bear on a side dish. Scintilla was rash

[1] The lowest seat on the middle couch, usually called the
consul's seat, but here the highest official present took it.

[2] She would pay a tax of 5 per cent, i.e. 2,500 sesterces, on
his value.

it; ego contra plus libram comedi, nam ipsum aprum
sapiebat. Et si, inquam, ursus homuncionem comest
quanto magis homuncio debet ursum comesse? In
summo habuimus caseum mollem ex sapa et cocleas
singulas et cordae frusta et hepatia in catillis et ova
pilleata et rapam et senape et catillum concacatum,
pax Palamedes. Etiam in alveo circumlata sunt oxy-
comina, unde quidam etiam improbe ternos pugnos[1]
sustulerunt. Nam pernae missionem dedimus. Sed
67 narra mihi, Gai, rogo, Fortunata quare non recumbit?"
"Quomodo nosti" inquit "illam" Trimalchio "nisi
argentum composuerit, nisi reliquias pueris diviserit,
aquam in os suum non coniciet." "Atqui" respondit
Habinnas "nisi illa discumbit, ego me apoculo" et
coeperat surgere, nisi signo dato Fortunata quater
amplius a tota familia esset vocata. Venit ergo galbino
succincta cingillo, ita ut infra cerasina appareret tunica et periscelides tortae phaecasiaeque inauratae.
Tunc sudario manus tergens, quod in collo habebat,
applicat se illi toro, in quo Scintilla Habinnae discumbebat uxor, osculataque plaudentem "est te"
inquit "videre?"

Eo deinde perventum est, ut Fortunata armillas
suas crassissimis detraheret lacertis Scintillaeque
miranti ostenderet. Ultimo etiam periscelides resolvit

---

[1] improbiter nos pugno *corrected by Buecheler.*

126

enough to taste it, and nearly brought up her own inside. I ate over a pound myself, for it tasted like proper wild boar. What I say is this, since bears eat up us poor men, how much better right has a poor man to eat up a bear? To finish up with we had cheese mellowed in new wine, and snails all round, and pieces of tripe, and liver in little dishes, and eggs in caps, and turnip, and mustard, and a dish of forcemeat. But hold hard, Palamedes.[1] Pickled olives were brought round in a dish too, and some greedy creatures took three handfuls. For we had let the ham go. But 67 tell me, Gaius, why is Fortunata not at dinner?" "Do you not know her better?" said Trimalchio. "Until she has collected the silver, and divided the remains among the slaves, she will not let a drop of water pass her lips." "Oh," replied Habinnas, "but unless she is here I shall take myself off," and he was just getting up, when at a given signal all the slaves called "Fortunata" four times and more. So she came in with a high yellow waist-band on, which allowed a cherry-red bodice to appear under it, and twisted anklets, and white shoes embroidered with gold. She wiped her hands on a cloth which she had round her neck, took her place on the sofa, where Scintilla, Habinnas's wife, was lying, kissed her as she was clapping her hands, and said, "Is it really you, dear?"

Fortunata then went so far as to take the bracelets off her fat arms to exhibit them to Scintilla's admiring gaze. At last she even took off her anklets

---

[1] *Pax* is an exclamation unconnected with the noun *pax*, "peace." The meaning of its conjunction with the word Palamedes is unknown: it may be merely due to the charm of alliteration.

et reticulum aureum, quem ex obrussa esse dicebat. Notavit haec Trimalchio iussitque afferri omnia et "Videtis" inquit "mulieris compedes: sic nos barcalae despoliamur. Sex pondo et selibram debet habere. Et ipse nihilo minus habeo decem pondo armillam ex millesimis Mercurii factam." Ultimo etiam, ne mentiri videretur, stateram iussit afferri et circumlatum approbari pondus. Nec melior Scintilla, quae de cervice sua capsellam detraxit aureolam, quam Felicionem appellabat. Inde duo crotalia protulit et Fortunatae in vicem consideranda dedit et "Domini" inquit "mei beneficio nemo habet meliora." "Quid?" inquit Habinnas "excatarissasti me, ut tibi emerem faham vitream. Plane si filiam haberem, auriculas illi praeciderem. Mulieres si non essent, omnia pro luto haberemus; nunc hoc est caldum meiere et frigidum potare."

Interim mulieres sauciae inter se riserunt ebriaeque iunxerunt oscula, dum altera diligentiam matris familiae iactat, altera delicias et indiligentiam viri. Dumque sic cohaerent, Habinnas furtim consurrexit pedesque Fortunatae correptos super lectum immisit. "Au au" illa proclamavit aberrante tunica super genna. Composita ergo in gremio Scintillae incensissimam[1] rubore faciem sudario abscondit.

68 Interposito deinde spatio cum secundas mensas Trimalchio iussisset afferri, sustulerunt servi omnes mensas et alias attulerunt, scobemque croco et minio tinctam sparserunt et, quod nunquam ante videram,

---

[1] incensissimam *Reinesius;* indecens imam.

128

and her hair-net, which she said was eighteen carat.
Trimalchio saw her, and ordered the whole lot to be
brought to him. "There," he said, "are a woman's
fetters; that is how we poor fools[1] are plundered. She
must have six pounds and a half of gold on her. I
have got a bracelet myself, made out of the per-
centage which I owe to Mercury, that weighs not an
ounce under ten pounds." At last, for fear we should
think he was lying, he ordered the scales to be brought,
and had the weight carried round and tested. Scintilla
was just as bad. She took off a little gold box from
her neck, which she called her lucky box. Then she
brought out two earrings, and gave them to Fortunata
to look at in her turn, and said, "Thanks to my husband's kindness, nobody has finer ones." "What?"
said Habinnas, "you bullied me to buy you a glass
bean. I declare if I had a daughter I would cut off
her ears. If there were no women, we should never
trouble about anything: as it is, we sweat for them
and get cold thanks."

Meanwhile the tipsy wives laughed together, and
gave each other drunken kisses, one prating of her
prudence as a housewife, the other of the favourites
of her husband and his inattention to her. While they
were hobnobbing, Habinnas got up quietly, took Fortunata by the legs, and threw her over on the sofa.
She shouted out, "Oh! goodness!" and her dress flew
up over her knees. She took refuge in Scintilla's arms,
and buried her burning red face in a napkin.

After an interval, Trimalchio ordered fresh relays 68
of food to be brought in. The slaves took away all the
tables, brought in others, and sprinkled about sawdust
coloured with saffron and vermilion, and, what I had

[1] *Barcala* is akin to *bardus* and *baro*, meaning "a blockhead."

ex lapide speculari pulverem tritum. Statim Trimalchio "poteram quidem" inquit "hoc fericulo esse contentus; secundas enim mensas habetis. Sed si quid belli habes, affer."

Interim puer Alexandrinus, qui caldam ministrabat, luscinias coepit imitari clamante Trimalchione subinde: "Muta." Ecce alius ludus. Servus qui ad pedes Habinnae sedebat, iussus, credo, a domino suo proclamavit subito canora voce:

"Interea medium Aeneas iam classe tenebat." Nullus sonus unquam acidior percussit aures meas; nam praeter errantis barbariae aut adiectum aut deminutum clamorem miscebat Atellanicos versus, ut tunc primum me etiam Vergilius offenderit. Plausum[1] tamen, cum aliquando desisset,[2] adiecit Habinnas et "nunquam"[3] inquit "didicit, sed ego ad circulatores eum mittendo erudibam.[4] Itaque parem non habet, sive muliones volet sive circulatores imitari. Desperatum[5] valde ingeniosus est: idem sutor est, idem cocus idem pistor, omnis musae mancipium. Duo tamen vitia habet, quae si non haberet, esset omnium numerum: recutitus est et stertit. Nam quod strabonus est, non curo: sicut Venus spectat. Ideo nihil 69 tacet, vix oculo mortuo unquam. Illum emi trecentis denariis." Interpellavit loquentem Scintilla et "plane" inquit "non omnia artificia servi nequam narras. Agaga est; at curabo, stigmam habeat." Risit Trimalchio et "adcognosco" inquit "Cappadocem: nihil

---

[1] plausum *Buecheler:* lassus.
[2] desisset *Scheffer:* dedisset.
[3] nunquam inquit *Buecheler:* nunquid.
[4] erudibam *Jahn:* audibant.
[5] desperatum *Buecheler:* desperatus.

never seen before, powdered tale. Trimalchio at once said, "I might really be satisfied with this course; for you have got your fresh relays. But if there is anything nice, put it on."

Meanwhile a boy from Alexandria, who was handing hot water, began to imitate a nightingale, and made Trimalchio shout, "Oh! change the tune." Then there was another joke. A slave, who was sitting at the feet of Habinnas, began, by his master's orders I suppose, suddenly to cry in a loud voice:

"Now with his fleet Aeneas held the main."[1]
No sharper sound ever pierced my ears; for besides his making barbarous mistakes in raising or lowering his voice, he mixed up Atellane verses[2] with it, so that Virgil jarred on me for the first time in my life. All the same, Habinnas supplied applause when he had at last left off, and said, "He never went to school, but I educated him by sending him round the hawkers in the market. So he has no equal when he wants to imitate mule-drivers or hawkers. He is terribly clever; he is a cobbler too, a cook, a confectioner, a slave of all the talents. He has only two faults, and if he were rid of them he would be simply perfect. He is a Jew and he snores. For I do not mind his being cross-eyed; he has a look like Venus. So that is why he cannot keep silent, and scarcely ever shuts his eyes. I bought him for three hundred denarii." Scintilla interrupted his story by saying, "To be sure 69 you have forgotten some of the tricks of the vile slave. He is a Don Juan; but I will see to it that he is branded." Trimalchio laughed and said, "Oh! I perceive he is a Cappadocian; he does not deny himself,

[1] See Virgil, *Æneid* v, 1.
[2] Comic verse; probably improper. See note, p. 95.

sibi defraudit, et mehercules laudo illum; hoc enim
nemo parentat. Tu autem, Scintilla, noli zelotypa
esse. Crede mihi, et vos novimus. Sic me salvum
habeatis, ut ego sic solebam ipsumam meam debat-
tuere, ut etiam dominus suspicaretur; et ideo me in
vilicationem relegavit. Sed tace, lingua, dabo panem."
Tanquam laudatus esset nequissimus servus, lucernam
de sinu fictilem protulit et amplius semihora tubicines
imitatus est succinente Habinna et inferius labrum
manu deprimente. Ultimo etiam in medium processit
et modo harundinibus quassis choraulas imitatus est,
modo lacernatus cum flagello mulionum fata egit,
donec vocatum ad se Habinnas basiavit, potionemque
illi porrexit et "Tanto melior" inquit "Massa, dono
tibi caligas."

Nec ullus tot malorum finis fuisset, nisi epidipnis
esset allata, turdi siliginei uvis passis nucibusque
farsi. Insecuta sunt Cydonia etiam mala spinis confixa,
ut echinos efficerent. Et haec quidem tolerabilia
erant, si non fericulum longe monstrosius effecisset,
ut vel fame perire mallemus. Nam cum positus esset,
ut nos putabamus, anser altilis circaque pisces et
omnia genera avium, "Amici"[1] inquit Trimalchio
"quicquid videtis hic positum, de uno corpore est
factum." Ego, scilicet homo prudentissimus, statim
intellexi quid esset, et respiciens Agamemnonem
"mirahor" inquam "nisi omnia ista de fimo[2] facta sunt
aut certe de luto. Vidi Romae Saturnalibus eiusmodi
70 cenarum imaginem fieri." Necdum finieram sermonem,
cum Trimalchio ait: "Ita crescam patrimonio, non

---

[1] amici *added by Buecheler.*
[2] fimo *added by Buecheler.*

and, upon my word, I admire him; for no one can send a dead man any fun. And please do not be jealous, Scintilla. Take my word for it, we know you women too. By my hope of salvation, I used to amuse my own mistress, until even the master became suspicious; and so he banished me to a country stewardship. But peace, my tongue, and you shall have some bread." The worthless slave took a clay lamp out of his dress, as if he had been complimented, and imitated trumpeters for more than half an hour, Habinnas singing with him and pulling his lower lip down. Finally, he came right into the middle of the room, and shook a pipe of reeds in imitation of flute-players, or gave us the mule-driver's life, with a cloak and a whip, till Habinnas called him and gave him a kiss, and offered him a drink, saying, "Better than ever, Massa. I will give you a pair of boots."

There would have been no end to our troubles if a last course had not been brought in, thrushes made of fine meal and stuffed with raisins and nuts. There followed also quinces, stuck all over with thorns to look like sea-urchins. We could have borne this, if a far more fantastic dish had not driven us even to prefer death by starvation. What we took to be a fat goose, with fish and all kinds of birds round it, was put on, and then Trimalchio said, "My friends, whatever you see here on the table is made out of one body." With my usual intelligence, I knew at once what it was; I looked at Agamemnon and said, "I shall be surprised if the whole thing is not made out of filth, or at any rate clay. I have seen sham dinners of this kind served in Rome at the Saturnalia." I had not finished speaking when Trimalchio said, "As I hope to grow in gains and not in girth, my cook

70

corpore, ut ista cocus meus de porco fecit. Non potest esse pretiosior homo. Volueris, de vulva faciet piscem, de lardo palumbum, de perna turturem, de colaepio gallinam. Et ideo ingenio meo impositum est illi nomen bellissimum; nam Daedalus vocatur. Et quia bonam mentem habet, attuli illi Roma munus cultros Norico ferro." Quos statim iussit afferri inspectosque miratus est. Etiam nobis potestatem fecit, ut mucronem ad buccam probaremus.

Subito intraverunt duo servi, tanquam qui rixam ad lacum fecissent; certe in collo[1] adhuc amphoras habebant. Cum ergo Trimalchio ius inter litigantes diceret, neuter sententiam tulit decernentis, sed alterius amphoram fuste percussit. Consternati nos insolentia ebriorum intentavimus oculos in proeliantes notavimusque ostrea pectinesque e gastris labentia, quae collecta puer lance circumtulit. Has lautitias aequavit ingeniosus cocus; in craticula enim argentea cochleas attulit et tremula taeterrimaque voce cantavit.

Pudet referre, quae secuntur: inaudito enim more pueri capillati attulerunt unguentum in argentea pelve pedesque recumbentium unxerunt, cum ante crura talosque corollis vinxissent. Hinc ex eodem unguento in vinarium atque lucernam aliquantum[2] est infusum.

Iam coeperat Fortunata velle saltare, iam Scintilla frequentius plaudebat quam loquebatur, cum Trimalchio "Permitto" inquit "Philargyre et Cario, etsi

---

[1] collo *Heinsius:* loco.
[2] aliquantum *Heinsius:* liquatum.

made the whole thing out of a pig. There could not be a more valuable fellow. If you want it, he will make you a fish out of a sow's belly, a woodpigeon out of bacon, a turtledove out of a ham, and a chicken out of a knuckle of pork. That gave me the idea of putting a very pretty name on him; he is called Daedalus.[1] And because he is so intelligent, I brought him back from Rome some knives, made of steel of Noricum, as a present." He had these knives brought in at once, and contemplated them with admiration. He even allowed us to try the edge on our checks.

Suddenly two slaves came in who had apparently been fighting at a water-tank; at least they still had waterpots on their necks. Trimalchio sat in judgment on the dispute, but neither of them accepted his decision, and they smashed each other's waterpots with sticks. We were amazed at their drunken folly, and stared at them fighting, and then we saw oysters and cockles fall out of the pots, and a boy picked them up and brought them round on a dish. The clever cook was a match for this exhibition; he offered us snails on a silver gridiron, and sang in an extremely ugly quavering voice.

I am ashamed to tell you what followed: in defiance of all convention, some long-haired boys brought ointment in a silver basin, and anointed our feet as we lay, after winding little garlands round our feet and ankles. A quantity of the same ointment was then poured into the mixing-bowl and the lamp.

Fortunata had now grown anxious to dance; Scintilla clapped her hands more often than she spoke, when Trimalchio said, "Philargyrus, you and Cario,

' A common nickname for a Jack of all trades.

prasinianus es famosus, dic et Menophilae, contuber-
nali tuae, discumbat." Quid multa? pacue de lectis
deiecti sumus, adeo totum triclinium familia occupaverat. Certe ego notavi super me positum cocum,
qui de porco anserem fecerat, muria condimentisque
fetentem. Nec contentus fuit recumbere, sed continuo
Ephesum tragoedum coepit imitari et subinde dominum suum sponsione provocare "si prasinus proximis
circensibus primam palmam."

71　Diffusus hac contentione Trimalchio "amici" inquit
"et servi homines sunt et aeque unum lactem bibe-
runt, etiam si illos malus fatus oppressit.[1]　Tamen me
salvo cito aquam liberam gustabunt.　Ad summam,
omnes illos in testamento meo manu mitto.　Philargyro
etiam fundúm lego et contubernalem suam, Carioni
quoque insulam et vicesimam et lectum stratum.　Nam
Fortunatam meam heredem facio, et commendo illam
omnibus amicis meis.　Et haec ideo omnia publico, ut
familia mea iam nunc sic me amet tanquam mortuum."
Gratias agere omnes indulgentiae coeperant domini,
cum ille oblitus nugarum exemplar testamenti iussit
afferri et totum a primo ad ultimum ingemescente
familia recitavit.　Respiciens deinde Habinnam "quid
dicis" inquit "amice carissime? Aedificas monumentum meum, quemadmodum te iussi? Valde te rogo,
ut secundum pedes statuae meae catellam ponas[2] et
coronas et unguenta et Petraitis omnes pugnas, ut

[1] oppressit *Buecheler:* oppresserit.
[2] ponas *Buecheler:* pingas.

though you are a damned wearer of the green,[1] may sit down and tell your good woman, Menophila, to do the same." I need hardly say that we were nearly pushed off the sofas with the slaves crowding into every seat. Anyhow, I noticed that the cook, who had made a goose out of the pig, sat stinking of pickle and sauces just above me. Not satisfied with having a seat, he at once began to imitate the tragedian Ephesus, and then invited his own master to make a bet on the green being first in the next games.

Trimalchio cheered up at this dispute and said, 71 "Ah, my friends, a slave is a man and drank his mother's milk like ourselves, even if cruel fate has trodden him down. Yes, and if I live they shall soon taste the water of freedom. In fact I am setting them all free in my will. I am leaving a property and his good woman to Philargyrus as well, and to Cario a block of buildings, and his manumission fees, and a bed and bedding. I am making Fortunata my heir, and I recommend her to all my friends. I am making all this known so that my slaves may love me now as if I were dead." They all began to thank their master for his kindness, when he turned serious, and had a copy of the will brought in, which he read aloud from beginning to end, while the slaves moaned and groaned. Then he looked at Habinnas and said, "Now tell me, my dear friend: you will erect a monument as I have directed? I beg you earnestly to put up round the feet of my statue my little dog, and some wreaths, and bottles of perfume, and all the fights of Petraites,[2]

[1] These persons were two of Trimalchio's slaves. Trimalchio addresses one of them, Philargyrus, as a supporter of the green colours in competitions in the circus. Competitors wore four colours, blue, green, white, and red.

[2] See note, p. 91.

mihi contingat tuo beneficio post mortem vivere; praeterea ut sint in fronte pedes centum, in agrum pedes ducenti. Omne genus enim poma volo sint circa cineres meos, et vinearum largiter. Valde enim falsum est vivo quidem domos cultas esse, non curari eas, ubi diutius nobis habitandum est. Et ideo ante omnia adici volo: 'hoc monumentum heredem non sequitur.'[1] Ceterum crit mih icurae, ut testamento caveam, ne mortuus iniuriam accipiam. Praeponam enim unum ex libertis sepulcro meo custodiae causa, ne in monumentum meum populus cacatum currat. Te rogo, ut naves etiam . . . . monumenti mei facias plenis velis euntes, et me in tribunali sedentem praetextatum cum anulis aureis quinque et nummos in publico de sacculo effundentem; scis enim, quod epulum dedi binos denarios. Faciatur, si tibi videtur, et triclinia. Facias et totum populum sibi suaviter faci-cutem. Ad dexteram meam ponas statuam Fortunatae mcae columbam tenentem: et catellam cingulo alliga-tam ducat: et cicaronem meum, et amphoras copiosas gypsatas, ne effluant vinum. Et urnam licet fractam sculpas, et super eam puerum plorantem. Horologium in medio, ut quisquis horas inspiciet, velit nolit, nomen

---

[1] sequitur *Buecheler*: sequatur. *The phrase, like* in fronte *and* in agrum *above, is written with Horace Satires* i, 8, 12-13, *in mind.* H.M.H.N.S. *is a common inscription on tombs.*

so that your kindness may bring me a life after death; and I want the monument to have a frontage of one hundred feet and to be two hundred feet in depth. For I should like to have all kinds of fruit growing round my ashes, and plenty of vines. It is quite wrong for a man to decorate his house while he is alive, and not to trouble about the house where he must make a longer stay. So above all things I want added to the inscription, 'This monument is not to descend to my heir.' I shall certainly take care to provide in my will against any injury being done to me when I am dead. I am appointing one of the freedmen to be caretaker of the tomb and prevent the common people from running up and defiling it. I beg you to put ships in full sail on the monument, and me sitting in official robes on my official seat, wearing five gold rings and distributing coin publicly out of a bag;[1] you remember that I gave a free dinner worth two denarii a head. I should like a dining-room table put in too, if you can arrange it. And let me have the whole people there enjoying themselves. On my right hand put a statue of dear Fortunata holding a dove, and let her be leading a little dog with a waistband on; and my dear little boy, and big jars sealed with gypsum, so that the wine may not run out. And have a broken urn carved with a boy weeping over it. And a sundial in the middle, so that anyone who looks at the time will read my name whether he likes it or

[1] Members of the college of Augustus were allowed on important public occasions to sit on a throne and to wear a *toga praetexta*. Trimalchio may have earned the right to wear gold rings by giving a public dinner: after his term of office as a Sevir Augusti (see note, p. 43) expired, he would not be entitled to wear them. See c. 32, where he wears a ring made to look like gold at a distance.

meum legat. Inscriptio quoque vide diligenter si
haec satis idonea tibi videtur: "C. Pompeius Trimalchio Maecenatianus hic requiescit. Huic seviratus
absenti decretus est. Cum posset in omnibus decuriis
Romae esse, tamen noluit. Pius, fortis, fidelis, ex
parvo crevit, sestertium reliquit trecenties, nec unquam philosophum audivit. Vale: et tu.'"

72   Haec ut dixit Trimalchio, flere coepit ubertim.
Flebat et Fortunata, flebat et Habinnas, tota denique
familia, tanquam in funus rogata, lamentatione trich-
nium implevit. Immo iam coeperam etiam ego plorare, cum Trimalchio "Ergo" inquit "cum sciamus
nos morituros esse, quare non vivamus? Sic vos feli-
ces videam, coniciamus nos in balneum, meo periculo,
non paenitebit. Sic calet tanquam furnus." "Vero,
vero," inquit Habinnas "de una die duas facere, nihil
malo" nudisque consurrexit pedibus et Trimalchionem
plaudentem[1] subsequi coepit.

    Ego respiciens ad Ascylton "Quid cogitas?" inquam
"ego enim si videro balneum, statim expirabo."
"Assentemur" ait ille "et dum illi balneum petunt,

---

[1] plaudentem *Jacobs*: gaudentem.

not. And again, please think carefully whether this in
scription seems to you quite appropriate: 'Here heth
Caius Pompeius Trimalchio, freedman of Maecenas.[1]
The degree of Priest of Augustus was conferred upon
him in his absence. He might have been attendant on
any magistrate in Rome, but refused it.[2] God-fearing,
gallant, constant, he started with very little and left
thirty millions. He never listened to a philosopher.
Fare thee well, Trimalchio: and thou too, passer-by.'"

After saying this, Trimalchio began to weep floods 72
of tears. Fortunata wept, Habinnas wept, and then
all the slaves began as if they had been invited to his
funeral, and filled the dining-room with lamentation.
I had even begun to lift up my voice myself, when
Trimalchio said, "Well, well, if we know we must die,
why should we not live? As I hope for your happiness, let us jump into a bath. My life on it, you will
never regret it. It is as hot as a furnace." "Very
true, very true," said Habinnas, "making two days out
of one is my chief delight." And he got up with bare
feet and began to follow Trimalchio, who was clapping
his hands.

I looked at Ascyltos and said, "What do you think?
I shall die on the spot at the very sight of a bath."
"Oh! let us say yes," he replied, "and we will slip

[1] Trimalchio was allowed to have this name because he had
been in the service of a master named Maecenas before he
became a slave in the family of the Pompeii. Slaves were
allowed to retain their old master's name on transfer in order
to prevent confusion arising from similarities in their names
where they were very numerous.

[2] Trimalchio boasts that if he had chosen to go to Rome as
a freedman he could have become a member of the decuries,
the orders or guilds which supplied the lower branches of
the public service, e.g. lictors, scribes, criers, and street
officers.

nos in turba exeamus." Cum haec placuissent, ducente per porticum Gitone ad ianuam venimus, ubi
canis catenarius tanto nos tumultu excepit, ut Ascyltos
etiam in piscinam ceciderit. Nec non ego quoque
ebrius, qui etiam pictum timueram canem, dum na-
tanti opem fero, in eundem gurgitem tractus sum.
Servavit nos tamen atriensis, qui interventu suo et
canem placavit et nos trementes extraxit in siccum.
Et Giton quidem iam dudum se ratione acutissima re-
demerat a cane; quicquid enim a nobis acceperat de
cena, latranti sparserat, [at] ille avocatus cibo furorem
suppresserat. Ceterum cum algentes utique petis-
semus ab atriense, ut nos extra ianuam emitteret,
" Erras " inquit "si putas te exire hac posse, qua venisti. Nemo unquam convivarum per candem ianuam
emissus est; alia intrant, alia exeunt." Quid faciamus
73 homines miserrimi et novi generis labyrintho inclusi,
quibus lavari iam coeperat votum esse? Ultro ergo
rogavimus, ut nos ad balneum duceret, proiectisque
vestimentis, quae Giton in aditu siccare coepit, balneum intravimus, angustum scilicet et cisternae frigida-
riae simile, in quo Trimalchio rectus stabat. Ac ne
sic quidem putidissimam eius iactationem[1] licuit effu-
gere; nam nihil melius esse dicebat quam sine turba
lavari, et eo ipso loco aliquando pistrinum fuisse.
Deinde ut lassatus consedit, invitatus balnei sono
diduxit usque ad cameram os ebrium et coepit Mene-
cratis cantica lacerare, sicut illi dicebant, qui lingnam

---

[1] eius iactationem *Heinsius* : ei actionem.

142

away in the crowd while they are looking for the bath."
This was agreed, and Giton led us through the gallery
to the door, where the dog on the chain welcomed us
with such a noise that Ascyltos fell straight into the
fish-pond. As I, who had been terrified even of a painted
dog, was drunk too, I fell into the same abyss while I
was helping him in his struggles to swim. But the porter
saved us by intervening to pacify the dog, and pulled us
shivering on to dry land.   Giton had ransomed himself from the dog some time before by a very cunning
plan; when it barked he threw it all the pieces we
had given him at dinner, and food distracted the
beast from his anger.   But when, chilled to the bone,
we asked the porter at least to let us out of the door, he
replied, "You are wrong if you suppose you can go out
at the door you came in by.   None of the guests are
ever let out by the same door; they come in at one
and go out by another."   There was nothing to be 73
done, we were victims enwound in a new labyrinth,
and the idea of washing had begun to grow pleasant,
so we asked him instead to show us the bath, and
after throwing off our clothes, which Giton began to
dry in the front hall, we went in.   It was a tiny place
like a cold-water cistern, and Trimalchio was standing
upright in it.   We were not allowed to escape his filthy
bragging even there; he declared that there was
nothing nicer than washing out of a crowd, and told
us that there had once been a bakery on that very
spot.   He then became tired and sat down, and the
echoes of the bathroom encouraged him to open his
tipsy jaws to the ceiling and begin to murder Menecrates's songs,[1] as I was told by those who could under-

---

[1] Menecrates was specially honoured by Nero (Suetonius,
Nero, c. 30).

eius intellegebant. Ceteri convivae circa labrum
manibus nexis currebant et gingilipho ingenti clamore
exsonabant. Ahi autem [aut] restrictis manibus anulos de pavimento conabantur tollere aut posito genu
cervices post terga flectere et pedum extremos polli-
ces tangere. Nos, dum alii sibi ludos faciunt, in solium,
quod Trimalchioni vaporabatur,[1] descendimus.

Ergo ebrietate discussa in aliud triclinium deducti
sumus, ubi Fortunata disposuerat lautitias [suas][2]
ita ut supra lucernas . . . aeneolosque piscatores
notaverim et mensas totas argenteas calicesque circa
fictiles inauratos et vinum in conspectu sacco defluens.
Tum Trimalchio "Amici" inquit "hodie servus meus
barbatoriam fecit, homo praefiscini frugi et micarius.
74 Itaque tangomenas faciamus et usque in lucem cenemus." Haec dicente eo gallus gallinaceus cantavit.
Qua voce confusus Trimalchio vinum sub mensa iussit
effundi lucernamque etiam mero spargi. Immo anulum traiecit in dexteram manum et "non sine causa"
inquit "hic bucinus signum dedit; nam aut incendium
oportet fiat, aut aliquis in vicinia animam abiciet.
Longe a nobis. Itaque quisquis hunc indicem attulerit,
corollarium accipiet." Dieto citius de vicinia gallus
allatus est, quem Trimalchio occidi[3] iussit, ut aeno co-
ctus fieret. Laceratus igitur ab illo doctissimo coco, qui
paulo ante de porco aves piscesque fecerat, in cacca-
bum est coniectus. Dumque Daedalus potionem fer-

[1] vaporabatur *Buecheler*: pervapatur (*in marg.* paraba-
tur).
[2] suas *marked for deletion in MS.*
[3] occidi *added by Buecheler.*

stand what he said. Other guests joined hands and ran round the edge of the bath, roaring with obstreperous laughter at the top of their voices. Some again had their hands tied behind their backs and tried to pick up rings from the floor, or knelt down and bent their heads backwards and tried to touch the tips of their toes. While the others were amusing themselves, we went down into a deep bath which was being heated for Trimalchio.

Then, having got rid of the effects of our liquor, we were led into another dining-room, where Fortunata had laid out her treasures, so that over the lamps I saw . . . . little bronze fishermen, and tables of solid silver, and china cups with gold settings, and wine being strained through a cloth before our eyes. Then Trimalchio said, "Gentlemen, a slave of mine is celebrating his first shave to-day: an honest, cheeseparing fellow, in a good hour be it spoken. So let us drink deep[1] and keep up dinner till dawn."

Just as he was speaking, a cock crew. The noise 74 upset Trimalchio, and he had wine poured under the table, and even the lamp sprinkled with pure wine. Further, he changed a ring on to his right hand, and said, "That trumpeter does not give his signal without a reason. Either there must be a fire, or some one close by is just going to give up the ghost. Lord, save us! So anyone who catches the informer shall have a reward." He had scarc l spoken, when the cock was brought in from somewhere near. Trimalchio ordered him to be killed and cooked in a saucepan. So he was cut up by the learned cook who had made birds and fishes out of a pig a little while before, and thrown into a cooking-pot. And while Daedalus took a long

[1] See note, p. 51.

145

ventissimam haurit, Fortunata mola buxea piper trivit.

Sumptis igitur matteis respiciens ad familiam Trimalchio "Quid vos" inquit "adhuc non cenastis?
Abite, ut alii veniant ad officium." Subiit igitur alia
classis, et illi quidem exclamavere: "Vale Gai," hi
autem: "Ave Gai." Hinc primum hilaritas nostra
turbata est; nam cum puer non inspeciosus inter
novos intrasset ministros, invasit eum Trimalchio et
osculari diutius coepit. Itaque Fortunata, ut ex aequo
ius firmum approbaret, male dicere Trimalchioni
coepit et purgamentum dedecusque praedicare, qui
non contineret libidinem suam. Ultimo etiam adiecit:
"canis." Trimalchio contra offensus convicio calicem
in faciem Fortunatae immisit. Illa tanquam oculum
perdidisset, exclamavit manusque trementes ad faciem
suam admovit. Consternata est etiam Scintilla trepi-
dantemque sinu suo texit. Immo puer quoque officio-
sus urceolum frigidum ad malam eius admovit, super
quem incumbens Fortunata gemere ac flere coepit.
Contra Trimalchio "Quid enim?" inquit "ambubaia
non meminit,[1] sed de[2] machina[3] illam sustuli,
hominem inter homines feci. At inflat se tanquam
rana, et in sinum suum non spuit,[4] codex, non mulier.
Sed hic, qui in pergula natus est, aedes non somniatur.
Ita genium meum propitium habeam, curabo, domata
sit Cassandra caligaria. Et ego, homo dipundiarius, sestertium centies accipere potni. Scis tu me non mentiri. Agatho, unguentarius herae proximae, seduxit
me et 'Suadeo' inquit 'non patiaris genus tuum inter-
ire.' At ego dum bonatus ago et nolo videri levis,

[1] meminit *Heinsius:* me misit.
[2] sed de *Buecheler:* sede.
[3] machina *Reiske:* machillam.
[4] non spuit *Reiske:* conspuit.

146

drink very hot, Fortunata ground up pepper in a box-wood mill.

After the good things were done, Trimalchio looked at the slaves and said, "Why have you not had dinner yet? Be off, and let some others come and wait." So another brigade appeared, and the old lot shouted, "Gaius, good-bye," and the new ones, "Hail! Gaius." After this, our jollity received its first shock; a rather com l boy came in among the fresh waiters, and Trimalchio took him and began to kiss him warmly. So Fortunata, to assert her rights at law, began to abuse Trimalchio, and called him a dirty disgrace for not behaving himself. At last she even added, "You bound." Her cursing annoyed Trimalchio, and he let fly a cup in her face. She shrieked as if her eye had been put out, and lifted her trembling hands to her face. Scintilla was frightened too, and shielded her quivering friend with her arms. While an officious slave held a cool little jar to her check, Fortunata leaned over it and began to groan and cry. But Tri-malchio said, "What is it all about? This chorus-girl has no memory, yet I took her off the sale-platform and made her one of ourselves. But she puffs herself up like a frog, and will not spit for luck; a log she is, not a woman. But if you were born in a slum you cannot sleep in a palace. Damn my soul if I do not properly tame this shameless Cassandra.[1] And I might have married ten million, wretched fool that I was! You know I am speaking the truth. Agatho, the perfumer of the rich woman next door, took me aside and said, 'I entreat you not to let your family die out.' But I, being a good chap, didn't wish to

[1] Cassandra is a type of passion, and a Cassandra in top-boots (caligaria) is a brutal, strong woman.

ipse mihi asciam in crus impegi. Recte, curabo, me
unguibus quaeras. Et ut depraesentiarum intelligas,
quid tibi feceris: Habinna, nolo, statuam eius in monumento meo ponas, ne mortuus quidem lites habeam.
Immo, ut seiat me posse malum dare, nolo, me mortuum basiet."

75 Post hoc fulmen Habinnas rogare coepit, ut iam
HL desineret irasci et | "Nemo" inquit "nostrum non
H peccat. Homines sumus, non dei." | Idem et Scintilla
flens dixit ac per genium eius Gaium appellando
rogare coepit, ut se frangeret.[1] Non tenuit ultra lacrimas Trimalchio et "Rogo" inquit "Habinna, sic peen-
lium tuum fruniscaris: si quid perperam feci, in faciem
meam inspue. Puerum basiavi frugalissimum, non
propter formam, sed quia frugi est: decem partes
dicit, librum ab oculo legit, thraecium sibi de diariis
fecit, arcisellium de suo paravit et duas trullas. Non
est dignus quem in oculis feram? sed Fortunata vetat.
Ita tibi videtur, fulcipedia? suadeo, bonum tuum con-
coquas, milva, et me non facias ringentem, amasiun-
cula: alioquin experieris cerebrum meum. Nosti me:
quod semel destinavi, clavo tabulari fixum est. Sed
vivorum meminerimus. Vos rogo, amici, ut vobis suaviter sit. Nam ego quoque tam fui quam vos estis, sed
virtute mea ad hoc perveni. Corcillum est quod homines facit, cetera quisquilia omnia. 'Bene emo,
bene vendo'; alius alia vobis dicet. Felicitate dissilio.

[1] se frangeret *Heinsius;* effrangeret.

148

seem fickle, and so I have stuck the axe into my own leg. Very well, I will make you want to dig me up with your finger-nails. But you shall understand what you have done for yourself straight away. Habinnas, do not put any statue of her on my tomb, or I shall have nagging even when I am dead. And to show that I can do her a bad turn, I will not have her kiss me even when I am laid out."

After this flash of lightning Habinnas began to im- 75 plore him to moderate his wrath. "We all have our faults," he said, "we are men, not angels." Scintilla cried and said the same, called him Gaius and besought him by his guardian angel to unbend. Trimalchio no longer restrained his tears, and said, "Habinnas, please, as you hope to enjoy your money, spit in my face if I have done anything wrong. I kissed that excellent boy not because he is beautiful, but because he is excellent: he can do division and read books at sight, he has bought a suit of Thracian armour out of his day's wages, purchased a round-backed chair with his own money, and two ladles. Does he not deserve to be treated well by me? But Fortunata will not have it. Is that your feeling, my high-heeled hussy? I advise you to chew what you have bitten off, you vulture, and not make me show my teeth, my little dear: otherwise you shall know what my anger is. Mark my words: when once my mind is made up, the thing is fixed with a ten-inch nail. But we will think of the living. Please make yourselves comfortable, gentlemen. I was once just what you are, but by my own merits I have come to this. A bit of sound sense is what makes men; the rest is all rubbish. 'I buy well and sell well': some people will tell you differently. I am bursting with happiness.

Tu autem, sterteia, etiamnum ploras? iam curabo, fatum tuum plores. Sed, ut coeperam dicere, ad hanc me fortunam frugalitas mea perduxit. Tam magnus ex Asia veni, quam hic candelabrus est. Ad summam, quotidie me solebam ad illum metiri, et ut celerius rostrum barbatum haberem, labra de lucerna ungebam. Tamen ad delicias [femina][1] ipsimi [domini] annos quattuordecim fui. Nec turpe est, quod dominus iubet. Ego tamen et ipsimae [dominae] satis faciebam. Scitis, quid dicam: tacco, quia non sum de gloriosis. 76 Ceterum, quemadmodum di volunt, dominus in domo factus sum, et ecce cepi ipsimi cerebellum. Quid multa? coheredem me Caesari fecit, et accepi patrimonium laticlavium. Nemini tamen nihil satis est. Concupivi negotiari. Ne multis vos morer, quinque naves aedificavi, oneravi vinum—et tune erat contra aurum—misi Romam. Putares me hoc iussisse: omnes naves naufragarunt, factum, non fabula. Uno die Neptunus trecenties sestertium devoravit. Putatis me defecisse? Non mehercules mi haec iactura gusti fuit, tanquam nihil facti. Alteras feci maiores et meliores et feliciores, ut nemo non me virum fortem diceret. Scitis, magna navis magnam fortitudinem habet. Oneravi rursus vinum, lardum, faham, seplasium, mancipia. Hoc loco Fortunata rem piam fecit; omne enim aurum suum, omnia vestimenta vendidit et mi centum aureos in manu posuit. Hoc fuit peculii mei fermentum. Cito fit, quod di volunt.

---

[1] femina, domini, dominae *bracketed by Buechele*r.

What, you snorer in bed, are you still whining? I will take care that you have something to whine over. Well, as I was just saying, self-denial has brought me into this fortune. When I came from Asia I was about as tall as this candle-stick. In fact I used to measure myself by it every day, and grease my lips from the lamp to grow a moustache the quicker. Still, I was my master's favourite for fourteen years. No disgrace in obeying your master's orders. Well, I used to amuse my mistress too. You know what I mean; I say no more, I am not a conceited man. Then, as the Gods willed, I became the real master 76 of the house, and simply had his brains in my pocket. I need only add that I was joint residuary legatee with Caesar,[1] and came into an estate fit for a senator. But no one is satisfied with nothing. I conceived a passion for business. I will not keep you a moment— I built five ships, got a cargo of wine—which was worth its weight in gold at the time—and sent them to Rome. You may think it was a put-up job; every one was wrecked, truth and no fairy-tales. Neptune gulped down thirty million in one day. Do you think I lost heart? Lord! no, I no more tasted my loss than if nothing had happened. I built some more, bigger, better and more expensive, so that no one could say I was not a brave man. You know, a huge ship has a certain security about her. I got another cargo of wine, bacon, beans, perfumes, and slaves. Fortunata did a noble thing at that time; she sold all her jewellery and all her clothes, and put a hundred gold pieces into my hand. They were the leaven of my fortune. What God wishes soon happens. I made

[1] It was not uncommon, and often prudent, for a rich man under the early Empire to mention the Emperor in his will.

Uno cursu centies sestertium corrotundavi. Statim redemi fundos omnes, qui patroni mei fuerant. Aedifico domum, venalicia coemo iumenta; quicquid tangeham, crescebat tanquam favus. Postquam coepi plus habere, quam tota patria mea habet, manum de tabula: sustuli me de negotiatione et coepi libertos faenerare. Et sane nolentem me negotium meum agere exhortavit mathematicus, qui venerat forte in coloniam nostram, Graeculio, Serapa nomine, consiliator deorum. Hic mihi dixit etiam ea, quae oblitus eram; ab acia et acu mi omnia exposuit; intestinas meas noverat; tantum quod mihi non dixerat, quid pridie cenaveram.

77 Putasses illum semper mecum habitasse. Rogo, Habinna—puto, interfuisti—: 'Tu dominam tuam de rebus illis fecisti. Tu parum felix in amicos es. Nemo unquam tibi parem gratiam refert. Tu latifundia possides. Tu viperam sub ala nutricas' et, quod vobis non dixerim, et nunc mi restare vitae annos triginta et menses quattuor et dies duos. Praeterea cito accipiam hereditatem. Hoc mihi dicit fatus meus. Quod si contigerit fundos Apuliae iungere, satis vivus pervenero. Interim dum Mercurius vigilat, aedificavi hanc domum. Ut scitis, casula[1] erat; nunc templum est. Habet quattuor cenationes, cubicula viginti, porticus marmoratos duos, susum cenationem,[2] cubiculum in quo ipse dormio, viperae huius sessorium, ostiarii cel-

---

[1] casula *Heinsius:* cnsue.
[2] cenationem *Scheffer:* cellationem.

a clear ten million on one voyage. I at once bought
up all the estates which had belonged to my patron.
I bui't a house, and bought slaves and cattle; whatever I touched grew like a honey-comb. When I
came to have more than the whole revenues of my
own country, I threw up the game: I retired from
active work and began to finance freedmen. I
was quite unwilling to go on with my work when
I was encouraged by an astrologer who happened
to come to our town, a little Greek called Serapa,
who knew the secrets of the Gods. He told
me things that I had forgotten myself; explained
everything from needle and thread upwards; knew
my own inside, and only fell short of telling me what
I had had for dinner the day before. You would 77
have thought he had always lived with me. You
remember, Habinnas?—I believe you were there?—
'You fetched your wife from you know where. You
are not lucky in your friends. No one is ever as grate-
ful to you as you deserve. You are a man of property.
You are nourishing a viper in your bosom,' and, though
I must not tell you this, that even now I had thirty
years four months and two days left to live. Moreover I shall soon come into an estate. My oracle tells
me so. If I could only extend my boundaries to
Apulia I should have gone far enough for my lifetime.
Meanwhile I built this house while Mercury watched
over me.[1] As you know, it was a tiny place; now it
is a palace. It has four dining-rooms, twenty bed-
rooms, two marble colonnades, an upstairs dining-
room, a bedroom where I sleep myself, this viper's
boudoir, an excellent room for the porter; there is

[1] Mercury was Trimalchio's patron. See nore, p. 43. Also
he was the god of gain and good luck.

lam perbonam; hospitium hospites capit. Ad summam, Scaurus cum huc venit, nusquam mavoluit hospitari, et habet ad mare paternum hospitium. Et multa alia sunt, quae statim vobis ostendam. Credite mihi: assem habeas, assem valeas; habes, habeberis. Sic amicus vester, qui fuit rana, nunc est rex. Interim. Stiche, profer vitalia, in quibus volo me efferri. Profer et unguentum et ex illa amphora gustum, ex qua iubeo lavari ossa mea."

78   Non est moratus Stichus, sed et stragulam albam et praetextam in triclinium attulit . . . . . . iussitque nos temptare, an bonis lanis essent confecta. Tum subridens "Vide tu" inquit "Stiche, ne ista mures tangant aut tineae? alioquin te vivum comburam. Ego gloriosus volo efferri, ut totus mihi populus bene imprecetur." Statim ampullam nardi aperuit omnesque nos unxit et "Spero" inquit "futurum ut acque me mortuum iuvet tanquam vivum." Nam vinum quidem in vinarium iussit infundi et "Putate vos" ait "ad parentalia mea invitatos esse."

Ihat res ad summam nauseam, cum Trimalchio ebrietate turpissima gravis novum acroama, cornicines, in triclinium iussit adduci, fultusque cervicalibus multis extendit se super torum extremum et "Fingite me" inquit "mortuum esse. Dicite aliquid belli." Consonuere cornicines funebri strepitu. Unus praecipue servus libitinarii illius, qui inter hos honestissimus erat, tam valde intonuit, ut totam concitaret viciniam,

154

plenty of spare room for guests. In fact when Scaurus came he preferred staying here to anywhere else, and he has a family place by the sea. There are plenty of other things which I will show you in a minute. Take my word for it: if you have a penny, that is what you are worth; by what a man hath shall he be reckoned. So your friend who was once a worm is now a king. Meanwhile, Stichus, bring me the grave-clothes in which I mean to be carried out. And some ointment, and a mouthful out of that jar which has to be poured over my bones."

In a moment Stichus had fetched a white winding- 78 sheet and dress into the dining-room and . . . [Trimalchio] asked us to feel whether they were made of good wool. Then he gave a little laugh and said, "Mind neither mouse nor moth corrupts them, Stichus; otherwise I will burn you alive. I want to be carried out in splendour, so that the whole crowd calls down blessings on me." He immediately opened a flask and anointed us all and said, "I hope I shall like this as well in the grave as I do on earth." Besides this he ordered wine to be poured into a bowl, and said, "Now you must imagine you have been asked to my funeral."

The thing was becoming perfectly sickening, when Trimalchio, now deep in the most vile drunkenness, had a new set of performers, some trumpeters, brought into the dining-room, propped himself on a heap of cushions, and stretched himself on his death-bed, saying, "Imagine that I am dead. Play something pretty." The trumpeters broke into a loud funeral march. One man especially, a slave of the undertaker who was the most decent man in the party, blew such a mighty blast that the whole neighbourhood was

TITUS PETRONIUS ARBITER

Itaque vigiles, qui custodiebant vicinam regionem, rati
ardere Trimalchionis domum, effregerunt ianuam
subito et cum aqua securibusque tumultuari suo iure
coeperunt. Nos occasionem opportunissimam naeti
Agamemnoni verba dedimus raptimque tam plane
quam ex incendio fugimus.

79 *L* | Neque fax ulla in praesidio erat, quae iter aperiret
errantibus, nec silentium noctis iam mediae promitte-
bat occurrentium lumen. Accedebat huc ebrietas et
imprudentia locorum etiam interdiu obfutura.[1] Itaque
cum hora paene tota per omnes scrupos gastrarumque
eminentium fragmenta traxissemus cruentos pedes,
tandem expliciti acumine Gitonis sumus. Prudens
enim [pridie], cum luce etiam clara timeret errorem,
omnes pilas columnasque notaverat creta, quae[2]
lineamenta evicerunt spississimam noctem et notabili
candore ostenderunt errantibus viam. Quamvis non
minus sudoris habuimus etiam postquam ad stabulum
pervenimus. Anus enim ipsa inter deversitores diutius
ingurgitata ne ignem quidem admotum sensisset. Et
forsitan pernoctassemus in limine, ni tabellarius
Trimalchionis intervenisset X vehiculis dives. Non
diu ergo tumultuatus stabuli ianuam effregit et nos
per eandem intro[3] admisit . . .

    Qualis nox fuit illa, di deaeque,
    quam mollis torus. Haesimus calentes
    et transfudimus hinc et hinc labellis
    errantes animas. Valete, curae
    mortalis. Ego sic perire coepi.

[1] obfutura *Buecheler:* obscura.
[2] creta, quae *Puteanus:* certaque.
[3] intro *Bourdelot:* terram.

56

roused. The watch,[1] who were patrolling the streets close by, thought Trimalchio's house was alight, and suddenly burst in the door and began with water and axes to do their duty in creating a disturbance. My friends and I seized this most welcome opportunity, outwitted Agamemnon, and took to our heels as quickly as if there were a real fire.

There was no guiding torch to show us the way as 79 we wandered; it was now midnight, and the silence gave us no prospect of meeting anyone with a light. Moreover we were drunk, and our ignorance of the quarter would have puzzled us even in the daytime. So after dragging our bleeding feet nearly a whole hour over the flints and broken pots which lay out in the road, we were at last put straight by Giton's cleverness. The careful child had been afraid of losing his way even in broad daylight, and had marked all the posts and columns with chalk; these lines shone through the blackest night, and their brilliant whiteness directed our lost footsteps. But even when we reached our lodgings our agitation was not relieved. For our friend the old woman had had a long night swilling with her lodgers, and would not have noticed if you had set a light to her. We might have had to sleep on the doorstep if Trimalchio's courier had not come up in state with ten carts. After making a noise for a little while he broke down the house-door and let us in by it...

Ah! gods and goddesses, what a night that was, how soft was the bed. We lay in a warm embrace and with kisses everywhere made exchange of our wandering spirits. Farewell, all earthly troubles. So began my destruction.

[1] Either a municipal or a private brigade of firemen or watchmen.

sine causa gratulor mihi. Nam cum solutus mero remisissem[1] ebrias manus, Ascyltos, omnis iniuriae inventor, subduxit mihi nocte puerum et in lectum transtulit suum, volutatusque liberius cum fratre non suo, sive non sentiente iniuriam sive dissimulante, indormivit alienis amplexibus oblitus iuris humani. Itaque ego ut experrectus pertrectavi gaudio despoliatum torum... Si qua est amantibus fides, ego dubitavi, an utrumque traicerem gladio somnumque morti iungerem. Tutius dein secutus consilium Gitona quidem verberibus excitavi, Ascylton autem truci intuens vultu "quoniam" inquam "fidem scelere violasti et communem amicitiam, res tuas ocius tolle et alium locum, quem polluas, quaere."

80 Non repugnavit ille, sed postquam optima fide partiti manubias sumus, "age" inquit "nunc et puerum dividamus." Iocari putabam discedentem. At ille gladium parricidali manu strinxit et "non frueris" inquit "hac praeda, super quam solus incumbis. partem meam necesse est vel hoc gladio contemptus abscidam."[2] Idem ego ex altera parte feci et intorto circa brachium pallio composui ad proeliandum gradum. Inter hanc miserorum dementiam infelicissimus puer tangebat utriusque genua cum fletu petebatque suppliciter, ne Thebanum par humilis taberna spectaret, neve sanguine mutuo pollueremus familiaritatis clarissimae sacra. "Quod si utique" proclamabat "facinore opus est, nudo ecce iugulum, convertite huc manus, imprimite mucrones. Ego mori debeo, qui amicitiae sacramentum delevi." Inhibuimus ferrum post has preces, et prior Ascyltos "ego" inquit "finem discordiae imponam. Puer ipse, quem vult,

[1] remisissem *Jacobs:* amisissem.
[2] contemptus *Burmann:* contentus.

158

I blessed my luck too soon. I was overcome with drink and let my shaking hands fall, and then Ascyltos, that fountain of all wickedness, took my little friend away et in lectum transtulit suum, volutatusque liberius cum fratre non suo, sive non sentiente iniuriam sive dissimulante, indormivit alienis amplexibus oblitus iuris humani. Itaque ego ut experrectus pertrectavi gaudio despoliatum torum ... Si qua est amantibus fides, ego dubitavi, an utrumque traicerem gladio somnumque morti iungerem. Tutius dein secutus cousilium Gitona quidem verberibus excitavi, I looked angrily at Ascyltos and said, "As you have wickedly broken our agreement and the friendship between us, collect your things at once, and find some other place to corrupt."

He did not resist, but after we had divided our 80 spoils with scrupulous honesty he said, "And now we must divide the boy too." I thought this was a parting joke. But he drew his sword murderously, and said, "You shall not enjoy this treasure that you brood over all alone. I am rejected, but I must carve off my share too, even with this sword."

So I did the same on my side; wrapped my cloak round my arm and put myself in position for a fight. As we raved in folly, the poor boy touched our knees, and humbly besought us with tears not to let that quiet lodging-house be the scene of a Theban duel, or stain the sanctity of a beautiful friendship with each other's blood. "But if you must commit your crime," he cried, "look here, here is my throat. Turn your hands this way and imbrue your blades. I deserve to die for breaking the oath of friendship." We put up our swords at his prayers, and Ascyltos spoke first, "I will put an end to this quarrel. Let the boy follow

159

sequatur, ut sit illi saltem in eligendo fratre [salva[
libertas." Ego qui vetustissimam consuetudinem
putabam in sanguinis pignus transisse, nihil timui,
immo condicionem praecipiti festinatione rapui com-
misique iudici litem. qui ne deliberavit quidem, ut
videretur cunctatus, verum statim ab extrema parte
verbi consurrexit *et* fratrem Ascylton elegit. Fulmi-
natus hac pronuntiatione, sic ut eram, sine gladio in
lectulum decidi, et attulissem mihi damnatus manus,
si non inimici victoriae invidissem. Egreditur superbus
cum praemio Ascyltos et paulo ante carissimum sibi
commilitonem fortunaeque etiam similitudine parem
in loco peregrino destituit abiectum.

LO | Nomen amicitiae sic, quatenus expedit, haeret;
          calculus in tabula mobile ducit opus.
     Cum fortuna manet, vultum servatis, amici ;
          cum cecidit, turpi vertitis ora fuga.

  ────────

     Grex agit in scaena mimum : pater ille vocatur,
          filius hic, nomen divitis ille tenet.
     Mox ubi ridendas inclusit pagina partes,
          vera redit facies, dum simulata[1] perit. . . .

81 Nec diu tamen lacrimis indulsi, sed veritus, ne
Menelaus etiam antescholanus inter cetera mala
solum me in deversorio inveniret, collegi sarcinulas
locumque secretum et proximum litori maestus
conduxi. Ibi triduo inclusus redeunte in animum
solitudine atque contemptu verberabam aegrum
L planctibus pectus | et inter tot altissimos gemitus

----

[1] dum simulata *Buecheler:* dissimulata.

160

the one he prefers, so that he at any rate may have a free choice of brothers."

I had no fears, imagining that long-standing familiarity had passed into a tie of blood, and I accepted the arrangement in hot haste, and referred the dispute to the judge. He did not even pretend to take time to consider, but got up at once as I finished speaking, and chose Ascyltos for his brother. I was thunderstruck at his choice, and fell down on the bed just as I was, without my sword; I should have committed suicide at the sentence if I had not grudged my enemy this triumph. Ascyltos went stalking out with his winnings, and left his comrade, whom he had loved a little while before, and whose fortunes had been so like his own, in despair in a strange place.

The name of friendship endures so long as there is profit in it: the counter on the board plays a changeable game. While my luck holds you give me your smiles, my friends; when it is out, you turn your faces away in shameful flight.

A company acts a farce on the stage: one is called the father, one the son, and one is labelled the Rich Man. Soon the comic parts are shut in a book, the men's real faces come back, and the make-up disappears.

But still I did not spend much time in weeping. I 81 was afraid that Menelaus the tutor[1] might increase my troubles by finding me alone in the lodgings, so I got together my bundles and took a room in a remote place right on the beach. I shut myself up there for three days; I was haunted by the thought that I was deserted and despised; I beat my breast, already worn with blows, groaned deeply and even cried aloud many

[1] See p. 37 note.

frequenter etiam proclamabam: "ergo me non ruina terra potuit haurire? Non iratum etiam innocentibus mare? Effugi iudicium, harenae imposui, hospitem occidi, ut inter *tot* audaciae nomina mendicns, exul, in deversorio Graecae urbis iacerem desertus? Et quis hanc mihi solitudinem imposuit? Adulescens omni libidine impurus et sua quoque confessione dignus exilio, stupro liber, stupro ingenuus, cuius anni ad tesseram venierunt, quem tanquam puellam conduxit etiam qui virum putavit. Quid ille alter? Qui [tanquam] die[1] togae virilis stolam sumpsit, qui ne vir esset, a matre persuasus est, qui opus muliebre in ergastulo fecit, qui postquam conturbavit et libidinis suae solum vertit, reliquit veteris amicitiae nomen et, pro pudor, tanquam mulier secutuleia unius noctis tactu omnia vendidit. Iacent nunc amatores obligati noctibus totis, et forsitan mutuis libidinibus attriti derident solitudinem meam. Sed non impune. Nam aut vir ego liberque non sum, aut noxio sanguine parentabo iniuriae mcae."

82   Haec locutus gladio latus cingo, et ne infirmitas militiam perderet, largioribus cibis excito vires. Mox in publicum prosilio furentisque more omnes circumeo porticus. Sed dum attonito vultu efferatoque nihil aliud quam caedem et sanguinem cogito frequentiusque manum ad capulum, quem devoveram, refero, notavit me miles, sive ille planus fuit sive nocturnus grassator, et "Quid tu" inquit "commilito, ex qua legione es aut cuius centuria?" Cum constantissime et centurionem et legionem essem ementitus, "Age ergo" inquit ille "in exercitu vestro

[1] alter die qui tanquam togae *MSS.*

162

times, "Could not the earth have opened and swallowed me, or the sea that shows her anger even against the innocent? I fled from justice, I cheated the ring, I killed my host, and with all these badges of courage I am left forsaken in lodgings in a Greek town, a beggar and an exile. And who condemned me to loneliness? A young man tainted by excess of every kind, deserving banishment even by his own admission, a free, yes, a free-born debauchee; his youth was wasted in gambling, and even those who supposed him to be a man treated him like a girl. And his friend? A boy who went into skirts instead of trousers, whose mother persuaded him never to grow up, who was the common sport of the slaves' quarters, who after going bankrupt, and changing the tune of his vices, has broken the ties of an old friendship, and shamelessly sold everything in a single night's work like a common woman. Now the lovers lie all night long in each other's arms, and very likely laugh at my loneliness when they are tired out. But they shall suffer for it. I am no man, and no free citizen, if I do not avenge my wrongs with their hateful blood."

With these words I put on my sword, and recruited 82 my strength with a square meal to prevent my losing the battle through weakness. I rushed out of doors at once, and went round all the arcades like a madman. My face was as of one dumbfoundered with fury, I thought of nothing but blood and slaughter, and kept putting my hand to the sword-hilt which I had consecrated to the work. Then a soldier, who may have been a swindler or a footpad, noticed me, and said, "Hullo, comrade, what regiment and company do you belong to?" I lied stoutly about my captain and my regiment, and he said, "Well, do soldiers in your

phaecasiati milites ambulant?" Cum deinde vultu atque ipsa trepidatione mendacium prodidissem, ponere *me* iussit arma et malo cavere. Despoliatus ergo, immo praecisa ultione retro ad deversorium tendo paulatimque temeritate laxata coepi grassatoris audaciae gratias agere . . .

    Non bibet inter aquas poma aut pendentia carpit
      Tantalus infelix, quem sua vota premunt.
    Divitis haec magni facies erit, omnia cernens
      qui timet et sicco concoquit ore famem. . . .

    Non multum oportet consilio credere, quia suam habet fortuna rationem . . .

83   In pinacothecam perveni vario genere tabularum mirabilem. Nam et Zeuxidos manus vidi nondum vetustatis iniuria vietas, et Protogenis rudimenta cum ipsius naturae veritate certantia non sine quodam horrore tractavi. Iam vero Apellis quam Graeci μονόκνημον appellant, etiam adoravi. Tanta enim subtilitate extremitates imaginum erant ad similitudinem praecisae, ut crederes etiam animorum esse picturam. Hinc aquila ferebat caelo sublimis Idaeum,[1] illinc candidus Hylas repellebat improbam Naida. Damnabat Apollo noxias manus lyramque resolutam modo nato flore honorabat. Inter quos etiam pictorum amantium vultus tanquam in solitudine exelamavi'

' Idaeum *Wehl:* deum.

force walk about in white shoes?" My expression and my trembling showed that I had lied, and he ordered me to hand over my arms and look out for myself. So I was not only robbed, but my revenge was nipped in the bud. I went back to the inn, and by degrees my courage cooled, and I began to bless the footpad's effrontery. . . .

Poor Tantalus stands in water and never drinks, nor plucks the fruit above his head: his own desires torment him. So must a rich great man look when, with everything before his eyes, he fears starvation, and digests hunger dry-mouthed. . . .

It is not much use depending upon calculation when Fate has methods of her own. . . .

I came into a gallery hung with a wonderful collection of various pictures. I saw the works of Zeuxis not yet overcome by the defacement of time, and I studied with a certain terrified wonder the rough drawings of Protogenes, which rivalled the truth of Nature herself. But when I came to the work of Apelles the Greek which is called the One-legged, I positiv ly worshipped it. For the outlines of his figures were defined with such subtle accuracy, that you would have declared that he had painted their souls as well. In one the eagle was carrying the Shepherd of Ida[1] on high to heaven, and in another fair Hylas resisted a tormenting Naiad. Apollo[2] passed judgement on his accursed hands, and adorned his unstrung lyre with the newborn flower. I cried out as if I were in a desert, among these faces of mere painted lovers, "So even

83

[1] Ganymede, who became the cupbearer of Jupiter.
[2] Apollo killed Hyacinthus, a Spartan boy whom he loved, by a mis-throw of the discus. The hyacinth flower sprang up from the boy's blood.

"Ergo amor etiam deos tangit. Iuppiter in caelo suo non invenit quod diligeret,[1] sed peccaturus in terris nemini tamen iniuriam fecit. Hylan Nympha praedata temperasset[2] amori suo, si venturum ad interdietum Herculem credidisset. Apollo pueri umbram revocavit in florem, et omnes fabulae quoque sine aemulo habuerunt complexus. At ego in societatem recepi hospitem Lycurgo crudeliorem."

Ecce autem, ego dum cum ventis litigo, intravit pinacothecam senex canus, exercitati vultus et qui videretur nescio quid magnum promittere, sed cultu non proinde speciosus, ut facile appareret eum *ex* hac nota litteratum esse, quos odisse divites solent. Is ergo ad latus constitit meum . . .

"Ego" inquit "poeta sum et ut spero, non humillimi spiritus, si modo coronis aliquid credendum est, quas etiam ad immeritos[3] deferre gratia solet. 'Quare ergo' inquis 'tam male vestitus es?' Propter hoc ipsum. Amor ingenii neminem unquam divitem fecit.

LO | Qui pelago credit, magno se faenore tollit;
    qui pugnas et castra petit, praecingitur auro;
    vilis adulator picto iacet ebrius ostro,
    et qui sollicitat nuptas, ad praemia peccat:
    sola pruinosis horret facundia pannis
    atque inopi lingua desertas invocat artes.

84 Non dubie ita est: si quis vitiorum omnium inimicus rectum iter vitae coepit insistere,[4] primum propter morum differentiam odium habet; quis enim potest probare diversa? Deinde qui solas extruere divitias

---

[1] diligeret sed *Jacobs :* eligeret et.
[2] temperasset *Buecheler :* imperasset.
[3] immeritos *Buecheler :* imperitos.
[4] insistere *cod. Messaniensis :* inspicere *other MSS.*

the gods feel love. Jupiter in his heavenly home could find no object for his passion, and came down on earth to sin, yet did no one any harm. The Nymph who ravished Hylas would have restrained her passion had she believed that Hercules would come to dispute her claim. Apollo recalled the ghost of a boy into a flower, and all the stories tell of love's embraces without a rival. But I have taken for my comrade a friend more cruel than Lycurgus himself."

Suddenly, as I strove thus with the empty air, a white-haired old man[1] came into the gallery. His face was troubled, but there seemed to be the promise of some great thing about him; though he was shabby in appearance, so that it was quite plain by this characteristic that he was a man of letters, of the kind that rich men hate. He came and stood by my side. . . .

"I am a poet," he said, "and one, I hope, of no mean imagination, if one can reckon at all by crowns of honour, which gratitude can set even on unworthy heads. 'Why are you so badly dressed, then?' you ask. For that very reason. The worship of genius never made a man rich.

"The man who trusts the sea consoles himself with high profits; the man who follows war and the camp is girded with gold; the base flatterer lies drunk on a couch of purple dye; the man who tempts young wives gets money for his sin; eloquence alone shivers in rags and cold, and calls upon a neglected art with unprofitable tongue.

"Yes, that is certainly true: if a man dislikes all 84 vices, and begins to tread a straight path in life, he is hated first of all because his character is superior; for who is able to like what differs from himself? Further, those who only trouble about heaping up riches,

---

[1] Eumolpus.

curant, nihil volunt inter homines melius credi, quam quod ipsi tenent. Insectantur[1] itaque, quacunque ratione possunt, litterarum amatores, ut videantur illi quoque infra pecuniam positi" . . .

L | "Nescio quo modo bonae mentis soror est paupertas" . . .

"Vellem, tam innocens esset frugalitatis meae hostis, ut deliniri posset. Nunc veteranus est latro et ipsis lenonibus doctior" . . .

85 "In Asiam cum a quaestore essem stipendio eductus, hospitium Pergami accepi. Ubi cum libenter habitarem non solum propter cultum aedicularum, sed etiam propter hospitis formosissimum filium, excogitavi rationem, qua non essem patri familiae suspectus amator. Quotiescunque enim in convivio de usu formosorum mentio facta est, tam vehementer excandui, tam severa tristitia violari aures meas obsceno sermone nolui, ut me mater praecipue tanquam unum ex philosophis intueretur. Iam ego coeperam ephebum in gymnasium deducere, ego studia eius ordinare, ego docere ac praecipere, ne quis praedator corporis admitteretur in domum . . .

Forte cum in triclinio iaceremus, quia dies sollemnis ludum artaverat pigritiamque recedendi imposuerat hilaritas longior, fere circa mediam noctem intellexi puerum vigilare. Itaque timidissimo murmure votum feci et 'domina' inquam 'Venus, si ego hunc puerum basiavero, ita ut ille non sentiat, cras illi par columbarum donabo.' Andito voluptatis pretio puer stertere coepit. Itaque aggressus simulantem aliquot basiolis invasi. Contentus hoc principio bene mane surrexi electumque par columbarum attuli expectanti

---

[1] insectantur *Buecheler:* iactantur.

do not want anything to be considered better than what is in their own hands. So they persecute men with a passion for learning in every possible way, to make them also look an inferior article to money. . . .

"Somehow or other poverty is own sister to good sense. . . .

"I wish he that hates me for my virtue were so guilt-less that he might be mollified. As it is he is a past master of robbery, and more clever than any pimp."

"In Asiam cum a quaestore essem stipendio eductus, 85 hospitium Pergami accepi. Ubi cum libenter habi-tarem non solum propter cultum aedicularum, sed etiam propter hospitis formosissimum filium, excogitavi rationem, qua non essem patri familiae suspectus amator. Quotiescunque enim in convivio de usu formosorum mentio facta est, tam vehementer ex-candui, tam severa tristitia violari aures meas obsceno sermone nolui, ut me mater praecipue tanquam unum ex philosophis intueretur. Iam ego coeperam ephebum in gymnasium deducere, ego studia eius ordinare, ego docere ac praecipere, ne quis praedator corporis ad-mitteretur in domum . . .

Forte cum in triclinio iaceremus, quia dies sollemnis ludum artaverat pigritiamque recedendi imposuerat hilaritas longior, fere circa mediam noctem intellexi puerum vigilare. Itaque timidissimo murmure votum feci et 'domina' inquam 'Venus, si ego hunc puerum basiavero, ita ut ille non sentiat, cras illi par colum-barum donaho.' Andito voluptatis pretio puer ster-tere coepit. Itaque aggressus simulantem aliquot basiolis invasi. Contentus hoc principio bene mane surrexi electumque par columbarum attuli expectanti

169

86 ac me voto exsolvi. Proxima nocte cum idem liceret, mutavi optionem et 'si hunc' inquam 'tractavero improba manu, et ille non senserit, gallos gallinaceos pugnacissimos duos donabo patienti.' Ad hoc votum ephebus ultro se admovit et, puto, vereri coepit, ne ego obdormiscerem. Indulsi ergo sollicito, totoque corpore citra summam voluptatem me ingurgitavi. Deinde ut dies venit, attuli gaudenti quicquid promiseram. Ut tertia nox licentiam dedit, consurrexi ... ad aurem male dormientis 'dii' inquam 'immortales, si ego buie dormienti abstulero coitum plenum et optabilem, pro hac felicitate cras puero asturconem Macedonicum optimum donabo, cum hac tamen exceptione, si ille non senserit.' Nunquam altiore somno ephebus obdormivit. Itaque primum implevi lactentibus papillis manus, mox basio inhaesi, deinde in unum omnia vota coniunxi. Mane sedere in cubiculo coepit atque expectare consuetudinem meam. Scis quanto facilius sit, columbas gallosque gallinaceos emere quam asturconem, et praeter hoc etiam timebam, ne tam grande munus suspectam faceret humanitatem meam. Ego aliquot boris spatiatus in hospitium reverti nihilque aliud quam puerum basiavi. At ille circumspiciens ut cervicem meam iunxit amplexu, 'rogo' inquit 'domine, ubi est asturco?'' ...

87 Cum ob hanc offensam praeclusissem mihi aditum, quem feceram, iterum ad licentiam redii. Interpositis enim paucis diebus, cum similis casus nos in candem fortunam rettulisset, ut intellexi stertere patrem, rogare coepi ephebum, ut reverteretur in gratiam mecum, id est ut pateretur satis fieri sibi, et cetera quae libido distenta dictat. At ille plane iratus nihil aliud dicebat nisi hoc: "aut dormi, aut ego iam dicam patri." Nihil est tam arduum, quod non improbitas

ac me voto exsolvi. Proxima nocte cum idem liceret, 86
mutavi optionem et 'si hunc' inquam 'tractavero improba manu, et ille non senserit, gallos gallinaceos
pugnacissimos duos donabo patienti.' Ad hoc votum
ephebus ultro se admovit et, puto, vereri coepit, ne
ego obdormiscerem. Indulsi ergo sollicito, totoque
corpore citra summam voluptatem me ingurgitavi.
Deinde ut dies venit, attuli gaudenti quicquid promiseram. Ut tertia nox licentiam dedit, consurrexi . . .
ad aurem male dormientis 'dii' inquam 'immortales,
si ego buie dormienti abstulero coitum plenum et
optabilem, pro hac felicitate cras puero asturconem
Macedonicum optimum donabo, cum hac tamen exceptione, si ille non senserit.' Nunquam altiore
somno ephebus obdormivit. Itaque primum implevi
lactentibus papillis manus, mox basio inhaesi, deinde
in unum omnia vota coniunxi. Mane sedere in
cubiculo coepit atque expectare consuetudinem meam.
Scis quanto facilius sit, columbas gallosque gallinaceos
emere quam asturconem, et praeter hoc etiam timebam,
ne tam grande munus suspectam faceret humanitatem
meam. Ego aliquot boris spatiatus in hospitium reverti
nihilque aliud quam puerum basiavi. At ille circumspiciens ut cervicem meam iunxit amplexu, 'rogo'
inquit 'domine, ubi est asturco?'' . . .

Cum ob hanc offensam praeclusissem mihi aditum, 87
quem feceram, iterum ad licentiam redii. Interpositis
enim paucis diebus, cum similis casus nos in candem
fortunam rettulisset, ut intellexi stertere patrem,
rogare coepi ephebum, ut reverteretur in gratiam
mecum, id est ut pateretur satis fieri sibi, et cetera
quae libido distenta dictat. At ille plane iratus nihil
aliud dicebat nisi hoc: "aut dormi, aut ego iam dicam
patri." Nihil est tam arduum, quod non improbitas

extorqueat. Dum dicit: "patrem excitabo," irrepsi tamen et male repugnanti gaudium extorsi. At ille non indelectatus nequitia mea, postquam diu questus est deceptum se et derisum traductumque inter condiscipulos, quibus iactasset censum meum, "videris tamen" inquit "non ero tui similis. Si quid vis, fac iterum." Ego vero deposita omni offensa cum puero in gratiam redii ususque beneficio eius in somnum delapsus sum. Sed non fuit contentus iteratione ephebus plenae maturitatis et annis ad patiendum gestientibus. Itaque excitavit me sopitum et "numquid vis?" inquit. Et non plane iam molestum erat munus. Utcunque igitur inter anhelitus sudoresque tritus, quod voluerat, accepit, rursusque in somnum decidi gaudio lassus. Interposita minus hora pungere me manu coepit et dicere: "quare non facimus?" tum ego totiens excitatus plane vehementer excandui et reddidi illi voces suas: 'aut dormi, aut ego iam patri dicam'" . . .

88   Erectus his sermonibus consulere prudentiorem coepı aetates tabularum et quaedam argumenta mihi obscura simulque causam desidiae praesentis excutere, cum pulcherrimae artes perissent, inter quas pictura ne minimum quidem sui vestigium reliquisset. Tum ille "pecuniae" inquit "cupiditas haec tropica insti-
LO tuit. | Priscis enim temporibus, cum adhuc nuda virtus placeret, vigebant artes ingenuae summumque certamen inter homines erat, ne quid profuturum saeculis diu lateret. Itaque herbarum omnium sucos Democritus expressit, et ne lapidum virgultorumque vis lateret, aetatem inter experimenta consumpsit. Eudoxos [quidem] in cacumine excelsissimi montis con-

172

extorqueat. Dum dicit: "patrem excitabo," irrepsi tamen et male repugnanti gaudium extorsi. At ille non indelectatus nequitia mea, postquam diu questus est deceptum se et derisum traductumque inter condiscipulos, quibus iactasset censum meum, "videris tamen" inquit "non ero tui similis. Si quid vis, fac iterum." Ego vero deposita omni offensa cum puero in gratiam redii ususque beneficio eius in somnum delapsus sum. Sed non fuit contentus iteratione ephebus plenae maturitatis et annis ad patiendum gestientibus. Itaque excitavit me sopitum et "numquid vis?" inquit. Et non plane iam molestum erat munus. Utcunque igitur inter anhelitus sudoresque tritus, quod voluerat, accepit, rursusque in somnum decidi gaudio lassus. Interposita minus hora pungere me manu coepit et dicere: "quare non facimus?" tum ego totiens excitatus plane vehementer excandui et reddidi illi voces suas: 'aut dormi, aut ego iam patri dicam'" . . .

Encouraged by his conversation, I began to draw on 88 his knowledge about the age of the pictures, and about some of the stories which puzzled me, and at the same time to discuss the decadence of the age, since the fine arts had died, and painting, for instance, had left no trace of its existence behind. "Love of money began this revolution," he replied. "In former ages virtue was still loved for her own sake, the noble arts flourished, and there were the keenest struggles among mankind to prevent anything being long undiscovered which might benefit posterity. So Democritus extracted the juice of every plant on earth, and spent his whole life in experiments to discover the virtues of stones and twigs. Eudoxos grew old on the top of a high mountain in order to trace the move-

senuit, ut astrorum caelique motus deprehenderet, et Chrysippus, ut ad inventionem sufficeret, ter elleboro animum detersit. Verum ut ad plastas convertar, Lysippum statuae unius lineamentis inhaerentem inopia extinxit, et Myron, qui paene animas hominum ferarumque aere comprehenderat, non invenit heredem. At nos vino scortisque demersi ne paratas quidem artes audemus cognoscere, sed accusatores antiquitatis vitia tantum docemus et discimus. Ubi est dialectica? Ubi astronomia? Ubi sapientiae cultissima[1] via? Quis unquam venit in templum et votum fecit, si ad eloquentiam pervenisset? Quis, si philosophiae fontem attigisset? Ac ne bonam quidem mentem aut bonam valitudinem petunt, sed statim antequam limen Capitolii tangant, alius donum promittit, si propinquum divitem extulerit, alius, si thesaurum effoderit, alius, si ad trecenties sestertium salvus pervenerit. Ipse senatus, recti bonique praeceptor, mille pondo auri Capitolio promittere solet, et ne quis dubitet pecuniam concupiscere, Iovem quoque peculio exornat. Noli ergo mirari, si pictura defecit, cum omnibus diis hominibusque formosior videatur massa auri, quam quicquid Apelles Phidiasque, Graeculi delirantes, fecerunt. Sed video te totum in illa haerere tabula, quae Troiae halosin ostendit. Itaque conabor opus versibus pandere:

89

> Iam decima maestos inter ancipites metus
> Phrygas obsidebat messis et vatis fides
> Calchantis atro dubia pendebat metu,
> cum Delio profante caesi vertices
> Idae trahuntur scissaque in molem cadunt

[1] cultissima *cod. Paris. 6842 D:* consultissima *other MSS.*

174

ments of the stars and the sky, and Chrysippus three times cleared his wits with hellebore to improve his powers of invention. If you turn to sculptors, Lysippus died of starvation as he brooded over the lines of a single statue, and Myron, who almost caught the very soul of men and beasts in bronze, left no heir behind him. But we are besotted with wine and women, and cannot rise to understand even the arts that are developed; we slander the past, and learn and teach nothing but vices. Where is dialectic now, or astronomy? Where is the exquisite way of wisdom? Who has ever been to a temple and made an offering in order to attain to eloquence, or to drink of the waters of philosophy? They do not even ask for good sense or good health, but before they even touch the threshold of the Capitol, one promises an offering if he may bury his rich neighbour, another if he may dig up a hid treasure, another if he may make thirty millions in safety. Even the Senate, the teachers of what is right and good, often promise a thousand pounds in gold to the Capitol, and decorate even Jupiter with pelf, that no one need be ashamed of praying for money. So there is nothing surprising in the decadence of painting, when all the gods and men think an ingot of gold more beautiful than anything those poor crazy Greeks, Apelles and Phidias, ever did.

"But I see your whole attention is riveted on that 89 picture, which represents the fall of Troy. Well, I will try and explain the situation in verse:

"'It was now the tenth harvest of the siege of the Trojans, who were worn with anxious fear, and the honour of Calchas the prophet stood wavering in dark dread, when at Apollo's bidding the wooded peaks of Ida were felled and dragged down, and the sawn

175

robora, minacem quae figurarent[1] equum.
Aperitur ingens antrum et obducti specus,
qui castra caperent.   Huc decenni proelio
irata virtus abditur, stipant graves
Danai recessus, in suo voto latent.
O patria, pulsas mille credidimus rates
solumque bello liberum: hoc titulus fero
incisus, hoc ad furta[2] compositus Sinon
firmabat et mens semper[3] in damnum potens.
    Iam turba portis libera ac bello carens
in vota properat.   Fletibus manant genae
mentisque pavidae gaudium lacrimas habet,
quas metus abegit.   Namque Neptuno sacer
crinem solutus omne Laocoon replet
clamore vulgus.   Mox reducta cuspide
uterum notavit, fata sed tardant manus,
ictusque resilit et dolis addit fidem.
Iterum tamen confirmat invalidam manum
altaque bipenni latera pertemptat.   Fremit
captiva pubes intus et, dum murmurat,
roborea moles spirat alieno metu.
Ihat iuventus capta, dum Troiam capit,
bellumque totum fraude ducebat nova.
    Ecce alia monstra: celsa qua Tenedos mare
dorso replevit, tumida consurgunt freta
undaque resultat scissa tranquillo minor,
qualis silenti nocte remorum sonus
longe refertur, cum premunt classes mare
pulsumque marmor abiete imposita gemit.
Respicimus: angues orbibus geminis ferunt
ad saxa fluctus, tumida quorum pectora

[1] figurarent *Pithoeus, Tomaesius:* figurabat.
[2] furta *Buecheler* : fata.
[3] mens semper *cod. Autissiodurensis :* mendatium semper
cod. Paris. 6842 D : mendacium *other MSS.*

176

planks fitted to a shape that resembled a war-horse. Within it a great hollow was opened, and a hidden cave that could shelter a host. In this the warriors who chafed at a war ten years long were packed away; the baleful Greeks fill every corner, and lie waiting in their own votive offering. Ah! my country! we thought the thousand ships were beaten off, and the land released from strife. The inscription carved on the horse, and Sinon's crafty bearing, and his mind ever powerful for evil, all strengthened our hope.

"'Now a crowd hurries from the gate to worship, care-less and free of the war. Their checks are wet with tears, and the joy of their trembling souls brings to their eyes tears that terror had banished. Laocoon, priest of Neptune, with hair unbound, stirs the whole assembly to cry aloud. He drew back his spear and gashed the belly of the horse, but fate stayed his hand, the spear leaped back, and won us to trust the fraud. But he nerved his feeble hand a second time, and sounded the deep sides of the horse with an axe. The young soldiers shut within breathed loud, and while the sound lasted the wooden mass gasped with a terror that was not its own. The prisoned warriors went forward to make Troy prisoner, and waged all the war by a new subtlety.

"'There followed further portents; where the steep ridge of Tenedos breaks the sea, the billows rise and swell, and the shattered wave leaps back hollowing the calm, sounding like the noise of oars horne far through the silent night, when ships bear down the ocean, and the calm is stirred and splashes under the burden of the keel. We look back: the tide carries two coiling snakes towards the rocks, their swollen breasts

N

rates ut altae lateribus spumas agunt.
Dat cauda sonitum, liberae ponto[1] inbae
consentiunt luminibus, fulmineum iubar
incendit aequor sibilisque undae fremunt.
Stupuere mentes.   Infulis stabant sacri
Phrygioque cultu gemina nati pignora
Lauconte.   Quos repente tergoribus ligant
angues corusci.   Parvulas illi manus
ad ora referunt, neuter auxilio sibi,
uterque fratri: transtulit pietas vices
morsque ipsa miseros mutuo perdit metu.
Accumulat ecce liberum funus parens,
infirmus auxiliator.   Invadunt virum
iam morte pasti membraque ad terram trahunt.
Iacet sacerdos inter aras victima
terramque plangit.   Sic profanatis sacris
peritura Troia perdidit primum deos.

    Iam plena Phoebe candidum extulerat inbar
minora ducens astra radianti face,
cum inter sepultos Priamidas nocte et mero
Danai relaxant claustra et effundunt viros.
Temptant in armis se duces, ceu ubi solet
nodo remissus Thessali quadrupes ingi
cervicem et altas quatere ad excursum iubas.
Gladios retractant, commovent orbes manu
bellumque sumunt.   Hic graves alius mero
obtruncat et continuat in mortem ultimam
somnos, ab aris alius accendit faces
contraque Troas invocat Troiae sacra." . . .

90 L | Ex is, qui in porticibus spatiabantur, lapides in
Eumolpum recitantem miserunt.   At ille, qui plausum ingenii sui noverat, operuit caput extraque tem-

---

[1] ponto *Sambucus, Tornaesius :* pontem L : pontum O.

like tall ships throwing the foam from their sides. Their tails crash through the sea, their crests move free over the open water, fierce as their eyes; a brilliant beam kindles the waves, and the waters resound with their hissing. Our heartbeats stopped. The priests stood wreathed for sacrifice with the two sons of Laocoon in Phrygian raiment. Suddenly the gleaming snakes twine their bodies round them. The boys throw up their little hands to their faces, neither helping himself, but each his brother: such was the exchange of love, and death himself slew both poor children by their unselfish fear. Then before our eyes the father, a feeble helper, laid his own body down upon his children's. The snakes, now gorged with death, attacked the man and dragged his limbs to the ground. The priest lies a victim before his altars and beats the earth. Thus the doomed city of Troy first lost her gods by profaning their worship.

"'Now Phoebe at the full lifted up her white beam, and led forth the smaller stars with her glowing torch, and the Greeks unbarred the horse, and poured out their warriors among Priam's sons drowned in darkness and wine. The leaders try their strength in arms, as a steed untied from the Thessalian yoke will toss his head and lofty mane as he rushes forth. They draw their swords, brandish their shields, and begin the fight. One slays Trojans heavy with drink, and prolongs their sleep to death that endeth all, another lights torches from the altars, and calls on the holy places of Troy to fight against the Trojans.'"...

Some of the people who were walking in the galleries threw stones at Eumolpus as he recited. He recognized this tribute to his genius, covered his head, and fled out of the temple. I was afraid that he

N2   179

plum profugit. Timui ego, ne me poetam vocaret.
Itaque subsecutus fugientem ad litus perveni, et ut
primum extra teli coniectum licuit consistere, "Rogo"
inquam "quid tibi vis cum isto morbo? Minus quam
duabus boris mecum moraris, et saepius poetice quam
humane locutus es. Itaque non miror, si te populus
lapidibus persequitur. Ego quoque sinum meum saxis
onerabo, ut quotiescunque coeperis a te exire, sanguinem tibi a capite mittam." Movit ille vultum et "O
mi" inquit "adulescens, non hodie primus auspicatus
sum. Immo quoties theatrum, ut recitarem aliquid,
intravi, hac me adventicia excipere frequentia solet.
Ceterum ne [et] tecum quoque habeam rixandum,
toto die me ab hoc cibo abstinebo." "Immo" inquam
ego "si cinras hodiernam bilem, una cenabimus" . . .

Mando aedicularum custodi cenulae officium . . .

91   Video Gitona cum linteis et strigilibus parieti appli-
citum tristem confusumque. Seires, non libenter
servire. Itaque ut experimentum oculorum caperem
convertit ille solutum gaudio vultum et "Miserere"
inquit "frater. Ubi arma non sunt, libere loquor.
Eripe me latroni cruento et qualibet saevitia paenitentiam indicis tui puni. Satis magnum erit misero
solacium, tua voluntate cecidisse." Supprimere ego
querellam iubeo, ne quis consilia deprehenderet, re-
lictoque Eumolpo—nam in balneo carmen recitabat—
per tenebrosum et sordidum egressum extraho Gitona
raptimque in hospitium meum pervolo Praeclusis

would call me a poet. So I followed him in his flight, and came to the beach, and as soon as we were out of range and could stop, I said, "Tell me, cannot you get rid of your disease? You have been in my company less than two hours, and you have talked more often like a poet than like a man. I am not surprised that the crowd pursue you with stones. I shall load my pockets with stones too, and whenever you begin to forget yourself I shall let blood from your head." His expression altered, and he said, "My dear young friend, I have been blessed like this before to-day. Whenever I go into the theatre to recite anything, the people's way is to welcome me with this kind of present. But I do not want to have anything to quarrel with you about, so I will keep off this food for a whole day." "Well," said I, "if you forswear your madness for to-day, we will dine together." . . .

I gave the house-porter orders about our supper. . . .

I saw Giton, with some towels and scrapers, hugging the wall in sad embarrassment. You could see he was not a willing slave. So to enable me to catch his eye he turned round, his face softened with pleasure, and he said, "Forgive me, brother. As there are no deadly weapons here, I speak freely. Take me away from this bloody robber and punish me as cruelly as you like, your penitent judge.[1] It will be quite enough consolation for my misery to die because you wish it." I told him to stop his lamentation, for fear anyone should overhear our plans. We left Eumolpus behind—he was reciting a poem in the bathroom—and I took Giton out by a dark, dirty exit, and flew with all speed to my lodgings. Then

[1] The words refer to the phrase in c. 80 *commisi iudici* (sc. *Gitoni*) *litem*, where Encolpius left Giton to choose between himself and Ascyltos.

91

deinde foribus invado pectus amplexibus et perfusum os lacrimis vultu meo contero. Diu vocem neuter invenit; nam puer etiam singultibus crebris amabile pectus quassaverat. "O facinus" inquam "indignum, quod amo te quamvis relictus, et in hoc pectore, cum vulnus ingens fuerit, cicatrix non est. Quid dicis, peregrini amoris concessio? Dignus hac iniuria fui?" Postquam se amari sensit, supercilium altius sustulit . . .

"Nec amoris arbitrium ad alium iudicem detuli.[1] Sed nihil iam queror, nihil iam memini, si bona fide paenitentiam emendas." Haec cum inter gemitus lacrimasque fudissem, detersit ille pallio vultum et "Quaeso" inquit "Encolpi, fidem memoriae tuae appello: ego te reliqui, an tu me prodidisti? Equidem fateor et prae me fero: cum duos armatos viderem, ad fortiorem confugi." Exosculatus pectus sapientia plenum inieci cervicibus manus, et ut facile intellegeret redisse me in gratiam et optima fide reviviscentem amicitiam, toto pectore adstrinxi.

92 Et iam plena nox erat mulierque cenae mandata curaverat, cum Eumolpus ostium pulsat. Interrogo ego: "quot estis?" obiterque per rimam foris speenlari diligentissime coepi, num Ascyltos una venisset. Deinde ut solum hospitem vidi, momento recepi. Ille ut se in grabatum reiecit viditque Gitona in conspectu ministrantem, movit caput et "Laudo" inquit "Ganymedem. Oportet hodie bene sit." Non delectavit me tam curiosum principium timuique, ne in coutu-

[1] detuli *Buecheler:* tuli *and* tulit.

I shut the door and warmly embraced him, and rubbed my face against his cheek, which was wet with tears. For a time neither of us could utter a sound; the boy's fair body shook with continuous sobs. "It is a shame and a wonder!" I cried, "You left me, and yet I love you, and no scar is left over my heart, where the wound was so deep. Have you any excuse for yielding your love to a stranger? Did I deserve this blow?" As soon as he felt that I loved him, he began to hold his head up. . . .

"I laid our love's cause before no other judge. But I make no complaint, I will forget all, if you will prove your penitence by keeping your word." I poured out my words with groans and tears, but Giton wiped his face on his cloak, and said, "Now, Eucolpins, I ask you, I appeal to your honest memory; did I leave you, or did you betray me? I admit, I confess it openly, that when I saw two armed men before me, I hurried to the side of the stronger." I pressed my lips to his dear wise heart, and put my arms round his neck, and hugged him close to me, to make it quite plain that I was in amity with him again, and that our friendship lived afresh in perfect confidence.

It was now quite dark, and the woman had seen 92 to our orders for supper, when Eumolpus knocked at the door. I asked, "How many of you are there?" and began as I spoke to look carefully through a chink in the door to see whether Ascyltos had come with him. When I saw that he was the only visitor, I let him in at once. He threw himself on a bed, and when he saw Giton before his eyes waiting at table, he wagged his head and said, "I like your Ganymede. To-day should be a fine time for us." I was not pleased

bernium recepissem Ascylti parem. Instat Eumolpus, et cum puer illi potionem dedisset, "Malo te" inquit "quam balneum totum" siccatoque avide poculo negat sibi unqnam acidius fuisse. "Nam et dum lavor" ait "paene vapulavi, quia conatus sum circa solium sedentibus carmen recitare, et postquam de balneo tanquam de theatro eiectus sum, circuire omnes angulos coepi et clara voce Encolpion clamitare. Ex altera parte iuvenis nudus, qui vestimenta perdiderat, non minore clamoris indignatione Gitona flagitabat. Et me quidem pueri tanquam insanum imitatione petulantissima deriserunt, illum autem frequentia ingens circumvenit cum plausu et admiratione timidissima. Habebat enim inguinum pondus tam grande, ut ipsum hominem laciniam fascini crederes. O iuvenem laboriosum: puto illum pridie incipere, postéro die finire. Itaque statim invenit auxilium; nescio quis enim, eques Romanus ut aiebant infamis, sua veste errantem circumdedit ac domum abduxit, credo, ut tam magna fortuna solus uteretur. At ego ne mea quidem vestimenta ab officioso *custode* recepissem, nisi notorem dedissem. Tanto magis expedit inguina quam ingenia fricare." Haec Eumolpo dicente mutabam ego frequentissime vultum, iniuriis scilicet inimici mei hilaris, commodis tristis. Utcunque tamen, tanquam non agnoscerem fabulam, tacui et cenae ordinem explicui . . .

93 "Vile est, quod licet, et animus errori intentus[1] iniurias diligit.

[1] errori intentus *Buecheler:* errore lentus.

at this inquisitive opening; I was afraid I had let
Ascyltos's double into the lodgings. Eumolpus persisted, and, when the boy brought him a drink, said,
"I like you better than the whole bathful." He
greedily drank the cup dry, and said he had never
taken anything with a sharper tang in it. "Why, I
was nearly flogged while I was washing," he cried,
"because I tried to go round the bath and recite
poetry to the people sitting in it, and when I was
thrown out of the bathroom as if it were a theatre, I
began to look round all the corners, and shouted for
Encolpius in a loud voice. In another part of the
place a naked young man who had lost his clothes
kept clamouring for Giton with equally noisy indignation. The boys laughed at me with saucy mimicry as
if I were crazy, but a large crowd surrounded him,
clapping their hands and humbly admiring. Habebat
enim inguinum pondus tam grande, ut ipsum hominem
laciniam fascini crederes. O iuvenem laboriosum:
puto illum pridie incipere, postero die finire. So he
found an ally at once: some Roman knight or other,
a low fellow, they said, put his own clothes on him as
he strayed round, and took him off home, I suppose,
ut tam magna fortuna solus uteretur. I should never
have got my own clothes back from the troublesome
attendant if I had not produced a voucher. Tanto
magis expedit inguina quam ingenia fricare." As
Eumolpus told me all this, my expression kept
changing, for of course I laughed at my enemy's
straits and frowned on his fortune. But anyhow
I kept quiet as if I did not know what the story was
about, and set forth our bill of fare. . . .

"What we may have we do not care about; our 93
minds are bent on folly and love what is troublesome.

Ales Phasiacis petita Colchis
atque Afrae volucres placent palato,
quod non sunt faciles : at albus anser
et pictis anas enovata[1] pennis
plebeium sapit.   Ultimis ab oris
attractus scarus atque arata Syrtis,
si quid naufragio dedit, probatur :
mullus iam gravis est.   Amica vincit
uxorem.   Rosa cinnamum veretur.
Quicquid quaeritur, optimum videtur."
    " Hoc est" inquam "quod promiseras, ne quem
hodie versum faceres? per fidem, saltem nobis parce,
qui te nunquam lapidavimus.   Nam si aliquis ex is,
qui in eodem synoecio potant, nomen poetae olfecerit,
totam concitabit viciniam et nos omnes sub eadem
causa obruet.   Miserere et aut pinacothecam aut balneum cogita."   Sic me loquentem obiurgavit Giton,
mitissimus puer, et negavit recte facere, quod seniori
conviciarer simulque oblitus officii mensam, quam
humanitate posuissem, contumelia tollerem, multaque
alia moderationis verecundiaeque verba, quae formam
eius egregie decebant. . . .

94 *LO* | " O felicem " inquit " matrem tuam, quae te talem
peperit : macte virtute esto.   Raram fecit mixturam
cum sapientia forma.   Itaque ne putes te tot verba
perdidisse, amatorem invenisti.   Ego laudes tuas carminibus implebo.   Ego paedagogus et custos etiam
quo non iusseris, sequar.   Nec iniuriam Encolpius
accipit, alium amat."   Profuit etiam Eumolpo miles
ille, qui mihi abstulit gladium ; alioquin quem animum
adversus Ascylton sumpseram, eum in Eumolpi sanguinem exercuissem.   Nec fefellit hoc Gitona.   Itaque extra cellam processit, tanquam aquam peteret,

---

[1] enovata *Pithoeus :* renovata.

"The bird won from Colchis where Phasis flows, and fowls from Africa, are sweet to taste because they are not easy to win; but the white goose and the duck with bright new feathers have a common savour. The wrasse drawn from far-off shores, and the yield of wrinkled Syrtis is praised if first it wrecks a boat: the mullet by now is a weariness. The mistress eclipses the wife, the rose hows down to the cinnamon. What men must seek after seems ever best."

"What about your promise, that you would not make a single verse to-day?" I said. "On your honour, spare us at least: we have never stoned you. If a single one of the people who are drinking in the same tenement with us scents the name of a poet, he will rouse the whole neighbourhood and ruin us all for the same reason. Spare us then, and remember the picture-gallery or the baths." Giton, the gentle boy, reproved me when I spoke thus, and said that I was wrong to rebuke my elders, and forget my duty so far as to spoil with my insults the dinner I had ordered out of kindness, with much more tolerant and modest advice which well became his beautiful self. . . .

"Happy was the mother who bore such a son as you," 94 he said, "be good and prosper. Beauty and wisdom make a rare conjunction. And do not think that all your words have been wasted. In me you have found a lover. I will do justice to your worth in verse. I will teach and protect you, and follow you even where you do not bid me. I do Encolpius no wrong; he loves another."

That soldier who took away my sword did Eumolpus a good turn too; otherwise I would have appeased the wrath raised in me against Ascyltos with the blood of Eumolpus. Giton was not blind to this. So he went out of the room on a pretence of fetching water, and

iramque meam prudenti absentia extinxit. Paululum ergo intepescente saevitia "Eumolpe" inquam "iam malo vel carminibus loquaris, quam eiusmodi tibi vota proponas. Et ego iracundus sum, et tu libidinosus: vide, quam non conveniat his moribus. Puta igitur me furiosum esse, cede insaniae, id est ocius foras exi."

LI Confusus hac denuntiatione Eumolpus non quaesiit iracundiae causam, sed continuo limen egressus adduxit repente ostium cellae meque nihil tale expectantem inclusit, exemitque raptim clavem et ad Gitona investigandum cucurrit.

Inclusus ego suspendio vitam finire constitui. Et iam semicinctio *lecti*[1] stantis ad parietem spondam vinxeram cervicesque nodo condebam, cum reseratis foribus intrat Eumolpus cum Gitone meque a fatali iam meta revocat ad lucem. Giton praecipue ex dolore in rabiem efferatus tollit clamorem, me utraque manu impulsum praecipitat super lectum, "erras" inquit "Encolpi, si putas contingere posse, ut ante moriaris. Prior coepi; in Ascylti hospitio gladium quaesivi. Ego si te non invenissem, periturus per praecipitia fui. Et ut scias non longe esse quaerentibus mortem, specta invicem, quod me spectare voluisti." Haec locutus mercennario Eumolpi novaculam rapit et semel iterumque cervice percussa ante pedes collabitur nostros. Exclamo ego attonitus, secutusque labentem eodem ferramento ad mortem viam quaero. Sed neque Giton ulla erat suspicione vulneris laesus, neque ego ullum sentiebam dolorem. Rudis enim

[1] lecti *added by Buecheler.*

188

quenched my wrath by his tactful departure. Then,
as my fury cooled a little, I said, "I would prefer even
that you should talk poetry now, Eumolpus, rather
than harbour such hopes. I am choleric, and you are
lecherous: you understand that these dispositions do
not suit each other. Well, regard me as a maniac,
yield to my infirmity, in short, get out quick."
Eumolpus was staggered by this attack, and never
asked why I was angry, but went out of the room at
once and suddenly banged the door, taking me completely by surprise and shutting me in. He pulled out
the key in a moment and ran off to look for Giton.

I was locked in. I made up my mind to hang myself and die. I had just tied a belt to the frame of a
bed which stood by the wall, and was pushing my neck
into the noose, when the door was unlocked, Eumolpus
came in with Giton, and called me back to light from
the very bourne of death. Nay, Giton passed from
grief to raving madness, and raised a shout, pushed me
with both hands and threw me on the bed, and cried,
"Encolpius, you are wrong if you suppose you could
possibly die before me. I thought of suicide first; I
looked for a sword in Ascyltos's lodgings. If I had
not found you I would have hurled myself to death
over a precipice. I will show you that death stands
close by those who seek him: behold in your turn the
scene you wished me to behold."

With these words he snatched a razor from Eumolpus's servant, drew it once, twice across his throat, and
tumbled down at our feet. I gave a cry of horror,
rushed to him as he fell, and sought the road of death
with the same steel. But Giton was not marked with
any trace of a wound, and I did not feel the least
pain. The razor was untempered, and specially blunted

novacula et in hoc retusa, ut pueris discentibus audaciam tonsoris daret, instruxerat thecam.   Ideoque nec
mercennarius ad raptum ferramentum expaverat, nec
Eumolpus interpellaverat mimicam mortem.

95 *LO* | Dum haec fabula inter amantes luditur, dever-
sitor cum parte cenulae intervenit, contemplatusque
foedissimam volutationem iacentium "rogo" inquit
"ebrii estis, an fugitivi, an utrumque? Quis autem
grabatum illum erexit, aut quid sibi vult tam furtiva
molitio? Vos mehercules ne mercedem cellae daretis,
fugere nocte in publicum voluistis.   Sed non impune.
Iam enim faxo sciatis non viduae hanc insulam esse
sed M. Mannicii." Exclamat Eumolpus "etiam
minaris?" simulque os hominis palma excussissima
pulsat.   Ille tot hospitum potionibus liberum nreco-
lum fictilem in Eumolpi caput iaculatus est solvitque
clamantis frontem et de cella se proripuit.   Eumolpus
contumeliae impatiens rapit ligneum candelabrum
sequiturque abeuntem et creberrimis ictibus supercilium suum vindicat.   Fit concursus familiae hospi-
tumque ebriorum frequentia.   Ego autem nactus
occasionem vindictae Eumolpum excludo, redditaque
scordalo vice sine aemulo scilicet et cella utor et
nocte.

Interim coctores insulariique mulcant exclusum et
alius veru extis stridentibus plenum in oculos eius
intentat, alius furca de carnario rapta statum proelian-
tis componit.   Anus praecipue lippa, sordidissimo
praecincta linteo, soleis ligueis imparibus imposita,

190

in order to give boy pupils the courage of a barber: and so it had grown a sheath. So the servant had not been alarmed when the steel was snatched from him, and Eumolpus did not interrupt our death-scene.

While this lover's play was being performed, an 95 inmate of the house came in with part of our little dinner, and after looking at us rolling in disarray on the ground he said, "Are you drunk, please, or runaway slaves, or both? Who turned the bed up there, and what do all these sneaking contrivances mean? I declare you meant to run off in the dark into the public street rather than pay for your room. But you shall pay for it. I will teach you that these lodgings do not belong to a poor widow, but to Marcus Mannicius." "What?" shouted Eumolpus, "you dare threaten us.' And as he spoke he struck the man in the face with all the force of his outstretched band. The man hurled a little earthenware pot, which was empty, all the guests having drunk from it, at Eumolpus's head, broke the skin of his forehead in the midst of his clamour, and rushed out of the room. Eumolpus would not brook an insult; he seized a wooden candlestick and followed the lodger out, and avenged his bloody forehead with a rain of blows. All the household ran up, and a crowd of drunken lodgers. I had a chance of punishing Eumolpus, and I shut him out, and so got even with the bully, and of course had the room and my sleep to myself without a rival.

Meanwhile cooks and lodgers belaboured him now that he was locked out, and one thrust a spit full of hissing meat into his eyes, another took a fork from a dresser and struck a fighting attitude. Above all, a blear-eyed old woman with a very dirty linen wrap round her. balancing herself on an uneven pair of

canem ingentis magnitudinis catena trahit instigatque
in Eumolpon. Sed ille candelabro se ab omni periculo vindicabat. Videbamus nos omnia per foramen
96 valvae, quod paulo ante ansa ostioli rupta laxaverat,
favebamque ego vapulanti. Giton autem non oblitus
misericordiae suae reserandum esse ostium succurren-
dumque periclitanti censebat. Ego durante adhuc
iracundia non continui manum, sed caput miserantis
stricto acutoque articulo percussi. Et ille quidem
flens consedit in lecto. Ego autem alternos oppone-
L bam foramini oculos iniuriaque Eumolpi | velut quo-
LO dam cibo me replebam ╎ advocationemque commen-
daham, cum procurator insulae Bargates a cena
excitatus a duobus lecticariis in mediam rixam per-
fertur; nam erat etiam pedibus aeger, is ut rabiosa
barbaraque voce in ebrios fugitivosque diu peroravit,
respiciens ad Eumolpon "o poetarum" inquit "diser-
tissime, tu eras? Et non discedunt ocius nequissimi
servi manusque continent a rixa?" . . .
L ╎ "Contubernalis mea mihi fastum facit. Ita si, me
amas, maledic illam versibus, ut habeat pudorem" . .
97 Dum Eumolpus cum Bargate in secreto loquitur,
intrat stabulum praeco cum servo publico aliaque
sane modica frequentia, facemque fumosam magis
quam lncidam quassans haec proclamavit: "puer in
balneo paulo ante aberravit, annorum circa xvi, crispus,
mollis, formosus, nomine Giton. Si quis eum reddere
aut commonstrare voluerit, accipiet nummos mille "

192

clogs, took the lead, brought up a dog of enormous size on a chain, and set him on to Eumolpus. But the candlestick was enough to protect him from all danger.

We saw everything through a hole in the folding 96 doors, which had been made by the handle of the door being broken a short time before; and I was delighted to see him thrashed. But Giton clung to compassion, and said we ought to open the door and go and rescue him from peril. My indignation was still awake; I did not hold my hand, I rapped his compassionate head with my sharp clenched knuckles. He cried and sat down on the bed. I put my eyes to the chink by turns, and gorged myself on the miseries of Eumolpus like a dainty dish, and approved their prolongation. Then Bargates, the man in charge of the lodging-house, was disturbed at his dinner, and two chairmen carried him right into the brawl; for he had gouty feet. In a furious vulgar voice he made a long oration against drunkards and escaped slaves, and then he looked at Eumolpus and said, "What, most learned bard, was it you? Get away quick, you damned slaves, and keep your hands from quarrelling." . .

"My mistress despises me. So curse her for me in rhyme, if you love me, and put shame into her." . .

While Eumolpus was talking privately to Bargates, 97 a crier came into the house with a municipal slave and quite a small crowd of other people, shook a torch which gave out more smoke than light, and made this proclamation: "Lost recently in the public baths, a boy aged about sixteen, hair curly, low habits, of attractive appearance, answers to the name of Giton. A reward of a thousand pieces will be paid to any person willing to bring him back or indicate his where-

TITUS PETRONIUS ARBITER

Nec longe a praecone Ascyltos stabat amictus dis-
coloria veste atque in lance argentea indicium et
fidem praeferebat. Imperavi Gitoni, ut raptim grabatum subiret annecteretque pedes et manus institis,
quibus sponda culcitam ferebat, ac sic ut olim Vlixes
Cyclopis arieti[1] adhaesisset, extentus infra grabatum
scrutantium eluderet manus.   Non est moratus Giton
imperium momentoque temporis inseruit vinculo manus
et Vlixem astu simillimo vicit.   Ego ne suspicioni re-
linquerem locum, lectulum vestimentis implevi uni-
usque hominis vestigium ad corporis mei mensuram
figuravi.

Interim Ascyltos ut pererravit omnes cum viatore
cellas, venit ad meam, et hoc quidem pleniorem spem
concepit, quo diligentius oppessulatas invenit fores.
Publicus vero servus insertans commissuris secures
claustrorum firmitatem laxavit.   Ego ad genna Ascylti
procubui et per memoriam amicitiae perque societatem miseriarum petii, ut saltem ostenderet fratrem.
Immo ut fidem haberent fictae preces, "scio te"
inquam "Ascylte, ad occidendum me venisse.   Quo
enim secures attulisti?   Itaque satia iracundiam tuam:
praebeo ecce cervicem, funde sanguinem, quem sub
praetextu quaestionis petisti."   Amolitur Ascyltos invidiam et se vero nihil aliud quam fugitivum suum
dixit quaerere, mortem nec hominis concupisse nec supplicis, utique eius quem post fatalem rixam habuisset[2]

---

[1] Cyclopis arieti *Buecheler :* pro ariete.
[2] habuisset *Buecheler :* habuit.

abouts." Ascyltos stood close by the crier in clothes
of many colours, holding out the reward on a silver
dish to prove his honesty. I told Giton to get under
the bed at once, and book his feet and hands into the
webbing which held up the mattress on the frame, so
that he might evade the grasp of searchers by staying stretched out under the bed, just as Ulysses of old
clung on to the ram of the Cyclops.[1] Giton obeyed
orders at once, and in a second had slipped his hands
into the webbing, and surpassed even Ulysses at his
own tricks. I did not want to leave any room for
suspicion, so I stuffed the bed with clothes, and
arranged them in the shape of a man about my own
height sleeping by himself.

Meanwhile Ascyltos went round all the rooms with
a constable, and when he came to mine, his hopes
swelled within him at finding the door bolted with
especial care. The municipal slave put an axe into the
joints, and loosened the bolts from their place. I fell
at Ascyltos's feet, and besought him, by the memory
of our friendship and the miseries we had shared, at
least to show me my brother. Further to win belief
in my sham prayers, I said, "I know you have come
to kill me, Ascyltos. Else why have you brought an
axe with you? Well, satisfy your rage. Here is my
neck, shed my blood, the real object of your pretended legal search." Ascyltos threw off his resent-
ment, and declared that he wanted nothing but his own
runaway slave, that he did not desire the death of any
man or any suppliant, much less of one whom he loved
very dearly now that their deadly dispute was over.

[1] See Homer's Odyssey, Book ix. Ulysses escaped from
the den of the Cyclops Polyphemus by clinging to the belly
of a ram, when Polyphemus sent out his flocks to graze.

98 carissimum. At non servus publicus tam languide
agit, sed raptam cauponi harundinem subter lectum
mittit omniaque etiam foramina parietum scrutatur.
Subducebat Giton ab ictu corpus et reducto timidis-
sime spiritu ipsos sciniphes ore tangebat...

Eumolpus autem, quia effractum ostium cellae neminem poterat excludere, irrumpit perturbatus et
"mille" inquit "nummos inveni; iam enim persequar
abeuntem praeconem et in potestate tua esse Gitonem
meritissima proditione[1] monstrabo." Genua ego per-
severantis amplector, ne morientes vellet occidere, et
"merito" inquam "excandesceres, si posses perditum[2]
ostendere. Nunc inter turbam puer fugit, nec quo
abierit, suspicari possum. Per fidem, Eumolpe, redue
puerum et vel Ascylto redde." Dum haec ego iam
credenti persuadeo, Giton collectione spiritus plenus
ter continuo ita sternutavit, ut grabatum concuteret.
Ad quem motum Eumolpus conversus salvere Gitona
iubet. Remota etiam culcita videt Vlixem, cui vel
esuriens Cyclops potuisset parcere. Mox conversus
ad me "quid est" inquit "latro? ne deprehensus
quidem ansus es mihi verum dicere. Immo ni deus
quidam humanarum rerum arbiter pendenti puero
excussisset indicium, elusus circa popinas errarem"...

Giton longe blandior quam ego, primum araneis
oleo madentibus vulnus, quod in supercilio factum
erat, coartavit. Mox palliolo suo laceratam mutavit

[1] proditone *Richard:* propositione.
[2] perditum *Jacobs:* proditum.

196

But the constable was not so deficient in energy. 98
He took a cane from the inn-keeper, and pushed it
under the bed, and poked into everything, even the
cracks in the walls. Giton twisted away from the
stick, drew in his breath very gently, and pressed his
lips close against the bugs in the bedding.. . The
broken door of the room could not keep anyone out,
and Eumolpus rushed in in a fury, and cried, "I have
found a thousand pieces; for I mean to follow the crier
as he goes away, and betray you as you richly deserve,
and tell him that Giton is in your hands." He persisted, I fell at his feet, besought him not to kill a
dying man, and said, "You might well be excited if you
could show him the lost one. As it is, the boy has
run away in the crowd, and I have not the least idea
where he has gone. As you love me, Eumolpus, get
the boy back, and give him to Ascyltos if you like."
I was just inducing him to believe me, when Giton
burst with holding his breath, and all at once sneezed
three times so that he shook the bed. Eumolpus
turned round at the noise, and said "Good day,
Giton." He pulled off the mattress, and saw an
Ulysses whom even a hungry Cyclops might have
spared. Then he turned on me, "Now, you thief;
you did not dare to tell me the truth even when you
were caught. In fact, unless the God who controls
man's destiny had wrung a sign from this boy as
he hung there, I should now be wandering round the
pot-bouses like a fool." . . .

Giton was far more at ease than I. He first stanched
a cut which had been made on Eumolpus's forehead
with spider's webs soaked in oil. He then took off
his torn clothes, and in exchange gave him a short
cloak of his own, then put his arms round him, for

197

vestem, amplexusque iam mitigatum osculis tanquam fomentis aggressus est et "in tua" inquit "pater carissime, in tua sumus custodia. Si Gitona tuum amas, incipe velle servare. Utinam me solum inimicus ignis hauriret vel hibernum invaderet mare. Ego enim omnium scelerum materia, ego causa sum. Si perirem, conveniret inimicis" . . .

99 "ego sic semper et ubique vixi, ut ultimam quamque lucem tanquam non redituram consumerem" . . .

profusis ego lacrimis rogo quaesoque, ut mecum quoque redeat in gratiam: neque enim in amantium esse potestate furiosam aemulationem. Daturum tamen operam, ne aut dicam aut faciam amplius, quo possit offendi. Tantum omnem scabitudinem animo tanquam bonarum artium magister deleret sine cicatrice. "Incultis asperisque regionibus diutius nives haerent, ast ubi aratro domefacta tellus nitet, dum loqueris, levis pruina dilabitur. Similiter in pectoribus ira considit: feras quidem mentes obsidet, eruditas praelabitur." "Ut scias" inquit Eumolpus "verum esse, quod dicis, ecce etiam osculo iram finio. Itaque, quod bene eveniat, expedite sarcinulas et vel sequimini me vel, si mavultis, ducite." Adhuc loquebatur, cum crepuit ostium impulsum, stetitque in limine barbis horrentibus nauta et "moraris" inquit "Eumolpe, tanquam propudium ignores." Haud mora, omnes consurgimus, et Eumolpus quidem mercennarium suum iam olim dormientem exire cum sarcinis inhet. Ego cum Gitone quicquid erat, in iter[1] compono et adoratis sideribus intro navigium . . .

[1] iter *Buecheler :* alter.

he was now softening, poulticed him with kisses, and said, "Dearest father, we are in your hands, yours entirely. If you love your Giton, make up your mind to save him. I wish the cruel fire might engulf me alone, or the wintry sea assail me. I am the object of all his transgressions, I am the cause. If I were gone, you two might patch up your quarrel." . .

"At all times and in all places I have lived such a 99 life that I spent each passing day as though that light would never return." . .

I burst into tears, and begged and prayed him to be friends again with me too: a true lover was incapable of mad jealousy. At the same time I would take care to do nothing more in word or deed by which he could possibly be hurt. Only he must remove all irritation from his mind like a man of true culture, and leave no scar. "On the wild rough uplands the snow lies late, but when the earth is beautiful under the mastery of the plough, the light frost passes while you speak. Thus anger dwells in our hearts; it takes root in the savage, and glides over the man of learning." "There," said Eumolpus, "you see what you say is true. Behold, I banish my anger with a kiss. So good luck go with us. Get ready your luggage and follow me, or lead the way if you like." He was still talking, when a knock sounded on the door, and a sailor with a straggly beard stood at the entrance and said, "You hang about, Eumolpus, as if you did not know a Blue Peter by sight." We all got up in a hurry, and Eumolpus ordered his slave, who had now been asleep for some time, to come out with his baggage. Giton and I put together all we had for a journey; I asked a blessing of the stars, and went aboard.

100 "molestum est quod puer hospiti placet. Quid autem? Non commune est, quod natura optimum fecit? Sol omnibus lucet. Luna innumerabilibus comitata sideribus etiam feras ducit ad pabulum. Quid aquis dici formosius potest? In publico tamen manant. Solus ergo amor furtum potins quam praemium erit? Immo vero nolo habere bona, nisi quibus populus inviderit. Unus, et senex, non erit gravis; etiam cum voluerit aliquid sumere, opus anhelitu prodet." Haec ut infra fiduciam posui fraudavique animum dissidentem, coepi somnum obruto tunicula capite mentiri.

Sed repente quasi destruente fortuna constantiam meam eiusmodi vox super constratum puppis congemuit: "ergo me derisit?" Et haec quidem virilis et paene auribus meis familiaris animum palpitantem percussit. Ceterum eadem indignatione mulier lacerata ulterius excanduit et "Si quis deus manibus meis" inquit "Gitona imponeret, quam bene exulem exciperem."[1] Uterque nostrum tam inexpectato ictus sono amiserat sanguinem. Ego praecipue quasi somnio quodam turbulento circumactus diu vocem collegi tremebundisque manibus Eumolpi iam in soporem labentis laciniam duxi et "Per fidem" inquam "pater, cuius haec navis est, aut quos vehat, dicere potes?" Inquietatus ille moleste tulit et "Hoc erat" inquit "quod placuerat tibi, ut supra constratum navis occuparemus secretissimum locum, ne nos patereris requiescere? Quid porro ad rem pertinet, si dixero Licham

---

[1] exciperem *margin ed. of Tornaesius :* exciperet.

"I am annoyed because the boy takes a stranger's 100
fancy. But are not all the finest works of nature
common property? The sun shines upon all men.
The moon with countless troops of stars in her train
leads even the beasts to their food. Can we imagine
anything more lovely than water? yet it flows
for all the world. Then shall love alone be stolen
rather than enjoyed? The truth is that I do not care for
possessions unless the common herd are jealous of
them. One rival, and he too an old man, will not be
troublesome; even if he wants to gain an advantage,
his shortness of breath will give him away." When I
had made these points without any confidence, de-
ceiving my protesting spirit, I covered my head in my
cloak and pretended to be asleep.

But suddenly, as though fate were in arms against
my resolution, a voice on the ship's deck said with a
groan, like this: "So he deceived me, then?" These
manly tones were somehow familiar to my ear, and my
heart beat fast as they struck me. But then a woman
torn by the same indignation broke out yet more
vehemently: "Ah, if the gods would deliver Giton
into my hands, what a fine welcome I would give
the runaway." The shock of these unexpected
sounds drove all the blood out of both of us. I felt
as if I were being hunted round in some troubled
dream; I was a long while finding my voice, and then
pulled Eumolpus's clothes with a shaking band, just
as he was falling into a deep sleep, and said, "Tell
me the truth, father; can you say who owns this ship,
or who is on board?" He was annoyed at being disturbed, and replied, "Was this why you chose a quiet
corner on deck, on purpose to prevent us from getting
any rest? What on earth is the use of my telling you

201

'Tarentinum esse dominum huiusce navigii, qui Try-
101 phaenam exulem Tarentum ferat?" Intremui post
hoc fulmen attonitus, iuguloque detecto "aliquando"
inquam "Totum me, Fortuna, vicisti." Nam Giton
quidem super pectus meum positus diu animam egit.
Deinde ut effusus sudor utriusque spiritum revocavit,
comprehendi Eumolpi genua et "Miserere" inquam
"morientium et pro consortio studiorum commoda
manum; mors venit, quae nisi per te non licet, potest
esse pro munere." Inundatus hac Eumolpus invidia
iurat per deos deasque se neque scire quid acciderit,
nec ullum dolum malum consilio adhibuisse, sed mente
simplicissima et vera fide in navigium comites in-
duxisse, quo ipse iam pridem fuerit usurus. "Quae
autem hic insidiae sunt" inquit "aut quis nobiscum
Hannibal navigat? Lichas Tarentinus, homo vere-
cundissimus et non tantum huius navigii dominus,
quod regit, sed fundorum etiam aliquot et familiae
negotiantis, onus deferendum ad mercatum conducit.
Hic est Cyclops ille et archipirata, cui vecturam de-
bemus; et praeter hunc Tryphaena, omnium femina-
rum formosissima, quae voluptatis causà huc atque illuc
vectatur." "Hi sunt" inquit Giton "quos fugimus"
simulque raptim causas odiorum et instans periculum
trepidanti Eumolpo exponit. Confusus ille et consilii
egens iubet quemque suam sententiam promere et
"Fingite" inquit "nos antrum Cyclopis intrasse.
Quaerendum est aliquod effugium. nisi naufragium

that Lichas of Tarentum is the master of this boat, and is carrying Tryphaena to Tarentum under a sentence of banishment?" I was thunderstruck at this 101 blow. I bared my throat, and cried, "Ah, Fate, at last you have smitten me hip and thigh." For Giton, who was sprawling over me, had already fainted. Then the sweat broke out on us and called us both back to life. I took Eumolpus by the knees, and cried, "Mercy on us! We are dead men. Help us, I implore you by our fellowship in learning; death is upon us, and we may come to welcome death, unless you prevent us from doing so."

Eumolpus was overwhelmed by this attack, and swore by gods and goddesses that he did not understand what had happened, and had no sinister intentions in his mind, but had taken us to share the voyage with him in perfect honesty and absolute good faith; he had been meaning to sail himself some time before. "Is there any trap here?" he said, "and who is the Hannibal we have on board? Lichas of Tarentum is a respectable person. He is not only owner and captain of this ship, but has several estates and some slaves in business. He is carrying a cargo consigned to a market. This is the ogre and pirate king to whom we owe our passage; and besides, there is Tryphaena, loveliest of women, who sails from one place to another in search of pleasure." "But it is these two we are running away from," said Giton, and poured out the story of our feud, and explained our imminent danger, till Eumolpus shook. He became muddled and helpless, and asked us each to put forward our views. "I would have you imagine that we have entered the ogre's den," he said. "We must find some way out, unless we run the ship aground and

ponimus et omni nos periculo liberamus." "Immo"
inquit Giton "persuade gubernatori, ut in aliquem
portum navem deducat, non sine praemio scilicet, et
affirma ei impatientem maris fratrem tuum in ultimis
esse. Poteris hanc simulationem et vultus confusione
et lacrimis obumbrare, ut misericordia permotus gubernator indulgeat tibi." Negavit hoc Eumolpus fieri
posse, "quia magna" inquit "navigia portubus se
curvatis insinuant, nec tam cito fratrem defecisse veri
simile erit. Accedit his, quod forsitan Lichas officii
causa visere languentem desiderabit. Vides, quam
valde nobis expediat, ultro dominum ad fugientes
accersere.[1] Sed finge navem ab ingenti posse cursu
deflecti et Licham non utique circumiturum aegrorum
cubilia: quomodo possumus egredi nave, ut non con-
spiciamur a cunctis? Opertis capitibus, an nudis?
Opertis, et quis non dare manum languentibus volet?
102 Nudis, et quid erit aliud quam se ipsos proscribere?"
"Quin potius" inquam ego "ad temeritatem confugi-
mus et per funem lapsi descendimus in scapham prae-
cisoque vinculo reliqua fortunae committimus? Nec
ego in hoc periculum Eumolpon arcesso. Quid enim
attinet innocentem alieno periculo imponere? Contentus sum, si nos descendentes adiuverit casus."
"Non imprudens" inquit "consilium" Eumolpos "si
aditum haberet. Quis enim non euntes notabit?
Utique gubernator, qui pervigil nocte siderum quoque
motus custodit. Et utcunque imponi nihil[2] dormienti
posset, si per aliam partem navis fuga quaereretur:
nunc per puppim, per ipsa gubernacula delabendum
est, a quorum regione funis descendit, qui scaphae

---

[1] accersere *Buecheler*: accedere.
[2] nihil *Buecheler*: vel.

free ourselves from all danger." "No," said Giton, "persuade the helmsman to run the boat into some harbour. Pay him well, of course, and tell him your brother cannot stand the sea, and is at his last gasp. You will be able to hide your deception by the confused look and the tears on your face. You will touch the helmsman's heart, and he will do you a favour." Eumolpus declared that this was impossible: "These large boats only steer into landlocked harbours, and it is incredible that our brother should collapse so soon. Besides, Lichas may perhaps ask to see the sick man as a matter of kindness. You realize what a fine turn we should do ourselves by leading the master up to his runaways with our own hands. But supposing the ship could be turned aside from her long passage, and Lichas did not after all go round the patient's beds; how could we leave the ship without being seen by every one? Cover our heads, or bare them? Cover them, and every one will want to lend his arm to the poor sick man! Bare them, that is nothing more or less than proscribing ourselves." "No," I said, "I 102 should prefer to take refuge in boldness, slip down a rope into the boat, cut the painter, and leave the rest to luck. I do not invite Eumolpus to share the risk. It is not fair to load an innocent person with another's troubles. I am satisfied if chance will help us to get down." "It is a clever plan," said Eumolpus, "if there were any way of starting it. But every one will see you going: especially the helmsman, who watches all night long, and keeps guard even over the motions of the stars. Of course you might elude his unsleeping watchfulness, if you wanted to escape off another part of the ship; but as it is, you want to slip off the stern close to the helm itself, where the rope which

custodiam tenet. Praeterea illud miror, Encolpi, tibi non succurrisse, unum nautam stationis perpetuae interdiu noctuque iacere in scapha, nec posse inde custodem nisi aut caede expelli aut praecipitari viribus. Quod an fieri possit, interrogate audaciam vestram. Nam quod ad meum quidem comitatum attinet, nullum recuso periculum, quod salutis spem ostendit. Nam sine causa [quidem] spiritum tanquam rem vacuam impendere ne vos quidem existimo velle. Videte, numquid hoc placeat: ego vos in duas iam pelles coniciam vinctosque loris inter vestimenta pro sarcinis habebo, apertis scilicet aliquatenus lahris, quibus et spiritum recipere possitis et cibum. Conclamabo deinde nocte servos poenam graviorem timentes praecipitasse se in mare. Deinde cum ventum fuerit in portum, sine ulla suspicione pro sarcinis vos efferam."
"Ita vero" inquam ego "tanquam solidos alligaturus, quibus non soleat venter iniuriam facere? An tanquam eos qui sternutare non soleamus nec stertere? An quia hoc genus furti semel [mea] feliciter cessit? Sed finge una die vinctos posse durare: quid ergo,.si diutius aut tranquillitas nos tenuerit aut adversa tempestas? Quid facturi sumus? Vestes quoque diutius vinetas ruga consumit, et chartae alligatae mutant figuram. Iuvenes adhuc laboris expertes statuarum ritu patiemur pannos et vincla?" . . .
"Adhuc aliquod iter salutis quaerendum est. Inspicite, quod ego inveni. Eumolpus tanquam litterarum

206

holds the boat safe hangs just by. Again, I am surprised that it did not occur to you, Encolpius, that one sailor is always on duty night and day lying in the boat, and you cannot turn this sentry out except by killing him, or throw him out except by force. You must ask your own bold heart whether that can be done. As far as my coming with you goes, I do not shirk any danger which offers a chance of safety. But I suppose that even you do not wish to squander your lives like a vain trifle without any reason. Now see whether you approve of this. I will roll you in two bales, tie you up, and put you among my clothes as luggage, of course leaving the ends a bit open, so that you can get your breath and your food. Then I will raise the cry that my slaves have jumped overboard in the dark, being afraid of some heavier punishment. Then after we have arrived in harbour, I will carry you out like baggage without arousing any suspicion."
"What," I cried, "tie us up like wholly solid people whose stomachs never make them unhappy? Like people who never sneeze nor suore? Just because this kind of trick on one occasion turned out a success[1]? But even supposing we could endure one day tied up: what if we were detained longer by a calm or by rough weather? What should we do? Even clothes that are tied up too long get creased and spoilt, and papers in bundles lose their shape. Are we young fellows who never worked in our lives to put up with bondage in dirty cloths as if we were statues?... No, we still have to find some way of salvation. Look at what I thought of. Eumolpus, as a man of learning,

[1] Cleopatra had herself conveyed to Julius Caesar at Alexandria wrapped up in a carpet. Plutarch: *Life of Caesar*, c. 49. Shaw: *Caesar and Cleopatra*, Act iii.

studiosus utique atramentum habet. Hoc ergo remedio
mutemus colores a capillis usque ad ungues. Ita tanquam servi Aethiopes et praesto tibi erimus sine
tormentorum iniuria hilares, et permutato colore im-
ponemus inimicis." "Quidni?" inquit Giton "etiam
circumcide nos, ut Iudaei videamur, et pertunde aures,
ut imitemur Arabes, et increta facies, ut suos Gallia
cives putet: tanquam hic solus color figuram possit
pervertere et non multa una oporteat consentiant [et
non] ratione, ut^1 mendacium constet. Futa infectam
medicamine faciem diutius durare posse; finge nec
aquae asperginem imposituram aliquam corpori macu-
lam, nec vestem atramento adhaesuram, quod frequenter etiam non accersito ferrumine infigitur: age,
numquid et labra possumus tumore taeterrimo implere?
Numquid et crines calamistro convertere? Numquid
et frontes cicatricibus scindere? Numquid et crura
in orhem pandere? Numquid et talos ad terram deducere? Numquid *et* barbam peregrina ratione
figurare? Color arte compositus inquinat corpus, non
mutat. Audite, quid amenti[2] succurrerit: praeligemus
vestibus capita et nos in profundum mergamus."

103 "Ne istud dii hominesque patiantur" Eumolpus exclamat "ut vos tam turpi exitu vitam finiatis. Immo
potius facite, quod iubeo. Mercennarius meus, ut ex
novacula comperistis, tonsor est: hic continuo radat

---

[1] et non *bracketed*, ut *added by Buecheler.*
[2] amenti *Buecheler :* timenti.

is sure to have some ink. We will use this medicine to dye ourselves, hair, nails, everything. Then we will stand by you with pleasure like Aethiopian slaves, without undergoing any tortures, and our change of colour will take in our enemies." "Oh! yes," said Giton, "and please circumcise us too, so that we look like Jews, and bore our ears to imitate Arabians, and chalk our faces till Gaul takes us for her own sons; as if this colour alone could alter our shapes, when it takes a number of points in unison to make a good lie. Suppose the stain of dye on the face could last for some time; imagine that never a drop of water could make any mark on our skins, nor our clothes stick to the ink, which often clings to us without the use of any cement: but, tell me, can we make our lips swell to a hideous thickness? Or transform our hair with curling-tongs? Or plough up our foreheads with scars? Or walk bow-legged? Or bend our ankles over to the ground? Or trim our beards in a foreign cut? Artificial colours dirty one's body without altering it. Listen, I have thought of this in desperation. Let us tie our heads in our clothes, and plunge into the deep."

God and man forbid," cried Eumolpus, "that you 103 should make such a vile conclusion of your lives. No; better take my advice. My slave, as you learned by his razor, is a barber. Let him shave the head of

utriusque non solum capita, sed etiam supercilia. Sequar ego frontes notans inscriptione sollerti, ut videamini stigmate esse puniti. Ita eaedem litterae et suspicionem declinabunt quaerentium et vultus umbra supplicii tegent."

Non est dilata fallacia, sed ad latus navigii furtim processimus capitaqne cum superciliis denudanda tonsori praebuimus. Implevit Eumolpus frontes utriusque ingentibus litteris et notum fugitivorum epigramma per totam faciem liberali manu duxit. Unus forte ex vectoribus, qui acclinatus lateri navis exonerabat stomachum nausea gravem, notavit sibi ad lunam tonsorem intempestivo inhaerentem ministerio, execratusque omen, quod imitaretur naufragorum ultimum votum, in cubile reiectus est. Nos dissimulata nauseantis devotione ad ordinem tristitiae redimus, silentioque compositi reliquas noctis horas male soporati consumpsimus . . .

104 "Videbatur mihi secundum quietem Priapus dicere: 'Encolpion quod quaeris, scito a me in navem tuam esse perductum.'" Exhorruit Tryphaena et "Putes" inquit "una nos dormiisse; nam et mihi simulacrum Neptuni, quod Baiis *in* tetrastylo[1] notaveram, videbatur dicere: 'in nave Lichae Gitona invenies.'" "Hinc scies" inquit Eumolpus "Epicurum esse hominem divinum, qui eiusmodi ludibria facetissima ratione condemnat" . . .

ceterum Lichas ut Tryphaenae somnium expiavit, "quis" inquit "prohibet navigium scrutari, ne videamur divinae mentis opera damnare?"

[1] Baiis in tetrastylo *Buecheler :* Baistor asylo.

210

each of you this minute, **and** your eyebrows as well.
Then I will come and mark your foreheads with some
neat inscription, so that you look like slaves punished
by branding. These letters will divert inquisitive
people's suspicions, and at the same time conceal your
faces with the shadow of punishment." We tried the
trick at once, and walked cautiously to the side of the
ship, and yielded up our heads and eyebrows to the
barber to be shorn. Eumolpus covered both our fore-
beads with enormous letters, and scrawled the usual
mark of runaway slaves all over our faces with a generous
hand. But one of the passengers, who was extremely
seasick, happened to be leaning over the side of the
ship to relieve his stomach, and observed the barber
in the moonlight busy with his ill-timed work. The
man cursed this for an omen, because it looked like
the last offering of a doomed crew, and then threw
himself back into his bunk. We pretended not to
hear his puking curses, and went on with the gloomy
business, and then lay down in silence and passed
the remaining hours of the night in uneasy sleep. . .

"I thought I heard Priapus say in my dream: 'I 104
tell you, Encolpius whom you seek has been led by me
on board your ship.'" Tryphaena gave a scream and
said, "You would think we had slept together; I
dreamed that a picture of Neptune, which I noticed in
a gallery at Baiae, said to me: 'You will find Giton on
board Lichas's ship.'" "This shows you," said Eumolpus, "that Epicurus was a superhuman creature; he
condemns jokes of this kind in a very witty fashion." . .
However, Lichas first prayed that Tryphaena's dream
might mean no harm, and then said, "There is no
objection to searching the ship to show that we do
not despise the workings of Providence." Then the

TITUS PETRONIUS ARBITER

.. Is qui nocte miserorum furtum deprehenderat, Hesus nomine, subito proclamat: "Ergo illi qui sunt, qui nocte ad lunam radebantur pessimo medius fidius exemplo? Audio enim non licere cuiquam mortalium in nave neque ungues neque capillos deponere, nisi 105 cum pelago ventus irascitur." Excanduit Lichas hoc sermone turbatus et "Itane" inquit "capillos aliquis in nave praecidit, et hoc nocte intempesta? Attrahite ocius nocentes in medium, ut sciam, quorum capitibus debeat navigium lustrari." "Ego" inquit Eumolpus "hoc iussi. Nec in[1] eodem futurus navigio auspicium mihi feci, sed quia nocentes horridos longosque habebant capillos, ne viderer de nave carcerem facere, iussi squalorem damnatis auferri; simul ut notae quoque litterarum non adumbratae comarum praesidio totae ad oculos legentium acciderent. Inter cetera apud communem amicam consumpserunt pecuniam meam, a qua illos proxima nocte extraxi mero unguentisque perfusos. Ad summam, adhuc patrimonii mei reliquias olent" . . .

itaque ut tutela navis expiaretur, placuit quadragenas utrique plagas imponi. Nulla ergo fit mora; aggrediuntur nos furentes nautae cum funibus temptantque vilissimo sanguine tutelam placare. Et ego quidem tres plagas Spartana nobilitate concoxi. Ceterum Giton semel ictus tam valde exclamavit, ut Tryphaenae aures notissima voce repleret. Non solum era[2] turbata est, sed ancillae etiam omnes familiari sono inductae ad vapulantem decurrunt. Iam Giton mirabili forma

[1] nec in *Buecheler :* nec non.
[2] era *Buecheler :* ergo.

man who had caught us at our wretched tricks the
night before, whose name was Hesus, suddenly shouted,
"Then who are those fellows who were being shaved
in the dark by moonlight? A mighty bad precedent,
I swear. I am told that no man alive ought to shed
a nail or a hair on board ship, unless winds and waves
are raging." At this speech Lichas fired up in alarm, 105
and said, "What, has anyone cut his hair on board
my ship, and at dead of night too? Quick, bring the
villains out here. I want to know who is to be punished to give us a clear voyage." "Oh," said Eumolpus, "I gave those orders. I was not doing anything
unlucky, considering that I had to share the voyage
myself. It was because these ruffians had long, dirty
hair. I did not want to turn the ship into a prison,
so I ordered the filth to be cleared off the brutes.
Besides, I did not want the marks of branding to be
screened and covered by their hair. They ought to
show at full length for every one to read. Further-
more, they squandered my money on a certain lady
friend of ours; I pulled them away from her the night
before, reeking with wine and scent. In fact, they
still stink of the shreds of my inheritance." . .

So it was decided that forty stripes should be inflicted on each of us to appease the guardian angel of
the ship. Not a moment was lost; the angry sailors advanced upon us with ropes-ends, and tried to soften
their guardian angel's heart with our miserable blood.
For my part I bore three full blows with Spartan
pride. But Giton cried out so lustily the moment he
was touched, that his familiar voice filled Tryphaena's
ears. Not only was the lady in a flutter, but all her
maids were drawn by the well-known tones, and came
running to the victim. Giton's loveliness had already

exarmaverat nautas coeperatque etiam sine voce saevientes rogare, cum ancillae pariter proclamant: "Giton est, Giton, inhibete crudelissimas manus; Giton est, domina, succurre." Deflectit aures Tryphaena iam sua sponte credentes raptimque ad puerum devolat. Lichas, qui me optime noverat, tanquam et ipse vocem audisset, accurrit et nec manus nec faciem meam consideravit, sed continuo ad inguina mea luminibus deflexis movit officiosam manum et "Salve" inquit "Encolpi." Miretur nunc aliquis Vlixis nutricem post vicesimum annum cicatricem invenisse originis indicem, cum homo prudentissimus confusis omnibus corporis orisque[1] lineamentis ad unicum fugitivi argumentum tam docte pervenerit. Tryphaena lacrimas effudit decepta supplicio—vera enim stigmata credebat captivorum frontibus impressa—sciscitarique submissius coepit, quod ergastulum intercepisset errantes, aut cuius tam crudeles manus in hoc supplicium durassent. Meruisse quidem contumeliam aliquam fugitivos, quibus in odium bona sua venissent . . .

106 concitatus iracundia prosiliit Lichas et "O te" inquit "feminam simplicem, tanquam vulnera ferro praeparata litteras biberint. Utinam quidem hac se inscriptione frontis maculassent: haberemus nos extremum solacium. Nunc mimicis artibus petiti sumus et adumbrata inscriptione derisi."

Volebat Tryphaena misereri, quia non totam voluptatem perdiderat, sed Lichas memor adhuc uxoris

---

[1] orisque *Buecheler :* indiciorumque.

disarmed the sailors; even without speaking he appealed to his tormentors. Then all the maids screamed out together: "It is Giton, it is; stop beating him, you monsters. Help, ma'am, Giton is here." Tryphaena had already convinced herself, and inclined her ear to them, and flew on wings to the boy. Lichas, who knew me intimately, ran up as though he had heard my voice too, and did not glance at my hands or face, sed continuo ad inguina mea luminibus deflexis movit officiosam manum, and said, "How are you, Encolpius?" No one need be surprised that Ulysses's nurse discovered the scar¹ which revealed his identity after twenty years, when a clever man hit upon the one test of a runaway so brilliantly, though every feature of his face and body was disguised. Tryphaena, thinking that the marks on our foreheads were real prisoners' brands, cried bitterly over our supposed punishment, and began to inquire more gently what prison had stayed us in our wanderings, and what band had been so ruthless as to inflict such marks upon us. "But, of course," she said, "runaway slaves who come to hate their own happiness, do deserve some chastisement." . .

Lichas leaped forward in a transport of rage and 106 cried, "You silly woman, as if these letters were made by the scars of the branding-iron. I only wish they had defiled their foreheads with this inscription: we should have some consolation left. As it is, we are being assailed by an actor's tricks, and befooled by a sham inscription."

Tryphaena besought him to have pity, because she had not lost all her desire for Giton, but the seduction

¹ See Homer's Odyssey, Book xix. She recognized Ulysses by an old scar on his leg.

215

corruptae contumeliarumque, quas in Herculis porticu acceperat, turbato vehementius vultu proclamat: "Deos immortales rerum humanarum agere curam, puto, intellexisti, o Tryphaena. Nam imprudentes noxios in nostrum induxere navigium, et quid fecissent, ad-monuerunt pari somniorum consensu. Ita vide, ut possit illis ignosci, quos ad poenam ipse deus deduxit. Quod ad me attinet, non sum crudelis, sed vereor, ne quod remisero, patiar." Tam superstitiosa oratione Tryphaena mutata negat se interpellare supplicium, immo accedere etiam iustissimae ultioni. Nec se minus grandi vexatam iniuria quam Licham, cuius pudoris dignitas in contione proscripta sit . . .

107 "Me, ut puto, hominem non ignotum, elegerunt ad hoc officium [legatum] petieruntque, ut se recon-ciliarem aliquando amicissimis. Nisi forte putatis iuvenes casu in has plagas incidisse, cum omnis vector nihil prius quaerat, quam cuius se diligentiae credat. Flectite ergo mentes satisfactione lenitas, et patimini liberos homines ire sine iniuria, quo destinant. Saevi quoque implacabilesque domini crudelitatem suam im-pediunt, si quando paenitentia fugitivos reduxit, et dediticiis hostibus parcimus. Quid ultra petitis aut quid vultis? In conspectu vestro supplices iacent iuvenes ingenui, honesti, et quod utroque potentius est, familiaritate vobis aliquando coniuncti. Si mehercules intervertissent pecuniam vestram, si fidem proditione

216

of his wife and the insults offered to him in the Porch of Hercules were still in Lichas's mind, and he cried out with a look of still more profound agitation, "Tryphaena, I believe you admit that the Gods in Heaven take some trouble about men's affairs. They brought these sinners on board my boat without their knowledge, and told us what they had done by a coincidence in dreams. Then do consider; how can we possibly pardon people whom a God himself has handed over to us for punishment? I am not a bloodthirsty man, but personally I am afraid that if I let them off anything it will fall on me." Tryphaena veered round at this appeal to superstition, declined to interfere with the punishment, and declared that she approved of this most proper vengeance. She had been just as grav l wronged as Lichas, considering that her reputation for chastity had been publicly impugned. . .

"I believe I am a man of some reputation, and they 107 have chosen me for this duty, and begged me to make it up between them and their old friends. I suppose you do not imagine that these young men have fallen into the snare by chance, when the first care of every one who goes a voyage is to find a trustworthy person to depend on. So unbend the sternness which has been softened by revenge, and let the men go free without hindrance to their destination. Even a harsh and unforgiving master reins in his cruelty if his runaways are at last led back by penitence, and we all spare an enemy who surrenders. What do you want or wish for more? These free and respectable young men lie prostrate before your eyes, and what is more important, they were once bound to you by close friendship I take my oath that if they had embezzled your money, or hurt you by betraying your confidence, you

217

laesissent, satiari tamen potuissetis hac poena, quam
videtis. Servitia ecce in frontibus cernitis et vultus
ingenuos voluntaria poenarum lege proscriptos." Interpellavit deprecationem supplicii[1] Lichas et "Noli"
inquit "causam confundere, sed impone singulis modum.
Ac primum omnium, si ultro venerunt, cur nudavere
crinibus capita? Vultum enim qui permutat, fraudem
parat, non satisfactionèm. Deinde, si gratiam a legato
moliebantur, quid ita omnia fecisti, ut quos tuebaris,
absconderes? Ex quo apparet casu incidisse noxios in
plagas et te artem quaesisse, qua nostrae animad-
versionis impetum eluderes. Nam quod invidiam facis
nobis ingenuos honestosque clamando, vide, ne deteri-
orem facias confidentia causam. Quid debent laesi
facere, ubi rei ad poenam confugiunt? At enim amici
fuerunt nostri: eo maiora meruerunt supplicia; nam
qui ignotos laedit, latro appellatur, qui amicos, paulo
minus quam parricida." Resolvit Eumolpos tam ini-
quam declamationem et "Intellego" inquit "nihil
magis obesse iuvenibus miseris, quam quod nocte de-
posuerunt capillos: hoc argumento incidisse videntur
in navem, non venisse. Quod velim tam candide ad
aures vestras perveniat, quam simpliciter gestum est.
Voluerunt enim antequam conscenderent, exonerare
capita molesto et supervacuo pondere, sed celerior
ventus distulit curationis propositum. Nec tamen
putaverunt ad rem pertinere, ubi inciperent, quod
placuerat ut fieret, quia nec omen nec legem navigan-

---

[1] supplicii *Buecheler*: supplicis.

might still be satisfied with the punishment you have
seen inflicted. Look, you see slavery on their foreheads, and their free faces branded under a self-
imposed sentence of punishment." Lichas interrupted
this plea for mercy, saying, "Do not go confusing the
issue, but let each single point have its place. And
first of all, if they came of their own accord, why have
they stripped all the hair off their heads? A man who
disguises himself wants to play a trick, not to make
amends. Again, if they were contriving some act of
grace through a mediator, why did you do everything
in your power to hide your protégés away? All this
makes it clear that the ruffians fell into the net by
accident, and that you hunted for some device to avoid
the force of our displeasure. When you try to pre-
judice us by calling them free and respectable, mind
you do not spoil your case by impudence. What
should an injured party do, when the guilty run into
punishment? Oh! you say, they were once our friends!
Then they deserve the harsher treatment. A person
who injures a stranger is called a robber, but a man
who hurts his friends is practically a parricide."
Eumolpus put an end to this unfair harangue by saying,
"I know that nothing is more against the poor young
men than their cutting their hair at night. This looks
like a proof that they came by chance upon the ship
and did not come on purpose. Now I want the plain
truth to come to your ears just as simply as it happened.
They wanted to relieve their heads of the troublesome
and useless weight before they came aboard, but the
wind got up and postponed their scheme of treatment.
They never thought that it made any difference where
they began what they had decided to do; they were
quite ignorant of sailors' omens and sea-law." "But

219

tium noverant." "Quid" inquit Lichas "attinuit supplices radere? Nisi forte miserabiliores calvi solent esse. Quamquam quid attinet veritatem per interpretem quaerere? quid dicis tu, latro? quae salamandra supercilia tua exussit? cui deo 'crinem vovisti? pharmace, responde."

108   Obstupueram ego supplicii metu pavidus, nec quid in re manifestissima dicerem, inveniebam turbatus . . . et deformis praeter spoliati capitis dedecus superciliorum etiam aequalis 'cum fronte calvities, ut nihil nec facere deceret nec dicere. Ut vero spongia uda facies plorantis detersa est et liquefactum per totum os atramentum omnia scilicet lineamenta fuliginea nube confudit, in odium se ira convertit. Negat Eumolpus passurum se, ut quisquam ingenuos contra fas legemque contaminet, interpellatque saevientium minas non solum voce sed etiam manibus. Aderat interpellanti mercennarius comes et unus alterque infirmissimus vector, solacia magis litis quam virium auxilia. Nec quicquam pro me deprecabar, sed intentans in oculos Tryphaenae manus usurum me viribus meis clara liberaque voce clamavi, ni abstineret a Gitone iniuriam mulier damnata et in toto navigio sola verberanda. Accenditur audacia mea iratior Lichas, indignaturque quod ego relicta mea causa tantum pro aho clamo. Nec minus Tryphaena contumelia saevit accensa totiusque navigii turbam diducit in partes. Hinc mercennarius tonsor ferramenta sua nobis et ipse armatus distribuit, illinc Tryphaenae

why should they shave themselves to excite pity?" said Lichas, "Unless of course bald people are naturally more pitiable. But what is the use of trying to discover the truth through a third person? Now speak up, you ruffian! Who was the salamander that singed off your eyebrows? What God had the promise of your hair? Answer me, gallows-bird!"

I was dumb with terror of being punished, and too 108 upset to find a word to say, for the case was only too clear....We were in no position to speak, or do anything, for to say nothing of the disgrace of our shaven heads, our eyebrows were as bald as our pates. But when a wet sponge was wiped down my doleful countenance, and the ink ran over all my face and of course blotted out every feature in a cloud of smut, anger passed into loathing. Eumolpus cried out that he would not allow anyone to disfigure free young men without right or reason, and cut short the angry sailors' threats not only by argument but by force. His slave stood by him in his protest, and one or two of the most feeble passengers, who rather consoled him for having to fight than increased his strength. For my part I shirked nothing. I shook my fist in Tryphaena's face, and declared in a loud open voice that I would use violence to her if she did not leave off hurting Giton, for she was a wicked woman and the only person on the ship who deserved flogging. Lichas's wrath blazed hotter at my daring, and he taunted me with throwing up my own case and only shouting for somebody else. Tryphaena was equally hot and angry and abusive, and divided the whole ship's company into factions. On our side, the slave barber handed out his blades to us, and kept one for himself, on the other side Tryphaena's slaves were ready with bare

familia nudas expedit manus, ac ne ancillarum quidem clamor aciem destituit, uno tantum gubernatore relicturum se navis ministerium denuntiante, si non desinat rabies libidine perditorum collecta. Nihilo minus tamen perseverat dimicantium furor, illis pro ultione, nobis pro vita pugnantibus. Multi ergo utrinque sine morte labuntur, plures cruenti vulneribus referunt veluti ex proelio pedem, nec tamen cuiusquam ira laxatur. Tune fortissimus Giton ad virilia sua admovit novaculam infestam, minatus se abscisurum tot miseriarum causam, inhibuitque Tryphaena tam grande facinus non dissimulata missione. Saepius ego cultrum tonsorium super iugulum meum posui, non magis me occisurus, quam Giton, quod minabatur, facturus. Audacius tamen ille tragoediam implebat, quia sciebat se illam habere novaculam, qua iam sibi cervicem

LO praeciderat. | Stante ergo utraque acie, cum appareret futurum non tralaticium bellum, aegre expugnavit gubernator, ut caduceatoris more Tryphaena indutias faceret. Data ergo acceptaque ex more patrio fide praetendit ramum oleac a tutela navigii raptum, atque in colloquium venire ausa

"Quis furor" exclamat "pacem convertit in arma?
Quid nostrae meruere manus? Non Troius heros
hac in classe vehit decepti pignus Atridae,
nec Medea furens fraterno sanguine pugnat.
Sed contemptus amor vires habet. Ei mihi, fata
hos inter fluctus quis raptis evocat armis?

222

fists, and even the cries of women were not unheard on the field. The helmsman alone swore that he would give up minding the ship if this madness, which had been stirred up to suit a pack of scoundrels, did not stop. None the less, the fury of the combatants persisted, the enemy fighting for revenge and we for dear life. Many fell on both sides without fatal results, still more got bloody wounds and retired in the style of a real battle, and still we all raged implacably. Then the gallant Giton turned a razor on himself and threatened to put an end to our troubles by self-mutilation, and Tryphaena averted the horrible disaster by a fair promise of freedom. I lifted a barber's knife to my throat several times, no more meaning to kill myself than Giton meant to do what he threatened. Still he filled the tragic part more recklessly, because he knew that he was holding the very razor with which he had already made a cut on his throat. Both sides were drawn up in battle array, and it was plain that the fight would be no ordinary affair, when the helmsman with difficulty induced Tryphaena to conclude a treaty like a true diplomat. So the usual formal undertakings were exchanged, and she waved an olive-branch which she took from the ship's figure-bead, and ventured to come up and talk to us: "What madness," she cried, "is turning peace into war? What have our hands done to deserve it? No Trojan hero[1] carries the bride of the cuckold son of Atreus in this fleet, nor does frenzied Medea[2] fight her foe by slaying her brother. But love despised is powerful. Ah! who courts destruction among these waves by drawing

---

[1] Paris.

[2] Absyrtus, Medea's brother, and son of Aietes, king of Colchis, plotted against Jason, who had come seeking the Golden Fleece. Medea killed him and fled with Jason.

Cui non est mors una satis? Ne vincite pontum
gurgitibusque feris alios imponite fluctus."

109   Haec ut turbato clamore mulier effudit, haesit
paulisper acies, revocataeque ad pacem manus inter-
misere bellum. Utitur paenitentiae occasione dux
Eumolpos et castigato ante vehementissime Licha
tabulas foederis signat, quis haec formula erat: "Ex
tui animi sententia, ut tu, Tryphaena, neque iniuriam
tibi factam a Gitone quereris, neque si quid ante hunc
diem factum est, obicies vindicabisve aut ullo alio
genere persequendum curabis; ut tu nihil imperabiṣ
puero repugnanti, non amplexum, non osculum, non
coitum venere constrictum, nisi pro qua re praesentes
numeraveris denarios centum. Item, Licha, ex tui
animi sententia, ut tu Encolpion nec verbo contume-
lioso insequeris nec vultu, neque quaeres ubi nocte
dormiat, aut si quaesieris, pro singulis iniuriis numera-
bis praesentes denarios ducenos." In haec verba
L foederibus compositis arma deponimus, | et ne residua
in animis etiam post iusiurandum ira remaneret, praeterita aboleri osculis placet. Exhortantibus universis
odia detumescunt, epulaeque ad certamen prolatae
LO conciliant hilaritate concordiam.[1] | Exsonat ergo can-
tibus totum navigium, et quia repentina tranquillitas
intermiserat cursum, alius exultantes quaerebat fuscina
pisces, alius hamis blandientibus convellebat praedam
repugnantem. Ecce etiam per antemnam pelagiae
consederant volucres, quas textis harundinibus peritus

---

[1] concordiam *Buecheler:* concilium.

the sword? Who does not find a single death
enough? Do not strive to outdo the sea and heap
fresh waves upon its savage floods."

The woman poured out these words in a loud excited 109
voice, the fighting died away for a little while, our
hands were recalled to the way of peace, and dropped
the war. Our leader Eumolpus seized the occasion
of their relenting, and after making a warm attack
on Lichas, signed the treaty, which ran as follows:
"Agreed on your part, Tryphaena, that you will
not complain of any wrong done to you by Giton, and
if any has been done to you before this date will
not bring it up against him or punish him or take
steps to follow it up in any other way whatsoever;
that you will give the boy no orders which he dislikes,
for a hug, a kiss, or a lover's close embrace, without
paying a hundred pieces for it cash down. Further-
more, it is agreed on your part, Lichas, that you will
not pursue Encolpius with insulting words or grimaces,
nor inquire where he sleeps at night, or if you do inquire will pay two hundred pieces cash down for every
injurious act done to him." Peace was made on these
terms, and we laid down our arms, and for fear any
vestige of anger should be left in our minds, even
after taking the oath, we decided to wipe out the
past with a kiss. There was applause all round, our
hatred died down, and a feast which had been brought
for the fight cemented our agreement with joviality.
Then the whole ship rang with songs; and a sudden
calm having stayed us in our course, one man pursued
the leaping fish with a spear, another pulled in his
struggling prey on alluring hooks. Besides all this,
some sea-birds settled on one of the yards, and a
clever sportsman took them in with jointed rod of

Q

artifex tetigit; illae viscatis illigatae viminibus defe-
rebantur ad manus.   Tollebat plumas aura volitantes,
pinnasque per maria inanis spuma torquebat.

Iam Lichas redire mecum in gratiam coeperat, iam
Tryphaena Gitona extrema parte potionis spargebat,
cum Eumolpus et ipse vino solutus dieta voluit in
calvos stigmososque iaculari, donec consumpta frigidis-
sima urbanitate rediit ad carmina sua coepitque capillorum elegidarion dicere:

"Quod solum formae decus est, cecidere capilli,
   vernantesque comas tristis abegit hiemps.
Nunc umbra nudata sua iam tempora maerent,
   areaque attritis ridet adulta[1] pilis.
O fallax natura deum: quae prima dedisti
   aetati nostrae gaudia, prima rapis."

"Infelix, modo crinibus nitebas
   Phoebo pulchrior et sorore Phoebi.
At nunc levior aere vel rotundo
   horti tubere, quod creavit unda,
ridentes fugis et times puellas.
Ut mortem citius venire credas,
   scito iam capitis perisse partem."

110   Plura volebat proferre, credo, et ineptiora praeteri-
tis, cum ancilla Tryphaenae Gitona in partem navis
inferiorem ducit corymbioque dominae pueri adornat
caput.   Immo supercilia etiam profert de pyxide seite-
qué iacturae lineamenta secuta totam illi formam
suam reddidit.   Agnovit Tryphaena verum Gitona,
lacrimisque turbata tune primum bona fide puero

---

[1] adulta *Buecheler:* adusta.

rushes; they were snared by these limed twigs and brought down into our hands. The breeze caught their feathers as they flew, and the light foam lashed their wings as they skimmed the sea.

Lichas was just beginning to be friendly with me again, Tryphaena was just pouring the dregs of a drink over Giton, when Eumolpus, who was unsteady with drink himself, tried to aim some satire at bald persons and branded criminals, and after exhausting his chilly wit, went back to his poetry and began to declaim a little dirge on Hair:

"The hair that is the whole glory of the body is fallen, dull winter has carried away the bright locks of spring. Now the temples are bare of their shade and are downcast, and the wide naked space on my old head shines where the hair is worn away. Ye Gods that love to cheat us; ye rob us first of the first joys ye gave to our youth.

"Poor wretch, a moment ago thy hair shone bright and more beautiful than Phœbus and the sister of Phœbus. Now thou art smoother than bronze or the round garden mushroom that is born in rain, and turnest in dread from a girl's mockery. To teach thee how quickly death shall come, know that a part of thine head hath died already."

He wanted to produce some more lines even more 110 silly than the last, I believe, when Tryphaena's maid took Giton below decks, and ornamented the boy's head with some of her mistress's artificial curls. Further, she also took some eyebrows out of a box, and by cunningly following the lines where he was defaced she restored his proper beauty complete. Tryphaena recognized the true Giton, there was a storm of tears, and she then for the first time gave the boy a kiss

L basium dedit. | Ego etiam si repositum in pristinum
decorem puerum gaudebam, abscondebam tamen frequentius vultum intellegebamque me non tralaticia
deformitate esse insignitum, quem alloquio dignum ne
Lichas quidem crederet. Sed buie tristitiae eadem
illa succurrit ancilla, sevocatumque me non minus de-
coro exornavit capillamento; immo commendatior
vultus enituit, quia flavum[1] corymbion erat . . .

LO | Ceterum Eumolpos, et periclitantium advocatus et
praesentis concordiae auctor, ne sileret sine fabulis
hilaritas, multa in muliebrem levitatem coepit iactare:
quam facile adamarent, quam cito etiam filiorum obli-
viscerentur, nullamque esse feminam tam pudicam,
quae non peregrina libidine usque ad furorem averte-
retur. Nec se tragoedias veteres curare aut nomina
saeculis nota, sed rem sua memoria factam, quam
expositurum se esse, si vellemus audire. Conversis
igitur omnium in se vultibus auribusque sic orsus est:

111 "Matrona quaedam Ephesi tam notae erat pudicitiae, ut vicinarum quoque gentium feminas ad spectaculum sui evocaret. Haec ergo cum virum extulisset,
non contenta vulgari more funus passis prosequi crinibus aut nudatum pectus in conspectu frequentiae
plangere, in conditorium etiam prosecuta est defun-
etum, positumque in hypogaeo Graeco more corpus
custodire ac flere totis noctibus diebusque coepit. Sic
afflictantem se ac mortem inedia persequentem non
parentes potuerunt abducere, non propinqui; magistratus ultimo repulsi abierunt, complorataque singularis

---

[1] flavum *margin ed. of Tornaesius:* flaucorum.

with real affection. Of course, I was glad to see him clothed again in his former loveliness, but still I kept hiding my own face continually, for I realized that I was marked with no common ugliness, since not even Lichas considered me fit to speak to. But the same maid came and rescued me from gloom, called me aside, and decked me with equally becoming curls. Indeed, my face shone with a greater glory. My curls were golden! . . .

Then Eumolpus, our spokesman in peril and the begetter of our present peace, to save our jollity from falling dumb for want of good stories, began to hurl many taunts at the fickleness of women; how easily they fell in love, how quickly they forgot even their own sons, how no woman was so chaste that she could not be led away into utter madness by a passion for a stranger. He was not thinking of old tragedies or names notorious in history, but of an affair which happened in his lifetime. He would tell it us if we liked to listen. So all eyes and ears were turned upon him, and he began as follows : ·

"There was a married woman in Ephesus of such 111 famous virtue that she drew women even from the neighbouring states to gaze upon her. So when she had buried her husband, the common fashion of following the procession with loose hair, and beating the naked breast in front of the crowd, did not satisfy her. She followed the dead man even to his resting-place, and began to watch and weep night and day over the body, which was laid in an underground vault in the Greek fashion. Neither her parents nor her relations could divert her from thus torturing herself, and courting death by starvation; the officials were at last rebuffed and left her; every one mourned for her as a woman of unique character, and she was now

exempli femina ab omnibus quintum iam diem sine
alimento trahebat. Assidebat aegrae fidissima ancilla,
simulque et lacrimas commodabat Ingenti, et quotiens-
cunque defecerat positum in monumento lumen
renovabat. Una igitur in tota civitate fabula erat,
solum illud affulsisse verum pudicitiae amorisque exemplum omnis ordinis homines confitebantur, cum
interim imperator provinciae latrones iussit crucibus
affigi secundum illam casulam, in qua recens cadaver
matrona deflebat. Proxima ergo nocte, cum miles,
qui cruces asservabat, ne quis ad sepulturam corpus
detraheret, notasset sibi [et] lumen inter monumenta
clarins fulgens et gemitum lugentis audisset, vitio
gentis humanae concupiit scire, quis aut quid faceret.
Descendit igitur in conditorium, visaque pulcherrima
muliere primo quasi quodam monstro infernisque
imaginibus turbatus substitit. Deinde ut et corpus
iacentis conspexit et lacrimas consideravit faciemque
unguibus sectam, ratus scilicet id quod erat, desiderium extincti non posse feminam pati, attulit in
monumentum cenulam suam coepitque bortari Ingentem, ne perseveraret in dolore supervacuo ac nihil
profuturo gemitu pectus diduceret: omnium eundem
esse exitum [sed] et idem domicilium, et cetera quibus
exulceratae mentes ad sanitatem revocantur. At illa
ignota consolatione percussa laceravit vehementius
pectus ruptosque crines super corpus[1] iacentis imposuit.
Non recessit tamen miles, sed eadem exhortatione
temptavit dare mulierculae cibum, donec ancilla vini

---

[1] corpus *Nodot:* pectus.

passing her fifth day without food. A devoted maid sat by the failing woman, shed tears in sympathy with her woes, and at the same time filled up the lamp, which was placed in the tomb, whenever it sank. There was but one opinion throughout the city, every class of person admitting this was the one true and brilliant example of chastity and love. At this moment the governor of the province gave orders that some robbers should be crucified near the small building where the lady was bewailing her recent loss. So on the next night, when the soldier who was watching the crosses, to prevent anyone taking down a body for burial, observed a light shining plainly among the tombs, and heard a mourner's groans, a very human weakness made him curious to know who it was and what he was doing. So he went down into the vault, and on seeing a very beautiful woman, at first halted in confusion, as if he had seen a portent or some ghost from the world beneath. But afterwards noticing the dead man lying there, and watching the woman's tears and the marks of her nails on her face, he came to the correct conclusion, that she found her regret for the lost one unendurable. He therefore brought his supper into the tomb, and began to urge the mourner not to persist in useless grief, and break her heart with unprofitable sobs: for all men made the same end and found the same resting-place, and so on with the other platitudes which restore wounded spirits to health. But she took no notice of his sympathy, struck and tore her breast more violently than ever, pulled out her hair, and laid it on the dead body. Still the soldier did not retire, but tried to give the poor woman food with similar encouragements, until the maid, who was no doubt seduced by the smell of his

231

certe ab eo odore corrupta primum ipsa porrexit ad
humanitatem invitantis victam manum, deinde refecta
potione et cibo expugnare dominae pertinaciam coepit
et 'Quid proderit' inquit 'hoc tibi, si soluta inedia
fueris, si te vivam sepelieris, si antequam fata poscant,
indemnatum spiritum effuderis?

  Id cinerem aut manes credis sentire sepultos?
Vis tu reviviscere? Vis discusso muliebri errore, quam
diu licuerit, lucis commodis frui? Ipsum te iacentis
corpus admonere debet, ut vivas.' Nemo invitus audit,
cum cogitur aut cibum sumere aut vivere. Itaque
mulier aliquot dierum abstinentia sicca passa est frangi
pertinaciam suam, nec minus avide replevit se cibo
quam ancilla, quae prior vieta est. Ceterum scitis,
quid plerumque soleat temptare humanam satietatem.
Quibus blanditiis impetraverat miles, ut matrona vellet vivere, isdem etiam pudicitiam eius aggressus est.
Nec deformis aut infacundus iuvenis castae videbatur,
conciliante gratiam ancilla ac subinde dicente:
                 'Placitone etiam pugnabis amori?
  Nec venit in mentem, quorum consederis arvis?'
quid diutius moror? ne hanc quidem partem corporis
mulier abstinuit, victorque miles utrumque persuasit.
Iacuerunt ergo una non tantum illa nocte, qua nuptias
fecerunt, sed postero etiam ac tertio die, praeclusis
videlicet conditorii foribus, ut quisquis ex notis igno-
tisque ad monumentum venisset, putaret expirasse
super corpus viri pudicissimam uxorem. Ceterum

112

232

wine, first gave in herself, and put out her hand at his kindly invitation, and then, refreshed with food and drink, began to assail her mistress's obstinacy, and say, 'What will you gain by all this, if you faint away with hunger, if you bury yourself alive, if you breathe out your undoomed soul before Fate calls for it?' 'Believest thou that the ashes or the spirit of the buried dead can feel thy woe?[1] Will you not begin life afresh? Will you not shake off this womanish failing, and enjoy the blessings of the light so long as you are allowed? Your poor dead husband's body here ought to persuade you to keep alive.' People are always ready to listen when they are urged to take a meal or to keep alive. So the lady, being thirsty after several days' abstinence, allowed her resolution to be broken down, and filled herself with food as greedily as the maid, who had been the first to yield.

· "Well, you know which temptation generally assails 112 a man on a full stomach. The soldier used the same insinuating phrases which had persuaded the lady to consent to live, to conduct an assault upon her virtue. Her modest eye saw in him a young man, handsome and eloquent. The maid begged her to be gracious, and then said, 'Wilt thou fight love even when love pleases thee? Or dost thou never remember in whose lands thou art resting?'[2] I need hide the fact no longer. The lady ceased to hold out, and the conquering hero won her over entire. So they passed not only their wedding night together, but the next and a third, of course shutting the door of the vault, so that any friend or stranger who came to the tomb would imagine that this most virtuous lady had breathed her last over her husband's body. Well, the

[1] See Virgil, *Æneid* iv, 34. [2] See Virgil, *Æneid* iv, 38.

delectatus miles et forma mulieris et secreto, quicquid boni per facultates poterat, coemebat et prima statim nocte in monumentum ferebat. Itaque unius cruciarii parentes ut viderunt laxatam custodiam, detraxere nocte pendentem supremoque mandaverunt officio. At miles circumscriptus dum desidet, ut postero die vidit unam sine cadavere crucem, veritus supplicium, mulieri quid accidisset exponit: nec se exspectaturum indicis sententiam, sed gladio ius dicturum ignaviae suae. Commodaret ergo illa perituro locum et fatale conditorium familiari ac viro faceret. Mulier non minus misericors quam pudica 'ne istud' inquit 'dii sinaut, ut eodem tempore duorum mihi carissimorum hominum duo funera spectem. Malo mortuum impendere quam vivum occidere.' Secundum hanc orationem inhet ex arca corpus mariti sui tolli atque illi, quae vacabat, cruci affigi. Usus est miles ingenio prudentissimae feminae, posteroque die populus miratus est, qua ratione mortuus isset in crucem."

113 Risu excepere fabulam nautae, [et] erubescente non mediocriter Tryphaena vultumque suum super cervicem Gitonis amabiliter ponente. At non Lichas risit, sed iratum commovens caput "Si iustus" inquit "imperator fuisset, debuit patris familiae corpus in monumentum referre, mulierem affigere cruci."

Non dubie redierat in animum Hedyle expilatumque libidinosa migratione navigium. Sed nec foederis

soldier was delighted with the woman's beauty, and
his stolen pleasure; he bought up all the fine things
his means permitted, and carried them to the tomb
the moment darkness fell. So the parents of one
of the crucified, seeing that the watch was ill-
kept, took their man down in the dark and adminis-
tered the last rite to him. The soldier was eluded
while he was off duty, and next day, seeing one of
the crosses without its corpse, he was in terror of
punishment, and explained to the lady what had
happened. He declared that he would not wait for
a court-martial, but would punish his own neglect
with a thrust of his sword. So she had better get
ready a place for a dying man, and let the gloomy
vault enclose both her husband and her lover. The
lady's heart was tender as well as pure. 'Heaven
forbid,' she replied, 'that I should look at the same
moment on the dead bodies of two men whom I love.
No, I would rather make a dead man useful, than
send a live man to death.' After this speech she
ordered her husband's body to be taken out of the
coffin and fixed up on the empty cross. The soldier
availed himself of this far-seeing woman's device, and
the people wondered the next day by what means the
dead man had ascended the cross."

The sailors received this tale with a roar; Try- 113
phaena blushed deeply, and laid her face caressingly
on Giton's neck. But there was no laugh from
Lichas; he shook his head angrily and said: "If the
governor of the province had been a just man, he
should have put the dead husband back in the tomb,
and hung the woman on the cross."

No doubt he was thinking once more of Hedyle
and how his ship had been pillaged on her passionate

235

verba permittebant meminisse, nec hilaritas, quae occupaverat mentes, dabat iracundiae locum. Ceterum Tryphaena in gremio Gitonis posita modo implebat osculis pectus, interdum concinnabat spoliatum crini-
L bus vultum. | Ego maestus et impatiens foederis novi non cibum, non potionem capiebam, sed obliquis truci-busque oculis utrumque spectabam. Omnia me oscula vulnerabant, omnes blanditiae, quascunque mulier libidinosa fingebat. Nec tamen adhuc sciebam, utrum magis puero irascerer, quod amicam mihi auferret, an amicae, quod puerum corrumperet: utraque inimi-cissima oculis meis et captivitate praeterita tristiora. Accedebat huc, quod neque Tryphaena me alloque-batur tanquam familiarem et aliquando gratum sibi amatorem, nec Giton me aut tralaticia propinatione dignum iudicabat, aut quod minimum est, sermone communi vocabat, credo, veritus ne inter initia coeuntis gratiae recentem cicatricem rescinderet. Inundavere pectus lacrimae dolore paratae, gemitusque suspirio tectus animam paene submovit . . .

In partem voluptatis temptabat admitti, nec domini supercilium induebat, sed amici quaerebat obse-quium . . .

"Si quid ingenui sanguinis habes, non pluris illam facies, quam scortum. Si vir fueris, non ibis ad spin-triam"[1] . . .

Me nihil magis pungebat,[2] quam ne Eumolpus sen-sisset, quicquid illud fuerat, et homo dicacissimus carminibus vindicaret . . .

Iurat Eumolpus verbis conceptissimis . . .

[1] spintriam *margin ed. of Tornaesius:* spuicam *or* spuitam.
[2] pungebat *Buecheler:* pudebat.

236

elopement. But the terms of our treaty forbade us to bear grudges, and the joy which had filled our souls left no room for wrath. Tryphaena was now lying in Giton's lap, covering him with kisses one moment, and sometimes patting his shaven head. I was gloomy and uneasy about our new terms, and did not touch food or drink, but kept shooting angry looks askance at them both. Every kiss was a wound to me, every pleasing wile that the wanton woman conjured up. I was not yet sure whether I was more angry with the boy for taking away my mistress, or with my mistress for leading the boy astray: both of them were hateful to my sight and more depressing than the bondage I had escaped. And besides all this, Tryphaena did not address me like a friend whom she was once pleased to have for a lover, and Giton did not think fit to drink my health in the ordinary way, and would not even so much as include me in general conversation. I suppose he was afraid of reopening a tender sear just as friendly feeling began to draw it together. My unhappiness moved me till tears overflowed my heart, and the groan I hid with a sigh almost stole my life away. . .

He tried to gain admission to share their joys, not wearing the proud look of a master, but begging him to yield as a friend. . .

"If you have a drop of honest blood in you you will think no more of her than of a common woman. Si vir fueris, non ibis ad spintriam" . . .

Nothing troubled me more than the fear that Eumolpus might have got some idea of what was going on, and might employ his powers of speech in attacking me in verse. . .

Eumolpus swore an oath in most formal language. . .

237

114   Dum haec taliaque iactamus, inhorruit mare nu-
besque undiqne adductae obruere tenebris diem. Dis-
currunt nautae ad officia trepidantes velaque tempe-
stati subducunt. Sed nec certos fluctus ventus impulerat,
nec quo destinaret cursum, gubernator sciebat. Siciliam
modo ventus dabat, saepissime [in oram] Italici litoris
aquilo possessor convertebat huc illuc obnoxiam ratem,[1]
et quod omnibus procellis periculosius erat, tam spissae
repente tenebrae lucem suppresserant, ut ne proram
quidem totam gubernator videret. Itaque hercules
postquam maris ira infesta[2] convaluit, Lichas trepidans
ad me supinas porrigit manus et "tu" inquit "Encolpi,
succurre periclitantibus et vestem illam divinam si-
strumque redde navigio. Per fidem, miserere, quemadmodum quidem soles."

Et illum quidem vociferantem in mare ventus excussit, repetitumque infesto gurgite procella circumegit
atque hausit. Tryphaenam autem prope iam fide-
lissimi rapuerunt servi, scaphaeque impositam cum
maxima sarcinarum parte abduxere certissimae morti...

Applicitus cum clamore flevi et "Hoc" inquam "a
diis meruimus, ut nos sola morte coniungerent? Sed
non crudelis fortuna concedit. Ecce iam ratem fluctus
evertet, ecce iam amplexus amantium iratum dividet
mare. Igitur, si vere Encolpion dilexisti, da oscula,
dum licet, et ultimum hoc gaudium fatis properantibus
rape." Haec ut ego dixi, Giton vestem deposuit

[1] ratem *Goldast:* partem.
[2] maris era infesta *Buecheler:* manifesta.

SATYRICON

While we talked over this matter and others, the **114**
sea rose, clouds gathered from every quarter, and
overwhelmed the day in darkness. The sailors ran
to their posts in terror, and furled the sails before the
storm. But the wind did not drive the waves in any
one direction, and the helmsman was at a loss which
way to steer. One moment the wind set towards
Sicily, very often the north wind blew off the Italian
coast, mastered the ship and twisted her in every
direction; and what was more dangerous than any
squall, such thick darkness had suddenly blotted out
the light that the steersman could not even see the
whole prow. Then for a wonder, as the hostile fury of
the storm gathered, Lichas trembled and stretched out
his hands to me imploringly, and said, "Help us in
our peril, Encolpius; let the ship have the goddess's
robe again and her holy rattle.[1] Be merciful, I implore
you, as your way is."

But even as he shouted the wind blew him into
the water, a squall whirled him round and round
repeatedly in a fierce whirlpool, and sucked him
down. Tryphaena's faithful slaves carried her off
almost by force, put her in a boat with most of her
luggage, and so rescued her from certain death. . .

I embraced Giton, and wept and cried aloud: "Did
we deserve this from the gods, that they should unite
us only when they slay? But cruel Fate does not
grant us even this. Look! even now the waves will
upset the boat; even now the angry sea will sunder a
lover's embrace. So if you ever really loved Encolpius,
kiss him while you may, and snatch this last joy as
Fate swoops down upon you." As I spoke Giton took

[1] Sacred emblems of Isis which Encolpius had probably
stolen.

meaque tunica contectus exeruit ad osculum caput.
Et ne sic cohaerentes malignior fluctus distraheret,
utrumque zona circumvenienti praecinxit et "Si nihil
aliud, certe diutius" inquit "iunctos nos mare[1] feret,
vel si voluerit misericors ad idem litus expellere, aut
praeteriens aliquis tralaticia humanitate lapidabit, aut
quod ultimum est iratis etiam fluctibus, imprudens
harena componet." Patior ego vinculum extremum,
et veluti lecto funebri aptatus exspecto mortem iam
non molestam. Peragit interim tempestas mandata
fatorum omnesque reliquias navis expugnat. Non
arbor erat relicta, non gubernacula, non funis aut
remus, sed quasi rudis atque infecta materies ihat cum
fluctibus . . .

Procurrere piscatores parvulis expediti navigiis ad
praedam rapiendam. Deinde ut aliquos viderunt, qui
suas opes defenderent, mutaverunt crudelitatem in
auxilium . . .

115 Audimus murmur insolitum et sub diaeta magistri
quasi cupientis exire beluae gemitum. Persecuti igitur
sonum invenimus Eumolpum sedentem membranaeque
ingenti versus ingerentem. Mirati ergo, quod illi
vacaret in vicinia mortis poema facere, extrahimus
clamantem iubemusque bonam babere mentem. At
ille interpellatus excanduit et "Sinite me" inquit
"sententiam explere; laborat carmen in fine." Inicio
ego phrenitico manum iubeoque Gitona accedere et in
terram trahere poetam mugientem . . .

Hoc opere tandem elaborato casam piscatoriam
subimus maerentes, cibisque naufragio corruptis

[1] iunctos nos mare *Faber :* iuncta nos mors.

240

off his clothes, and I covered him with my shirt as he put up his head to be kissed. And that no envious wave should pull us apart as we clung to each other, he put his belt round us both and tied it tight, saying, "Whatever happens to us, at least we shall be locked together a long while as the sea carries us, and if the sea has pity and will cast us up on the same shore, some one may come by and put stones over us out of ordinary human kindness, or the last work of the waves even in their wrath will be to cover us with the unconscious sand." I let him bind me for the last time, and then waited, like a man dressed for his death-bed, for an end that had lost its bitterness. Meanwhile by Fate's decree the storm rose to its height, and took by violence all that was left of the ship. No mast, no helm, no rope or oar remained on her. She drifted on the waves like a rough and unshapen lump of wood. . . .

Some fishermen in handy little boats put out to seize their prey. When they saw some men alive and ready to fight for their belongings, they altered their savage plans and came to the rescue. . .

We heard a strange noise, and a groaning like a 115 wild beast, coming from under the master's cabin. So we followed the noise, and found Eumolpus sitting there inscribing verses on a great parchment. We were surprised at his having time to write poetry with death close at hand, and we pulled him out, though he protested, and implored him to be sensible. But he was furious at our interruption, and cried: "Let me complete my design; the poem balts at the close." I laid hands on the maniac, and told Giton to help me to drag the bellowing hard ashore. . .

When this business was at last completed, we came sadly to a fisherman's cottage, refreshed our-

utcunque curati tristissimam exegimus noctem. Postero die, cum poneremus consilium, cui nos regioni
crederemus, repente video corpus humanum circum-
actnm levi vertice ad litus deferri. Substiti ergo tristis
coepique umentibus[1] oculis maris fidem inspicere et
"Hunc forsitan" proclamo "in aliqua parte terrarum
secura exspectat uxor, forsitan ignarus tempestatis
filius aut pater;[2] utique reliquit aliquem, cui pro-
ficiscens osculum dedit. Haec sunt consilia mortalium,
haec vota magnarum cogitationum. En homo quemadmodum natat." Adhuc tanquam ignotum defle-
bam, cum inviolatum os fluctus convertit in terram,
agnovique terribilem paulo ante et implacabilem Licham pedibus meis paene subiectum. Non tenui
igitur diutius lacrimas, immo percussi semel iterumque
manibus pectus et "Ubi nunc est" inquam "iracundia
tua, ubi impotentia tua? nempe piscibus beluisque
expositus es, et qui paulo ante iactabas vires imperii
tui, de tam magna nave ne tabulam quidem naufragus
habes. Ite nunc mortales, et magnis cogitationibus
pectora implete. Ite cauti, et opes fraudibus captas
per mille annos disponite. Nempe hic proxima luce
patrimonii sui rationes inspexit, nempe diem etiam,
quo venturus esset in patriam, animo suo fixit.[3] Dii
deaeque, quam longe a destinatione sua iacet. Sed
non sola mortalibus maria hanc fidem praestant. Illum
bellantem arma decipiunt, illum diis vota reddentem
penatium suorum ruina sepelit. Ille vehiculo lapsus
properantem spiritum excussit, cibus avidum strangu-

[1] umentibus *margin ed. of Tornaesius :* viventibus.
[2] pater *Buecheler :* patrem.
[3] fixit *Oeveringius :* finxit.

selves more or less with food spoilt by sea-water, and passed a very miserable night. Next morning, as we were trying to decide into what part of the country we should venture, I suddenly saw a man's body caught in a gentle eddy and carried ashore. I stopped gloomily, and, with moist eyes, began to reflect upon the treachery of the sea. "Maybe," I cried, "there is a wife waiting cheerfully at home for this man in a far-off land, or a son or a father, maybe, who know nothing of this storm; he is sure to have left some one behind whom he kissed before he went. So much for mortal men's plans, and the prayers of high ambition. Look how the man floats." I was still crying over him as a perfect stranger, when a wave turned his face towards the shore without a mark upon it, and I recognized Lichas, but a while ago so fierce and so relentless, now thrown almost under my feet. Then I could restrain my tears no longer; I beat my breast again and again, and cried, "Where is your temper and your hot head now? Behold! you are a prey for fish and savage beasts. An hour ago you boasted the strength of your command, and you have not one plank of your great ship to save you. Now let mortal men fill their hearts with proud imaginations if they will. Let misers lay out the gains they win by fraud for a thousand years. Lo! this man but yesterday looked into the accounts of his family property, and even settled in his own mind the very day when he would come home again. Lord, Lord, how far he lies from his consummation! But it is not the waves of the sea alone that thus keep faith with mortal men. The warrior's weapons fail him; another pays his vows to Heaven, and his own house falls and buries him in the act. Another slips from his coach and dashes out his eager soul: the glutton

lavit, abstinentem frugalitas. Si bene calculum ponas, ubique naufragium est. At enim fluctibus obruto non contingit sepultura. Tanquam intersit, periturum corpus quae ratio consumat, ignis an fluctus an mora. Quicquid feceris, omnia haec eodem ventura sunt. Ferae tamen corpus lacerabunt. Tanquam melius ignis accipiat; immo hanc poenam gravissimam credimus, ubi servis irascimur. Quae ergo dementia est, omnia facere, ne quid de nobis relinquat sepultura?" . . .

Et Licham quidem rogus inimicis collatus manibus adolebat. Eumolpus autem dum epigramma mortuo facit, oculos ad arcessendos sensus longius mittit . . .

116 Hoc peracto libenter officio destinatum carpimus iter ac momento temporis in montem sudantes con scendimus, ex quo hand procul impositum aree sub-limi oppidum cernimus. Nec quod esset, sciebamus errantes, donec a vilico quodam Crotona esse cognovimus, urbem antiquissimam et aliquando Italiae primam. Cum deinde diligentius exploraremus, qui homines inhabitarent nobile solum, quodve genus negotiationis praecipue probarent post attritas bellis frequentibus opes, "O mi" inquit "hospites, si negotiatores estis, mutate propositum aliudque vitae praesidium quaerite. Sin autem urbanioris notae homines sustinetis semper mentiri, recta ad lucrum curritis. In hac enim urbe non litterarum studia celebrantur, non eloquentia locum habet, non frugalitas sanctique mores laudibus ad fructum perveniunt, sed quoscunque homines in

chokes at dinner, the sparing man dies of want. Make a fair reckoning, and you find shipwreck everywhere. You tell me that for those the waters whelm there is no burial. As if it mattered how our perishable flesh comes to its end, by fire or water or the lapse of time! Whatever you may do, all these things achieve the same goal. But beasts will tear the body, you say, as though fire would give it a more kindly welcome! When we are angry with our slaves, we consider burning their heaviest punishment. Then what madness to take such trouble to prevent the grave from leaving aught of us behind!" . . .

So Lichas was burned on a pyre built by his enemy's hands. Eumolpus proceeded to compose an epitaph on the dead man, and looked about in search of some far-fetched ideas. . .

We gladly performed this last office, and then took 116 up our proposed way, and in a short while came sweating to a mountain top, from which we saw, not far off, a town set on a high peak. We had lost ourselves, and did not know what it was, until we learned from a farm-bailiff that it was Croton, a town of great age, and once the first city in Italy. When we went on to inquire particularly what men lived on such honoured soil, and what kind of business pleased them best, now that their wealth had been brought low by so many wars, the man replied, "My friends, if you are business men, change your plans and look for some other safe way of life. But if you profess to be men of a superior stamp and thorough-paced liars, you are on the direct road to wealth. In this city the pursuit of learning is not esteemed, eloquence has no place, economy and a pure life do not win their reward in honour: know that the whole of

245

hac urbe videritis, scitote in duas partes esse divisos.
Nam aut captantur aut captant. In hac urbe nemo
liberos tollit, quia quisquis suos heredes habet, non ad
cenas,[1] non ad spectacula admittitur, sed omnibus pro-
hibetur commodis, inter ignominiosos latitat. Qui vero
nec uxores unquam duxerunt nec proximas necessitu-
dines habent, ad summos honores perveniunt, id est
soli militares, soli fortissimi atque etiam innocentes
habentur. Adibitis" inquit "oppidum tamquam in
pestilentia campos, in quibus nihil aliud est nisi cada-
vera, quae lacerantur, aut corvi, qui lacerant" . . .

117   prudentior Eumolpus convertit ad novitatem rei
mentem genusque divinationis sibi non displicere confessus est. Iocari ego senem poetica levitate credebam,
cum ille "Utinam quidem sufficeret largior scaena, id
est vestis humanior, instrumentum lautius, quod prae-
beret mendacio fidem: non mehercules penam istam
differrem, sed continuo vos ad magnas opes ducerem.
Atquin promitto, quicquid exigeret, dummodo placeret
vestis, rapinae comes, et quicquid Lycurgi villa gras-
santibus praebuisset. Nam nummos in praesentem
usum deum matrem pro fide sua reddituram" . . .

"Quid ergo" inquit Eumolpus "cessamus mimum
componere? Facite ergo me dominum, si negotiatio
placet." Nemo ansus est artem damnare nihil anfe-
rentem. Itaque ut duraret inter omnes tutum mendacium, in verba Eumolpi sacramentum iuravimus:
uri, vinciri, verberari ferroque necari, et quicquid
aliud Eumolpus iussisset. Tanquam legitimi gladia-

---

[1] cenas *Bongarsius:* scenas.

the men you see in this city are divided into two classes. They are either the prey of legacy-hunting or legacy-hunters themselves. In this city no one brings up children, because anyone who has heirs of his own stock is never invited to dinner or the theatre; he is deprived of all advantages, and lies in obscurity among the base-born. But those who have never married, and have no near relations, reach the highest positions; they alone, that is, are considered soldierly, gallant, or even good. Yes," he went on, "you will go into a town that is like a plague-stricken plain, where there is nothing but carcasses to be devoured, and crows to devour them." . . .

Eumolpus was more cautious, and directed his 117 attention to the novelty of the case, declaring that this kind of prophecy did not make him uneasy. I thought the old man was joking with the light heart of a poet, but then he said, "I only wish I had a more ample background, I mean a more gentlemanly dress, and finer ornaments, to lend colour to my strange tale; I declare I would not put off the business, I would bring you into great wealth in a moment. Anyhow, I promise to do whatever my fellow-robber demands, so long as my clothes are satisfactory, and whatever we may find in Lycurgus's house when we break in. I am sure that our mother goddess for her honour's sake will pay up some coin to us for present needs." . . . "Well then," said Eumolpus, "Why shouldn't we make up a farce? Now appoint me your master, if you like the business." No one dared to grumble at this harmless device. So to keep the lie safe among us all, we took an oath to obey Eumolpus; to endure burning, bondage, flogging, death by the sword, or anything else that Eumolpus ordered. We

tores domino corpora animasque religiosissime addici-
mus. Post peractum sacramentum serviliter ficti
dominum consalutamus, elatumque ab Eumolpo filium
pariter condiscimus, iuvenem ingentis eloquentiae et
spei, ideoque de civitate sua miserrimum senem exisse,
ne aut clientes sodalesque filii sui aut sepulcrum
quotidie causam lacrimarum cerneret. Accessisse
huic tristitiae proximum naufragium, quo amplius
vicies sestertium amiserit; nec illum iactura moveri,
sed destitutum ministerio non agnoscere dignitatem
suam. Praeterea habere in Africa trecenties sestertium fundis nominibusque depositum; nam familiam
quidem tam magnam per agros Numidiae esse sparsam,
ut possit vel Carthaginem capere. Secundum hanc
formulam imperamus Eumolpo, ut plurimum tussiat,
ut sit modo solutioris stomachi cibosque omnes palam
damnet; loquatur aurum et argentum fundosque
mendaces et perpetuam terrarum sterilitatem; sedeat
praeterea quotidie ad rationes tabulasque testamenti
omnibus *mensibus* renovet. Et ne quid scaenae deesset,
quotiescunque aliquem nostrum vocare temptasset,
alium pro alio vocaret, ut facile appareret dominum
etiam eorum meminisse, qui praesentes non essent.

His ita ordinatis, "quod bene feliciterque eveniret"
precati deos viam ingredimur. Sed neque Giton sub
insolito fasce durabat, et mercennarius Corax, detracta-
tor ministerii, posita frequentius sarcina male dicebat
properantibus affirmabatque se aut proiecturum sarcinas
aut cum onere fugiturum. "Quid vos" inquit "iumen-

pledged our bodies and souls to our master most solemnly, like regular gladiators. When the oath was over, we posed like slaves and saluted our master, and learned all together that Eumolpus had lost a son, a young man of great eloquence and promise, and that the poor old man had left his own country for this reason, to escape seeing his son's dependants and friends, or the tomb which was the source of his daily tears. His grief had been increased by a recent shipwreck, in which he lost over two million sesterces: it was not the loss that troubled him, but with no servant to wait upon him he could not recognize his own importance. Besides, he had thirty millions invested in Africa in estates and bonds; such a horde of his slaves was scattered over the fields of Numidia that he could positively have saeked Carthage. Under this scheme we ordered Eumolpus to cough frequently, sometimes to be bilious, and to find fault openly with all his food; he must talk of gold and silver and his disappointing farms and the obstinate barrenness of the soil; further, he must sit over his accounts daily, and revise the sheets of his will every month. To make the setting quite complete, he was to use the wrong names whenever he tried to call one of us, so that it would clearly look as though our master had also in his mind some servants who were not present. This was all arranged; we offered a prayer to Heaven for a prosperous and happy issue, and started on our journey. But Giton was not used to a burden and could not bear it, and the slave Corax, a shirker of work, kept putting down his bundle and cursing our hurry, and declaring that he would either throw the baggage away or run off with his load. "You seem to think I am a beast of burden or

249

tum me putatis esse aut lapidariam 'navem? Hominis operas locavi, non caballi. Nec minus liber sum
quam vos, etiam si pauperem pater me reliquit."
Nec contentus maledictis tollebat subinde altius
pedem et strepitu obsceno simul atque odore viam
implebat. Ridebat contumaciam Giton et singulos
crepitus eius pari clamore prosequebatur . . .

118LO | "Multos [inquit Eumolpos, o] iuvenes carmen
decepit. Nam ut quisque versum pedibus instruxit
sensumque teneriorem verborum ambitu intexuit,
putavit se continuo in Heliconem venisse. Sic forensi-
bus ministeriis exercitati frequenter ad carminis tran-
quillitatem tanquam ad portum feliciorem[1] refugerunt,
credentes facilius poema exstrui posse, quam controversiam sententiolis ibrantibus pictam. Ceterum
neque generosior spiritus vanitatem[2] amat, neque concipere[3] aut edere partum mens potest nisi ingenti
flumine litterarum inundata. Refugiendum est ab omni
verborum, ut ita dicam, vilitate et sumendae voces a
plebe semotae,[4] ut fiat 'odi profanum vulgus et arceo.'
Praeterea curandum est, ne sententiae emineant extra
corpus orationis expressae, sed intexto vestibus colore
niteant. Homerus testis et lyrici Romanusque Vergilius et Horatii curiosa felicitas. Ceteri enim aut
non viderunt viam, qua iretur ad carmen, aut visam[5]
timuerunt calcare. Ecce belli civilis ingens opus

---

[1] feliciorem *cod. Messaniensis:* faciliorem *other MSS.*
[2] vanitatem *cod. Messaniensis:* sanitatem *other MSS.*
[3] concipere *cod. Bernensis:* conspicere *L:* conspici *O.*
[4] semotae *Buecheler:* summotae.
[5] visam *Faber:* versum.

250

a ship for carrying stones," he cried. "You paid for the services of a man, not a horse. I am just as free as you are, although my father did leave me a poor man." Not satisfied with curses, he kept lifting his leg up and filling the whole road with a disgusting noise and smell. Giton laughed at his impudence and matched every noise he made. . . .

"Yes, my young friends," said Eumolpus, "poetry 118 has led many astray. As soon as a man has shaped his verse in feet and woven into it a more delicate meaning with an ingenious circumlocution, he thinks that forthwith he has sealed Helicon. In this fashion people who are tired out with forensic oratory often take refuge in the calm of poetry as in some happier haven, supposing that a poem is easier to construct than a declamation adorned with quivering epigrams. But nobler souls do not love such coxcombry, and the mind cannot conceive or bring forth its fruit unless it is steeped in the vast flood of literature. One must flee away from all diction that is, so to speak, cheap, and choose words divorced from popular use, putting into practice, "I hate the common herd and hold it afar." [1] Besides, one must take care that the epigrams do not stand out from the body of the speech: they must shine with a brilliancy that is woven into the material. Homer proves this, and the lyric poets, and Roman Virgil, and the studied felicity of Horace. The others either did not see the path that leads to poetry, or saw it and were afraid to walk in it For instance, anyone who attemps the vast theme of the Civil War [2] will sink under the burden

[1] Horace, *Odes* iii, 1.
[2] The theme of the Pharsalia of Lucan, against whom Eumolpus's criticisms seem to be directed.

251

quisquis attigerit, nisi plenus litteris, sub onere
labetur. Non enim res gestae versibus comprehen-
dendae sunt, quod longe melius historiei faciunt, sed
per ambages deorumque ministeria et fabulosum
sententiarum tormentum praecipitandus est liber
spiritus, ut potins furentis animi vaticinatio appareat
quam religiosae orationis sub testibus fides: tanquam
si placet hic impetus, etiam si nondum recepit ultimam
manum" . . .

119   "Orhem iam totum victor Romanus habebat,
qua mare, qua terrae, qua sidus currit utrumque.
Nec satiatus erat.   Gravidis freta pulsa carinis
iam peragebantur; si quis sinus abditus ultra,
si qua foret tellus, quae fulvum mitteret aurum,
hostis erat, fatisque in tristia bella paratis
quaerebantur opes. Non vulgo nota placebant
gaudia, non usu plebeio trita voluptas.
Aes Ephyreiacum[1] laudabat miles in unda;
quaesitus tellure nitor certaverat ostro;   10
hinc Numidae accusant,[2] illinc nova vellera Seres,
atque Arabum populus sua despoliaverat arva.
Ecce aliac clades et laesae vulnera pacis.
Quaeritur in silvis auro fera, et ultimus Hammon
Afrorum excutitur, ne desit belua dente
ad mortes pretiosa; fames premit advena classes,
tigris et aurata gradiens vectatur in aula,
ut hibat humanum populo plaudente cruorem.
Heu, pudet effari perituraque prodere fata,
Persarum ritu male pubescentibus annis   20

---

[1] Aes Ephyreiacum *Heinsius:* aes epyrecum *and the like
most MSS.:* spolia Tum (cum *Dr*) Senius *codd. Monacensis et
Dresdensis.*
[2] accusant *L:* accusatius *O.*

252

unless he is full of literature. It is not a question of recording real events in verse; historians can do that far better. The free spirit of genius must plunge headlong into allusions and divine interpositions, and rack itself for epigrams coloured by mythology, so that what results seems rather the prophecies of an inspired seer than the exactitude of a statement made on oath before witnesses: the following effusion will show what I mean, if it take your fancy, though it has not yet received my final touches. . . .

"The conquering Roman now held the whole world, 119 sea and land and the course of sun and moon. But he was not satisfied. Now the waters were stirred and troubled by his loaded ships; if there were any hidden bay beyond, or any land that promised a yield of yellow gold, that place was Rome's enemy, fate stood ready for the sorrows of war, and the quest for wealth went on. There was no happiness in familiar joys, or in pleasures dulled by the common man's use. The soldier out at sea would praise the bronze of Corinth; bright colours dug from earth rivalled the purple; here the African curses Rome, here the Chinaman plunders his marvellous silks, and the Arabian hordes have stripped their own fields bare.

"Yet again more destruction, and peace hurt and bleeding. The wild beast is searched out in the woods at a great price, and men trouble Hammon deep in Africa to supply the beast whose teeth make him precious for slaying men; strange ravening creatures freight the fleets, and the padding tiger is wheeled in a gilded palace to drink the blood of men while the crowd applauds.

"I shrink from speaking plain and betraying our destiny of ruin; boys whose childhood is hardly begun

TITUS PETRONIUS ARBITER

surripuere viros exsectaque viscera ferro
in venerem fregere, atque ut fuga nobilis aevi
circumscripta mora properantes differat annos,
quaerit se natura nec invenit.   Omnibus ergo
scorta placent fractique enervi corpore gressus
et laxi crines et tot nova nomina vestis,
quaeque virum quaerunt.   Ecce Afris cruta terris
citrea mensa greges servorum ostrumque renidens,
ponitur ac maculis imitatur vilius[1] aurum
quae sensum trahat. Hoc sterile ac male nobile lignum
turba sepulta mero circum venit, omniaque orbis   31
praemia corruptis[2] miles vagus esurit armis.
Ingeniosa gula est.   Siculo scarus aequore mersus
ad mensam vivus perducitur, atque Lucrinis
cruta litoribus vendunt conchylia cenas,
ut renovent per damna famem.   Iam Phasidos unda
orbata est avibus, mutoque in litore tantum
solac desertis adspirant frondibus aurae.
Nec minor in campo furor est, emptique Quirites
ad praedam strepitumque lucri suffragia vertunt.   40
Venalis populus, venalis curia patrum,
est favor in pretio. Senibus quoque libera virtus
exciderat, sparsisque opibus conversa potestas
ipsaque maiestas auro corrupta iacebat.
Pellitur a populo victus Cato; tristior ille est,

[1] vilius *Gronovius:* vilibus. *For* imitatur *some MSS. give*
mutatur.
[2] corruptis *Buecheler:* correptis.

254

are kidnapped in the Persian way, and the powers the knife has shorn are forced to the service of lust, and in order that the passing of man's finest age may be hedged round with delay and hold back the hurrying years, Nature seeks for herself, and finds herself not. So all take their pleasure in harlotry, and the halting steps of a feeble body, and in flowing hair and numberless clothes of new names, everything that ensnares mankind.

"Tables of citron-wood are dug out of the soil of Africa and set up, the spots on them resembling gold which is cheaper than they, their polish reflecting hordes of slaves and purple clothes, to lure the senses. Round this barren and low-born wood there gathers a crowd drowned in drink, and the soldier of fortune gorges the whole spoils of the world while his weapons rust.

"Gluttony is a fine art. The wrasse is brought alive to table in sea-water from Sicily, and the oysters torn from the banks of the Lucrine lake make a dinner famous, in order to renew men's hunger by their extravagance. All the birds are now gone from the waters of Phasis; the shore is quiet; only the empty air breathes on the lonely boughs.

"The same madness is in public life, the true-born Roman is bought, and changes his vote for plunder and the cry of gain. The people are corrupt, the house of senators is corrupt, their support hangs on a price. The freedom and virtue of the old men had decayed, their power was swayed by largesse, even their dignity was stained by money and trodden in the dust.

"Cato is beaten and driven out by the mob; his conqueror is more unhappy than he, and is ashamed to have torn the rods of office from Cato. For the

255

qui vicit, fascesque pudet rapuisse Catoni.
Namque—hoc dedecoris populo morumque ruina—
non homo pulsus erat, sed in uno vieta potestas
Romanumque decus.   Quare tam perdita Roma
ipsa sui merces erat et sine vindice praeda.   50
Praeterea gemino deprensam gurgite plebem[1]
faenoris illuvies ususque exederat acris.
Nulla est certa domus, nullum sine pignore corpus,
sed veluti tabes tacitis concepta medullis
intra membra furens curis latrantibus errat.
Arma placent miseris, detritaque commoda luxu
vulneribus reparantur.   Inops audacia tuta est.
Hoc mersam caeno Romam somnoque iacentem
quae poterant artes sana ratione movere,
ni furor et bellum ferroque excita[2] libido?   60
120   Tres tulerat Fortuna duces, quos obruit omnes
armorum strue diversa feralis Enyo.
Crassum Parthus habet, Libyco iacet aequore Magnus,
Iulius ingratam perfudit sanguine Romam,
et quasi non posset tot tellus ferre sepulcra,
divisit cineres.   Hos gloria reddit honores.
Est locus exciso penitus demersus hiatu
Parthenopen inter magnaeque Dicarchidos arva,
Cocyti perfusus aqua; nam spiritus, extra
qui furit effusus, funesto spargitur aestu.   70
Non haec autumno tellus viret aut alit herbas

[1] plebem *Crusius:* praedam.
[2] excita *cod. Messaniensis:* excisa.

shame of the nation and the fall of their character lay in this, that here was not only one man's defeat. In his person the power and glory of Rome was humbled. So Rome in her deep disgrace was herself both price and prize, and despoiled herself without an avenger. Moreover filthy usury and the handling of money had caught the common people in a double whirlpool, and destroyed them. Not a house is safe, not a man but is mortgaged; the madness spreads through their limbs, and trouble bays and hounds them down like some disease sown in the dumb flesh. In despair they turn to violence, and bloodshed restores the good things lost by luxury. A beggar can risk everything in safety. Could the spell of healthful reason stir Rome from the filth where she rolled in heavy sleep, or only madness and war and the lust wakened by the sword?

"Fortune brought forth three generals, and the god- 120 dess of War and Death buried them all, each beneath a pile of arms. The Parthian has Crassus in keeping,[1] Pompey the Great lies by the Libyan water,[2] Julius stained ungrateful Rome with his blood; and as though the earth could not endure the burden of so many graves, she has separated their ashes. These are the wages paid by fame.

"Between Parthenope and the fields of the great town of Dicarchis there lies a spot[3] plunged deep in a cloven chasm, wet with the water of Cocytus: for the air that rushes furiously outward is laden with

[1] M. Licinius Crassus was defeated and killed by the Parthians at Carrhae, 53 B.C.

[2] C. Pompeius Magnus was killed on the shore at Pelusium in Egypt after his defeat at Pharsalus, 48 B.C.

[3] The Phlegraean Plain, between Naples and Puteoli. The latter town is here called Dicarchis after its founder Dicaearchus.

caespite laetus ager, non verno persona cantu
mollia discordi strepitu virgulta locuntur,
sed chaos et nigro squalentia pumice saxa
gaudent ferali circum tumulata cupressu.
Has inter sedes Ditis pater extulit ora
bustorum flammis et cana sparsa favilla,
ac tali volucrem Fortunam voce lacessit:
'Rerum humanarum divinarumque potestas,
Fors, cui nulla placet nimium secura potestas,   80
quae nova semper amas et mox possessa relinquis,
ecquid Romano sentis te pondere victam,
nec posse ulterius perituram extollere molem?
Ipsa suas vires odit Romana iuventus
et quas struxit opes, male sustinet.   Aspice late
luxuriam spoliorum et censum in damna furentem.
Aedificant auro sedesque ad sidera mittunt,
expelluntur aquae saxis, mare nascitur arvis,   ·
et permutata rerum statione rebellant.
En etiam mea regna petunt.   Perfossa dehiscit   90
molibus insanis tellus, iam montibus haustis
antra gemunt, et dum vanos[1] lapis invenit usus,
inferni manes caelum sperare fatentur.
Quare age, Fors, muta pacatum in proelia vultum
Romanosque cie ac nostris da funera reguis.
Iam pridem nullo perfundimus ora crnore,
nec mea Tisiphone sitientis perluit artus,

> [1] vanos *Delbenius:* vanus *O:* varios *L.*

that baleful spray. The ground here is never green in autumn, the field does not prosper or nurture herbage on its turf, the soft thickets never ring nor are loud in springtime with the songs of rival birds, but chaos is there, and gloomy rocks of black pumice-stone lie happy in the gloom of the cypresses that mound them about. From this place the father of Dis lifted his head, lit with funeral flames and flecked with white ashes, and provoked winged Fortune with these words:

"'Disposer of life in earth and heaven, Chance, always angry against power too firmly seated, everlasting lover of change and quick forsaker of thy conquests, dost not thou feel thy spirit crushed under the weight of Rome, and that thou canst not further raise up the mass that is doomed to fall? The youth of Rome contemns its own strength, and groans under the wealth its own hands have heaped up. See, everywhere they squander their spoils, and the mad use of wealth brings their destruction. They have buildings of gold and thrones raised to the stars, they drive out the waters with their piers, the sea springs forth amid the fields: rebellious man turns creation's order upside down. Aye, they grasp even at my kingdom. The earth is hewn through for their madmen's foundations and gapes wide, now the mountains are hollowed out until the caves groan, and while men turn precious stones to their empty purposes, the ghosts of hell declare their hopes of winning heaven. Arise, then, Chance, change thy looks of peace to war, harry the Roman, and let my kingdom have the dead. It is long now since my lips were wet with blood, and never has my loved Tisiphone bathed her thirsty limbs since the sword

ex quo Sullanus bibit ensis et horrida tellus
extulit in lucem nutritas sanguine fruges.'

121   Haec ubi dieta dedit, dextrae coniungere dextram
conatus rupto tellurem solvit biatu.   101
Tune Fortuna levi defudit pectore voces:
'*O* genitor, cui Cocyti penetralia parent,
si modo vera mihi fas est impune profari,
vota tibi cedent; nec enim minor ira rebellat
pectore in hoc leviorque exurit flamma medullas.
Omnia, quae tribui Romanis arcibus, odi
muneribusque meis irascor.   Destruct istas
idem, qui posuit, moles deus.   Et mihi cordi
quippe cremare viros et sanguine pascere luxum. 110
Cerno equidem gemina iam stratos morte Philippos
Thessaliaeque rogos et funera gentis Hiberae.
Iam fragor armorum trepidantes personat aures.
Et Libyae cerno tua, Nile, gementia claustra
Actiacosque sinus et Apollinis arma timentes.
Pande, age, terrarum sitientia regna tuarum
atque animas accerse novas.   Vix navita Porthmeus
sufficiet simulacra virum traducere cumba;

260

of Sulla[1] drank deep, and the earth stood thick with
corn fattened on blood and thrust up to the sun.'

"He spoke and ended, and strained to take her hand 121
in his, till he broke and clove the earth asunder. Then
Fortune poured forth words from her fickle heart:
'Father, whom the inmost places of Cocytus obey,
thy prayer shall prosper, if at least I may foretell the
truth without fear; for the anger that rises in my
heart is stern as thine, and the flame that burns deep
in my bones as fierce. I hate all the gifts I have made
to towering Rome, and am angry at my own blessings.
The god that raised up those high palaces shall destroy
them too. It will be my delight also to burn the men
and feed my lust with blood. Lo, already I see
Philippi's field strewn with the dead of two battles,[2]
and the blazing pyres of Thessaly[3] and the burial of
the people of Iberia.[4] Already the crash of arms rings
in my trembling ears. And in Libya I see the barriers
of the Nile[5] groan, and the people in terror at the gulf
of Actium and the army loved by Apollo.[6] Open, then,
the thirsty realms of thy dominion, and summon fresh
souls. The old sailor, the Ferryman, will scarc l have
strength to carry over the ghosts of the men in his

[1] The massacre of the supporters of Marius in 82 B.C.,
Sulla being Dictator.
[2] In the battles of Pharsalus, 48 B.C., the final defeat of
Pompey, and Philippi, 42 B.C., the defeat of the Republican
army under Brutus and Cassius.
[3] Again referring to Pharsalus, which is in Thessaly.
[4] Killed in Caesar's Spanish campaigns against the Pom-
peians, 49 and 45 B.C.
[5] The reference is to Caesar's Egyptian campaigns.
[6] The Emperor Augustus ascribed his victory over Antony
and Cleopatra at Actium in 31 B.C. to the favour of Apollo.

classe opus est.   Tuque ingenti satiare ruina,
pallida Tisiphone, concisaque vulnera mande: 120
ad Stygios manes laceratus ducitur orbis.'

122   Vixdum finierat, cum fulgure rupta corusco
intremuit nubes elisosque abscidit ignes.
Subsedit pater umbrarum, gremioque reducto
telluris pavitans fraternos palluit ictus.
Continuo clades hominum venturaque damna
auspiciis patuere deum.   Namque ore cruento
deformis Titan[1] vultum caligine texit:
civiles acies iam tum spectare[2] putares.
Parte alia plenos exstinxit Cynthia vultus   130
et lucem sceleri subduxit.   Rupta tonabant
verticibus lapsis montis inga, nec vaga passim
flumina per notas ibant morientia ripas.
Armorum strepitu caelum furit et tuba Martem
sideribus tremefacta ciet, iamque Aetna voratur
ignibus insolitis et in aethera fulmina mittit.
Ecce inter tumulos atque ossa carentia bustis
umbrarum facies diro stridore minantur.
Fax stellis comitata novis incendia ducit,
sanguineoque recens descendit Iuppiter imbre.   140
Haec ostenta brevi solvit deus.   Exuit omnes
quippe moras Caesar, vindictaeque actus amore
Gallica proiecit, civilia sustulit arma.
   Alpibus aeriis, ubi Graio numine[3] pulsae
descendunt rupes et se patiuntur adiri,

----

[1] Titan *Delbenius:* titubans.
[2] spectare *Crusius:* spirare (spitare *Bernensis*).
[3] numine *Reiske:* nomine.

boat; a whole fleet is needed. And thou, pale Tisiphone, take thy fill of wide destruction, and tear the bleeding wounds; the whole world is rent in pieces and drawn down to the Stygian shades.'

"She had scarc 1 ceased to speak when a cloud 122 shook and was riven by a gleam of lightning, and flashed forth a moment's burst of flame. The father of darkness sank down, closed the chasm in earth's bosom, and grew white with terror at the stroke of his brother. Straightway the slaughter of men and the destruction to come were made plain by omens from on high. For Titan was disfigured and dabbled in blood, and veiled his face in darkness: thou hadst thought that even then he gazed on civil strife. In another quarter Cynthia darkened her full face, and denied her light to the crime. The mountain-tops slid down and the peaks broke in thunder, the wandering streams were dying, and no more ranged abroad between their familiar banks. The sky is loud with the clash of arms, the trumpet shakes to the stars and rouses the War God, and at once Aetna is the prey of unaccustomed fires, and casts her lightnings high into the air. The faces of the dead are seen visible among the tombs and the unburied bones, gibbering in dreadful menace. A blazing light girt with unknown stars leads the way for the flames of cities, and the sky rains down fresh showers of blood. In a little while God made these portents plain. For now Caesar shook off all his lingering, and, spurred by the passion of revenge, threw down his arms against Gaul and took them up against Rome.

"In the high Alps, where the rocks trodden by a Greek god[1] slope downward and allow men to ap-

[1] Hercules was said to have been the first to cross the Alps.

est locus Herculeis aris sacer: hunc nive dura
claudit hiemps canoque ad sidera vertice tollit.
caelum illinc cecidisse putes: non solis adulti[1]
mansuescit radiis, non verni temporis aura,
sed glacie concreta rigent hiemisque pruinis: 150
totum ferre potest umeris minitantibus orhem.
Haec ubi calcavit Caesar inga milite laeto
optavitque[2] locum, summo de vertice montis
Hesperiae campos late prospexit et ambas
intentans cum voce manus ad sidera dixit:
'Iuppiter omnipotens, et te,[3] Saturnia tellus,
armis laeta meis olimque onerata triumphis,
testor, ad has acies invitum accersere Martem,
LO invitas me ferre manus.   Sed vulnere cogor,
pulsus ab urbe mea, dum Rhenum sanguine tinguo,
dum Gallos iterum Capitolia nostra petentes   161
Alpibus excludo, vincendo certior exsul.
Sanguine Germano sexagintaque triumphis
esse nocens coepi.   Quanquam quos gloria terret,
aut qui sunt qui bella vident?   Mercedibus emptae
ac viles operae, quorum est mea Roma noverca.
At[4] reor, hand impune, nec hanc sine vindice dextram
vinciet ignavus.   Victores ite furentes,
ite mei comites, et causam dicite ferro.
Namque omnes unum crimen vocat, omnibus una 170
impendet clades.   Reddenda est gratia vobis,
non solus vici.   Quare, quia poena tropaeis
imminet et sordes meruit victoria nostra,

[1] adulti *cod. Messaniensis:* adusti *other MSS.*
[2] optavit *margin of L:* oravit.
[3] te *Buecheler:* tu *L:* eu *O.*
[4] at *Heinsius:* ut.

proach them, there is a place sacred to the altars of
Hercules: the winter seals it with frozen snow, and
heaves it up on its white top to the sky. It seems as
though the sky had fallen away from there: the beams
of the full sun do not soften the place, nor the breezes
of the springtime, but the soil stands stiff with ice and
winter's frost: its frowning shoulders could support
the whole globe. When Caesar with his exultant
army trod these heights and chose a place, he looked
far over the fields of Hesperia from the high mountain-
top, and lifted his voice and both hands to the stars
and said: 'Jupiter, Lord of all, and thou land of
Saturn, once proud of my victories and loaded with my
triumphs, I call you to witness that I do not willingly
summon the War God to these hosts, and that my hand
is not raised willingly to strike. But I am driven on by
wounds, by banishment from my own city, while I dye
the Rhine with blood and cut off the Gauls from the
Alps on their second march to our Capitol.[1] Victory
makes my exile doubly sure. My rout of the Germans
and my sixty triumphs were the beginning of my
offences. Yet who is it that fears my fame, who are
the men that watch me fight? Base hirelings bought
at a price, to whom my native Rome is a stepmother.
But I think that no coward shall bind my strong
arm unhurt without a blow in return. Come, men, to
victory while anger is hot, come, my comrades, and
plead our cause with the sword. For we are all
summoned under one charge, and the same doom
bangs over us all. My thanks are your due, my
victory is not mine alone. Wherefore, since punishment threatens our trophies, and disgrace is the meed

[1] The traditional date for the sack of Rome by the Gauls
is 390 B.C.

iudice Fortuna cadat alea.　Sumite bellum

et temptate manus.　Certe mea causa peracta est:

inter tot fortes armatus nescio vinci.'

　　Haec ubi personuit, de caelo Delphicus ales

omina laeta dedit pepulitque meatibus auras.

Nec non horrendi nemoris de parte sinistra

insolitae voces flamma sonuere sequenti.　　　　　180

Ipse nitor Phoebi vulgato laetior orbe

crevit et aurato praecinxit fulgure vultus.

123 Fortior ominibus movit Mavortia signa

Caesar et insolitos gressu prior occupat ansus.

Prima quidem glacies et cana vineta pruina

non pugnavit·humus mitique horrore quievit.

Sed postquam turmac nimbos fregere ligatos

et pavidus quadrupes undarum vincula rupit,

incaluere nives.　Mox flumina montibus altis

undabant modo nata, sed haec quoque—iussa

　　putares—　　　　　　　　　　　　　　190

stabant, et vineta fluctus stupuere ruina,[1]

et paulo ante lues iam concidenda iacebat.

Tum vero male fida prius vestigia lusit

decepitque pedes; pariter turmaeque virique

armaque congesta strue deplorata iacebant.

Ecce etiam rigido concussae flamine nubes

exonerabantur, nec rupti turbine venti

derant aut tumida confractum grandine caelum.

LO Ipsae iam nubes ruptae super arma cadebant,

et concreta gelu ponti velut unda ruebat.　　　　200

Victa erat ingenti tellus nive victaque caeli

sidera, vieta suis haerentia flumina ripis;

nondum Caesar erat, sed magnam nixus in bastam

　　　　　[1] ruina *Reiske:* pruina.

of conquest, let Chance decide how our lot shall fall. Raise the standard and prove your strength. My pleading at least is accomplished; armed amid so many warriors I cannot know defeat.' As he spoke these words aloud, the Delphic bird[1] in the sky gave a happy omen, and beat the air as it flew. And from the left quarter of a gloomy grove strange voices sounded and fire flashed thereafter. Even Phoebus glowed with orb brighter than his wont, and set a burning halo of gold about his face.

"Heartened by these omens, Caesar advanced the 123 standards of war, and marched first to open this strange tale of daring. At first indeed the ice and the ground fettered with white frost did not fight against them, and lay quiet in the kindly cold. But then the regiments broke the close-bound clouds, the trembling horses shattered the frozen bonds of the waters, and the snows melted. Soon new-born rivers rolled from the mountain heights, but they, too, stood still as if by some command, and the waves stopped short with ruining floods enchained, and the water that ran a moment before now halted, hard enough to cut. But then, treacherous before, it mocked their steps and failed their footing; horses and men and arms together fell heaped in misery and ruin. Lo! too, the clouds were shaken by a strong wind, and let fall their burden, and round the army were gusts of whirlwind and a sky broken by swollen hail. Now the clouds themselves burst and fell on the armed men, and a mass of ice showered upon them like a wave of the sea. Earth was overwhelmed in the deep snow, and the stars of heaven, and the rivers that clung to their banks. But Caesar was not yet overwhelmed; he

[1] The raven, consecrated to Apollo on account of its gift of prophecy.

horrida securis frangebat gressibus arva,
qualis Caucasea decurrens arduus aree
Amphitryoniades, aut torvo Iuppiter ore,
cum se verticibus magni demisit Olympi
et periturorum disiecit[1] tela Gigantum.
 Dum Caesar tumidas iratus deprimit arces,
interea volucer motis conterrita pinnis   210
Fama volat summique petit inga celsa Palati
atque hoc Romano tonitru ferit omnia signa:
iam classes fluitare mari totasque per Alpes
fervere Germano perfusas sanguine turmas.
Arma, cruor, caedes, incendia totaque bella
ante oculos volitant. Ergo pulsata tumultu
pectora perque duas scinduntur territa causas.
Huic fuga per terras, illi magis unda probatur
et patria pontus iam tutior. Est magis arma
qui temptare velit fatisque iubentibus uti.   220
Quantum quisque timet, tantum fugit. Ocior ipse
hos inter motus populus, miserabile visu,
quo mens ieta iuhet, deserta ducitur urbe.
Gaudet Roma fuga, debellatique Quirites
rumoris sonitu maerentia tecta relinquunt.
Ille manu pavida natos tenet, ille penates
occultat gremio deploratumque relinquit
limen et absentem votis interficit bostem.
Sunt qui coniugibus maerentia pectora iungant,
grandaevosque patres onerisque ignara iuventus   230
id pro quo metuit, tantum trahit. Omnia secum
hic vehit imprudens praedamque in proelia ducit:

---

[1] disiecit *Gulielmus:* deiecit.

leaned on his tall spear and crushed the rough ground with fearless tread, like the son of Amphitryon[1] hastening down from a high peak of Caucasus, or the fierce countenance of Jupiter, when he descended from the heights of great Olympus and scattered the arms of the doomed Giants.

"While Caesar treads down the swelling peaks in his wrath, Rumour flies swift in terror with beating wings, and seeks out the lofty top of the tall Palatine. Then she strikes all the images of the gods with her message of Roman thunder: how ships are now sweeping the sea, and the horsemen red with German blood pouring hotly over the range of the Alps. Battle, blood, slaughter, fire, and the whole picture of war flits before their eyes. Their hearts shake in confusion, and are fearfully divided between two counsels. One man chooses flight by land, another trusts rather to the water, and the open sea now safer than his own country. Some prefer to attempt a fight and turn Fate's decree to account. As deep as a man's fear is, so far he flies. In the turmoil the people themselves, a woeful sight, are led swiftly out of the deserted city, whither their stricken heart drives them. Rome is glad to·flee, her true sons are cowed by war, and at a rumour's breath leave their houses to mourn. One holds his children with a shaking hand, one hides his household gods in his bosom, and weeping, leaves his door and calls down death on the unseen enemy. Some clasp their wives to them in tears, youths carry their aged sires, and, unused to burdens, take with them only what they dread to lose. The fool drags all his goods after him, and marches laden with booty to the battle: and

[1] Hercules: he came down to rescue Prometheus.

ac velut ex alto cum magnus inhorruit auster

et pulsas evertit aquas, non arma ministris,

non regimen prodest, ligat alter pondera pinus,

alter tuta sinus tranquillaque litora quaerit:

hic dat vela fugae Fortunaeque omnia credit.

Quid tam parva queror? Gemino cum consule Magnus,

ille tremor Ponti saevique repertor Hydaspis

et piratarum scopulus, modo quem ter ovantem 240

Iuppiter horruerat, quem fracto gurgite Pontus

et veneratus erat submissa Bosporos unda,

pro pudor, imperii deserto nomine fugit,

ut Fortuna levis Magni quoque terga videret.

124 Ergo tanta lues divum quoque numina vicit,[1]

consensitque fugae caeli timor. Ecce per orhem

mitis turba deum terras exosa furentes

deserit atque hominum damnatum avertitur agmen.

Pax prima ante alias niveos pulsata lacertos

abscondit galea victum caput atque relicto 250

orbe fugax Ditis petit inplacabile regnum.

Huic comes it submissa Fides et crine soluto

Iustitia ac maerens lacera Concordia palla.

At contra, sedes Erebi qua rupta dehiscit,

<hr>

[1] vicit *Hermann:* vidit.

all now is as when on high the rush of a strong south wind tumbles and drives the waters, and neither rigging nor hehn avail the crews, and one girds together the heavy planks of pine, another heads for quiet inlets and a waveless shore: a third sets sail and flees, and trusts all to Chance. But why sorrow for these petty ills? Pompey the Great, who made Pontus tremble and explored fierce Hydaspes,[1] the rock that broke the pirates,[2] who of late, in his third triumph, shook the heart of Jupiter, to whom the troubled waters of Pontus and the conquered Sea of Bosporus[3] bowed, flees shamefully with the two consuls[4] and lets his imperial title drop, that fickle Chance might see the back of great Pompey himself turned in flight.

"So great a calamity broke the power of the gods 124 also, and dread in heaven swelled the rout. A host of gentle deities throughout the world abandon the frenzied earth in loathing, and turn aside from the doomed army of mankind.

"Peace first of all, with her snow-white arms bruised, hides her vanquished head beneath her helmet, and leaves the world and turns in flight to the inexorable realm of Dis. At her side goes humble Faith and Justice with loosened hair, and Concord weeping with her cloak rent in pieces. But where the hall of Erebus is open and gapes wide, the dreadful company of Dis

[1] Untrue, for he went no further than the Euphrates: the river Hydaspes is in India.

[2] He cleared the Mediterranean of Cilician pirates in forty days during the year 67 B.C.

[3] He passed over these waters in 66 B.C. in the course of his campaign against Mithridates.

[4] C. Claudius Marcellus and L. Cornelius Lentulus Crus, consuls, 49 B.C.

emergit late Ditis chorus, horrida Erinys
et Bellona minax facibusque armata Megaera
Letumque Insidiaeque et lurida Mortis imago.
Quas inter Furor, abruptis ceu liber habenis,
sanguineum late tollit caput oraque mille
vulneribus confossa cruenta casside velat: 260
haeret detritus laevae Mavortius umbo
innumerabilibus telis gravis, atque flagranti
stipite dextra minax terris incendia portat.

    Sentit terra deos mutataque sidera pondus
quaesivere suum; namque omnis regia caeli
in partes diducta ruit. Primumque Dione
Caesaris acta sui ducit, comes additur illi
Pallas et ingentem quatiens Mavortius hastam.
Magnum[1] cum Phoebo soror et Cyllenia proles
excipit ac totis similis Tirynthius actis.   270

    Intremuere tubae ac scisso Discordia crine
extulit ad superos Stygium caput. Huius in ore
concretus sanguis, contusaque lumina flebant,
stabant aerati[2] scabra rubigine dentes,
tabo lingua fluens, obsessa draconibus ora,
atque inter torto laceratam pectore vestem
LO sanguineam tremula quatiebat lampada dextra.
Haec ut Cocyti tenebras et Tartara liquit,
alta petit gradiens iuga nobilis Appennini,

    [1] Magnum *cod. Messaniensis:* Magnaque *other MSS.*
    [2] aerati *L:* irati *O.*

    272

ranges forth, the grim Fury, and threatening Bellona,
Megaera whirling her torches, and Destruction, and
Treachery, and the pale presence of Death. And
among them Madness, like a steed loosed when the
reins snap, flings up her bloody head and shields her
face, scarred by a thousand wounds, with a blood-
stained helm; her left hand grips her worn martial
shield, heavy with countless spear-points, her right
waves a blazing brand and carries fire through the
world.

"Earth felt that the gods were there, the stars were
shaken, and swung seeking their former poise; for the
whole palace of the sky broke and tumbled to ruin.
And first Dione[1] champions the deeds of Caesar, and
Pallas joins her side, and the child of Mars,[2] who bran-
dishes his tall spear. "The sister[3] of Phoebus and the
son of Cyllene[4] and the hero of Tiryns,[5] like to him
in all his deeds, receive Pompey the Great.

"The trumpets shook, and Discord with dishevelled
hair raised her Stygian head to the upper sky. Blood
had dried on her face, tears ran from her bruised eyes,
her teeth were mailed with a scurf of rust, her tongue
was dripping with foulness and her face beset with
snakes, her clothes were torn before her writhen breasts,
and she waved a red torch in her quivering hand.
When she had left behind the darkness of Cocytus
and Tartarus, she strode forward to the high ridges of

---

[1] Venus, though properly Dione is the mother of Venus.
Caesar by convention was descended from her through
Iulus and Aeneas.
[2] Romulus, as son of Mars.
[3] Diana.
[4] Mercury, son of Maia and Zeus, born on Mount Cyllene.
[5] Hercules, who lived at Tiryns while he served Eurystheus.

unde omnes terras atque omnia litora posset   280

aspicere ac toto fluitantes orbe catervas,

atque has erumpit furibundo pectore voces:

'Sumite nunc gentes accensis mentibus arma,

sumite et in medias immittite lampadas urbes.

Vincetur, quicunque latet; non femina cesset,

non puer aut aevo iam desolata senectus;

ipsa tremat tellus lacerataque tecta rebellent.

Tu legem, Marcelle, tene. Tu concute plebem,

Curio. Tu fortem ne supprime, Lentule, Martem.

Quid porro tu, dive, tuis cunctaris in armis,   290

non frangis portas, non muris oppida solvis

thesaurosque rapis? Nescis tu, Magne, tueri

Romanas arces? Epidamni moenia quaere

Thessalicosque sinus humano sanguine tingue.'

    Factum est in terris, quicquid Discordia iussit."

    Cum haec Eumolpos ingenti volubilitate verborum effudisset, tandem Crotona intravimus. Ubi quidem parvo deversorio refecti, postero die amplioris fortunae domum quaerentes incidimus in turbam heredipetarum sciscitantium, quod genus hominum aut unde veniremus. Ex praescripto ergo consilii communis exaggerata

proud Apennine, to gaze down thence upon all the
earth and all its shores, and the armies streaming
over the whole globe; then these words were wrung
from her angry soul: 'To arms now, ye peoples,
while your spirit is hot, to arms, and set your
torches to the heart of cities. He that would hide
him shall be lost: let no women halt, nor children,
nor the old who are now wasted with age; let the
earth herself quake, and the shattered houses join the
fight. Thou Marcellus,[1] hold fast the law. Thou,
Curio,[2] make the rabble quail. Thou, Lentulus,[1] give
brave Mars no check. And thou, divine Caesar, why
art thou a laggard with thine arms? Crash down the
gates, strip towns of their walls and seize their treasure.
So Magnus knows not how to hold the hills of Rome?
Let him take the bulwarks of Epidamnus[3] and dye the
bays of Thessaly[4] with the blood of men.' Then all
the commands of Discord were fulfilled upon the
earth."

Eumolpus poured out these lines with immense
fluency, and at last we came into Croton. There we
refreshed ourselves in a little inn, but on the next day
we went to look for a house of greater pretensions,
and fell in with a crowd of fortune-hunters, who inquired what kind of men we were, and where we had
come from. Then, as arranged by our common council,

---

[1] See note on c. 123. The law was the Senatus consultum
of 49 B.C. ordering Caesar to give up his army.

[2] C. Scribonius Curio, a supporter of Caesar, who was
defeated and killed by Juba in Africa, 49 B.C.

[3] Dyrrhachium in Epirus, where Pompey entrenched himself on the outbreak of war.

[4] Cf. note on c. 121.

verborum volubilitate, unde aut qui essemus, hand
L dubie credentibus indicavimus. | Qui statim opes suas
summo cum certamine in Eumolpum congesserunt.

Certatim omnes heredipetae muneribus gratiam
Eumolpi sollicitant . . .

125 dum haec magno tempore Crotone aguntur . . .
et Eumolpus felicitate plenus prioris fortunae esset
oblitus statim adeo, ut suis iactaret, neminem gratiae
suae ibi posse resistere impuneque suos, si quid deli-
quissent in ea urbe, beneficio amicorum laturos.
Ceterum ego, etsi quotidie magis magisque super-
fluentibus bonis saginatum corpus impleveram puta-
bamque a custodia mei removisse vultum Fortunam,
tamen saepius tam consuetudinem meam cogitabam
quam causam, et "quid" aiebam "si callidus captator
exploratorem in Africam miserit mendaciumque de-
prehenderit nostrum? Quid, si etiam mercennarius
[Eumolpi] praesenti felicitate lassus indicium ad amicos detulerit totamque fallaciam invidiosa proditione
detexerit? Nempe rursus fugiendum erit et tandem
expugnata paupertas nova mendicitate revocanda.
Dii deaeque, quam male est extra legem viventibus:
quicquid meruerunt, semper exspectant." . . .

126 "Quia nosti venerem tuam, superbiam captas vendis-
que amplexus, non commodas. Quo enim spectant
flexae pectine comae, quo facies medicamine attrita
et oculorum quoque mollis petulantia, quo incessus
arte[1] compositus et ne vestigia quidem pedum extra
mensuram aberrantia, nisi quod formam prostituis, ut

[1] arte *Dousa:* tute.

276

a torrent of ready words burst from us, and they gave easy credence to our account of ourselves and our country. They at once quarrelled fiercely in their eagerness to heap their own riches on Eumolpus.

The fortune-hunters all competed to win Eumolpus's favour with presents. . . .

This went on for a long while in Croton, ... 125 Eumolpus was flushed with success, and so far forgot the former state of his fortunes as to boast to his intimates that no one there could cross his good pleasure; and that his own dependants would escape unpunished by the kindness of his friends if they committed any crime in that city. But though I had lined my belly well every day with the ever-growing supply of good things, and believed that Fortune had turned away her face from keeping a watch on me, still I often thought over my old life and my history, and kept saying to myself, "Supposing some cunning legacy-hunter sends a spy over to Africa and finds out our lies? Or supposing the servant grows weary of his present luck and gives his friends a hint, or betrays us out of spite, and exposes the whole plot? Of course we shall have to run away again; we must start afresh as beggars, and call back the poverty we have now at last driven out. Ah! gods and goddesses! the outlaw has a hard life; he is always waiting to get what he deserves." . . .

"Because you know your beauty you are haughty, 126 and do not bestow your embraces, but sell them. What is the object of your nicely combed hair, your face plastered with dyes, and the soft fondness even in your glance, and your walk arranged by art so that never a footstep strays from its place? It means of

277

vendas? Vides me: nec anguria novi nec mathemati-
corum caelum curare solco, ex vultibus tamen hominum
mores colligo, et cum spatiantem vidi, quid cogitet[1]
scio. Sive ergo nobis vendis quod peto, mercator paratus est, sive quod humanius est, commodas, effice ut
beneficium debeamus. Nam quod servum te et humilem
fateris, accendis desiderium aestuantis. Quaedam enim
feminae sordibus calent, nec libidinem concitant, nisi
aut servos viderint aut statores altius cinctos. Harena
alias accendit aut perfusus pulvere mulio aut histrio
scaenae ostentatione traductus. Ex hac nota domina
est mea: usque ab orchestra quattuordecim transilit
et in extrema plebe quaerit quod diligat."

Itaque oratione blandissima plenus "rogo" inquam
"numquid illa, quae me amat, tu es?' 'Multum risit
ancilla post tam frigidum schema et "nolo" inquit
"tibi tam valde placeas. Ego adhuc servo nunquam
succubui, nec hoc dii sinaut, ut amplexus meos in
crucem mittam. Viderint matronae, quae flagellorum
vestigia osculantur; ego etiam si ancilla sum, nunquam
tamen nisi in equestribus sedco." Mirari equidem
tam discordem libidinem coepi atque inter monstra
numerare, quod ancilla haberet matronae superbiam
et matrona ancillae humilitatem.

LO | Procedentibus deinde longius iocis rogavi ancillam,
ut in platanona perduceret dominam. Placuit puellae
consilium. Itaque collegit altius tunicam flexitque se

---

[1] cogitet *Burmann:* cogites.

course that you offer your comeliness freely for sale. Look at me; I know nothing of omens, and I never attend to the astrologer's sky, but I read character in a man's face, and when I see him walk I know his thoughts. So if you will sell us what I want, there is a buyer ready: if you will be more gracious and bestow it upon us, let us be indebted to you for a favour. For when you admit that you are a slave of low degree, you fan the passion of a lady who burns for you. Some women kindle for vile fellows, and cannot rouse any desire unless they have a slave or a servant in short garments in their eye. Some burn for a gladiator, or a muleteer smothered in dust, or an actor disgraced by exhibiting himself on the stage. My mistress is of this class; she skips fourteen rows away from the orchestra, and hunts for a lover among the low people at the back."

With my ears full of her winning words I then said, "It is not you, I suppose, who love me so?" The girl laughed loudly at such a clumsy turn of speech, and said, "Pray do not be so conceited. I never yielded to a slave yet, and God forbid that I should throw my arms round a gallows-bird. The married women may see to that, and kiss the scars of a flogging; I may be only a lady's maid, for all that I never sit down in any seats but the knights'." I began to marvel at their contrary passions, and to count them as portents, the maid having the pride of a married lady, and the married lady the low tastes of a wench.

Then as our jokes proceeded further, I asked the maid to bring her mistress into the grove of plane-trees. The plan pleased the girl. So she gathered her skirts up higher, and turned into the laurel grove

279

in eum daphnona, qui ambulationi haerebat. Nec diu
morata dominam producit e latebris laterique meo
applicat, mulierem omnibus simulacris emendatiorem.
Nulla vox est quae formam eius possit comprehendere,
nam quicquid dixero, minus erit. Crines ingenio suo
flexi per totos se umeros effuderant, frons minima et
quae radices capillorum retro flexerat, supercilia usque
ad malarum scripturam currentia et rursus confinio
luminum paene permixta, oculi clariores stellis extra
lunam fulgentibus, nares paululum inflexae et osculum
quale Praxiteles habere Dianam credidit. Iam mentum, iam cervix, iam manus, iam pedum candor intra
auri gracile vinculum positus: Parium marmor exstin-
xerat. Itaque tune primum Dorida vetus amator con-
tempsi . . .

Quid factum est, quod tu proiectis, Iuppiter, armis
    inter caelicolas fabula muta taces?
Nunc erat a torva submittere cornua fronte,
    nunc pluma canos dissimulare tuos.
Haec vera est Danae. Tempta modo tangere corpus,
    iam tua flammifero membra calore fluent . . .

127   Delectata illa risit tam blandum, ut videretur mihi
plenum os extra nubem luna proferre. Mox digitis
gubernantibus vocem "Si non fastidis" inquit "femi-

which grew close to our path. She was not long away before she led the lady out of her hiding-place, and brought her to my side. The woman was more perfect than any artist's dream. There are no words that can include all her beauty, and whatever I write must fall short of her. Her hair grew in natural waves and flowed all over her shoulders, her forehead was small, and the roots of her hair brushed back from it, her brows ran to the edge of her cheekbones and almost met again close beside her eyes, and those eyes were brighter than stars far from the moon, and her nose had a little curve, and her mouth was the kind that Praxiteles[1] dreamed Diana had. And her chin and her neck, and her hands, and the gleam of her foot under a light band of gold! She had turned the marble of Paros dull. So then at last I put my old passion for Doris to despise. . . .

"What is come to pass, Jupiter,[2] that thou hast cast away thine armour, and now art silent in heaven and become an idle tale? Now were a time for thee to let the horns sprout on thy lowering forehead, or hide thy white hair under a swan's feathers. This is the true Danae. Dare only to touch her body, and all thy limbs shall be loosened with fiery heat." . . .

She was happy, and smiled so sweetly that I thought 127 the full moon had shown me her face from behind a cloud. Then she said, letting the words escape through her fingers, "If you do not despise a rich

[1] The celebrated 4th century sculptor made for Mantinea a group (not extant) of Leto with Apollo and Artemis, a statue of Artemis Brauronia for Athens, and an Artemis for Anticyra.

[2] Jupiter, when he loved Europa, Leda, and Danae, appeared to them as a bull, a swan, and a shower of gold respectively.

nam ornatam et hoc primum anno virum expertam, concilio tibi, o iuvenis, sororem. Habes tu quidem et fratrem, neque enim me piguit inquirere, sed quid prohibet et sororem adoptare? Eodem gradu venio. Tu tantum dignare et meum osculum, cum libuerit, agnoscere." "Immo" inquam ego "per formam tuam te rogo, ne fastidias hominem peregrinum inter cultores admittere. Invenies religiosum, si te adorari permiseris. Ac ne me indices ad hoc templum Amoris gratis accedere, dono tibi fratrem meum." "Quid? tu"[1] inquit illa "donas mihi eum, sine quo non potes vivere, ex cuius osculo pendes, quem sic tu amas, quemadmodum ego te volo?" Haec ipsa cum diceret, tanta gratia conciliabat vocem loquentis, tam dulcis sonus pertemptatum mulcebat aëra, ut putares inter auras canere Sirenum concordiam. Itaque miranti [et] toto mihi caelo clarins nescio quid relucente libuit deae nomen quaerere. "Ita" inquit "non dixit tibi ancilla mea me Circen vocari? Non sum quidem Solis progenies, nec mea mater, dum placet, labentis mundi cursum detinuit. Habebo tamen quod caelo imputem, si nos fata coniunxerint. Immo iam nescio quid tacitis cogitationibus deus agit. Nec sine causa Polyaenon Circe amat: semper inter haec nomina magna fax surgit. Sume ergo amplexum, si placet. Neque est

[1] quid tu *Pithoeus:* quidni.

woman who has known a man first this very year, dear youth, I will give you a new sister. True, you have a brother, too, for I made bold to inquire, but why should you not take to yourself a sister as well? I will come as the same kind of relation. Deign only to recognize my kiss also when it is your good pleasure."

"I should rather implore you by your beauty," I replied, "not to scorn to enrol a stranger among your worshippers. You will find me a true votary, if you allow me to kneel before you. And do not think that I would enter this shrine of Love without an offering; I will give you my own brother."

"What," she said, "you give me the one without whom you cannot live, on whose lips you hang, whom you love as I would have you love me?" Even as she spoke grace made her words so attractive, the sweet noise fell so softly upon the listening air, that you seemed to have the harmony of the Sirens ringing in the breeze. So as I marvelled, and all the light of the sky somehow fell brighter upon me, I was moved to ask my goddess her name. "Then my maid did not tell you that I am called Circe?" she said. "I am not the Sun-child indeed, and my mother has never stayed the moving world in its course while she will. But I shall have a debt to pay to Heaven if fate brings you and me together. Sur l now, the Gods with their quiet thoughts have some plan in the making. Circe does not love Polyaenus [1] without good reason; when these two names meet, a great fire is always set ablaze. Then take me in your embrace if you like.

[1] Polyaenus is the name assumed by Encolpius at Croton. Circe in the Odyssey (Book X) is daughter of the Sun. Cf. c. 134: *Phoebeia Circe.*

283

quod curiosum aliquem extimescas: longe ab hoc loco frater est." Dixit haec Circe, implicitumque me brachiis mollioribus pluma deduxit in terram vario gramine indutam.

Idaeo quales fudit de vertice flores
terra parens, cum se concesso[1] iunxit amori
Iuppiter et toto concepit pectore flammas:
emicuere rosae violaeque et molle cyperon,
albaque de viridi riserunt lilia prato:
talis humus Venerem molles clamavit in herbas,
candidiorque dies secreto favit amori.

In hoc gramine pariter compositi mille osculis lusimus, quaerentes voluptatem robustam . . .

128L | "Quid est?" inquit "numquid te osculum meum offendit? Numquid spiritus ieiunio marcens?[2] Numquid alarum negligens sudor? Aut[3] si haec non sunt, numquid Gitona times?" Perfusus ego rubore manifesto etiam si quid habueram virium, perdidi, totoque corpore velut luxato[4] "quaeso" inquam "regina, noli suggillare miserias. Veneficio contactus sum" . . .

"Dic, Chrysis, sed verum: numquid indecens sum? Numquid incompta? Numquid ab aliquo naturali vitio formam meam excaeco? Noli decipere dominam tuam. Nescio quid peccavimus." Rapuit deinde tacenti speculum, et postquam omnes vultus temptavit, quos solet inter amantes risus fingere, excussit vexatam solo vestem raptimque aedem Veneris intravit. Ego contra damnatus et quasi quodam visu in horrorem perductus interrogare animum meum coepi, an vera voluptate fraudatus essem.

[1] concesso *Sambucus:* confesso.
[2] marcens *Buecheler:* macer.
[3] Aut *Buecheler:* puto.
[4] luxato *Jungermann:* laxato.

You need have no fear of any spy; your brother is far away from here."

Circe was silent, folded me in two arms softer than a bird's wing, and drew me to the ground on a carpet of coloured flowers.

"Such flowers as Earth, our mother, spread on Ida's top when Jupiter embraced her and she yielded her love, and all his heart was kindled with fire: roses glowed there, and violets, and the tender flowering rush; and white lilies laughed from the green grass: such a soil summoned Venus to the soft grasses, and the day grew brighter and looked kindly on their hidden pleasure."

We lay together there among the flowers and exchanged a thousand light kisses, but we looked for sterner play. . . .

"Tell me," she cried, "do you find no joy in my 128 lips? Nor in the breath that faints with hunger? Nor in my body wet with heat? If it is none of these, are you afraid of Giton?" I crimsoned with blushes under her eyes, and lost any strength I might have had before, and cried as though there were no whole part in my body, "Dear lady, have mercy, do not mock my grief. Some poison has infected me." . . .

"Speak to me, Chrysis, tell me true: am I ugly or untidy? Is there some natural blemish that darkens my beauty? Do not deceive your own mistress. I know not how, but I have sinned." She then snatched a glass from the silent girl, and after trying every look that raises a smile to most lovers' lips, she shook out the cloak the earth had stained, and hurried into the temple of Venus. But I was lost and horror-stricken as if I had seen a ghost, and began to inquire of my heart whether I was cheated of my true delight.

TITUS PETRONIUS ARBITER

LO | Nocte soporifera veluti cum somnia ludunt
errantes oculos effossaque protulit aurum
in lucem tellus: versat manus improba furtum
thesaurosque rapit, sudor quoque perluit ora
et mentem timor altus habet, ne forte gravatum
excutiat gremium secreti conscius auri:
mox ubi fugerunt elusam gaudia mentem
veraqne forma redit, animus, quod perdidit, optat
atque in praeterita se totus imagine versat . . .

L | "Itaque hoc nomine tibi gratias ago, quod me
Socratica fide diligis. Non tam intactus Alcibiades
in praeceptoris sui lecto iacuit" . . .

129 "Crede mihi, frater, non intellego me virum esse,
non sentio. Funerata est illa pars corporis, qua quondam Achilles eram" . . .

Veritus puer, ne in secreto deprehensus daret sermonibus locum, proripuit se et in partem aedium in-
teriorem fugit . . .

LO | cubiculum autem meum Chrysis intravit codicil-
losque mihi dominae suae reddidit, in quibus haec
erant scripta: "Circe Polyaeno salutem. Si libidinosa
essem, quererer decepta; nunc etiam languori tuo
gratias ago. In umbra voluptatis diutius lusi. Quid
tamen agas, quaero, et an tuis pedibus perveneris
domum; negant enim medici sine nervis homines
ámbulare posse. Narrabo tibi, adulescens, paralysin
cave. Nunquam ego aegrum tam magno periculo vidi;
medius fidius iam peristi. Quod si idem frigus genua
manusque temptaverit tuas, licet ad tubicines mittas.

As when dreams deceive our wandering eyes in the heavy slumber of night, and under the spade the earth yields gold to the light of day: our greedy hands finger the spoil and snatch at the treasure, sweat too runs down our face, and a deep fear grips our heart that maybe some one will shake out our laden bosom, where he knows the gold is hid: soon, when these pleasures flee from the brain they mocked, and the true shape of things comes back, our mind is eager for what is lost, and moves with all its force among the shadows of the past. . . .

"So in his name I give you thanks for loving me as true as Socrates. Alcibiades never lay so unspotted in his master's bed." . . .

"I tell you, brother, I do not realize that I am a man, I do not feel it. That part of my body where I was once an Achilles is dead and buried." . . .

The boy was afraid that he might give an opening for scandal if he were caught in a quiet place with me, and tore himself away and fled into an inner part of the house. . . .

Chrysis came into my room and gave me a letter from her mistress, who wrote as follows: "Circe greets Polyaenus. If I were a passionate woman, I should feel betrayed and hurt: as it is I can be thankful even for your coldness. I have amused myself too long with the shadow of pleasure. But I should like to know how you are, and whether your feet carried you safely home; the doctors say that people who have lost their sinews cannot walk. I tell you what, young man, you must beware of paralysis. I have never seen a sick person in such grave danger; I declare you are as good as dead. If the same mortal chill attacks your knees and hands, you may send for

129

287

Quid ergo est? Etiam si gravem iniuriam accepi,
bomini tamen misero non invideo medicinam. Si
vis sanus esse, Gitonem roga. Recipies, inquam, nervos
tuos, si triduo sine fratre dormieris. Nam quod ad me
attinet, non timeo, ne quis inveniatur cui minus pla-
ceam. Nec speculum mihi nec fama mentitur. Vale,
si potes."

Ut intellexit Chrysis perlegisse me totum convicium,
"Solent" inquit "haec fieri, et praecipue in hac civitate, in qua mulieres etiam lunam deducunt . . . itaque
huius quoque rei cura agetur. Rescribe modo blandins
dominae animumque eius candida humanitate restitue.
Verum enim fatendum est: ex qua hora iniuriam accepit, apud se non est." Libenter quidem parui an-
130 cillae verhaque codicillis talia imposui: "Polyaenos
Circae salutem. Fateor me, domina, saepe peccasse;
nam et homo sum et adhuc iuvenis. Nunquam tamen
ante hunc diem usque ad mortem deliqui. Habes con-
fitentem reum: quicquid iusseris, merui. Proditionem
feci, hominem occidi, templum violavi: in haec faci-
nora quaere supplicium. Sive occidere placet, ferro
meo venio, sive verberibus contenta es, curro nudus
ad dominam. Illud unum memento, non me sed instrumenta peccasse. Paratus miles arma non habui.
Quis hoc turbaverit, nescio. Forsitan animus antecessit
corporis moram, forsitan dum omnia concupisco, voluptatem tempore consumpsi. Non invenio, quod feci.
Paralysin tamen eavere iubes: tanquam ea[1] maior fieri

----

[1] ea *Buecheler:* iam.

the funeral trumpeters. And what about me? Well,
even if I have been deeply wounded, I do not grudge
a poor man a cure. If you want to get well, ask
Giton. I think you will recover your sinews if you
sleep for three days without your brother. So far as
I am concerned, I am not afraid of finding anyone
who dislikes me more. My looking-glass and my
reputation do not lie. Keep as well as you can."

When Chrysis saw that I had read through the
whole of this complaint, she said: "These things
often happen, especially in this town, where the women
can even draw down the moon from the sky, and so
attention will be paid to this matter also. Only do
write back more gently to my mistress, and restore her
spirits by your frank kindness. For I must tell you
the truth: she has never been herself from the
moment you insulted her."

I obeyed the girl with pleasure and wrote on 130
a tablet as follows: "Polyaenus greets Circe.
Dear lady, I admit my many failings; for I am
human, and still young. But never before this day
have I committed deadly sin. The culprit confesses
to you; I have deserved whatever you may order. I
have been a traitor, I have destroyed a man, and pro-
faned a temple: demand my punishment for these
crimes. If you decide on execution, I will come with
my sword; if you let me off with a flogging, I will run
naked to my lady. Illud unum memento, non me
sed instrumenta peccasse. Paratus miles arma non
habui. Who upset me so I know not. Perhaps my
will ran on while my body lagged behind, perhaps I
wasted all my pleasure in delay by desiring too much.
I cannot discover what I did. But you tell me to
beware of paralysis: as if the disease could grow

possit, quae abstulit mihi, per quod etiam te habere potui. Summa tamen excusationis meae haec est: placebo tibi, si me culpam emendare permiseris"...

L | Dimissa cum eiusmodi pollicitatione Chryside curavi diligentius noxiosissimum corpus, balneoque praeterito modica unctione usus, mox cibis validioribus pastus, id est hulhis cochlearumque sine iure cervicibus, hausi parcius merum. Hinc ante somnum levissima ambulatione compositus sine Gitone cubiculum intravi. Tanta erat placandi cura, ut timerem, ne

131 latus meum frater convelleret. Postero die, cum sine offensa corporis animique consurrexissem, in eundem platanona descendi, etiam si locum inauspicatum timebam, coepique inter arbores ducem itineris exspectare Chrysidem. Nec diu spatiatus consederam, ubi hesterno die fueram, cum illa intus venit[1] comitem aniculam trabens. Atque ut me consalutavit, "Quid est" inquit "fastose, ecquid bonam mentem habere coepisti?"

Illa de sinu licium protulit varii coloris filis intortum cervicemque vinxit meam. Mox turbatum sputo pulverem medio sustulit digito frontemque repugnantis signavit...

Hoc peracto carmine ter me iussit exspuere terque lapillos conicere in sinum, quos ipsa praecantatos purpura involverat, admotisque manibus temptare coepit inguinum vires. Dicto citius nervi paruerunt imperio manusque aniculae ingenti motu repleverunt. At illa

---

[1] intus venit *Buecheler*: intervenit.

worse, which has taken away from me the means of making you my own. But my apology amounts to this—I will do your pleasure if you allow me to mend my fault." ...

Chrysis was sent off with this promise, and I paid great attention to my offending body, and after leaving my bath anointed myself in moderation, and then fed on strong foods, onions, I mean, and snails' heads without sauce, and drank sparingly of wine. I then settled myself with a gentle walk before bed, and went into my room without Giton. I was so anxious to please her that I was afraid my brother might take away my strength. Next day I got up sound in mind 131 and body, and went down to the same grove of plane-trees, though I was rather afraid of the unlucky place, and began to wait among the trees for Chrysis to lead me on my way.

After walking up and down a short while, I sat where I had been the day before, and Chrysis came under the trees, bringing an old woman with her. When she had greeted me, she said, "Well, disdainful lover, have you begun to come to your senses?" Then the old woman took a twist of threads of different colours out of her dress, and tied it round my neck. Then she mixed some dust with spittle, and took it on her middle finger, and made a mark on my forehead despite my protest. ...

After this she ordered me in a rhyme to spit three times and throw stones into my bosom three times, after she had said a spell over them and wrapped them in purple, and laid her hands on me and began to try the force of her charm. ... Dieto citius nervi parue-runt imperio manusque aniculae ingenti motu reple-

gaudio exsultans "Vides" inquit "Chrysis mea, vides, quod aliis leporem excitavi?" . . .

LO | Nobilis aestivas platanus diffuderat umbras
et bacis redimita Daphne tremulaeque cupressus
et circum tonsae trepidanti vertice pinus.
Has inter ludebat aquis errantibus amnis
spumeus et querulo vexabat rore lapillos.
Dignus amore locus : testis silvestris aedon
atque urbana Procne, quae circum gramina fusae
ac molles violas cantu sua furta[1] colebant . . .

Premebat illa resoluta marmoreis cervicibus aureum torum myrtoque florenti quietum . . . verberabat. Itaque ut me vidit, paululum erubuit, hesternae scilicet iniuriae memor; deinde ut remotis omnibus secundum invitantem consedi, ramum super oculos meos posuit, et quasi pariete interiecto audacior facta "Quid est" inquit "paralytice? ecquid hodie totus venisti?" "Rogas" inquam ego "potins quam temptas?" Totoque corpore in amplexum eius immissus non praecantatis usque ad satietatem osculis fruor . . .

132L | Ipsa corporis pulchritudine me ad se vocante trahebat ad venerem. Iam pluribus osculis collisa labra crepitabant, iam implicitae manus omne genus amoris invenerant, iam alligata mutuo ambitu corpora animarum quoque mixturam fecerant . . .

Manifestis matrona·contumeliis verberata tandem ad ultionem decurrit vocatque cubicularios et me iubet catomidiari.[2] Nec contenta mulier tam gravi iniuria

---

[1] furta *Buecheler:* sura *or* rura.
[2] catomidiari *Salmasius:* catarogare.

292

verunt. At illa gaudio exsultans "Vides" inquit "Chrysis mea, vides, quod aliis leporem excitavi?"...

The stately plane-tree, and Daphne decked with berries, and the quivering cypresses, and the swaying tops of the shorn pines, cast a summer shade. Among them played the straying waters of a foamy river, lashing the pebbles with its chattering flow. The place was proper to love; so the nightingale of the woods bore witness, and Procne from the town, as they hovered about the grasses and the tender violets, and pursued their stolen loves with a song. . . .

She was stretched out there with her marble neck pressed on a golden bed, brushing her placid face with a spray of myrtle in flower. So when she saw me she blushed a little, of course remembering my rudeness the day before; then, when they had all left us, she asked me to sit by her, and I did; she laid the sprig of myrtle over my eyes, and then growing holder, as if she had put a wall between us, "Well, poor paralytic," she said, "have you come here to-day a whole man?" "Do not ask me," I replied, "try me." I threw myself eagerly into her arms, and enjoyed her kisses unchecked by any magic until I was tired. . . .

The loveliness of her body called to me and drew 132 us together. There was the sound of a rain of kisses as our lips met, our hands were clasped and discovered all the ways of love, then our bodies were held and bound by our embrace until even our souls were made as one soul. . . .

My open taunts stung the lady, and at last she ran to avenge herself, and called her chamber grooms, and ordered me to be hoisted for flogging. Not content with this black insult, the woman called up all her low

mea convocat omnes quasillarias familiaeque sordidissimam partem ac me conspui inhet. Oppono ego manus oculis meis, nullisque effusis precibus, quia sciebam quid meruissem, verberibus sputisque[1] . . . extra ianuam eiectus sum. Eicitur et Proselenos, Chrysis, vapulat, totaque familia tristis inter se mussat quaeritque, quis dominae hilaritatem confuderit . . .

Itaque pensatis vicibus animosior verberum notas arte contexi, ne aut Eumolpus contumelia mea hilarior *LO* fieret aut tristior Giton. | Quod solum igitur salvo pudore poteram, contingere languorem simulavi, conditusque lectulo totum ignem furoris in eam converti, quae mihi omnium malorum causa fuerat :

> ter corripui terribilem manu bipennem,
> ter languidior coliculi repente thyrso
> ferrum timui, quod trepido male dabat usum.
> Nec iam poteram, quod modo conficere libebat;
> namque illa metu frigidior rigente bruma
> confugerat in viscera mille operta rugis.
> Ita non potui supplicio caput aperire,
> sed furciferae mortifero timore lusus
> ad verba, magis quae poterant nocere, fugi.

Erectus igitur in cubitum hac fere oratione contumacem vexavi: "Quid dicis" inquam "omnium hominum deorumque pudor? Nam ne nominare quidem te inter res serias fas est. Hoc de te merui, ut me in *L* caelo positum ad inferos traheres? | Ut traduceres annos primo florentes vigore senectaeque ultimae mihi lassitudinem imponeres? Rogo te, mihi apodixin defunctoriam redde." Haec ut iratus effudi,

[1] *Buecheler would insert* obrutus.

spinsters, and the very dregs of her slaves, and invited them to spit upon me. I put my hands to my eyes and never poured forth any appeal, for I knew my deserts, and was beaten and spat upon and thrown out of doors. Proselenos was thrown out too, Chrysis was flogged, and all the slaves muttered gloomily to themselves, and asked who had upset their mistress's spirits. . . . So after considering my position I took courage, and carefully hid the marks of the lasb for fear Eumolpus should exult or Giton be depressed at my disgrace. | Quod solum igitur salvo pudore poteram, contingere languorem simulavi, conditusque lectulo totum ignem furoris in eam converti, quae mihi omnium malorum causa fuerat:

ter corripui terribilem manu bipennem,
ter languidior coliculi repente thyrso
ferrum timui, quod trepido male dabat usum.
Nec iam poteram, quod modo conficere libebat;
namque illa metu frigidior rigente bruma
confugerat in viscera mille operta rugis.
Ita non potui supplicio caput aperire,
sed furciferae mortifero timore lusus
ad verba, magis quae poterant nocere, fugi.

Erectus igitur in cubitum hac fere oratione contumacem vexavi: "Quid dicis" inquam "omnium hominum deorumque pudor? Nam ne nominare quidem te inter res serias fas est. Hoc de te merui, ut me in caelo positum ad inferos traheres? | Ut traduceres L annos primo florentes vigore senectaeque ultimae mihi lassitudinem imponeres? Rogo te, mihi apodixin defunctoriam redde." Haec ut iratus effudi,

295

TITUS PETRONIUS ARBITER

LO | illa solo fixos oculos aversa tenebat,
nec magis incepto vultum sermone movetur
quam lentae salices lassove papavera collo.

Nec minus ego tam foeda obiurgatione finita paenitentiam agere sermonis mei coepi secretoque rubore
perfundi, quod oblitus verecundiae meae cum ea parte
corporis verba contulerim, quam ne ad cognitionem
quidem admittere severioris notae homines solerent.
Mox perfricata diutius fronte "Quid autem ego" inquam "mali feci, si dolorem meum naturali convicio
exoneravi? Aut quid est quod in corpore humano
ventri male dicere solemus aut gulae capitique etiam,
cum saepius dolet? Quid? Non et Vlixes cum corde
L litigat suo, | et quidam tragici oculos suos tanquam
audientes castigant? Podagrici pedibus suis male
dicunt, chiragrici manibus, lippi oculis, et qui offen-
derunt saepe digitos, quicquid doloris habent, in pedes
deferunt:
LO | Quid me constricta spectatis fronte Catones
damnatisque novae simplicitatis opus?
Sermonis puri non tristis gratia ridet,
quodque facit populus, candida lingua refert.
Nam quis concubitus, Veneris quis gaudia nescit?
Quis vetat[1] in tepido membra calere toro?
Ipse pater veri doctos Epicurus amare[2]
iussit, et hoc vitam dixit habere τέλος" . . .
L | "Nihil est hominum inepta persuasione falsius nec
ficta severitate ineptius" . . .
133 LO | Hac declamatione finita Gitona voco et "Narra
mihi" inquam "frater, sed tua fide: ea nocte, qua te
mihi Ascyltos subduxit, usque in iniuriam vigilavit,

[1] vetat *Dousa:* petat.
[2] doctos — — amare *Dousa:* doctus — — in arte.

296

| illa solo fixos oculos aversa teuchat,   *LO*
nec magis incepto vultum sermone movetur
quam lentae salices lassove papavera collo.

Nec minus ego tam foeda obiurgatione finita paenitentiam agere sermonis mei coepi secretoque rubore
perfundi, quod oblitus verecundiae mcae cum ea parte
corporis verba contulerim, quam ne ad cognitionem
quidem admittere severioris notae homines solerent.

Then, after rubbing my forehead for a long while, I
said, "But what harm have I done if I have relieved
my sorrow with some free abuse?   And then there is
the fact that of our bodily members we often damn
our guts, our throats, even our heads, when they give
us much trouble.   Did not Ulysses argue with his own
heart,[1] while some tragedians curse their eyes as if
they could hear?   Gouty people damn their feet,
people with chalk-stones their hands, blear-eyed
people their eyes, and men who have often hurt their
toes put down all their ills to their poor feet:

"Why do ye, Cato's disciples, look at me with
wrinkled foreheads, and condemn a work of fresh simplicity? A cheerful kindness laughs through my pure
speech, and my clean mouth reports whatever the
people do. All men born know of mating and the
joys of love; all men are free to let their limbs glow
in a warm bed. Epicurus, the true father of truth,
bade wise men be lovers, and said that therein lay the
crown of life." . . .

There is nothing more insincere than people's silly
convictions, or more silly than their sham morality. . . .

When my speech was over, I called Giton, and said, **133**
"Now tell me, brother, on your honour. That night
when Ascyltos took you away from me, did he keep

[1] In the line τέτλαθι δὴ, κραδιή, καὶ κύντερον ἄλλο τοτ᾽ ἔτλης.

297

an contentus fuit vidua pudicaque nocte?" Tetigit
puer oculos suos conceptissimisque iuravit verbis sibi
ab Ascylto nullam vim factam . . .

Positoque in limine genu sic deprecatus sum numina
versu:

"Nympharum Bacchique comes, quem pulchra Dione
divitibus silvis numen dedit, inclita paret
cui Lesbos viridisque Thasos, quem Lydus adorat
semper ovans[1] templumque suis[2] imponit Hypaepis:
huc ades et Bacchi tutor Dryadumque voluptas,
et timidas admitte preces.   Non sanguine tristi
perfusus venio, non templis impius hostis
admovi dextram, sed inops et rebus egenis
attritus facinus non toto corpore feci.
Quisquis peccat inops, minor est reus. Hac prece quaeso,
exonera mentem culpaeque ignosce minori,
et quandoque mihi fortunae arriserit hora,
non sine honore tuum patiar decus.   Ibit ad aras,
sancte tuas hircus, pecoris pater, ibit ad aras
corniger et querulae fetus[3] suis, bostia lactens.
Spumabit pateris bornus liquor, et ter ovantem
circa delubrum gressum feret ebria pubes" . . .

Dum haec ago curaque sollerti deposito meo caveo,
intravit delubrum anus laceratis crinibus nigraque
veste deformis, extraque vestibulum me iniecta manu
duxit . . .

134L   "Quae striges comederunt nervos tuos, aut quod
purgamentum nocte calcasti in trivio aut cadaver? Ne

---

[1] septifluus *most MSS.:* semperflavius *cod. Bernensis:* vesti-
fluus *Turnebus:* semper ovans *Buecheler.*
[2] suis *Jungermann:* tuis.
[3] fetus *Sambucus:* festus.

awake until he had wronged you, or was he satisfied with spending the night decently alone?" The boy touched his eyes and swore a most precise oath that Ascyltos had used no force to him. . . .

I kneeled down on the threshold and entreated the favour of the gods in these lines:

"Comrade of the Nymphs and Bacchus, whom lovely Dione set as god over the wide forests, whom famous Lesbos and green Thasos obey, whom the Lydian worships in perpetual celebration, whose temple he has set in his own city of Hypaepa: come hither, guardian of Bacchus and the Dryads' delight, and hear my humble prayer. I come not to thee stained with dark blood, I have not laid hands on a temple like a wicked enemy, but when I was poor and worn with want I sinned, yet not with my whole body. There is less guilt in a poor man's sin. This is my prayer; take the load from my mind, forgive a light offence; and whenever fortune's season smiles upon me, I will not leave thy glory without worship. A goat shall walk to thine altars, most holy one, a horned goat that is father of the flock, and the young of a grunting sow, a tender sacrifice. The new wine of the year shall foam in the bowls, and the young men full of wine shall trace their joyous steps three times round thy sanctuary." . . .

As I was doing this and making clever plans to guard my trust, an old woman in ugly black clothes, with her hair down, came into the shrine, laid hands on me, and drew me out through the porch. . . .

"What screech-owl has eaten your nerve away, **134** what foul thing or corpse have you trodden on at a cross-road in the dark? Never even in boyhood

a puero quidem te vindicasti, sed mollis, debilis, lassus
tanquam caballus in clivo, et operam et sudorem per-
didisti. Nec contentus ipse peccare, mihi deos iratos
excitasti"[1] . .

LO | Ac me iterum in cellam sacerdotis nihil recusantem
perduxit impulitque super lectum et harundinem ab
ostio rapuit iterumque nihil respondentem mulcavit.
Ac nisi primo ictu harundo quassata impetum verbe-
rantis minuisset, forsitan etiam brachia mea caputque
fregisset. Ingemui ego utique propter mascarpionem,
lacrimisque ubertim manantibus obscuratum dextra
caput super pulvinum inclinavi. Nec minus illa fletu
confusa altera parte lectuli sedit aetatisque longae
moram tremulis vocibus coepit accusare, donec intervenit sacerdos.

"Quid vos" inquit "in cellam meam tanquam ante
O recens bustum venistis? | Utique die feriarum, quo
etiam lngentes rident."

LO | "O" inquit "Oenothea, hunc adulescentem quem
vides : malo astro natus est; nam neque puero neque
L puellae bona sua vendere potest. | Nunquam tu homi-
nem tam infelicem vidisti : lorum in aqua, non inguina
LO habet. | Ad summam, qnalem putas esse, qui de Circes
L toro sine voluptate surrexit?" | His auditis Oenothea
inter utrumque consedit motoque diutius capite
"Istum" inquit "morbum sola sum quae emendare scio.
Et ne *me* putetis perplexe agere, rogo ut adulescentulus
mecum nocte dormiat . . .
nisi illud tam rigidum reddidero quam cornu :

[1] excitasti *Wouwer:* extricasti.

300

could you hold your own, but you were weakly, feeble, tired, and like a cab-horse on a hill you wasted your efforts and your sweat. And not content with failing yourself, you have roused the gods to wrath against me." . . .

And she took me unresisting into the priestess's room again, and pushed me over the bed, and took a cane off the door and beat me again when I remained unresponsive. And if the cane had not broken at the first stroke and lessened the force of the blow, I daresay she would have broken my head and my arm outright. Anyhow I groaned at her dirty tricks, and wept abundantly, and covered my head with my right arm, and leaned against the pillow. She was upset, and cried too, and sat on another piece of the bed, and began to curse the delays of old age in a quavering voice, when the priestess came in.

"Why have you come into my room as if you were visiting a fresh-made grave?" she said. "Especially on a holiday, when even mourners smile." "Ah, Oenothea," said the woman, "this young man was born under a bad planet; he cannot sell his treasure to boys or girls either. You never beheld such an unlucky creature: he is a piece of wash-leather, not a real man. Just to show you, what do you think of a man who can come away from Circe without a spark of pleasure?" When Oenothea heard this she sat down between us, shook her head for some time, and then said, "I am the only woman alive who knows how to cure that disease. Et ne *me* putetis perplexe agere, rogo ut adulescentulus mecum nocte dormiat . . .

nisi illud tam rigidum reddidero quam cornu:

LO | Quicquid in orbe vides, paret mihi. Florida tellus,
cum volo, siccatis arescit languida sueis,
cum volo, fundit opes, scopulique atque horrida saxa
Niliacas iaculantur aquas. Mihi pontus inertes
submittit fluctus, zephyrique tacentia ponunt
ante meos sua flabra pedes. Mihi flumina parent
Hyrcanaeque tigres et iussi stare dracones.
Quid leviora loquor? Lunae descendit imago
carminibus deducta meis, trepidusque furentes
flectere Phoebus equos revoluto cogitur orbe.
Tantum dicta valent. Taurorum flamma quiescit
virgineis exstincta sacris, Phoebeia Circe
carminibus magicis socios mutavit Vlixis,
Proteus esse solet quicquid libet. His ego callens
artibus Idaeos frutices in gurgite sistam
et rursus fluvios in summo vertice ponam."

135 Inhorrui ego tam fabulosa pollicitatione conterritus,
anumque inspicere diligentius coepi . . .
"Ergo" exclamat Oenothea "imperio parete" . . .
detersisque curiose manibus inclinavit se in lectulum
ac me semel iterumque basiavit . . .

L | Oenothea mensam veterem posuit in medio altari,
quam vivis implevit carbonibus, et camellam etiam
vetustate ruptam pice temperata refecit. Tum clavum,
qui detrahentem secutus cum camella lignea fuerat,
LO fumoso parieti reddidit. | Mox incincta quadrato pallio
cucumam ingentem foco apposuit, simulque pannum
de carnario detulit furca, in quo faba erat ad usum
L reposita | et sincipitis vetustissima particula mille

"Whatever thou seest in the world is obedient to me. The flowery earth, when I will, faints and withers as its juices dry, and, when I will, pours forth its riches, while rocks and rough crags spurt waters wide as the Nile. The great sea lays its waves lifeless before me, and the winds lower their blasts in silence at my feet. The rivers obey me, and Hyrcanian tigers, and serpents, whom I bid stand still. But I will not tell you of small things; the shape of the moon is drawn down to me by my spells, and Phoebus trembles and must turn his fiery steeds as I compel him back in his course. So great is the power of words. The flaming spirit of bulls is quenched and calmed by a maiden's rites, and Circe, the child of Phoebus, transfigured Ulysses's crew with magic songs, and Proteus can take what form he will. And I, who am cunning in these arts, can plant the bushes of Mount Ida in the sea, or set rivers back on lofty peaks."

I shrank in horror from her promised miracles, and 135 began to look at the old woman more carefully. . . . "Now," cried Oenothea, "obey my orders!" and she wiped her hands carefully, leaned over the bed, and kissed me once, twice . . . .

Oenothea put up an old table in the middle of the altar, and covered it with live coals, and repaired a wine-cup that had cracked from age with warm pitch. Then she drove in once more on the smoky wall a nail which had come away with the wooden wine-cup when she took it down. Then she put on a square cloak, and laid an enormous cooking-pot on the hearth, and at the same time took off the meat-hooks with a fork a bag which had in it some beans put by for use, and some very mouldy pieces of a brain smashed into

303

LO plagis dolata. | Ut solvit ergo licio pannum, partem leguminis super mensam effudit iussitque me diligenter purgare. Servio ego imperio granaque sordidissimis putaminibus vestita curiosa manu segrego. At illa inertiam meam accusans improba tollit, dentibusque folliculos pariter spoliat atque in terram veluti muscarum imagines despuit . . .

Mirabar equidem paupertatis ingenium singularumque rerum quasdam artes:

Non Indum fulgebat ebur, quod inhaeserat auro,
nec iam calcato radiabat marmore terra .
muneribus delusa suis, sed crate saligna
impositum Cereris vacuae nemus et nova terrae
pocula, quae facili vilis rota finxerat actu.[1]
Hinc molli stillae lacus et de candice lento
vimineae lances maculataque testa Lyaeo.
At paries circa palea satiatus inani
fortuitoque luto clavos[2] numerabat agrestes,
et viridi iunco gracilis pendebat harundo.
Praeterea quae fumoso suspensa tigillo
conservabat opes humilis casa, mitia sorba
inter odoratas pendebant texta coronas
et thymbrae veteres et passis uva racemis:
qualis in Actaea quondam fuit hospita terra,
digna sacris Hecales, quam Musa loquentibus annis
Battiadae vatis mirandam tradidit aevo . . .

136 Dum illa carnis etiam paululum delibat . . .
et dum coaequale natalium suorum sinciput in carnarium furca reponit, fracta est putris sella, quae

[1] actu *margin of L:* astu *or* bastu.
[2] clavos *Sambucus:* clavus.

a thousand fragments. After unfastening the bag she poured out some of the beans on the table, and told me to shell them carefully. I obeyed orders, and my careful fingers parted the kernels from their dirty covering of shell. But she reproved me for laziness, snatched them up in a hurry, tore off the shells with her teeth in a moment, and spat them on to the ground like the empty husks of flies. . .

I marvelled at the resources of poverty, and the art displayed in each particular. 'No Indian ivory set in gold shone here, the earth did not gleam with marble now trodden upon and mocked for the gifts she gave, but the grove of Ceres on her holiday was set round with hurdles of willow twigs and fresh cups of clay shaped by a quick turn of the lowly wheel. There was a vessel for soft honey, and wicker-work plates of pliant bark, and a jar dyed with the blood of Bacchus. And the wall round was covered with light chaff and spattered mud; on it hung rows of rude nails and slim stalks of green rushes. Besides this, the little cottage roofed with smoky beams preserved their goods, the soft service-berries hung entwined in fragrant wreaths, and dried savory and bunches of raisins; such a hostess was here as was once on Athenian soil, worthy of the worship of Hecale,[1] of whom the Muse testified for all ages to adore her, in the years when the poet of Cyrene sang.'

While she was having a small mouthful of meat as 136 well, . . . and was replacing the brain, which must have been born on her own birthday, on the jack with her fork, the rotten stool which she was using to increase

---

[1] Hecale was a poor woman who entertained Theseus. The poet Callimachus (a native of Cyrene, founded by Aristotle of Thera, called Battus) wrote a famous epic called after her.

staturae altitudinem adiecerat, anumque pondere
suo deiectam super foculum mittit. Frangitur ergo
cervix cucumulae ignemque modo convalescentem
L restinguit. | Vexat cubitum ipsa stipite ardenti |
LO faciemque totam excitato cinere perfundit. Consurrexi equidem turbatus anumque non sine risu
erexi . . .

L | Statimque, ne res aliqua sacrificium moraretur, ad
reficiendum ignem in viciniam cucurrit. . . .

O | Itaque ad casac ostiolum processi . . .

LO|L | cum ecce tres anseres sacri | qui, ut puto medio
LO die solebant ab anu diaria exigere, | impetum in
me faciunt foedoque ac veluti rabioso stridore
circumsistunt trepidantem. Atque alius tunicam
meam lacerat, abus vincula calceamentorum resolvit
ac trahit; unus etiam, dux ac magister saevitiae,
non dubitavit crus meum serrato vexare morsu.
Oblitus itaque nugarum pedem mensulae extorsi
coepique pugnacissimum animal armata elidere
manu. Nec satiatus defunctorio ictu, morte me
anseris vindicavi:

> Tales Herculea Stymphalidas arte coactas
> ad caelum fugisse reor, pennaeque fluentis
> Harpyias, cum Phineo maduere veneno
> fallaces epulae. Tremuit perterritus aether
> planctibus insolitis, confusaque regia caeli . . .

L | Iam reliqui revolutam passimque per totum effusam
pavimentum collegerant faham, orbatique, ut existimo,
duce redierant in templum, cum ego praeda simul
atque [hac] vindicta gaudens post lectum occisum
anserem mitto vulnusque cruris baud altum aceto

306

her height broke, and the old woman's weight sent her down on to the hearth. So the neck of the pot broke and put out the fire, which was just getting up. A glowing brand touched her elbow, and her whole face was covered with the ashes she scattered. I jumped up in confusion and put the old woman straight, not without a laugh. . . .. She ran off to her neighbours to see to reviving the fire, to prevent anything keeping the ceremony back. . . . So I went to the door of the house, . . . when all at once three sacred geese, who I suppose generally demanded their daily food from the old woman at mid-day, made a rush at me, and stood round me while I trembled, cackling borribly like. mad things. One tore my clothes, another untied the strings of my sandals and tugged them off; the third, the ringleader and chief of the brutes, lost no time in attacking my leg with his jagged bill. It was no laughing matter: I wrenched off a leg of the table and began to hammer the ferocious creature with this weapon in my hand. One simple blow did not content me. I avenged my honour by the death of the goose.

'Even so I suppose the birds of Stymphalus fled into the sky when the power of Hercules compelled them, and the Harpies whose reeking wings made the tantalizing food of Phineus run with poison. The air above trembled and shook with unwonted lamentation, and the palace of heaven was in an uproar.' . . .

The remaining geese had now picked up the beans, which were spilt and scattered all over the floor, and having lost their leader had gone back, I think, to the temple. Then I came in, proud of my prize and my victory, threw the dead goose behind the bed, and bathed the wound on my leg, which was not

diluo. Deinde convicium verens abeundi formavi consilium, collectoque cultu meo ire extra casam coepi. Necdum superaveram[1] cellulae limen, cum animadverto Oenotheam cum testo ignis pleno venientem. Reduxi igitur gradum proiectaque veste, tanquam exspectarem morantem, in aditu steti. Collocavit illa ignem cassis harundinibus collectum, ingestisque super pluribus lignis excusare coepit moram, quod amica se non dimisisset nisi tribus potionibus e lege siccatis. "Quid" porro "tu" inquit "me absente fecisti, aut ubi est faba?" Ego, qui putaveram me rem laude etiam dignam fecisse, ordine illi totum proelium exposui, et ne diutius tristis esset, iacturae pensionem anserem

LO obtuli. Quem | anus ut vidit, tam magnum acque clamorem sustulit, ut putares iterum anseres limen intrasse. Confusus itaque et novitate facinoris attoni-

137 tus quaerebam, quid excanduisset, aut quare anseris potins quam mei misereretur. At illa complosis manibus "Scelerate" inquit "etiam loqueris? Nescis quam magnum flagitium admiseris: occidisti Priapi delicias, anserem omnibus matronis acceptissimum. Itaque ne te putes nihil egisse, si magistratus hoc scierint, ibis in crucem. Polluisti sanguine domicilium meum ante hunc diem inviolatum, fecistique ut me, quisquis voluerit inimicus, sacerdotio pellat." ...

L | "Rogo" inquam "noli clamare: ego tibi pro ansere struthocamelum reddam" ...

---

[1] superaveram *Turnebus:* liberaveram *or* libaveram.

deep, with vinegar. Then, being afraid of a scolding, I made a plan for getting away, put my things together, and started to leave the house. I had not yet got outside the room, when I saw Oenothea coming with a jar full of live coals. So I drew back and threw off my coat, and stood in the entrance as if I were waiting for her return. She made up a fire which she raised out of some broken reeds, and after heaping on a quantity of wood, began to apologize for her delay, saying that her friend would not let her go until the customary three glasses had been emptied. "What did you do while I was away?" she went on, "and where are the beans?" Thinking that I had done something which deserved a word of praise, I described the whole of my fight in detail, and to put an end to her depression I produced the goose as a set-off to her losses. When the old woman saw the bird, she raised such a great shriek that you would have thought that the geese had come back into the room again. I was astonished and shocked to find so strange a crime at my door, and I asked her why she had flared up, and why she should be more sorry for the goose than for me. But she beat her hands together 137 and said, "You villain, you dare to speak. Do you not know what a dreadful sin you have committed? You have killed the darling of Priapus, the goose beloved of all married women. And do not suppose that it is not serious; if any magistrate finds out, on the cross you go. My house was spotless until to-day, and you have defiled it with blood, and you have given any enemy of mine who likes the power to turn me out of my priesthood." . . .

"Not such a noise, please," I said; "I will give you an ostrich to replace the goose." . . .

· Dum haec me stupente in lectulo sedet anserisque·
fatum complorat, interim Proselenos cum impensa
sacrificii venit, visoque ansere occiso sciscitata causam
tristitiae et ipsa flere vehementius coepit meique
misereri, tanquam patrem meum, non publicum
anserem, occidissem. Itaque taedio fatigatus "rogo".
inquam "expiare manus pretio liceat[1] . . .

si vos provocassem, etiam si homicidium fecissem.
Ecce duos aureos pono, unde possitis et deos et anseres
emere." Quos ut vidit Oenothea, "ignosce" inquit
"adulescens, sollicita sum tua causa. Amoris est hoc
argumentum, non malignitatis. Itaque dabimus operam, ne quis seiat. Tu modo deos roga, ut illi facto
tuo ignoscant."

LO | Quisquis habet nummos, secura navigat[2] aura
    fortunamque suo temperat arbitrio.
Uxorem ducat Danaen ipsumque licebit
    Acrisium iubeat credere quod Danaen.
Carmina componat, declamet, concrepet omnes
    et peragat causas sitque Catone prior.
Iurisconsultus "parret, non parret" habeto
    atque esto quicquid Servius et Labeo.
Multa loquor: quod vis, nummis praesentibus opta,
    et veniet. Clausum possidet arca Iovem . . .

L | Infra manus meas camellam vini posuit, et cum
digitos pariter extensos porris apioque lustrasset,
abellanas nuces cum precatione mersit in vinum. Et
sive in summum redierant, sive subsederant, ex hoc

----

[1]liceat *Dousa:* licet.
[2]navigat *Vincentius:* naviget.

. I was amazed, and the woman sat on the bed and wept over the death of the goose, until Proselenos came in with materials for the sacrifice, and seeing the dead bird, inquired why we were so depressed. When she found out she began to weep loudly, too, and to compassionate me as if I had killed my own father instead of a common goose. I grew tired and disgusted, and said, "Please let me cleanse my hands by paying; it would be another thing if I had insulted you or done a murder. Look, I will put down two gold pieces. You can buy both gods and geese for that." When Oenothea saw the money, she said, "Forgive me, young man, I am troubled on your account. I am showing my love and not my ill-will. So we will do our best to keep the secret. But pray the gods to pardon what you have done."

"Whoever has money sails in a fair wind, and directs his fortune at his own pleasure. Let him take Danae' to wife, and he can tell Acrisius to believe what he told Danae. Let him write poetry, make speeches, snap his fingers at the world, win his cases and outdo Cato. A lawyer, let him have his 'Proven' and his 'Not proven,' and be all that Servius and Labeo were. I have said enough: with money about you, wish for what you like and it will come. Your safe has Jupiter shut up in it." . . .

She stood a jar of wine under my hands, and made me stretch all my fingers out, and rubbed them with leeks and parsley, and threw filberts into the wine with a prayer. She drew her conclusions from them according

coniecturam ducebat.[1] Nec me fallebat inanes scilicet ac sine medulla ventosas nuces in summo umore consistere, graves autem et plenas integro fructu ad ima deferri . .

Recluso pectore extraxit fartissimum[2] iecur et inde mihi futura praedixit.

Immo, ne quod vestigium sceleris superesset, totum anserem laceratum verubus confixit epulasque etiam lautas paulo ante, ut ipsa dicebat, perituro paravit. . . .

Volabant inter haec potiones meracae . . .

138 ' Profert Oenothea scorteum fascinum, quod ut oleo et minuto pipere atque urticae trito circumdedit semine, paulatim coepit inserere ano meo. . . .

Hoc crudelissima anus spargit subinde umore femina mea . . .

Nasturcii sucum cum habrotono miscet perfusisque inguinibus meis viridis urticae fascem comprehendit omniaque infra umbilicum coepit lenta manu caedere...

Aniculae quamvis solutae mero ac libidine essent, eandem viam tentant et per aliquot vicos secutae fugientem "Prende furem" clamant. Evasi tamen omnibus digitis inter praecipitem decursum cruentatis . . .

"Chrysis, quae priorem fortunam tuam oderat, hanc vel cum periculo capitis persequi destinat" . . .

"Quid huic formae aut Ariadne habuit aut Leda simile? Quid contra hanc Helene, quid Venus posset? Ipse Paris, dearum litigantium[3] index, si hanc in compa-

---

[1] hoc *Goldast:* hac   coniecturam ducebat *Dousa:* coniectura dicebat.

[2] fartissimum *Heinsius:* fortissimum.

[3] litigantium *Dousa:* libidinantium.

as they rose to the top or sank. I noticed that the nuts which were empty and had no kernel, but were filled with air, stayed on the surface, while the heavy ones, which were ripe and full, were carried to the bottom. . . .

She cut the goose open, drew out a very fat liver, and foretold the future to me from it. Further, to remove all traces of my crime, she ran the goose right through with a spit, and made quite a fine meal for me, though I had been at death's door a moment ago, as she told me. . . .

Cups of neat wine went swiftly round with it. . . .

Profert Oenothea scorteum fascinum, quod ut oleo 138 et minuto pipere atque urticae trito circumdedit semine, paulatim coepit inserere ano meo. . . .

Hoc crudelissima anus spargit subinde umore femina mea . . .

Nasturcii sucum cum habrotono miscet perfusisque inguinibus meis viridis urticae fascem comprehendit omniaque infra umbilicum coepit lenta manu caedere . . .

Though the poor old things were silly with drink and passion they tried to take the same road, and pursued me through several streets, crying "Stop thief!" But I escaped, with all my toes running blood in my headlong flight. . . .

"Chrysis, who despised your lot before, means to follow you now even at peril of her life." . . .

"Ariadne and Leda had no beauty like hers. Helen and Venus would be nothing beside her. And Paris himself, who decided the quarrel of the goddesses,[1] would have made over Helen and the goddesses too to her, if his eager gaze had seen her to compare

[1] Paris judged the claims of Hera, Aphrodite and Athena to the golden apple inscribed "To the fairesr," which Eris threw among the guests at the wedding of Peleus and Thetis, and awarded it to Aphrodite.

ratione vidisset tam petulantibus oculis, et Helenen
huie donasset et deas. Saltem si permitteretur osen-
lum capere, si illud caeleste ac divinum pectus
amplecti forsitan rediret hoc corpus ad vires et
resipiscerent partes veneficio, credo, sopitae. Nec me
contumeliae lassant: quod verberatus sum, nescio;
quod eiectus sum, lusum puto. Modo redire in gratiam liceat"....

139 Torum frequenti tractatione vexavi, amoris mei
quasi quandam imaginem ...

"Non solum me numen et implacabile fatum
persequitur. Prius Inachia Tirynthius ora
exagitatus onus caeli tulit, ante profanam
Laomedon gemini satiavit numinis iram,
Iunonem Pelias sensit, tulit inscius arma
Telephus et regnum Neptuni pavit Vlixes.
Me quoque per terras, per cani Nereos aequor
Hellespontiaci sequitur gravis ira Priapi"....

Quaerere a Gitone meo coepi, num aliquis me
quaesisset. "Nemo" inquit "hodie. Sed hesterno die
mulier quaedam haud inculta ianuam intravit, cumque
diu mecum esset locuta et me accersito sermone las-
sasset, ultimo coepit dicere, te noxam meruisse datu-
rumque serviles poenas, si laesus in querella perseve-
rasset"....

314

with them. If only I were allowed a kiss, or could put my arms round the body that is heaven's own self; maybe my body would come back to its strength, and the part of me that is drowsed with poison, I believe, might be itself again. . No insult turns me back; I forget my floggings, and I think it fine sport to be flung out of doors. Only let her be kind to me again." . . .

I moved uneasily over the bed again and again, as 139 if I sought for the ghost of my love . . . .

'I am not the only one whom God and an inexorable doom pursues. Before me the son of Tiryns was driven from the Inachian shore and bore the burden of heaven, and Laomedon before me satisfied the ominous wrath of two gods.[1] Pelias felt Juno's power, Telephus [2] fought in ignorance, and Ulysses was in awe of Neptune's kingdom.[3] And me too the heavy wrath of Hellespontine Priapus follows over the earth and over the waters of hoary Nereus.' . . .

I began to inquire of Giton whether anyone had asked for me. "No one to-day," he said, "but yesterday a rather pretty woman came in at the door, and talked to me for a long while, till I was tired of her forced conversation, and then began to say that you deserved to be hurt and would have the tortures of a slave, if your adversary persisted with his complaint." . . .

[1] He cheated Apollo and Neptune of their wages for building Troy. *See* Homer, *Iliad* xxiii, 442: Horace, *Odes*, iii. 3.
[2] He was king of Mysia and fought the Greeks who were driven ashore in his country on their way to Troy. Achilles wounded him with the miraculous spear of Chiron. (Murray, *Euripides*, p. 345.)
[3] The Odyssey is the record of the wanderings of Ulysses by sea.

315

Nondum querellam finieram, cum Chrysis intervenit amplexuque effusissimo me invasit et "Teneo te" inquit "qualem speraveram: tu desiderium meum, tu voluptas mea, nunquam finies hunc ignem, nisi sanguine exstinxeris" . . .

Unus ex noviciis servulis subito accurrit et mihi dominum iratissimum esse affirmavit, quod biduo iam officio defuissem. Recte ergo me facturum, si excusationem aliquam idoneam praeparassem. Vix enim posse fieri, ut rabies irascentis sine verbere consideret . . .

140 Matrona inter primas honesta, Philomela nomine, quae multas saepe hereditates officio aetatis extorserat, tum anus et floris exstincti, filium filiamque ingerebat orbis senibus, et per hanc successionem artem suam perseverabat extendere. Ea ergo ad Eumolpum venit et commendare liberos suos eius prudentiae bonitatique.... credere se et vota sua. Illum esse solum in toto orbe terrarum, qui praeceptis etiam salubribus instruere iuvenes quotidie posset. Ad summam, relinquere se pueros in domo Eumolpi, ut illum loquentem audirent . . . quae sola posset hereditas iuvenibus dari. Nec aliter fecit ac dixerat, filiamque speciosissimam cum fratre ephebo in cubiculo reliquit simulavitque se in templum ire ad vota nuncupanda. Eumolpus, qui tam frugi erat ut illi etiam ego   viderer, non distulit puellam invitare ad pigiciaca puer sacra. Sed et podagricum se esse lumborumque solutorum omnibus dixerat, et si non servasset integram simulationem, periclitabatur totam paene tragoediam evertere. Itaque ut constaret mendacio fides, puellam quidem exoravit, ut sederet super commendatam bonitatem, Coraci autem imperavit, ut lectum, in quo ipse iacebat, subiret positisque

[1] pugesiaca *margin of L.*

I had not finished grumbling, when Chrysis came in, ran up and warmly embraced me, and said, "Now I have you as I hoped; you are my desire, my pleasure, you will never put out this flame unless you quench it in my blood." . . .

One of the new slaves suddenly ran up and said that my master was furious with me because I had now been away from work two days. The best thing I could do would be to get ready some suitable excuse. It was hardly possible that his savage wrath would abate without a flogging for me. . . .

Matrona inter primas honesta, Philomela nomine, 140 quae multas saepe hereditates officio aetatis extorserat, tum anus et floris extincti, filium filiamque ingerebat orbis senibus, et per hanc successionem artem suam perseverabat extendere. Ea ergo ad Eumolpum venit et commendare liberos suos eius prudentiae bonitatique . . . credere se et vota sua. Illum esse solum in toto orbe terrarum, qui praeceptis etiam salubribus instruere iuvenes quotidie posset. Ad summam, relinquere se pueros in domo Eumolpi, ut illum loquentem audirent . . . quae sola posset hereditas iuvenibus dari. Nec aliter fecit ac dixerat, filiamque speciosissimam cum fratre epheboin cubiculo reliquit simulavitque se in templum ire ad vota nuncupanda. Eumolpus, qui tam frugi erat ut illi etiam ego puer viderer, non distulit puellam invitare ad pigiciaca[1] sacra. Sed et podagricum se esse lumborumque solutorum omnibus dixerat, et si non servasset integram simulationem, periclitabatur totam paene tragoediam evertere. Itaque ut constaret mendacio fides, puellam quidem exoravit, ut sederet super commendatam bonitatem, Coraci autem imperavit, ut lectum, in quo ipse iacebat, subiret positisque

in pavimento manibus dominum lumbis suis commoveret. Ille lente[1] parebat imperio puellaeque artificium pari motu remunerabat. Cum ergo res ad effectum spectaret, clara Eumolpus voce exhortabatur Coraca, ut spissaret officium. Sic inter mercennarium amicamque positus senex veluti oscillatione ludebat. Hoc semel iterumque ingenti risn, etiam suo, Eumolpus fecerat. Itaque ego quoque, ne desidia consuetudinem perderem, dum frater sororis suae automata per clostellum miratur, accessi temptaturus, an pateretur iniuriam. Nec se reiciebat a blanditiis doctissimus puer, sed me numen inimicum ibi quoque invenit . . .

"Dii maiores sunt, qui me restituerunt in integrum. Mercurius enim, qui animas ducere et reducere solet, suis beneficiis reddidit mihi, quod manus irata praeciderat, ut scias me gratiosiorem esse quam Protesilaum aut' quemquam alium antiquorum." Haec locutus sustuli tunicam Eumolpoque me totum approbavi. At ille primo exhorruit, deinde ut plurimum crederet, utraque manu deorum beneficia tractat . . .

"Socrates, deorum hominumque . . ., gloriari solebat, quod nunquam neque in tabernam conspexerat nec ullius turbae frequentioris concilio oculos suos crediderat. Adeo nihil est commodius quam semper cum sapientia loqui."

"Omnia" inquam "ista vera sunt; nec ulli enim celerius homines incidere debent in malam fortunam, quam qui alienum concupiscunt. Unde plani autem, unde levatores viverent, nisi aut locellos aut sonantes aere sacellos pro hamis in turbam mitterent? Sicut muta animalia cibo inescantur, sic homines non caperentur nisi spei aliquid morderent" , . .

[1] lente *Scioppius:* lento.

in pavimento manibus dominum lumbis suis commoveret. Ille lente parebat imperio puellaeque artificium
pari motu remunerabat. Cum ergo res ad effectum
spectaret, clara Eumolpus voce exhortabatur Coraca,
ut spissaret officium. Sic inter mercennarium amicamque positus senex veluti oscillatione ludebat. Hoc
semel iterumque ingenti risu, etiam suo, Eumolpus
fecerat. Itaque ego quoque, ne desidia consuetudinem
perderem, dum frater sororis suae automata per clostellum miratur, accessi temptaturus, an pateretur
iniuriam. Nec se reiciebat a blanditiis doctissimus
puer, sed me numen inimicum ibi quoque invenit ... .

"Dii maiores sunt, qui me restituerunt in integrum.
Mercurius enim, qui animas ducere et reducere solet,
suis beneficiis reddidit mihi, quod manus irata praeciderat, ut scias me gratiosiorem esse quam Protesilaum [1]
aut quemquam alium antiquorum." Haec locutus
sustuli tunicam Eumolpoque me totum approbavi. At
ille primo exhorruit, deinde ut plurimum crederet,
utraque manu deorum beneficia tractat . . .

"Socrates, the friend of God and man, used to
boast that he had never peeped into a shop, or allowed
his eyes to rest on any large crowd. So nothing is
more blessed than always to converse with wisdom."

"All that is very true," I said, "and no one deserves
to fall into misery sooner than the covetous. But how
would cheats or pickpockets live, if they did not ex-
pose little boxes or purses jingling with money, like
hooks, to collect a crowd? Just as dumb creatures
are snared by food, human beings would not be caught
unless they had a nibble of hope." . . .

---

[1] He was allowed to revisit earth after death. *See* Words-
worth's *Laodamia*.

141 "Ex Africa navis, ut promiseras, cum pecunia tua et
familia non venit. Captatores iam exhausti liberali-
tatem imminuerunt. Itaque aut fallor, aut fortuna
communis coepit redire ad paenitentiam tuam"[1] . . .

"Omnes, qui in testamento meo legata habent,
praeter libertos meos hac condicione percipient, quae
dedi, si corpus meum in partes conciderint et astante
populo comederint" . . .

"Apud quasdam gentes scimus adhuc legem servari,
ut a propinquis suis consumantur defuncti, adeo quidem, ut obiurgentur aegri frequenter, quod carnem
suam faciant peiorem. His admoneo amicos meos, ne
recusent quae iubeo, sed quibus animis devoverint
spiritum meum, eisdem etiam corpus consumant" . . .

Excaecabat pecuniae ingens fama oculos animosque
miserorum.

Gorgia paratus erat exsequi . . .

"De stomachi tui recusatione non habeo quod
timeam. Sequetur imperium, si promiseris illi pro
unius horae fastidio multorum honorum pensationem.
Operi modo oculos et finge te non humana viscera sed
centies sestertium comesse. Accedit huc, quod aliqua
inveniemus blandimenta, quibus saporem mutemus.
Neque enim ulla carc per se placet, sed arte quadam
corrumpitur et stomacho conciliatur averso. Quod si
exemplis quoque vis probari consilium, Saguntini
oppressi ab Hannibale humanas edere carnes, nec

[1] tuam *Busch:* suam.

320

"The ship from Africa with your money and slaves 141 that you promised does not arrive. The fortune-hunters are tired out, and their generosity is shrinking. So that unless I am mistaken, our usual luck is on its way back to punish you."...

"All those who come into money under my will, except my own children, will get what I have left them on one condition, that they cut my body in pieces and eat it up in sight of the crowd."...

"We know that in some countries a law is still observed, that dead people shall be eaten by their relations, and the result is that sick people are often blamed for spoiling their own flesh. So I warn my friends not to disobey my orders, but to eat my body as heartily as they damned my soul."...

His great reputation for wealth dulled the eyes and brains of the fools. Gorgias was ready to manage the funeral....

"I am not at all afraid of your stomach turning. You will get it under control if you promise to repay it for one unpleasant hour with heaps of good things. Just shut your eyes and dream you are eating up a solid million instead of human flesh. Besides, we shall find some kind of sauce which will take the taste away. No flesh at all is pleasant in itself, it has to be artificially disguised and reconciled to the unwilling digestion. But if you wish the plan to be supported by precedents, the people of Saguntum,[1] when Hannibal besieged them, ate human flesh without any legacy in

---

[1] Saguntum fell in 218 B.C. after an eight months' siege.

ʜereditatem exspectabant. Petelini[1] idem fecerunt in ultima fame, nec quicquam aliud in hac epulatione captabant, nisi tantum ne esurirent. Cum esset Numantia a Scipione capta, inventae sunt matres, quae liberorum suorum tenerent semesa in sinu corpora" . . .

[1] Petelini *Puteanus:* Petavii.

prospect. The people of Petelia[1] did likewise in the extremities of famine, and gained nothing by the diet, except of course that they were no longer hungry. And when Numantia was stormed by Scipio,[2] some women were found with the half-eaten bodies of their children hidden in their bosoms." . . .

[1] A town in the territory of the Bruttii, who were subdued by Rome in the 3rd century B.C.

[2] In 133 B.C. after fifteen months' blockade. The fall of the city established the supremacy of Rome in Spain.

FRAGMENTA

I

Servius ad Vergili Aen. III 57: auri sacra fames]
sacra id est execrabilis. Tractus est autem sermo ex
more Gallorum. Nam Massilienses quotiens pestilentia laborabant, unus se ex pauperibus offerebat
alendus anno integro publicis *sumptibus* et purioribus
cibis. Hic postea ornatus verbenis et vestibus sacris
circumducebatur per totam civitatem cum exsecratio-
nibus, ut in ipsum reciderent mala totius civitatis, et
sic proiciebatur. Hoc autem in Petronio lectum est

II

*Servius ad Vergili Aen. XII 159 de feminino nominum
in* TOR *exeuntium genere:* Si autem a verbo non venerint, communia sunt. Nam similiter et masculina et
feminina in TOR exeunt, ut hic et haec senator, hic et
haec balneator, licet Petronius usurpaverit "balneatricem" dicens

III

Pseudacro ad Horati epod. 5, 48: Canidia rodens
pollicem] habitum et motum Canidiae expressit
furentis. Petronius ut monstraret furentem, "pollice"
ait "usque ad periculum roso"

324

FRAGMENTS

I

Servius on Virgil, Aeneid III, 57: " The sacred hunger for gold." "Sacred" means "accursed." This expression is derived from a Gallie custom. For whenever the people of Massilia were burdened with pestilence, one of the poor would volunteer to be fed for an entire year out of public funds on food of special purity. After this period he would be decked with sacred herbs and sacred robes, and would be led through the whole state while people cursed him, in order that the sufferings of the whole state might fall upon him, and so he would be cast out. This account has been given in Petronius.

II

Servius on Virgil, Aeneid XII, 159, on the feminine gender of nouns ending in -tor: But if they are not derived from a verb they are common in gender. For in these cases both the masculine and the feminine end alike in -tor, for example, senator, a male or female senator, balneator, a male or female bath attendant, though Petronius makes an exception in speaking of a "bath-woman" (*balneatricem*).

III

Pseud-Acro on Horace, Epodes 5, 48: " Canidia biting her thumb": He expressed the appearance and movements of Canidia in a rage. Petronius, wishing to portray a furious person, says "*biting his thumb to the quick.*"

FRAGMENTA

IV

Sidonius Apollinaris carminis XXIII:
quid vos eloquii canam Latini,
Arpinas, Patavine, Mantuane?—
Et te Massiliensium per hortos
sacri stipitis, Arbiter, colonum
Hellespontiaco parem Priapo?

V

*Priscianus institutionum VIII 16 p. 381 et XI 29
p. 567 Hertzii inter exempla quibus deponentium verborum participia praeteriti temporis passivam significationem
habere declarat:* Petronius "animam nostro amplexam
pectore"

V[b]

*Boethius in Porphyrium a Victorino translatum dialogo
II extremo p. 45 exemplarium Basiliensium:* Ego faciam,
inquit, libentissime. Sed quoniam iam matutinus, ut
ait Petronius, sol tectis arrisit, surgamus, et si quid
est illud, diligentiore postea consideratione tractabitur

VI*

Fulgentius mythologiarum I p. 23 Munckeri: Nescis
. . quantum saturam matronae formident. Licet
mulierum verbialibus undis et causidici cedant nec
grammatici muttiant, rhetor taceat et clamorem
praeco compescat, sola est quae modum imponit
furentibus, licet Petroniana subet Albucia

326

FRAGMENTS

IV

Sidonius Apollinaris Carmen XXIII, 145, 155 : Why should I hymn you, tuneful Latin writers, thou of Arpinum, thou of Patavium, thou of Mantua?[1] And thou, Arbiter, who in the gardens of the men of Massilia findest a home on the hallowed tree-trunk as the peer of Hellespontine Priapus?

V

Priscian Institutiones VIII, 16 and XI, 29 (pp. 381, 567 ed. Hertz) among the examples by which he shows that the past participles of deponent verbs have a passive meaning: Petronius, "*the soul locked (amplexam) in our bosoms.*"

V^b

Boethius on Victorinus's translation of Porphyry, Dialogue II (p. 45 ed. Basle): I shall be very glad to do it, he said. But since *the morning sun,* in Petronius's words, *has now smiled upon the roofs,* let us get up, and if there is any other point, it shall be treated later with more careful attention.

VI

Fulgentius Mythologiae I (p. 23 ed. Muncker): You do not know . . . how women dread satire. Lawyers may retreat and scholars may not utter a syllable before the flood of a woman's words, the rhetorician may be dumb and the herald may stop his cries; satire alone can put a limit to their madness, though it be Petronius's *Albucia* who is hot.

[1] The writers are Cicero, Livy, Virgil.

FRAGMENTA

VII*

Fulgentius mythologiarum III 8 p. 124 ubi sucum myrrhae valde fervidum esse dixit: Unde et Petronius Arbiter ad libidinis concitamentum myrrhinum se poculum bibisse refert

VIII*

Fulgentius in expositione Virgilianae continentiae p. 156: Tricerberi enim fabulam iam superius exposuimus in modum iurgii forensisque litigii positam. Unde et Petronius in Euscion ait "Cerberus forensis erat causidicus"

IX*

Fulgentius in expositione sermonum antiquorum 42 p. 565 Merceri: Ferculum dicitur missum carnium. Unde et Petronius Arbiter ait "postquam ferculum allatum est"

X*

Fulgentius ibidem 46 p. 565: Valgia vero sunt labellorum obtortiones in supinatione factae. Sicut et Petronius ait "obtorto valgiter labello"

XI*

Fulgentius ibidem 52 p. 566: Alucinare dicitur vana somniari, tractum ab alucitis, quos nos conopes dicimus. Sicut Petronius Arbiter ait "nam contubernalem alucitae molestabant"

FRAGMENTS

VII

Fulgentius Mythologiae III, 8 (p. 124), (where he remarked that essence of myrrh is very strong): hence too Petronius Arbiter says *that he drank a cup of myrrh in order to excite his passion.*

VIII

Fulgentius in his Treatise on the Contents of Virgil's works (p. 156): For we have already explained above the application of the myth of Cerberus with Three Heads to quarrels and litigation in the courts. Hence too Petronius says of *Euscios, "The barrister was a Cerberus of the courts."*

IX

Fulgentius in his Explanation of Old Words, 42 (p. 565 in Mercer's edition): *Ferculum* means a dish of flesh. Hence too Petronius Arbiter says, "*After the dish of flesh (ferculum) was brought in.*"·

X

Fulgentius ibid. 46 (p. 565): *Valgia* really means the twisting of the lips which occurs in vomiting. As Petronius also says, "*With lips twisted as in a vomit (valgiter).*"

XI

Fulgentius ibid. 52 (p. 566): *Alucinare* means to dream falsely, and is derived from *alucitae,* which we call *conopes* (mosquitoes). As Petronius Arbiter says, "*For the mosquitoes (alucitae) were troubling my companion.*"

FRAGMENTA

XII*

Fulgentius ibidem 60 p. 567: Manubiae dicuntur ornamenta regum. Unde et Petronius Arbiter ait "tot regum manubiae penes fugitivum repertae"

XIII*

Fulgentius ibidem 61 p. 567: Aumatium dicitur locum secretum publicum sicut in theatris aut in circo. Unde et Petronius Arbiter ait "in aumatium memet ipsum conieci"

XIV

Isidorus originum V 26, 7: Dolus est mentis calliditas ab eo quod deludat: aliud enim agit, aliud simulat. Petronius aliter existimat dicens "quid est, iudices, dolus? Nimirum ubi aliquid factum est quod legi dolct. Habetis dolum: accipite nunc malum"

XV

Glossarium S. Dionysii: Petaurus genus ludi. Petronius "petauroque iubente modo superior."

XVI

Petronius "satis constaret eos nisi inclinatos non solere transire cryptam Neapolitanam" *ex glossario S. Dionysii.*

XVII*[1]

In alia glossario:

   Suppes suppumpis, hoc est supinis pedibus.
   Tullia, media vel regia.

[1] Wrongly attributed to Petronius by Pithoeus through misunderstanding a marginal note of Scaliger.

FRAGMENTS

XII

Fulgentius ibid. 60 (p. 567): Manubiae means the ornaments of kings. Hence Petronius Arbiter also says, "*So many kingly ornaments (manubiae) found in the possession of a runaway.*"

XIII

Fulgentius ibid. 61 (p. 567): Aumatium means a private place in a public spot such as theatres or the circus. Hence Petronius Arbiter also says, "*I hurled myself into the privy-place (aumatium).*"

XIV

Isidorus Origines V, 26, 7: Dolus[1] is the mental cunning on the part of the deceiver: for he does one thing and pretends another. Petronius takes a different view when he says, "*What is a wrong (dolus), gentlemen? It occurs whenever anything offensive to the law is done. You understand what a wrong is: now take damage . . .*"

XV

Glossary of St. Dionysius: The spring-board is a kind of game. Petronius, "*Now lifted high at the will of the spring-board.*"

XVI

From the Glossary of St. Dionysius : Petronius, "*It was quite certainly their usual plan to go through the Grotto of Naples only with backs bent double.*"

XVII

Another Glossary :

Suppes suppumpis, that is with feet bent backwards.
Tullia, mediator (?) or princess.

[1] *Dolus* originally meant *a device* without moral connotation; hence the legal term for *fraud* was *dolus malus,* and the use of *dolus* alone in a bad sense is later.

FRAGMENTA

XVIII*

Nicolaus Perottus Cornu copiae p. 200, 26 editionis Aldinae anni 1513: Cosmus etiam excellens unguentarins fuit, a quo unguenta dieta sunt Cosmiana. idem [*Iuvenalis 8, 86*] "et Cosmi toto mergatur aheno." Petronius "affer nobis, inquit, alabastrum Cosmiani"

XIX

Terentianus Maurus de metris:
> Horatium videmus
> versus tenoris huius
> nusquam locasse inges,
> at Arbiter disertus
> libris suis frequentat.
> Agnoscere haec potestis,
> cantare quae solemus:
> "Memphitides puellae
> sacris deum paratae.
> Tinctus colore noctis
> manu puer loquaci"

Marius Victorinus III 17 (in Keilii grammaticis VI p. 138): Huius tenoris ac formae quosdam versus poetas lyricos carminibus suis indidisse cognovimus, ut et apud Arbitrum invenimus, cuius exemplum
> "Memphitides puellae
> sacris deum paratae."
> "Tinctus colore noctis
> Aegyptias choreas"

FRAGMENTS

XVIII

Nicolaus Perottus in the Cornucopia (p. 200, 26 in the Aldine Edition of 1513): Cosmus too was a superb perfumer, and ointments are called Cosmian after him. The same writer (Juvenal 8, 86) says, "and let him be plunged deep in a bronze vase of Cosmus." Petronius, "*Bring us, he said, an alabaster box of Cosmus ointment.*"

XIX

Terentianus Maurus on Metre :
We see that Horace nowhere employed verse of this rhythm continuously, but the learned Arbiter uses it often in his works. You will remember these lines, which we are used to sing : "*The maidens of Memphis, made ready for the rites of the Gods. The boy coloured deep as the night with speaking gestures.*"

Marius Victorinus III, 17 (Keil, Grammatici, VI,138):
We know that the lyric poets inserted some lines of this rhythm and form in their works, as we find too in Arbiter, for example : "*The maidens of Memphis, made ready for the rites of the Gods,*" and again "*Coloured deep as the night,* [dancing] *Egyptian dances.*"

FRAGMENTA

XX

Terentianus Maurus de metris:

Nunc divisio, quam loquemur, edet
metrum, quo memorant Anacreonta
dulces composuisse cantilenas.
Hoc Petronius invenitur usus,
Musis cum lyricum refert eundem
consonantia verba cantitasse,
et plures alii. Sed iste versus
quali compositus tome sit, edam.
"Inverunt segetes meum laborem."
"Iuverunt" caput est id hexametri—
quod restat "segetes meum laborem,"
tale est ceu "triplici vides ut ortu
Triviae rotetur ignis
volucrique Phoebus axe
rapidum pererret orhem"

XXI

Diomedes in arte III p. 518 Keilii: Et illud hinc est
comma quod Arbiter fecit tale
"Anus recocta vino
trementibus labellis"

XXII

Servius in artem Donati p. 432,22 Keilii: Item Quirites dicit numero tantum plurali. Sed legimus apud
Horatium hunc Quiritem, ut sit nominativus hic
334

FRAGMENTS

XX

Terentianus Maurus on Metre :

Now the analysis, which we will explain, will give us the metre in which they say that Anacreon wrote his sweet old songs. We find that Petronius, as well as many others, used this metre, when he says that this same lyric poet sang in words harmonious to the Muses. But I will explain with what kind of caesura this verse is written. In the line "*Iuverunt segetes meum laborem*" ("*The cornfields have lightened my labour*"), the word "*iuverunt*" is the beginning of a hexameter: the remaining words "*segetes meum laborem*" are in the same metre as

> "*triplici vides ut ortu*
> *Triviae rotetur ignis*
> *volucrique Phoebus axe*
> *rapidum pererret orbem*"

("*You see how the fire of Trivia spins round from her threefold rising,*[1] *and Phoebus on his winged wheel traverses the hurrying globe*".)

XXI

Diomede on Grammar III (Keil p. 518): Hence arises the caesura which Arbiter employed thus :
> "*Anus recocta vino*
> *trementibus labellis*"

("*An old woman soaked in wine, with trembling lips*")

XXII

Servius on the Grammar of Donatus (Keil p. 432, 22): Again, he uses "Quirites" ("Roman citizens") only in the plural number. But we read in Horace the accusative "hunc Quiritem" ("this Roman citizen") making

---

[1] I.e. as the new, the full, or the waning moon.

FRAGMENTA

Quiris. Item idem Horatius "quis te Quiritem?" cuius nominativus erit hic Quirites, ut dicit Petronius

Pompeius in commento artis Donati p. 167, 9 K: Nemo dicit "hic Quirites" sed "hi Quirites," licet legerimus hoc. Legite in Petronio, et invenietis de nominativo singulari hoc factum. Et ait Petronius "hic Quirites"

XXIII

grammaticus de dubiis nominibus p. 578,23 K: Fretum generis neutri et pluraliter freta, ut Petronius "freta Nereidum"

XXIV*

Hieronymus in epistula ad Demetriadem CXXX 19 p. 995 Vallarsii: Cincinnatulos pueros et calamistratos et peregrini muris olentes pelliculas, de quibus illud Arbitri est

"Non bene olet qui bene semper olet,"
quasi quasdam pestes et venena pudicitiae virgo devitet

XXV*

Fulgentius mythologiarum II 6 p. 80 de Prometheo: Quamvis Nicagoras . . . quod vulturi iecur praebeat, livoris quasi pingat imaginem. Unde et Petronius Arbiter ait

"qui voltur iecur intimum pererrat
et pectus trahit intimasque fibras,
non est quem lepidi vocant poetae,
sed cordis *mala,* livor atque luxus"

the nominative "hic Quiris." Again, the same Horace says "Quis te Quiritem?" and there the nominative will be "*hic Quirites*," as Petronius says.

Pompeias in his Commentary on the Art of Donatus (Keil p. 167, 9): No one says "this Roman citizen," but "these Roman citizens," although we find the former in books. Read Petronius, and you will find this use of the nominative singular. And Petronius says "*Hic Quirites*" ("*this Roman citizen*)."

XXIII

A Grammarian on Nouns of uncertain gender (Keil p. 578, 23): Fretum ("a strait") is of the neuter gender, and its plural is freta, as Petronius says "*Freta Nereidum*" ("*The straits of the Nereids*").

XXIV

Hieronymus in his Letter to Demetriades CXXX, 19 (Vallarsius p. 995): Boys with hair curled and crimped and skins smelling like foreign musk-rats, about whom Arbiter wrote the line, "*To smell good always is not to smell good*,"[1] showing how the virgin may avoid certain plagues and poisons of modesty.

XXV

Fulgentius Mythologiae II, 6 (p. 80, on Prometheus): Although Nicagoras ... represents his yielding his liver to a vulture, as an allegorical picture of envy. Hence too Petronius Arbiter says: "*The vulture who explores our inmost liver, and drags out our heart and inmost nerves, is not the bird of whom our dainty poets talk, but those diseases of the soul, envy and wantonness.*"

[1] The line occurs in Martial 2, 12, 4. The reference to Petronius may be due to a confusion with ch. 2, l. 1.

POEMS

TITUS PETRONIUS ARBITER

INTRODUCTION

Of the poems which follow, 1-17 are found in the cod. Vossianus L. Q. 86, a MS. of the 9th century. They follow a number of epigrams attributed to Seneca and are not attributed by the MS. to Petronius. But 3, 1 and 13, 6-9 are quoted by Fulgentius (myth. I, 1, p. 31 and III, 9, p. 126) as from Petronius, while the general resemblance to Petronius led Scaliger to attribute the remainder to the same author. Though absolute proof of the correctness of this attribution is lacking, most readers will feel little doubt that Scaliger was right.

18-29[1] were contained in a MS. once at Beauvais and now lost. The contents of this codex Bellovacensis were published by Claude Binet in 1579. The last two poems were not, according to Binet, given to Petronius by the MS., and I have included them with some hesitation. But as Binet saw, the resemblance to the style and tone of Petronius is considerable, and they are therefore given here. The six poems which followed in this MS. are given by Baehrens (*P.L.M.* iv. 103-8) to Petronius. But they have no particular affinity with the work of Petronius, and as they have inserted among them in Binet's book a number of poems which are admittedly by Luxorius (see Baehrens, *op. cit.* App. Crit. on *P.L.M.* iv. 104), they are not included here.

---

[1] No. 20 is also contained in cod. Paris, 10318 (Salmasianus), cod. Vossianus, *L.Q.* 86, cod. Paris, 8071 (Thuaneus).

POEMS

The remaining two poems are found in cod. Vossianus L.F. 111, a MS. of the 9th century. They are attributed to Petronius by the MS., and follow two poems found in the MSS of the novel (c. 14 and c. 83). Their general resemblance would betray their authorship.

For a discussion of these MSS. see Baehrens, *Poetae Latini Minores,* vol. iv, pp. 11, 13 and 19. Also p. 36 ff.

SIGLA

Cod. Voss. L.Q. 86 = *V.*
Cod. Bellovacensis = *W.*
Cod. Voss. L.F. 111 = *E*

H.E.B.

TITUS PETRONIUS ARBITER

74 *Poet. Lat. Min.* iv, ed. Baehrens.

1 Inveniet quod quisque velit: non omnibus unum est
    quod placet: hic spinas colligit, ille rosas.

75 *P.L.M.*

2 Iam nunc algentes autumnus fecerat umbras[1]
atque hiemem tepidis spectabat Phoebus habenis,
iam platanus iactare comas, iam coeperat uvas
adnumerare suas defecto palmite vitis:
ante oculos stabat quidquid promiserat annus.

76 *P.L.M.*

3 Primus in orbe deos fecit timor, ardua caelo
fulmina cum caderent discussaque moenia flammis
atque ictus flagraret Athos; mox Phoebus ab ortu[2]
lustrata deuectus humo, Lunaeque senectus
et reparatus honos; hinc signa effusa per orhem
et permutatis disiunctus mensibus annus.
Profecit[3] vitium iamque error iussit inanis
agricolas primos Cereri dare messis honores,
palmitibus plenis Bacchum vincire, Palemque
pastorum gaudere manu; natat obrutus omnis[4]
Neptunus demersus aqua; Pallasque tabernas
vindicat; et voti reus et qui vendidit orbem,[5]
iam sibi quisque deos avido certamine fingit.

77 *P.L.M.*

4 Nolo ego semper idem capiti suffundere costum
    nec noto[6] stomachum conciliare mero.

[1] algentes ... fecerat *Baehrens:* ardentes ... fregerat *V.*
[2] ab ortu *Butler:* ad ortus *V.*
[3] profecit *anon:* proiecit *V.*
[4] natat obrutus *probably corrupt:* portus tenet *Buecheler.*
[5] orhem *perhaps corrupt:* orbam *Barth:* urbem *Pithoeus*
[6] noto *Paulmier:* toto *V.*

342

POEMS

Every man shall find his own desire; there is no 1
one thing which pleases all: one man gathers thorns
and another roses.

Now autumn had brought its chill shades, and 2
Phoebus was looking winterwards with cooler reins.
Now the plane-tree had begun to shed down her
leaves, now the young shoots had withered on the
vine, and she had begun to number her grapes: the
whole promise of the year was standing before our
eyes.

It was fear first created gods in the world, when the 3
lightning fell from high heaven, and the ramparts of the
world were rent with flame, and Athos was smitten and
blazed. Soon 'twas Phoebus sank to earth, after he
had traversed earth from his rising; the Moon grew
old and once more renewed her glory; next the starry
signs were spread through the firmament, and the
year divided into changing seasons. The folly spread,
and soon vain superstition bade the labourer yield to
Ceres the harvest's chosen firstfruits, and garland
Bacchus with the fruitful vine, and made Pales to
rejoice in the shepherd's work; Neptune swims deep-
plunged beneath all the waters of the world, Pallas
watches over shops, and the man who wins his prayer
or has betrayed the world for gold now strives greedily
to create gods of his own.

I would not always steep my head with the same 4
sweet nard, nor strive to win my stomach with familiar

343

TITUS PETRONIUS ARBITER

Taurus amat gramen mutata carpere valle
    et fera mutatis sustinet ora cibis.
Ipsa dies ideo nos grato perluit haustu,
    quod permutatis hora recurrit equis.

78 *P.L.M.*
5 Uxor, legis onus,[1] debet quasi census amari.
    nec censum vellem semper amare meum.

79 *P.L.M.*
6 Linque tuas sedes alienaque litora quaere,
    o[2] iuvenis: maior rerum tibi nascitur ordo.
Ne succumbe malis: te noverit ultimus Hister,
te Boreas gelidus securaque regna Canopi,
quique renascentem Phoebum cernuntque cadentem:
maior in externas fit qui[3] descendit harenas.

80 *P.L.M.*
7 Nam nihil est, quod non mortalibus afferat usum;
    rebus in adversis quae iacuere iuvant.
Sic rate demersa fulvum deponderat aurum,
    remorum levitas naufraga membra vehit.
Cum sonuere tubae, iugulo stat divite ferrum
    barbaricum: tennis praebia pannus habet.[4]

[1] legis onus *Baehrens* : inus *V.*
[2] o *added by Scaliger, omitted by V.*
[3] fit qui *Baehrens* : itacui *V.*
[4] barbaricum *Baehrens* : tennis *Butler* : praebia *Baehrens* :
barbara contempnit praelia *V., retaining which* hebes *for*
habet *Scaliger.*

344

wine. The bull loves to change his valley-pasture, and the wild beast maintains his zest by change of food. Even to be bathed in the light of day is pleasant only because the night-hour races back with altered steeds.

A wife is a burden imposed by law, and should be 5 loved like one's fortune. But I do not wish to love even my fortune for ever.

Leave thine home, O youth, and seek out alien 6 shores : a larger range of life is ordained for thee. Yield not to misfortune; the far-off Danube shall know thee, the cold North-wind, and the untroubled kingdoms of Canopus, and the men who gaze on the new birth of Phoebus or upon his setting: he that disembarks on distant sands, becomes thereby the greater man

For there is naught that may not serve the need of 7 mortal men, and in adversity despised things help us. So when a ship sinks, yellow gold weighs down its possessor, while a flimsy oar bears up the shipwrecked body. When the trumpets sound, the savage's knife stands drawn at the rich man's throat; the poor man's rags wear the amulet of safety.

345

TITUS PETRONIUS ARBITER

81 *P.L.M.*

8 Parvula securo tegitur mihi culmine sedes
uvaque plena mero fecunda pendet ab ulmo.
Dant rami cerasos, dant mala rubentia silvae,
Palladiumque nemus pingui se vertice frangit.
Iam qua diductos potat levis area fontes,
Corycium mihi surgit olus maluaeque supinae
et non sollicitos missura papavera somnos.
Praeterea sive alitibus contexere fraudem
seu magis imbelles libuit circumdare cervos
aut tereti lino pavidum subducere piscem,
hos tantum novere dolos mea sordida rura.
I nunc et vitae fugientis tempora vende
divitibus cenis. Me si manet exitus idem,
hic precor inveniat consumptaque tempora poscat.

82 *P.L.M.*

9 Non satis est quod nos mergit[1] furiosa iuventus
      transversosque rapit fama sepulta probris?
En[2] etiam famuli cognataque facce caterva[3]
      inter conrasas luxuriantur opes.[4]
Vilis servus habet regni bona, cellaque capti
      deridet Vestam Romuleamque casam.
Idcirco virtus medio iacet obruta caeno,
      nequitiae classes candida vela ferunt.

83 *P.L.M.*

10 Sic et membra solent auras includere ventris,[5]
quae penitus mersae cum rursus abire laborant,

[1] mergis *V. corr. Buecheler.*
[2] en *L. Müller:* an *V.*
[3] caterva *Baehrens:* sepulti *V.*
[4] inter conrasas *Baehrens:* intesta merassas *V.*
[5] ventis *V., corr. Riese.*

My little house is covered by a roof that fears no 8
harm, and the grape swollen with wine hangs from the
fruitful elm. The boughs yield cherries, the orchards
ruddy apples, and the trees sacred to Pallas[1] break under
the wealth of their branches. And now where the
smooth soil drinks from the runnels of the spring,
Corycian kale springs up for me and creeping mallows,
and the poppy with promise of untroubled sleep.
Moreover, if my pleasure is to lay snares for birds, or
if I choose rather to entrap the timid deer, or draw out
the quivering fish on slender line, so much deceit is all
that is known to my humble fields. Go, then, and
barter the hours of flying life for rich banquets. My
prayer is that since at the last the same end waits for
me, it may find me here, here call me to account for
the time that I have spent.

Is it not enough that mad youth engulfs us, and 9
our good name is sunk in reproach and sweeps us
astray? Behold! even bondmen and the rabble that is
kindred to the mire wanton amid our gathered
boards! The low slave enjoys the treasure of a kingdom, and the thrall's room shames Vesta and the cottage of Romulus. So goodness lies obscured in the
deep mud, and the fleet of the unrighteous carries
snowy sails.

So, too, the body will shut in the belly's wind, 10
which, when it labours to come forth again from its
deep dungeon, prizes forth a way by sharp blows: and

[1] The olive, which she gave to Athens. By this gift, which
the Gods considered more useful than the horse given by
Poseidon, she became the presiding deity of the city.

verberibus rimantur iter ; nec desinit ante
frigidus, adstrictis[1] qui regnat in ossibus, horror
quam tepidus laxo manavit corpore sudor.

84 *P.L.M.*

11 O litus vita mihi dulcins, o mare! felix
   cui licet ad terras ire subinde meas!
O formosa dies! hoc quondam rure solebam
   Naiadas[2] alterna sollicitare manu!
Hic fontis lacns est, illic sinus egerit algas:
   haec statio est tacitis fida[3] cupidinibus.
Pervixi; neque enim fortuna malignior unquam
   eripiet nobis quod prior hora[4] dedit.

85 *P.L.M.*

12 Haec ait et tremulo deduxit vertice canos
consecuitque genas; oculis nec defuit imber,
sed qualis rapitur per vallis improbus amnis,
cum gelidae periere nives et languidus auster
non patitur glaciem resoluta vivere terra,
gurgite sic pleno facies manavit et alto
insonuit gemitu turbato murmure pectus.

86 *P.L.M.*

13 Nam citius flammas mortales ore tenebunt
quam secreta tegant. Quicquid dimittis in aula,
effluit et subitis rumoribus oppida pulsat.
Nec satis est vulgasse fidem. Cumulatius exit
proditionis opus famamque onerare laborat-

[1] et frigidus strictis *V., corr. Reiske.*
[2] Naiadas *Lindenbrog :* Iliadas *V.* alterna... manu *B*
armatas... manus *V.*
[3] fida *Pithoeus :* vieta *V.*
[4] prior hora *Scaliger :* priora *V.*

there is no end to the cold shiver which rules the cramped frame, till a warm sweat bedews and loosens the body.

O sea-shore and sea more sweet to me than life! 11 Happy am I who may come at once to the lands I love. O beauteous day! In this country long ago I used to rouse the Naiads with my bands' alternate stroke. Here is the fountain's pool, there the sea washes up its weeds: here is a sure haven for quiet love. I have had life in full; for never can harder fortune take away what was given us in time over-past.

With these words he tore the white hair from his 12 trembling head, and rent his checks; his eyes filled with tears, and as the impetuous river sweeps down the valleys when the cold snow has perished, and the gentle south-wind will not suffer the ice to live on the unfettered earth, so was his face wet with a full stream, and his heart rang with the troubled murmur of deep groaning.

For sooner will men hold fire in their months than 13 keep a secret. Whatever you let escape you in your hall flows forth and beats at city walls in sudden rumours. Nor is the breach of faith the end. The work of betrayal issues forth with increase, and strives

Sic commissa verens avidus reserare[1] minister
fodit humum regisque latentes prodidit aures.
Concepit nam terra sonos calamique loquentes
incinuere[2] Midam, qnalem narraverat index.

87 *P.L.M.*

14 Illic alternis depugnat pontus et aer,
    hic rivo tenui pervia ridet humus.
Illic demersas[3] complorat navita puppes,
    hic pastor miti perluit amne pecus.
Illic immanes mors obdita[4] solvit hiatus,
    hic gaudet curva falce recisa Ceres.
Illic inter aquas urit sitis arida fauces,
    hic data periuro[5] basia multa viro.
Naviget et fluctus lasset mendicus Vlixes,
    in terris vivet candida Penelope.

88 *P.L.M.*

15 Qui nolit properare[6] mori nec cogere fata
    mollia praecipiti rumpere fila manu,
hactenus irarum mare noverit. Ecce refuso
    gurgite securos obluit unda pedes.
Ecce inter virides iactatur mytilus algas
    et rauco trahitur lubrica concha sinu.
Ecce recurrentes qua versat fluctus arenas,
    discolor attrita calculus exit humo.
Haec quisquis calcare potest, in litore tuto
    ludat et hoc solum iudicet esse mare.

[1] verens reserare *Fulgentius:* ferens... seruare *V.*
[2] incinuere *Salmasius:* inuenerem *V.*
[3] demersas *Baehrens:* divisas *V.*
[4] obdita *Baehrens:* oblita *V.*
[5] data *Wernsdorf:* da *V.* periuro *probably corrupt: perhaps* quaeque suo *Butler.*
[6] nolit *Oudendorp:* moluit *V.* properare *Tollius:* propare *V.*

to add weight to the report. So was it that the greedy slave, who feared to unlock his knowledge, dug in the ground and betrayed the secret of the king's hidden ears. For the earth brought forth sounds, and the whispering reeds sang how Midas was even such an one as the tell-tale had revealed.

There sea and sky struggle and buffet each other, 14 bere the tiny stream runs through smooth and smiling country. There the sailor laments for his sunken ship, here the shepherd dips his flock in the gentle river. There death confronts and chokes the vast gape of greed, here the earth laughs to lie low before the curved sickle. There, with water everywhere, dry thirst burns the throat, here kisses are given in plenty to faithless man. Let Ulysses go sail and weary the waters in beggar's rags: the chaste Penelope dwells on land.

The man that would not haste to die, nor force the 15 Fates to snap the tender threads with impetuous hand, should know only this much of the sea's anger. Lo! where the tide flows back, and the wave bathes his feet without peril! Lo! where the mussel is thrown up among the green sea-weed, and the hoarse whorl of the slippery shell is rolled along! Lo! where the wave turns the sands to rush back in the eddy, there pebbles of many a hue appear on the wave-worn floor. Let the man who may have these things under his feet, play safely on the shore, and count this alone to be the sea.

TITUS PETRONIUS ARBITER

89 *P.L.M.*

16 Non est forma satis nec quae vult bella videri[1]
    debet vulgari more placere sibi.
Dicta, sales, lusus, sermonis gratia, risus
    vincunt naturae candidioris opus.
Condit enim formam quicquid consumitur artis,
    et nisi velle[2] subest, gratia nuda perit.

90 *P.L.M.*

17 Sic contra rerum naturae munera notae
    corvus maturis frugibus ova refert.
Sic format lingua fetum cum protulit ursa
    et piscis nullo iunctus amore parit.
Sic Phoebea chelys nutu[3] resoluta parentis
    Lucinae tepidis naribus ova fovet.
Sic sine concubitu textis apis excita ceris
    fervet et audaci milite castra replet.
Non uno contenta valet natura tenore,
    sed permutatas gaudet habere vices.

91 *P.L.M.*

18 Indica purpureo genuit me litore tellus,
    candidus accenso qua redit orbe dies.
Hic ego divinos inter generatus honores
    mutavi Latio barbara verba sono.
Iam dimitte tuos, Paean o Delphice, cycnos
    dignior haec vox est, quae tua templa colat.

[1] *The first couplet is to be found in Fulgentius, Myth.* I, 12, p. 44.
[2] velle subest *probably corrupt:* sal suberit *Baehrens.*
[3] nutu *Butler:* victo *W:* vinclo *Binetus.*

Outward beauty is not enough, and the woman who 16
would appear fair must not be content with any common manner. Words, wit, play, sweet talk and laughter, surpass the work of too simple nature. For all
expense of art seasons beauty, and naked loveliness is
wasted all in vain, if it have not the will to please.

So, contrary to the known operations of nature, the 17
raven lays her eggs when the crops are ripe. So the
she-bear shapes her cubs with her tongue, and the
fish is ignorant of love's embrace, yet brings forth
young. So the tortoise, sacred to Phoebus, delivered
by the will of mother Lucina, batches her eggs with
the warmth of her nostrils. So the bee, begotten
without wedlock from the woven cells, throbs with
life and fills her camp with bold soldiery. The strength
of nature lies not in holding on one even way, but she
loves to change the fashion of her laws.

My[1] birthplace was India's glowing shore, where the 18
day returns in brilliance with fiery orb. Here I was
born amid the worship of the gods, and exchanged
my barbarie speech for the Latin tongue. O healer of
Delphi, now dismiss thy swans; here is a voice more
worthy to dwell within thy temple.

[1] A parrot is speaking.

TITUS PETRONIUS ARBITER

92 *P.L.M.*

19 Naufragus eiecta nudus rate quaerit eodem
    percussum telo, cui sua fata fleat.[1]
Grandine qui segetes et totum perdidit annum,
    in simili deflet tristia fata sinu.
Funera conciliant miseros, orbique parentes
    coniungunt gemitus et facit hora pares.
Nos quoque confusis feriemus sidera verbis;
    fama est coniunctas[2] fortins ire preces.

93 *P.L.M.*

20 Aurea mala mihi, dulcis mea Martia, mittis,
    mittis et hirsutae munera castaneae.
Omnia grata putem, sed si magis ipsa venire
    ornares donum, pulcra puella, tuum.
Tu licet apportes stringentia mala palatum,
    tristia mandenti est mellens ore sapor.
At si dissimulas, multum mihi cara, venire,
    oscula cum pomis mitte; vorabo libens.

94 *P.L.M.*

21 Si Phoebi soror es, mando tibi, Delia, causam,
    scilicet ut fratri quae peto verba feras:
"Marmore Sicanio struxi tibi, Delphice, templum
    et levibus calamis candida verba dedi.
Nunc si nos audis atque es divinus, Apollo,
    dic mihi, qui nummos non habet, unde petat."

---

[1] fleat *Jacobs:* legat *W.*
[2] fama est coniunctas *Butler:* et fama est constans *W.*

PQEMS

The sailor, naked from the shipwreck, seeks out a 19
comrade stricken by the same blow to whom he may
bewail his fate. The farmer who has lost his crops and
the whole year's fruits in the hail, weeps his sad lot
on a bosom wounded like his own. Death draws the
unhappy together; bereaved parents utter their groans
with one voice, and the moment makes them equal.
We too will strike the stars with words in unison;
the saying is that prayers travel more strongly when
united.

You send me golden apples, my sweet Martia, and 20
you send me the fruit of the shaggy chestnut. Believe
me, I would love them all; but should you choose
rather to come in person, lovely girl, you would
beautify .your gift. Come, if you will, and lay sour
apples to my tongue, the sharp flavour will be like
honey as I bite. But if you feign you will not come,
dearest, send kisses with the apples; then gladly will
I devour them.

If you are sister to Phoebus, Delia, I entrust my 21
petition to you, that you may carry to your brother
the words of my prayer. "God of Delphi, I have
built for you a temple of Sicilian marble, and have
given you fair words of song from a slender pipe of
reed. Now if you hear us, Apollo, and are indeed
divine, tell me where a man who has no money is to
find it."

TITUS PETRONIUS. ARBITER

95 *P.L.M.*

22 Omnia quae miseras possunt finire querellas,
    in promptu voluit candidus esse deus.
Vile holus et duris haerentia mora rubetis
    pungentis[1] stomachi composuere famem.
Flumine vicino stultus sitit, et riget[2] euro
    cum calidus tepido consonat igne focus[3].
Lex armata sedet circum fera limina nuptae:
    nil metuit licito fusa puella toro.
Quod satiare potest dives natura ministrat;
    quod docet infrenis[4] gloria fine caret.

96 *P.L.M.*

23 Militis in galea nidum fecere columbae:
    apparet Marti quam sit amica Venus.

97 *P.L.M.*

24 Iudaeus licet et porcinum numen adoret
    et caeli summas advocet auriculas,
ni tamen et ferro succiderit inguinis oram
    et nisi nodatum solverit arte caput,
exemptus populo sacra[5] migrabit ab urbe
    et non ieiuna sabbata lege premet.[6]

98 *P.L.M.*

25 Una est nobilitas argumentumque coloris
    ingenui timidas non habuisse manus.

---

[1] pungentis *Dousa :* pugnantis **W.**
[2] et riget *Binet :* effugit **W.**
[3] focus *Buecheler :* rogus **W.**
[4] infrenis *Binet:* inferius **W.**
[5] sacra *Baehrens :* graia **W.**
[6] premet **W.**, *perhaps corrupt :* tremet *Buecheler.*

POEMS

Honest Heaven ordained that all things which can **22** end our wretched complaints should be ready to hand. Common green herbs and the berries that grow on rough brambles allay the gnawing hunger of the belly. A fool is he who goes thirsty with a river close by, and shivers in the east wind while a blazing fire roars on the warm hearth. The law sits armed by the threshold of a wanton bride; the girl who lies on a lawful bed knows no fear. The wealth of nature gives us enough for our fill: that which unbridled vanity teaches us to pursue has no end to it.

Doves have made a nest in the soldier's helmet: **23** see how Venus loveth Mars.

The Jew may worship his pig-god and clamour in **24** the ears of high heaven, but unless he also cuts back his foreskin with the knife, he shall go forth from the holy city cast forth from the people, and transgress the sabbath by breaking the law of fasting.

This is the one nobility and proof of honourable **25** estate, that a man's hands have shown no fear.

TITUS PETRONIUS ARBITER

99 *P.L.M.*

26 Lecto compositus vix prima silentia noctis
      carpebam et somno lumina vieta dabam,
cum me savus Amor prensat[1] sursumque capillis
      excitat et lacerum pervigilare inhet.
"Tu famulus meus," inquit, "ames cum mille puellas,
      solus, io, solus, dure, iacere potes?"
Exsilio et pedibus nudis tunicaque soluta
      omne iter ingredior,[2] nullum iter expedio.
Nunc propero, nunc ire piget, rursumque redire
      paenitet, et pudor est stare via media.
Ecce tacent voces hominum strepitusque viarum
      et volucrum cantus fidaque turba canum;
solus ego ex cunctis paveo somnumque torumque,
      et sequor imperium, magne Cupido, tuum.

100 *P.L.M.*

27 Sit nox illa diu nobis dilecta, Nealce,
      quae te prima meo pectore composuit:
sit torus et lecti genius secretaque lampas,[3]
      quis tenera in nostrum veneris arbitrium.
Ergo age duremus, quamvis adoleverit aetas,
      utamurque annis quos mora parva teret.
Fas et iura sinunt veteres extendere amores;
      fac cito quod coeptum est, non cito desinere.

101 *P.L.M.*

28 Foeda est in coitu et brevis voluptas
et taedet Veneris statim peractae.
Non ergo ut pecudes libidinosae
caeci protinus irruamus illuc
(nam languescit amor peritque flamma);

[1] prensat *Oudendorp:* prensum *W.*
[2] ingredior *Riese:* impedio *W.*
[3] lampas *Buecheler:* longa *W.*

358

At rest in bed, I had scarce begun to enjoy the first 26
silence of night, and to give up my conquered eyes
to sleep, when fierce Love took hold of me and drew
me up by the hair, and tore me, bidding me watch
till day. "Ah, my slave," he said, "thou lover of
a thousand girls, canst thou lie alone bere, alone, oh
hard of heart?" I leaped up, and with bare feet and
disordered raiment started on every path and found
a way by none. Now I run, now to move is weariness:
I repent of turning back, and am ashamed to halt in
the midst of the road. Lo, the voices of men and the
roar of the streets, the singing of birds and the faithful company of watchdogs are all silent. I alone of all
men dread both sleep and my bed, and follow thy
command, great Lord of desire.

Long may that night be dear to us, Nealce, that 27
first laid you to rest upon my heart. Dear be the
bed and the genius of the couch, and the silent lamp
that saw you come softly to do our pleasure. Come,
then, let us endure though we have grown older, and
employ the years which a brief delay will blot out.
It is lawful and right to prolong an old love: grant
that what we began in baste may not hastily be
ended.

The pleasure of the act of love is gross and brief, 28
and love once consummated brings loathing after it.
Let us then not rush blindly thither straightway like
lustful beasts, for love sickens and the flame dies
down; but even so, even so, let us keep eternal holi-

sed sic sic sine fine feriati
et tecum iaceamus osculantes.
Hic nullus labor est ruborque nullus:
hoc iuvit, iuvat et diu iuvabit;
hoc non deficit incipitque semper.

102 *P.L.M.*

29 Accusare et amare tempore uno
ipsi vix fuit Herculi ferendum.

120 *P.L.M.*

30 Pallunt nos oculi vagique sensus
oppressa ratione mentiuntur.
Nam turris prope quae quadrata surgit,
detritis procul angulis rotatur.
Hyblaeum refugit satur liquorem
et naris casiam frequenter odit.
Hoc illo magis aut minus placere
non posset nisi lite destinata
pugnarent dubio tenore sensus.

121 *P.L.M.*

31 Somnia quae mentes ludunt volitantibus umbris,
non delubra deum nec ab aethere numina mittunt,
sed sibi quisque facit. Nam cum prostrata sopore
urget membra quies et mens sine pondere ludit,
quidquid luce fuit tenebris agit. Oppida bello
qui quatit et flammis miserandas eruit urbes,
tela videt versasque acies et funera regum
atque exundantes profuso sanguine campos.
Qui causas orare solent, legesque forumque
et pavidi cernunt inclusum chorte[1] tribunal.
Condit avarus opes defossumque invenit aurum.

[1] chorte *Mommsen:* corde *E.*

day, and lie with thy lips to mine. No toil is here and no shame: in this, delight has been, and is, and long shall be; in this there is no diminution, but a beginning everlastingly.

To love and accuse at one time were a labour 29 Hercules himself could scarce have borne.

Our eyes deceive us, and our wandering senses 30 weigh down our reason and tell us falsehoods. For the tower which stands almost four-square has its corners blunted at a distance and becomes rounded. The full stomach turns from the honey of Hybla, and the nose often hates the scent of cinnamon. One thing could not please us more or less than another, unless the senses strove in set conflict with wavering balance.

It is not the shrines of the gods, nor the powers of 31 the air, that send the dreams which mock the mind with flitting shadows; each man makes dreams for himself. For when rest lies about the limbs subdued by sleep, and the mind plays with no weight upon it, it pursues in the darkness whatever was its task by daylight. The man who makes towns tremble in war, and overwhelms unhappy cities in flame, secs arms, and routed hosts, and the deaths of kings, and plains streaming with outpoured blood. They whose life is to plead cases have statutes and the courts before their eyes, and look with terror upon the judgement-seat surrounded by a throng. The miser hides his gains and discovers buried treasure.

TITUS PETRONIUS ARBITER

Venator saltus canibus quatit. Eripit undis
aut premit eversam periturus navita puppem.
Scribit amatori meretrix, dat adultera munus:
et canis in somnis leporis vestigia lustrat.
In noctis spatium miserorum vulnera durant.

POEMS

The hunter shakes the woods with his pack. The sailor snatches his shipwrecked bark from the waves, or grips it in death-agony.· The woman writes to her lover, the adulteress yields herself: and the dog follows the tracks of the hare as he sleeps. The wounds of the unhappy endure into the night-season.

SENECAE
ΑΠΟΚΟΛΟΚΥΝΤΩΣΙΣ DIVI CLAUDII

INTRODUCTION

This piece is ascribed to Seneca by ancient tradition; it is impossible to prove that it is his, and impossible to prove that it is not. The matter will probably continne to be decided by every one according to his view of Seneca's character and abilities: in the matters of style and of sentiment much may be said on both sides. Dion Cassius (lx, 35) says that Seneca composed an ἀποκολοκύντωσις or Pumpkinification of Claudius after his death, the title being a parody of the usual ἀποθέωσις; but this title is not given in the MSS. of the Ludus de Morte Claudii, nor is there anything in the piece which suits the title very well.

As a literary form, the piece belongs to the class called *Satura Menippea,* a satiric medley in prose and verse.

This text is that of Buecheler, with a few trifling changes, which are indicated in the notes. We have been courteously allowed by Messrs Weidmann to use this text. I have to acknowledge the help of Mr Ball's notes, from which I have taken a few references; but my translation was made many years ago.

W. H. D. ROUSE.

BIBLIOGRAPHY

Editio Princeps: Lucii Annaei Senecae in morte Claudii Caesaris Ludus nuper repertus: Rome, 1513.

Latest critical text: Franz Buecheler, Weidmann, 1904 (a reprint with a few changes of the text from a larger work, Divi Claudii Ἀποκολοκύντωσις in the Symbola Philologorum Bonnensium, fasc. i, 1864).

Translations and helps: The Satire of Seneca on the Apotheosis of Claudius, by A. P. Ball (with introduction, notes, and translations): New York: Columbia University Press; London, Macmillan, 1902.

SENECAE APOCOLOCYNTOSIS DIVI CLAUDII

Quid actum sit in caelo ante diem III idus Octobris anno novo, initio saeculi felicissimi, volo memoriae tradere. Nihil nec offensae nec gratiae dabitur. Haec ita vera. Si quis quaesiverit unde sciam, primum, si noluero, non respondebo. Quis coacturus est? Ego scio me liberum factum, ex quo suum diem obiit ille, qui verum proverbium fecerat, aut regem aut fatuum nasci oportere. Si libuerit respondere, dicam quod mihi in buccam venerit. Quis unquam ab historico iuratores exegit? Tamen si necesse fuerit auctorem producere, quaerito ab eo qui Drusillam euntem in caelum vidit: idem Claudium vidisse se dicet iter facientem "non passibus aequis." Velit nolit, necesse est illi omnia videre, quae in caelo aguntur: Appiae viae curator est, qua scis et divum Augustum et Tiberium Caesarem ad deos isse. Hunc si interrogaveris, soli narrabit: coram pluribus nunquam verbum faciet. Nam ex quo in senatu iuravit se Drusillam vidisse caelum ascendentem et illi pro tam bono nuntio nemo credidit, quod viderit, verbis conceptis affirmavit se non indicaturum, etiam si in medio foro hominem

370

SENECA

APOCOLOCYNTOSIS, OR LUDUS DE MORTE CLAUDII: THE PUMPKINIFICATION OF CLAUDIUS.

I wish to place on record the proceedings in heaven **1** October 13 last, of the new year which begins this auspicious age. It shall be done without malice or favour. This is the truth. Ask if you like how I know it? To begin with, I am not bound to please you with my answer. Who will compel me? I know the same day made me free, which was the last day for him who made the proverb true—One must be born either a Pharaoh or a fool. If I choose to answer, I will say whatever trips off my tongue. Who has ever made the historian produce witness to swear for him? But if an authority must be produced, ask of the man who saw Drusilla translated to heaven: the same man will aver he saw Claudius on the road, Virg. Aen. ii, 724 dot and carry one. Will he nill he, all that happens in heaven he needs must see. He is the custodian of the Appian Way; by that route, you know, both Tiberius and Augustus went up to the gods Question him, he will tell you the tale when you are alone; before company he is dumb. You see he swore in the Senate that he beheld Drusilla mounting heavenwards, and all he got for his good news was that everybody gave him the lie: since when he solemnly swears he will never bear witness again to what he has seen, not even if he had seen a man murdered in open market. What

occisum vidisset. Ab hoc ego quae tum audivi, certa
clara affero, ita illum salvum et felicem habeam.

2   Iam Phoebus breviore via contraxerat ortum
    lucis, et obscuri crescebant tempora somni,
    iamque suum victrix augebat Cynthia regnum,
    et deformis hiemps gratos carpebat honores
    divitis autumni, iussoque senescere Baccho
    carpebat raras serus vindemitor uvas.

Puto magis intellegi, si dixero: mensis erat October,
dies III idus Octobris. Horam non possum certam
tibi dicere, facilius inter philosophos quam inter horo-
logia conveniet, tamen inter sextam et septimam erat.
"Nimis rustice" inquies: "cum omnes poetae, non
contenti ortus et occasus describere, ut etiam medium
diem inquietent, tu sic transibis horam tam bonam?"

    Iam medium curru Phoebus diviserat orhem[1]
    et propior nocti fessas quatiebat habenas
    obliquo flexam deducens tramite lucem:

3 Claudius animam agere coepit nec invenire exitum
poterat. Tum Mercurius, qui semper ingenio eius
delectatus esset, unam e tribus Parcis seducit et ait:
"Quid, femina crudelissima, hominem miserum tor-
queri pateris? Nec unquam tam diu cruciatus cesset?

[1] *So MSS: Buecheler* orhem *unnecessarily.*

he told me I report plain and clear, as I hope for his health and happiness.

Now had the sun with shorter course drawn in his   **2**
    risen light,
And by equivalent degrees grew the dark hours of
    night:
Victorious Cynthia now held sway over a wider space,
Grim winter drove rich autumn out, and now usurped
    his place;
And now the fiat had gone forth that Bacchus must
    grow old,
The few last clusters of the vine were gathered ere
    the cold:

I shall make myself better understood, if I say the month was October, the day was the thirteenth. What hour it was I cannot certainly tell; philosophers will agree more often than clocks; but it was between midday and one after noon. "Clumsy creature!" you say. "The poets are not content to describe sunrise and sunset, and now they even disturb the midday siesta. Will you thus neglect so good an hour?"

Now the sun's chariot had gone by the middle of his
    way;
Half wearily he shook the reins, nearer to night than
    day,
And led the light along the slope that down before
    him lay.

Claudius began to breathe his last, and could not   **3**
make an end of the matter. Then Mercury, who had always been much pleased with his wit, drew aside one of the three Fates, and said: "Cruel beldame, why do you let the poor wretch be tormented? After

373

Annus sexagesimus quartus est, ex quo cum anima luctatur. Quid buic et rei publicae invides? Patere mathematicos aliquando verum dicere, qui illum, ex quo princeps factus est, omnibus annis, omnibus mensibus efferunt. Et tamen non est mirum si errant et horam eius nemo novit; nemo enim unquam illum natum putavit. Fac quod faciendum est:

Dede neci, melior vacua sine regnet in aula.' "

Sed Clotho "ego mehercules" inquit "pusillum temporis adicere illi volebam, dum hos pauculos, qui supersunt, civitate donaret (constituerat enim omnes Graecos, Gallos, Hispanos, Britannos togatos videre) sed quoniam placet aliquos peregrinos in semen relinqui et tu ita iubes fieri, fiat." Aperit tum capsulam et tres fusos profert: unus erat Augurini, alter Babae, tertius Claudii. "Hos" inquit "tres uno anno exiguis intervallis temporum divisos mori iubebo, nec illum incomitatum dimittam. Non oportet enim eum, qui modo se tot. milia hominum sequentia videbat, tot praecedentia, tot circumfusa, subito solum destitui. Contentus erit his interim convictoribus."

4   Haec ait et turpi convolvens stamina fuso
abrupit stolidae regalia tempora vitae.
374

all this torture cannot he have a rest? Four and sixty
years it is now since he began to pant for breath.
What grudge is this you bear against him and the
whole empire? Do let the astrologers tell the truth
for once; since he became emperor, they have never
let a year pass, never a month, without laying him
out for his burial. Yet it is no wonder if they are
wrong, and no one knows his hour. Nobody ever believed he was really quite born.[1] Do what has to be
done: "Kill him, and let a better man rule in his Virg.
empty court." Georg
iv, 90

Clotho replied: 'Upon my word, I did wish to
give him another hour or two, until he should make
Roman citizens of the half dozen who are still out-
siders. (He made up his mind, you know, to see the
whole world in the toga, Greeks, Gauls, Spaniards,
Britons, and all.) But since it is your pleasure to
leave a few foreigners for seed, and since you command me, so be it." She opened her box and out
came three spindles. One was for Augurinus, one
for Baba, one for Claudius.[2] "These three," she says,
"I will cause to die within one year and at no great
distance apart, and I will not dismiss him unattended.
Think of all the thousands of men he was wont to see
following after him, thousands going before, thousands
all crowding about him; and it would never do to
leave him alone on a sudden. These boon companions
will satisfy him for the nonce."

This said, she twists the thread around his ugly spindle 4
  once,
Snaps off the last bit of the life of that Imperial dunce.

[1] A proverb for a nobody, as Petron. 58 *qui te natum non
putat*.

[2] Augurinus: unknown. Baba: see Sen. Ep. 159, a fool.

375

LUCIUS ANNAEUS SENECA

At Lachesis redimita comas, ornata capillos,

Pieria crinem lauro frontemque coronans,

candida de niveo subtemina vellere sumit

felici moderanda manu, quae ducta colorem

assumpsere novum. Mirantur pensa sorores:

mutatur vilis pretioso lana metallo,

aurea formoso descendunt saecula filo.

Nec modus est illis, felicia vellera ducunt

et gaudent implere manus, sunt dulcia pensa.

Sponte sua festinat opus nulloque labore

mollia contorto descendunt stamina fuso.

Vincunt Tithoni, vincunt et Nestoris annos.

Phoebus adest cantuque iuvat gaudetque futuris,

et laetus nunc plectra movet, nunc pensa
    ministrat.

Detinet intentas cantu fallitque laborem.

Dumque nimis citharam fraternaque carmina
    laudant,

plus solito nevere manus, humanaque fata

laudatum transcendit opus. "Ne demite, Parcae"

Phoebus ait "vincat mortalis tempora vitae

APOCOLOCYNTOSIS

But Lachesis, her hair adorned, her tresses neatly
bound,
Pierian laurel on her locks, her brows with garlands
crowned,
Plucks me from out the snowy wool new threads as
white as snow,
Which handled with a happy touch change colour as
they go,
Not common wool, but golden wire; the Sisters wondering gaze,
As age by age the pretty thread runs down the golden
days.
World without end they spin away, the happy fleeces
pull;
What joy they take to fill their bands with that delightful wool!
Indeed, the task performs itself: no toil the spinners
know:
Down drops the soft and silken thread as round the
spindles go;
Fewer than these are Tithon's years, not Nestor's life
so long.
Phoebus is present: glad he is to sing a merry song;
Now helps the work, now full of hope upon the barp
doth play;
The Sisters listen to the song that charms their toil
away.
They praise their brother's melodies, and still the
spindles run,
Till more than man's allotted span the busy hands
have spun.
Then Phoebus says, "O sister Fates! I pray take none
away,
But suffer this one life to be longer than mortal day.

LUCIUS ANNAEUS SENECA

ille, mihi similis vultu similisque decore
nec cantu nec voce minor.   Felicia lassis
saecula praestabit legumque silentia rumpet.
Qualis discutiens fugientia *Lucifer* astra
aut qualis surgit redeuntibus Hesperus astris,
qualis cum primum tenebris Aurora solutis
induxit rubicunda diem, Sol aspicit orhem
lucidus, et primos a carcere concitat axes:
talis Caesar adest, talem iam Roma Neronem
aspiciet. Flagrat nitidus fulgore remisso
vultus, et adfuso cervix formosa capillo."

haec Apollo.   At Lachesis, quae et ipsa homini for-
mosissimo faveret, fecit illud plena manu, et Neroni
multos anuos de suo donat.   Claudium autem iubent
omnes

χαίροντας, εὐφημοῦντας ἐκπέμπειν δόμων.[1]

Et ille quidem animam ebulliit, et ex eo desiit vivere
videri. Exspiravit autem dum comoedos audit, ut
scias me non sine causa illos timere. Ultima vox eius
haec inter homines audita est, cum maiorem sonitum

---

[1] A fragment from the Cresphontes of Euripides (Nauck,
452).

APOCOLOCYNTOSIS

Like me in face and lovely grace, like me in voice and
    song,
He'll bid the laws at length speak out that have been
    dumb so long,
Will give unto the weary world years prosperous and
    bright.
Like as the daystar from on high scatters the stars of
    night,
As, when the stars return again, clear Hesper brings
    his light,
Or as the ruddy dawn drives out the dark, and brings
    the day,
As the bright sun looks on the world, and speeds along
    its way
His rising car from morning's gates: so Caesar doth
    arise,
So Nero shows his face to Rome before the people's
    eyes;
His bright and shining countenance illumines all the air,
While down upon his graceful neck fall rippling waves
    of hair."

Thus Apollo. But Lachesis, quite as ready to cast a
favourable eye on a handsome man, spins away by the
handful, and bestows years and years upon Nero out
of her own pocket. As for Claudius, they tell everybody
            to speed him on his way
    With cries of joy and solemn litany.

At once he bubbled up the ghost, and there was an
end to that shadow of a life. He was listening to a
troupe of comedians when he died, so you see I have
reason to fear those gentry. The last words he was
heard to speak in this world were these. When he had
made a great noise with that part of him which talked

379

emisisset illa parte, qua facilius loquebatur: "vae me,
puto, concacavi me." Quod an fecerit, nescio: omnia
certe concacavit.

5   Quae in terris postea sint acta, supervacuum est
referre.   Scitis enim optime, nec periculum est ne
excidant memoriae quae gaudium publicum impres-
serit: nemo felicitatis suae obliviscitur.   In caelo
quae acta sint, audite: fides penes auctorem erit.
Nuntiatur Iovi venisse quendam bonae staturae, bene
canum; nescio quid illum minari, assidue enim caput
movere; pedem dextrum trahere.   Quaesisse se, cuius
nationis esset: respondisse nescio quid perturbato
sono et voce confusa; non intellegere se linguam eius,
nec Graecum esse nec Romanum nec ullins gentis
notae.   Tum Iuppiter Herculem, qui totum orhem
terrarum pererraverat et nosse videbatur omnes nati-
ones, iubet ire et explorare, quorum hominum esset.
Tum Hercules primo aspectu sane perturbatus est, ut
qui etiam non omnia monstra timuerit.   Ut vidit novi
generis faciem, insolitum incessum, vocem nullius
terrestris animalis sed qualis esse marinis beluis solet,
raucam et implicatam, putavit sibi tertium decimum
laborem venisse.   Diligentius intuenti visus est quasi
homo.   Accessit itaque et quod facillimum fuit Grae-
culo, ait:

τίς πόθεν εἶς ἀνδρῶν, πόθι τοι πόλις ἠδὲ τοκῆες;

easiest, he cried out, "Oh dear, oh dear! I think I have made a mess of myself." Whether he did or no, I cannot say, but certain it is he always did make a mess of everything.

What happened next on earth it is mere waste of 5 time to tell, for you know it all well enough, and there is no fear of your ever forgetting the impression which that public rejoicing made on your memory. No one forgets his own happiness. What happened in heaven you shall hear: for proof please apply to my informant. Word comes to Jupiter that a stranger had arrived, a man of fair height and hair well sprinkled with grey; he seemed to be threatening something, for he wagged his head ceaselessly; he dragged the right foot. They asked him what nation he was of; he answered something in a confused mumbling voice: his language they did not understand. He was no Greek and no Roman, nor of any known race. On this Jupiter bids Hercules go and find out what country he comes from; you see Hercules had travelled over the whole world, and might be expected to know all the nations in it. But Hercules, the first glimpse he got, was really much taken aback, although not all the monsters in the world could frighten him; when he saw this new kind of object, with its extraordinary gait, and the voice of no terrestrial beast, but such as you might hear in the leviathans of the deep, hoarse and inarticulate, he thought his thirteenth labour had come upon him. When he looked closer, the thing seemed to be a kind of man. Up he goes, then, and says what your Greek finds readiest to his tongue:

"Who art thou, and what thy people? Who thy Od. i, 17 parents, where thy home?"

LUCIUS ANNAEUS SENECA

Claudius gaudet esse illic philologos homines, sperat futurum aliquem historiis suis locum.   Itaque et ipse Homerico versu Caesarem se esse significans ait:

Ἰλιόθεν με φέρων ἄνεμος Κικόνεσσι πέλασσεν.

Erat autem sequens versus verior, acque Homericus:

ἔνθα δ᾿ ἐγὼ πόλιν ἔπραθον, ὤλεσα δ᾿ αὐτούς.

6 Et imposuerat Herculi minime vafro, nisi fuisset illic Febris, quae fano suo relicto sola cum illo venerat ceteros omnes deos Romae reliquerat. "Iste" inquit "mera mendacia narrat.   Ego tibi dico, quae cum illo tot annis vixi: Luguduni natus est, Marci municipem vides.   Quod tibi narro, ad sextum decimum lapidem natus est a Vienna, Gallus germanus.   Itaque quod Gallum facere oportebat, Romam cepit.   Hunc ego tibi recipio Luguduni natum, ubi Licinus[1] multis annis regnavit.   Tu autem, qui plura loca calcasti quam ullus mulio perpetuarius, Lugudunenses scire debes, et[2] multa milia inter Xanthum et Rhodanum interesse." Excandescit hoc loco Claudius et quanto potest murmure irascitur.   Quid diceret, nemo intellegebat, ille autem Febrim duci iubebat, illo gestu solutae manus

[1] *Buecheler* Licinus *for* Licinius.
[2] *Buecheler omits* et *with one MS. and brackets* Lugudunenses.

382

APOCOLOCYNTOSIS

Claudius was delighted to find literary men in that place, and began to hope there might be some corner for his own historical works. So he caps him with another Homeric verse, explaining that he was Caesar:

"Breezes wafted me from Ilion unto the Ciconian Od. ix, 39 land."

But the next verse was more true, and no less Homeric:

"Thither come, I sacked a city, slew the people every one."

He would have taken in poor simple Hercules, but 6 that Our Lady of Malaria was there, who left her temple and came alone with him: all the other gods he had left at Rome. Quoth she, "The fellow's tale is nothing but lies. I have lived with him all these years, and I tell you, he was born at Lyons. You behold a fellow-burgess of Marcus.[1] As I say, he was born at the sixteenth milestone from Vienne, a native Gaul. So of course he took Rome, as a good Gaul ought to do. I pledge you my word that in Lyons he was born, where Licinus[2] was king so many years. But you that have trudged over more roads than any muleteer that plies for hire, you must have come across the people of Lyons, and you must know that it is a far cry from Xanthus to the Rhone." At this point Claudius flared up, and expressed his wrath with as big a growl as he could manage. What he said nobody understood; as a matter of fact, he was ordering my lady of Fever to be taken away, and making that sign with his trembling hand (which

[1] Reference unknown.
[2] A Gallic slave, appointed by Augustus Procurator of Gallia Lugudunensis, when he made himself notorious by his extortions. See Dion Cass. liv, 21.

et ad hoc unum satis firmae, quo decollare homines
7 solebat, iusserat illi collum praecidi.   Putares omnes
illius esse libertos : adeo illum nemo curabat.   Tum
Hercules "audi me" inquit "tu desine fatuari. Venisti
huc, ubi mures ferrum rodunt.   Citius mihi verum, ne
tibi alogias excutiam."   Et quo terribilior esset, tragi-
cus fit et ait :

"exprome propere, sede qua genitus cluas,
  hoc ne peremptus stipite ad terram accidas;
  haec clava reges saepe mactavit feros.
  Quid nunc profatu voeis incerto sonas ?
  Quae patria, quae gens mobile eduxit caput?
  Edissere.   Equidem regna tergemini petens
  longinqua regis, unde ab Hesperio mari
  Inachiam ad urbem nobile advexi peeus,
  vidi duobus imminens fluviis ingum,
  quod Phoebus ortu semper obverso videt,
  ubi Rhodanus ingens amne praerapido fluit,
  Ararque dubitans, quo suos cursus agat,
  tacitus quietis adluit ripas vadis.
  Estne illa tellus spiritus altrix tui?"

Haec satis animose et fortiter, nihilo minus mentis

was always steady enough for that, if for nothing else) by which he used to decapitate men.   He had ordered her head to be chopped off.   For all the notice the others took of him, they might have been his own freedmen.

Then Hercules said, "You just listen to me, and 7 stop playing the fool.   You have come to the place where the mice nibble iron.[1] Out with the truth, and look sharp, or I'll knock your quips and quiddities out of you."   Then to make himself all the more awful, he strikes an attitude and proceeds in his most tragic vein:

"Declare with speed what spot you claim by birth,
  Or with this club fall stricken to the earth!
  This club hath ofttimes slaughtered haughty kings!
  Why mumble unintelligible things?
  What land, what tribe produced that shaking head?
  Declare it!   On my journey when I sped
  Far to the Kingdom of the triple King,
  And from the Main Hesperian did bring
  The goodly cattle to the Argive town,
  There I beheld a mountain looking down
  Upon two rivers: this the Sun espies
  Right opposite each day he doth arise.
  Hence, mighty Rhone, thy rapid torrents flow,
  And Arar, much in doubt which way to go,
  Ripples along the banks with shallow roll.
  Say, is this land the nurse that bred thy soul?"

These lines he delivered with much spirit and a bold front.   All the same, he was not quite master of his

---

[1] A proverb, found also in Herondas iii, 76: apparently fairy-land, the land of Nowhere.

suae non est et timet μωροῦ πληγήν. Claudius ut vidit
virum valentem, oblitus nugarum intellexit neminem
Romae sibi parem fuisse, illic non habere se idem gratiae: gallum in suo sterquilino plurimum posse. Itaque
quantum intellegi potuit, haec visus est dicere: "Ego
te, fortissime deorum Hercule, speravi mihi adfuturum
apud alios, et si qui a me notorem petisset, te fui
nominaturus, qui me optime nosti. Nam si memoria
repetis, ego eram qui tibi[1] ante templum tuum ius
dicebam totis diebus mense Iulio et Augusto. Tu scis,
quantum illio miseriarum tulerim, cum causidicos audirem diem et noctem, in quos si incidisses, valde fortis
licet tibi videaris, maluisses cloacas Augeac purgare:
multo plus ego stercoris exhausi. Sed quoniam volo"

8 "Non mirum quod in curiam impetum fecisti: nihil
tibi clausi est. Modo dic nobis, qnalem deum istum
fieri velis. Ἐπικούρειος θεὸς non potest esse: οὔτε
αὐτὸς πρᾶγμα ἔχει τι οὔτε ἄλλοις παρέχει; Stoicus?
Quomodo potest 'rotundus' esse, ut ait Varro, 'sine
capite, sine praeputio'? Est aliquid in illo Stoici dei,
iam video: nec cor nec caput habet. Si mehercules
a Saturno petisset hoc beneficium, cuius mensem toto
anno celebravit, Saturnalicius princeps, non tulisset
illud, nedum ab Iove, quem quantum quidem in illo

---

[1] *So MSS. Buecheler reads* Tiburi, *quoting Suet. Aug. 72.*

---

[1] A parody of the phrase, θεοῦ πληγή, god's blow, or as in
Apostolius viii, 89, C, θεοῦ δὲ πληγὴν οὐχ ὑπερπηδᾷ βροτός (from
Menander): no mortal can escape god's blow.

[2] *Gallum* means both Gaul and cock; the proverb plays on
his birthplace.

[3] Compare Diogenes Laertius x, 139: τὸ μακάριον καὶ ἄφθαρτον
οὔτε αὐτὸ πρᾶγμά τι ἔχει οὔτε ἄλλῳ παρέχει: "The Blessed and
Incorruptible neither itself has trouble nor causes trouble to
another."

[4] Author or *Saturae Menippeae* (now lost), which no doubt
burlesqued the Stoic "perfect man," *totus teres ataue rotundus.*

wits, and had some fear of a blow from the fool.[1]
Claudius, seeing a mighty man before him, forgot his
trifling and understood that here he had not quite the
same pre-eminence as at Rome, where no one was his
equal: the Gallic cock[2] was worth most on his own
dunghill. So this is what he was thought to say, as
far as could be made out: "I did hope, Hercules,
bravest of all the gods, that you would take my part
with the rest, and if I should need a voucher, that I
might name you who know me so well. Do but call
it to mind, how it was I used to sit in judgment before
your temple whole days together during July and
August. You know what miseries I endured there, in
hearing the lawyers plead day and night. If you had
fallen amongst these, you may think yourself very
strong, but you would have found it worse than the
sewers of Augeas: I drained out more filth than you
did. But since I want..."

(Some pages have fallen out, in which Hercules
must have been persuaded. The gods are now discus-
sing what Hercules tells them).

"No wonder you have forced your way into the 8
Senate House: no bars or bolts can hold against you.
Only do say what species of god you want the fellow
to be made. An Epicurean god he cannot be: for
they take no trouble and cause none.[3] A Stoic,
then? How can he be globular, as Varro[4] says, without a head or any other projection? There *is* in him
something of the Stoic god, as I can see now: he has
neither heart nor head. Upon my word, if he had
asked this boon from Saturn, he would not have got
it, though he kept up Saturn's feast all the year round,
a truly Saturnalian prince. A likely thing he will get
it from Jove, whom he condemned for incest as far as

fuit, damnavit incesti. Silanum enim generum suum
occidit propterea quod sororem suam, festivissimam
omnium puellarum, quam omnes Venerem vocarent,
maluit Iunonem vocare. 'Quare' inquit 'quaero
enim, sororem suam?' Stulte, stude: Athenis dimi-
dium licet, Alexandriae totum. 'Quia Romae' inquis
'mures molas lingunt.' Hic nobis curva corriget?
quid in cubiculo suo faciat, nescit, et iam 'caeli
scrutatur plagas'? Deus fieri vult: parum est quod
templum in Britannia habet, quod hunc barbari colunt
et ut deum orant μωροῦ εὐιλάτου τυχεῖν?"

9 Tandem Iovi venit in mentem, privatis intra curiam
morantibus senatoribus non licere[1] sententiam dicere
nec disputare. "Ego" inquit "p. c. interrogare vobis
permiseram, vos mera mapalia fecistis. Volo ut
servetis disciplinam curiae. Hic qualiscunque est,
quid de nobis existimabit?" Illo dimisso primus
interrogatur sententiam Ianus pater. Is designatus
erat in kal. Iulias postmeridianus consul, homo quan-
tumvis vafer, qui semper videt ἅμα πρόσσω καὶ ὀπίσσω.

[1] senatoribus non licere: *added by Buecheler.*

---

[1] Because Juno was *et soror et coniunx.*

[2] Marriage with a half-sister was allowed at Athens; the
Egyptian royal family married brother and sister.

[3] Another proverb of uncertain meaning; probably "because people like nice things at Rome, as they do everywhere."

in him lay :[1] for he killed his son-in-law Silanus,
because Silanus had a sister, a most charming girl,
called Venus by all the world, and he preferred to call
her Juno. Why, says he, I want to know why, his
own sister? Read your books, stupid: you may go
half-way at Athens, the whole way at Alexandria.[2]
Because the mice lick meal[3] at Rome, you say. Is
this creature to mend our crooked ways? What goes
on in his own closet he knows not;[4] and now he
searches the regions of the sky, wants to be a god.
Is it not enough that he has a temple in Britain, that
savages worship him and pray to him as a god, so that
they may find a fool[5] to have mercy upon them?"

At last it came into Jove's head, that while strangers 9
were in the House it was not lawful to speak or debate.
"My lords and gentlemen," said he, "I gave you
leave to ask questions, and you have made a regular
farmyard[6] of the place. Be so good as to keep the
rules of the House. What will this person think of
us, whoever he is?" So Claudius was led out, and
the first to be asked his opinion was Father Janus:
he had been made consul elect for the afternoon of
the next first of July,[7] being as shrewd a man as you
could find on a summer's day: for he could see, as they
say, before and behind.[8] He made an eloquent

[4] Perhaps alluding to a mock marriage of Silius and
Messalina.

[5] Again μωροῦ for θεοῦ as in ch. 6.

[6] Proverb: meaning unknown.

[7] Perhaps an allusion to the shortening of the consul's
term, which was done to give more candidates a chance of
the honour.

[8] Il. iii, 109; alluding here to Janus's double face.

389

LUCIUS ANNAEUS SENECA

Is multa diserte, quod in foro vivebat, dixit, quae notarius persequi non potuit, et ideo non refero, ne aliis verbis ponam, quae ab illo dicta sunt. Multa dixit de magnitudine deorum : non debere hunc vulgo dari honorem. "Ohm" inquit "magna res erat deum fieri : iam famam mimum fecistis. Itaque ne videar in personam, non in rem dicere sententiam, censeo ne quis post hunc diem deus fiat ex his, qui ἀρούρης καρπὸν ἔδουσιν, aut ex his, quos alit ζείδωρος ἄρουρα. Qui contra hoc senatus consultum deus factus, dictus pictusve erit, eum dedi Laruis et proximo munere inter novos auctoratos ferulis vapulare placet." Proximus interrogatur sententiam Diespiter Vicae Potae filius, et ipse designatus consul, nummariolus : hoc quaestu se sustinebat, vendere civitatulas solebat. Ad hunc belle accessit Hercules et auriculam illi tetigit Censet itaque in haec verba : "Cum divus Claudius et divum Augustum sanguine contingat nec minus divam Augustam aviam suam, quam ipse deam esse iussit, longeque omnes mortales sapientia antecellat, sitque e re publica esse aliquem qui cum Romulo possit ʻferventia rapa vorare,ʼ censeo uti divus Claudius ex hac die deus sit, ita uti ante eum qui optimo iure factus sit, eamque rem ad metamorphosis Ovidi adiciendam." Variae erant sententiae, et vide-

---

[1] No one knows what this phrase really means. Cic. Att. i, 16[13] has *fabam mimum*, which makes it likely that there should be the same reading here ; but as the meaning is so uncertain it seems best not to alter the text.

[2] Il. vi, 142 and other phrases.

[3] Part of the training.

[4] Apparently sometimes identified with Pluto, Dis.

[5] A quotation from some unknown poet. Martial speaks of Romulus eating turnips, xiii, 16.

390

harangue, because his life was passed in the forum, but too fast for the notary to take down. That is why I give no full report of it, for I don't want to change the words he used. He said a great deal of the majesty of the gods, and how the honour ought not to be given away to every Tom, Dick, or Harry. " Once," said he, "it was a great thing to become a god ; now you have made it a farce.[1] Therefore, that you may not think I am speaking against one person instead of the general custom, I propose that from this day forward the godhead be given to none of those who eat the fruits of the earth, or whom mother earth doth nourish.[2] After this bill has been read a third time, whosoever is made, said, or portrayed to be god, I vote he be delivered over to the bogies, and at the next public show be flogged with a birch amongst the new gladiators."[3] The next to be asked was - Diespiter, son of Vica Pota, he also being consul elect, and a moneylender ;[4] by this trade he made a living, used to sell rights of citizenship in a small way. Hercules trips me up to him daintily, and tweaks him by the ear. So he uttered his opinion in these words : " Inasmuch as the blessed Claudius is akin to the blessed Augustus, and also to the blessed Augusta, his grandmother, whom he ordered to be made a goddess, and whereas he far surpasses all mortal men in wisdom, and seeing that it is for the public good that there be some one able to join Romulus in devouring boiled turnips,[5] I propose that from this day forth blessed Claudius be a god, to enjoy that honour with all its appurtenances in as full a degree as any other before him, and that a note to that effect be added to Ovid's Metamorphoses." The meeting was divided, and it looked as though Claudius was to

batur Claudius sententiam vincere. Hercules enim,
qui videret ferrum suum in igne esse, modo huc modo
illuc cursabat et aichat: "Noli mihi invidere, mea res
agitur; deinde tu si quid volueris, in vicem faciam;
manus manum lavat."

10   Tune divus Augustus surrexit sententiae suae loco
dicendae, et summa facundia disseruit: "Ego" inquit
"p. c. vos testes babeo, ex quo deus factus sum, nullum me verbum fecisse: semper meum negotium ago.
Sed non possum amplius dissimulare, et dolorem, quem
graviorem pudor facit, continere. In hoc terra mari-
que pacem peperi? Ideo civilia bella compescui? Ideo
legibus urbem fundavi, operibus ornavi, ut—quid
dicam p. c. non invenio: omnia infra indignationem
verba sunt. Confugiendum est itaque ad Messalae
Corvini, disertissimi viri, illam sententiam "pudet
imperii." Hic, p. c., qui vobis non posse videtur
muscam excitare, tam facile homines occidebat, quam
canis adsidit. Sed quid ego de tot ac talibus viris
dicam? Non vacat deflere publicas clades intuenti
domestica mala. Itaque illa omittam, haec referam;
nam etiam si soror[1] mea Graece nescit, ego scio:
ἔγγιον γόνυ κνήμης. Iste quem videtis, per tot annos

[1] *MSS.* sormea.

wın the day.   For Hercules saw his iron was in the
fire, trotted here and trotted there, saying, "Don't
deny me; I make a point of the matter.   I'll do as
much for you again, when you like; you roll my log,
and I'll roll yours: one hand washes another."

Then arose the blessed Augustus, when his turn 10
came, and spoke with much eloquence.[1]   "I call you
to witness, my lords and gentlemen," said he, "that
since the day I was made a god I have never uttered
one word.   I always mind my own business.   But
now I can keep on the mask no longer, nor conceal the
sorrow which shame makes all the greater.   Is it for
this I have made peace by land and sea?   For this
have I calmed intestine wars?   For this, laid a firm
foundation of law for Rome, adorned it with buildings,
and all that—gentlemen, words fail me; there are
none can rise to the height of my indignation.   I
must borrow that saying of the eloquent Messala
Corvinus, I am ashamed of my authority.[2]   This man,
my lords, who looks as though he could not worry a
fly, used to chop off heads as easily as a dog sits down.
But why should I speak of all those men, and such
men?   There is no time to lament for public disasters,
when one has so many private sorrows to think of.   I
leave that, therefore, and say only this; for even if
my sister knows no Greek, I do: The knee is nearer
than the shin.[3]   This man you see, who for so many

[1] The speech seems to contain a parody of Augustus's
style and sayings.
[2] M. Valerius Messalas Corvinus, appointed praefectus urbi,
resigned within a week.
[3] A proverb, like "Charity begins at home." The reading of
the passage is uncertain; "sister" is only a conjecture, and
it is hard to see why his sister should be mentioned.

393

sub meo nomine latens, hanc mihi gratiam rettulit, ut duas Iulias proneptes meas occideret, alteram ferro, alteram fame ; unum abnepotem L. Silanum. videris Iuppiter an in causa mala, certe in tua, si aequus futurus es. Dic mihi, dive Claudi, quare quemquam ex his, quos quasque occidisti, antequam de causa cognosceres, antequam audires, damnasti? Hoc ubi 11 fieri solet? In caelo non fit. Ecce Iuppiter, qui tot annos regnat, uni Volcano crus fregit, quem

ῥῖψε ποδὸς τεταγὼν ἀπὸ βηλοῦ θεσπεσίοιο,

et iratus fuit uxori et suspendit illam: numquid occidit? Tu Messalinam, cuius acque avunculus maior eram quam tuns, occidisti. "Nescio" inquis. Di tibi male faciant: adeo istuc turpins est, quod nescisti, quam quod occidisti. C. Caesarem non desiit mortuum persequi. Occiderat ille socerum: hic et generum. Gaius Crassi filium vetuit Magnum vocari: hic nomen illi reddidit, caput tulit. Occidit in una domo Crassum, Magnum, Scriboniam, Tristionias, Assarionem, nobiles tamen, Crassum vero tam fatuum, ut etiam regnare posset. Hune nunc deum facere vultis? Videte corpus eius dis iratis natum. Ad summam, tria verba cito dicat, et servum me ducat. Hunc deum quis colet? Quis credet? Dum tales deos facitis, nemo vos deos esse credet. Summa rei, p. c.,
394

years has been masquerading under my name, has done me the favour of murdering two Julias, great-granddaughters of mine, one by cold steel and one by starvation; and one great-grandson, L. Silanus. See, Jupiter, whether in a bad cause (at least it is your own) you will be fair. Come tell me, blessed Claudius, why of all those you killed, both men and women, without a hearing, why you did not hear their side of the case first, before putting them to death? Where do we find that custom? It is not done in heaven. Look at Jupiter: all these years he has been king, and 11 never did more than once to break Vulcan's leg,

> 'Whom seizing by the foot he cast from the   Iliad i, 591
> threshold of the sky,'

and once he fell in a rage with his wife and strung her up: did he do any killing¨ You killed Messalina, whose great-uncle I was no less than yours. 'I don't know,' did you say? Curse you! that is just it: not to know was worse than to kill. Caligula he went on persecuting even when he was dead. Caligula murdered his father-in-law, Claudius his son-in-law to boot. Caligula would not have Crassus' son called Great; Claudius gave him his name back, and took away his head. In one family he destroyed Crassus, Magnus, Scribonia, the Tristionias, Assario, noble though they were; Crassus indeed such a fool that he might have been emperor. Is this he you want now to make a god? Look at his body, born under the wrath of heaven! In fine, let him say as many as three words quickly, and he may have me for a slave. God! who will worship this god, who will believe him? While you make gods of such as he, no one will believe you to be gods. To be brief, my lords: if I have lived

si honeste me[1] inter vos gessi, si nulli clarins respondi, vindicate iniurias meas. Ego pro sententia mea hoc censeo:" atque ita ex tabella recitavit: "quando quidem divus Claudius occidit socerum suum Appium Silanum, generos duos Magnum Pompeium et L. Silanum, socerum filiae suae Crassum Frugi, hominem tam similem sibi quam ovo ovum, Scriboniam socrum filiae suae, uxorem suam Messalinam et ceteros quorum numerus iniri non potuit, placet mihi in eum severe animadverti, nec illi rerum iudicandarum vacationem dari, eumque quam primum exportari, et caelo intra triginta dies excedere, Olympo intra diem tertium."

Pedibus in hanc sententiam itum est. Nec mora, Cyllenius illum collo obtorto trahit ad inferos, a caelo

"illuc[1] unde negant redire quemquam."

12 Dum descendunt per viam sacram, interrogat Mercurius, quid sibi velit ille concursus hominum, num Claudii funus esset. Et erat omnium formosissimum et impensa cura, plane ut scires deum efferri: tubicinum, cornicinum, omnis generis aenatorum tanta turba, tantus concentus, ut etiam Claudius audire posset. Omnes laeti, hilares: populus Romanus ambulabat tanquam liber. Agatho et pauci causidici plorabant, sed plane ex animo. Iurisconsulti e tenebris procedebant, pallidi, graciles, vix animam habentes, tanquam qui tum maxime reviviscerent.

[1] *Added by Buecheler.*

honourably among you, if I have never given plain speech to any, avenge my wrongs. This is my motion": then he read out his amendment, which he had committed to writing: "Inasmuch as the blessed Claudius murdered his father-in-law Appius Silanus, his two sons-in-law, Pompeius Magnus and L. Silanus, Crassus Frugi his daughter's father-in-law, as like him as two eggs in a basket, Scribonia his daughter's mother-in-law, his wife Messalina, and others too numerous to mention; I propose that strong measures be taken against him, that he be allowed no delay of process, that immediate sentence of banishment be passed on him, that he be deported from heaven within thirty days, and from Olympus within thirty hours."

A division was taken upon this without further debate. Not a moment was lost: Mercury got a grip of his throat, and haled him to the lower regions, to that bourne "from which they say no traveller returns."[1] As they passed downwards along the 12 Sacred Way, Mercury asked what was that great concourse of men? could it be Claudius' funeral? It was certainly a most gorgeous spectacle, got up regardless of expense, clear it was that a god was being borne to the grave: tootling of flutes, roaring of horns, an immense brass band of all sorts, such a din that even Claudius could hear it. Joy and rejoicing on every side, the Roman people walking about like free men. Agatho and a few pettifoggers were weeping for grief, and for once in a way they meant it. The Barristers were crawling out of their dark corners, pale and thin, with hardly a breath in their bodies, as though just coming to life again. One of them when he saw the

[1] Catullus iii, 12.

397

LUCIUS ANNAEUS SENECA

Ex his unus cum vidisset capita conferentes et fortunas suas deplorantes causidicos, accedit et ait: "dicebam vobis: non semper Saturnalia crunt."

Claudius ut vidit funus suum, intellexit se mortuum esse. Ingenti eum μεγάλῳ χορικῷ nenia cantabatur anapaestis:

"Fundite fletus, edite planctus,
resonet tristi clamore forum:
cecidit pulchre cordatus homo,
quo non alius fuit in toto
fortior orbe.
Ille citato vincere cursu
poterat celeres, ille rebelles
fundere Parthos levibusque sequi
Persida telis, certaque manu
tendere nervum, qui praecipites
vulnere parvo figeret hostes,
pictaque Medi terga fugacis.
Ille Britannos ultra noti
litora ponti
et caeruleos senta Brigantas
dare Romuleis colla catenis
iussit et ipsum nova Romanae
iura securis tremere Occanum.
Deflete virum, quo non alius
potuit citius discere causas,
una tantum parte audita,
saepe ne utra. Quis nunc index
toto lites audiet anno?
Tibi iam cedet sede relicta,
qui dat populo iura silenti,

pettifoggers putting their heads together, and lamenting their sad lot, up comes he and says: "Did not I tell you the Saturnalia could not last for ever?"

When Claudius saw his own funeral train, he realized that he was dead. For they were chanting his dirge in anapaests, with much mopping and mouthing:

"Pour forth your laments, your sorrow declare,
Let the sounds of grief rise high in the air:
For he that is dead had a wit most keen,
Was bravest of all that on earth have been.
Racehorses are nothing to his swift feet:
Rebellious Parthians he did defeat;
Swift after the Persians his light shafts go:
For he well knew how to fit arrow to bow,
Swiftly the striped barbarians fled:
With one little wound he shot them dead.
And the Britons beyond in their unknown seas,
Blue-shielded Brigantians too, all these
He chained by the neck as the Romans' slaves.
He terrified Ocean with all his waves,
Made fear a new master to lay down the law.
O weep for the man! This world never saw
One quicker a troublesome suit to decide,
When only one part of the case had been tried,
(He could do it indeed and not hear either side).
Who'll now sit in judgment the whole year round?
Now he that is judge of the shades underground

399

Cretaea tenens oppida centum.
Caedite maestis pectora palmis,
o causidici, venale genus.
Vosque poetae lugete novi,
vosque in primis qui concusso
magna parastis lucra fritillo."

13 Delectabatur laudibus suis Claudius, et cupiebat diutius spectare. Inicit illi manum Talthybius deorum[1] et trahit capite obvoluto, ne quis eum possit agnoscere, per campum Martium, et inter Tiberim et viam tectam descendit ad inferos. Antecesserat iam compendiaria Narcissus libertus ad patronum excipiendum, et venienti nitidus, ut erat a balineo, occurrit et ait: "Quid di ad homines?" "celerius" inquit Mercurius "et venire nos nuntia." Dicto citius Narcissus evolat. Omnia proclivia sunt, facile descenditur. Itaque quamvis podagricus esset, momento temporis pervenit ad ianuam Ditis, ubi iacebat Cerberus vel ut ait Horatius "belua centiceps." Pusillum perturbatur—subalbam canem in deliciis habere adsueverat—ut illum vidit canem nigrum, villosum, sane non quem velis tibi in tenebris occurrere, et magna voce "Claudius" inquit "veniet." Cum plausu procedunt cantantes: εὑρήκαμεν, συγχαίρωμεν.[2] Hic erat C. Silius consul designatus, Iunens praetorius, Sex. Traulus, M. Hel-

---

[1] *The MSS. add* nuntius.
[2] *Buecheler alters the MS. reading to* συγχαίρομεν, *the actual word of the cry.*

APOCOLOCYNTOSIS

Once ruler of fivescore cities in Crete,
Must yield to his better and take a back seat.
Mourn, mourn, pettifoggèrs, ye venal crew,
And you, minor poets, woe, woe is to you!
And you above all, who get rich quick
By the rattle of dice and the three card trick."

Claudius was charmed to hear his own praises sung, 13
and would have stayed longer to see the show.   But
the Talthybius[1] of the gods laid a band on him, and
led him across the Campus Martins, first wrapping his
head up close that no one might know him, until be-
twixt Tiber and the Subway he went down to the
lower regions.   His freedman Narcissus had gone
down before him by a short cut, ready to welcome his
master.   Out he comes to meet him, smooth and
shining (he had just left the bath), and says he:
"What make the gods among mortals?"   "Look
alive," says Mercury, "go and tell them we are
coming."   Away he flew, quicker than tongue can tell
it.   It is easy going by that road, all down hill.   So
although Claudius had a touch of the gout, in a trice
they were come to Dis's door.   There lay Cerberus,
or, as Horace puts it, the hundred-headed monster. Odes ii,
Claudius was a trifle perturbed (it was a little white 13, 35
bitch he used to keep for a pet) when he spied this
black shag-haired bound, not at all the kind of thing
you could wish to meet in the dark.   In a loud voice
he cried, "Claudius is coming!"   All marched before
him singing, "The lost is found, O let us rejoice
together!"[2]   Here were found C. Silius consul elect,
Juncus the ex-praetor, Sextus Traulus, M. Helvius,

[1] Talthybius was a herald, and *nuntius* is obviously a gloss
on this.   He means Mercury.
[2] With a slight change, a cry used in the worship of Osiris.

vius, Trogus, Cotta, Vettius Valens, Fabius equites R. quos Narcissus duci iusserat. Medius erat in hac cantantium turba Mnester pantomimus, quem Claudius decoris causa minorem fecerat. Ad Messalinam—cito rumor percrebuit Claudium venisse—convolant: primi omnium liberti Polybius, Myron, Harpocras, Amphaeus, Pheronactus, quos Claudius omnes, necubi imparatus esset, praemiserat. Deinde praefecti duo Iustus Catonius et Rufrius Pollio. Deinde amici Saturninus Lusius et Pedo Pompeius et Lupus et Celer Asinius consulares. Novissime fratris filia, sororis filia, generi, soceri, socrus, omnes plane consanguinei. Et agmine facto Claudio occurrunt. Quos cum vidisset Claudius, exclamat: πάντα φίλων πλήρη "quomodo huc venistis vos?" Tum Pedo Pompeius: "Quid dicis, homo crudelissime? Quaeris, quomodo? Quis enim nos alius huc misit quam tu, omnium amicorum interfector? In ius camus, ego tibi hic sellas ostendam."

14   Ducit illum ad tribunal Aeaci: is lege Cornelia quae de sicariis lata est, quaerebat. Postulat, nomen eius recipiat; edit subscriptionem: occisos senatores XXXV, equites R. CCXXI, ceteros ὅσα ψάμαθός τε κόνις τε. Advocatum non invenit. Tandem procedit P. Petronius, vetus convictor eius, homo Claudiana lingua disertus, et postulat advocationem. Non datur. Accusat Pedo Pompeius magnis clamoribus. Incipit patronus velle respondere. Aeacus, homo iustissimus,

APOCOLOCYNTOSIS

Trogus, Cotta, Vettius Valens, Fabius, Roman Knights whom Narcissus had ordered for execution. In the midst of this chanting company was Mnester the mime, whom Claudius for honour's sake had made shorter by a head. The news was soon blown about that Claudius had come: to Messalina they throng: first his freedmen, Polybius, Myron, Harpocras, Amphaeus, Pheronactus, all sent before him by Claudius that he might not be unattended anywhere; next two prefects, Justus Catonius and Rufrius Pollins; then his friends, Saturninus Lusius and Pedo Pompeius and Lupus and Celer Asinius, these of consular rank; last came his brother's daughter, his sister's daughter, sons-in-law, fathers and mothers-in-law, the whole family in fact. In a body they came to meet Claudius; and when Claudius saw them, he exclaimed, "Friends everywhere, on my word! How came you all here?" To this Pedo Pompeius answered, "What, cruel man? How came we here? Who but you sent us, you, the murderer of all the friends that ever you had? To court with you! I'll show you where their lordships sit.'

Pedo brings him before the judgement seat of 14 Aeacus, who was holding court under the Lex Cornelia to try cases of murder and assassination. Pedo requests the judge to take the prisoner's name, and produces a summons with this charge: Senators killed, 35; Roman Knights, 221; others as the sands of the seashore for multitude. Claudius finds no counsel. At ll. ix, 385 length out steps P. Petronius, an old chum of his, a finished scholar in the Claudian tongue, and claimed a remand. Not granted. Pedo Pompeius prosecutes with loud outcry. The counsel for the defence tries to reply; but Aeacus, who is the soul of justice, will

vetat, et illum altera tantum parte audita condemnat
et ait: αἴκε πάθοι τά τ' ἔρεξε, δίκη κ' ἰθεῖα γένοιτο. Ingens silentium factum est. Stupebant omnes novitate
rei attoniti, negabant hoc unquam factum. Claudio
magis iniquum videbatur quam novum. De genere
poenae diu disputatum est, quid illum pati oporteret.
Erant qui dicerent, Sisyphum satis diu laturam fecisse,
Tantalum siti periturum nisi illi succurreretur, aliquando Ixionis miseri rotam sufflaminandam. Non
placuit ulli ex veteribus missionem dari, ne vel Claudius unquam simile speraret. Placuit novam poenam
constitui debere, excogitandum illi laborem irritum
et alicuius cupiditatis speciem sine effectu. Tum
Aeacus inhet illum alea ludere pertuso fritillo. Et iam
coeperat fugientes semper tesseras quaerere et nihil
proficere.

15   Nam quotiens missurus erat resonante fritillo,
     utraque subducto fugiebat tessera fundo.
     Cumque recollectos auderet mittere talos,
     fusuro similis semper semperque petenti,
     404

not have it. Aeacus bears the case against Claudius, refuses to hear the other side and passes sentence against him, quoting the line:

"As he did, so be he done by, this is justice undefiled."[1]

A great silence fell. Not a soul but was stupefied at this new way of managing matters; they had never known anything like it before. It was no new thing to Claudius, yet he thought it unfair. There was a long discussion as to the punishment he ought to endure. Some said that Sisyphus had done his job of porterage long enough; Tantalus would be dying of thirst, if he were not relieved; the drag must be put at last on wretched Ixion's wheel. But it was determined not to let off any of the old stagers, lest Claudius should dare to hope for any such relief. It was agreed that some new punishment must be devised: they must devise some new task, something senseless, to suggest some craving without result. Then Aeacus decreed he should rattle dice for ever in a box with no bottom. At once the poor wretch began his fruitless task of hunting for the dice, which for ever slipped from his fingers.

"For when he rattled with the box, and thought he 15
    now had got 'em,
The little cubes would vanish thro' the perforated
    bottom.
Then he would pick 'em up again, and once more set
    a-trying:
The dice but served him the same trick: away they
    went a-flying.
So still he tries, and still he fails; still searching long
    he lingers;

[1] A proverbial line.

LUCIUS ANNAEUS SENECA

decepere fidem: refugit digitosque per ipsos
fallax adsiduo dilabitur alea furto.
Sic cum iam summi tanguntur culmina montis,
irrita Sisyphio volvuntur pondera collo.

Apparuit subito C. Caesar et petere illum in servitutem coepit; producit testes, qui illum viderant ab
illo flagris, ferulis, colaphis vapulantem.   Adiudicatur
C. Caesari; Caesar illum Aeaco donat.   Is Menandro
liberto suo tradidit, ut a cognitionibus esset.

And every time the tricksy things go slipping thro'
    his fingers.
Just so when Sisyphus his rock once gets atop the
    mountain,
To his dismay he secs it come down on his poor head
    bounding!"

All on a sudden who should turn up but Caligula,
and claims the man for a slave: brings witnesses,
who said they had seen him being flogged, caned,
fisticuffed by him. He is handed over to Caligula,
and Caligula makes him a present to Aeacus. Aeacus
delivers him to his freedman Menander, to be his
law-clerk.

INDEX TO PETRONIUS

INDEX OF NAMES

The references are to chapters in the English translation. The Fragments and Poems are indicated by numbers with the letter F or P respectively prefixed.

A

Achilles, son of Peleus and Thetis; leader of the Greeks against Troy, 59, 129

Acrisius, father of Danae, was told by an oracle that her son would kill him. He therefore shut her up in a brazen tower; Zeus however visited her in the form of a shower of gold, and she became the mother of Perseus, 137

Actium, a promontory in Acarnania, 121

Aeneas, son of Anchises and Venus; hero of Virgil's Aeneid as mythical founder of Rome, 68

Aethiopian, 102

Aetna, a volcanic mountain in north-east Sicily, 122

Africa, 48, 93, 117, 119, 125, 141

African, 35, 119

Agamemnon, a teacher of rhetoric, 3, 6, 26, 28, 46, 48, 49, 50, 52, 65, 69, 78

Agamemnon, leader of the Greeks against Troy, 59

Agatho, a perfumer, 74

Ajax, son of Telamon; after the death of Achilles he was worsted in the contest for Achilles's arms by Odysseus, went mad, and, having killed a flock of sheep in madness, killed himself, 59

Albucia, a character in the lost portion of Petronius, F6

Alcibiades, son of Clinias and Dinomache, b. about 450 B.C.; pupil and friend of Socrates, by whom his life was saved at the battle of Potidaea, 432 B.C., and whom he saved at Delium, 424 B.C., 128

Alexandria, 31, 68

Alps, 122, 123

Amphitryon, son of Alcaeus king of Tiryns, and reputed father of Heracles by Alcmene his wife, who was visited by Zeus, 123

Anacreon of Teos, lyric poet of the sixth century n.o., F20

Apelles, a celebrated fourth century painter who lived at the court of Philip and Alexander 83, 88

Apelles, an actor, 64

Apennine, 124

Apollo, 83, 89, 121, P2I

Apulia, 77

Aquarius, 35, 39

Arabian, 102, 119

Aratus of Soli, an astronomer of the third century, author of the poems Phaenomena and Dioseme a, which Cicero translated, 40 i

Arbiter: Nero called Gaius Petronius "arbiter elegantiarum," and the author of the Satyricon is often cited as Petronius Arbiter, F4, 19, 21, 24 (in conjunction with the name Petronius) F7, 9, 11, 12, 13, 25

Ariadne, daughter of Minos, fled with Theseus to Naxos, where he left her; she was found by Dionysus and became his bride, 138

Arpinum, a town in Latium, birthplace of Cicero, F4

Ascyltos, companion of Encolpius and Giton, 6, 7, 9, 10, 11, 12, 13, 14, 15, 19, 20, 21, 22, 24, 57, 58, 59, 72, 79, 80, 92, 94, 97. 98, 133

Asia, 2, 44, 75, 85

Asiatic, 44

Assafoetida, a musical play no longer extant, 35

Atellane, 53, 68

Athena, 59

Athenian, 185

Athens, 2, 38

Athos, a mountain at the extremity of the peninsula Acte in Macedonia, P3

Atreus, father of Menelaus, 108

Attic, 38

Augustus, first emperor of Rome, b. 63 B.C., d. 14 A.D., 57, 60, 71

410

INDEX OF NAMES

INDEX OF NAMES

INDEX OF NAMES

INDEX OF NAMES

INDEX OF NAMES

INDEX OF NAMES

THE LOEB CLASSICAL LIBRARY.

VOLUMES ALREADY PUBLISHED

Latin Authors.

APULEIUS. The Golden Ass (Metamorphoses), W. Adlington (1566). Revised by S. Gaselee. (*3rd Imp.*)
AUSONIUS. H. G. Evelyn White. 2 Vols.
BOETHIUS: TRACTS AND DE CONSOLATIONE PHILOSO PHIAE. Rev. H. F. Stewart and E. K. Band.
CAESAR: CIVIL WARS. A. G. Peskett. (*2nd Imp.*)
CAESAR: GALLIC WAR. H. J. Edwards. (*3rd Imp.*)
CATULLUS. F. W. Cornish; TIBULLUS. J. P. Postgate; and PERVIGILIUM VENERIS. J. W. Mackail. (*7th Imp.*)
CICERO: DE FINIBUS. H. Rackham. (*2nd Imp.*)
CICERO: DE OFFICIIS. Walter Miller. (*2nd Imp.*)
CICERO: DE SENECTUTE, DE AMICITIA, DE DIVINATIONE. W. A. Falconer.
CICERO: LETTERS TO ATTICUS. E. O. Winstedt. 3 Vols. (Vol. I, *3rd Imp.* Vols. II and III, *2nd Imp.*)
CICERO: PRO ARCHIA POETA, POST REDITUM IN SENATU POST REDITUM AD QUIRITES, DE DOMO SUA, DE HARUSPICUM RESPONSIS, PRO PLANCIO. N. H. Watts.
CLAUDIAN. M. Platnauer. 2 Vols.
CONFESSIONS OF ST. AUGUSTINE. W. Watts (1631). 2 Vols. (*3rd Imp.*)
FRONTINUS, STRATEGEMATA AND DE AQUIS. C. E. Bennett.
FRONTO: CORRESPONDENCE. C. R. Haines. 2 Vols.
HORACE: ODES AND EPODES. C. E. Bennett. (*6th Imp.*)
JUVENAL AND PERSIUS. G. G. Ramsay. (*2nd Imp.*)
LIVY. B. O. Poster. 13 Vols. Vols. I, II and III. (Vol. I, *2nd Imp.*)
LUCRETIUS. W. H. D. Rouse.
MARTIAL. W. C. Ker. 2 Vols.
OVID: HEROIDES AND AMORES. Grant Showerman. (*2nd Imp.*)
OVID: METAMORPHOSES. F. J. Miller. 2 Vols. (*3rd Imp.*)
OVID: TRISTIA AND EX PONTO. A. L. Wheeler.
PETRONIUS. M. Heseltine; SENECA: APOCOLOCYNTOSIS. W. H. D. Rouse. (*6th Imp.*)
PLAUTUS. Paul Nixon. 5 Vols. Vols. I—III. (Vol. I *2nd Imp.*)
PLINY: LETTERS. Melmoth's Translation revised by W. M. L. Hutchinson. 2 Vols. (*2nd Imp.*)
PROPERTIUS. H. E. Butler. (*3rd Imp.*)
QUINTILIAN. H. E. Butler. 4 Vols.
SCRIPTORES HISTORIAE AUGUSTAE. D. Magie. 4 Vols. Vols. I and II
SALLUST. J. C. Rolfe.
SENECA: EPISTULAE MORALES. R. M. Gummere. 3 Vols. Vols. I and II. (*2nd Imp.*)
SENECA: TRAGEDIES. F. J. Miller. 2 Vols. (*2nd Imp.*)
SUETONIUS. J. C. Rolfe. 2 Vols. (*3rd Imp.*)

Latin Authors.

(Continued.)

TACITUS: DIALOGUS, Sir Wm. Peterson: and AGRICOLA AND
GERMANIA. Maurice Hutton. (3rd Imp.)

TERENCE. John Sargeaunt. 2 Vols. (4th Imp.)

VELLEIUS PATERCULUS AND RES GESTAE DIVI AUGUSTI.
F. W. Shipley.

VIRGIL. H. R. Fairclough. 2 Vols. (Vol. I, 4h Imp. Vol. II, 3rd
Imp.)

Greek Authors.

AENEAS TACTICUS, ASCLEPIODOTUS AND ONASANDER.
The Illinois Club.

ACHILLES TATIUS. S. Gaselee.

AESCHINES. C. D. Adams.

AESCHYLUS. H. Weir Smyth. 2 Vols. Vol. I.

APOLLODORUS. Sir James G. Frazer. 2 Vols.

APOLLONIUS RHODIUS. R. C. Seaton. (3rd Imp.)

THE APOSTOLIC FATHERS. Kirsopp Lake. 2 Vols. (Vol. I,
4th Imp. Vol. II, 3rd Imp.)

APPIAN'S ROMAN HISTORY. Horace White. 4 Vols.

ARISTOPHANES. Benjamin Bickley Rogers. 3 Vols. [G. R. Mair.

CALLIMACHUS AND LYCOPHRON. A. W. Mair; and ARATUS.

CLEMENT OF ALEXANDRIA. Rev. G. W. Butterworth.

DAPHNIS AND CHLOE. Thornley's Translation revised by J. M.
Edmonds; and PARTHENIUS. S. Gaselee. (2nd Imp.)

DIO CASSIUS: ROMAN HISTORY. E. Cary. 9 Vols. Vols. I to
VII.

EURIPIDES. A. S. Way. 4 Vols. (Vols. I and II, 4th Imp. Vol.
III, 2nd Imp. Vol. IV, 3rd Imp.)

GALEN: ON THE NATURAL FACULTIES. A J. Brock.

THE GREEK ANTHOLOGY. W. R. Paton. 5 Vols. (Vols. I and
III, 2nd Imp. Vol. II, 3rd Imp.)

THE GREEK BUCOLIC POETS (THEOCRITUS, BION, MOS-
CHUS). J. M. Edmonds. (4th Imp.)

HERODOTUS. A. D. Godley. 4 Vols.

HESIOD AND THE HOMERIC HYMNS. H. G. Evelyn White.
(2nd Imp.)

HIPPOCRATES. W. H. S. Jones. 4 Vols. Vols. I and II.

HOMER: ILIAD. A. T. Murray. 2 Vols.

HOMER: ODYSSEY. A. T. Murray. 2 Vols. (2nd Imp.)

JULIAN. Wilmer Cave Wright. 3 Vols.

LUCIAN. A. M. Harmon. 8 Vols. Vols. I to IV. (Vols. I and II,
2nd Imp.)

LYRA GRAECA. J. M. Edmonds. 3 Vols. Vols. 1 and II.

MARCUS AURELIUS. C. R. Haines. (2nd Imp.)

MENANDER. F. G. Allinson.

PAUSANIAS: DESCRIPTION OF GREECE. W. H. S. Jones. 5
Vols. and Companion Vol. Vol. 1.

PHILOSTRATUS: THE LIFE OF APOLLONIUS OF TYANA.
F. C. Conybeare. 2 Vols. (2nd Imp.)

PHILOSTRATUS AND EUNAPIUS, LIVES OF THE SOPHISTS.
Wilmer Cave Wright.

Greek Authors.

(Continued.)

PINDAR. Sir J. E. Sandys. (*3rd Imp.*)

PLATO: EUTHYPHRO. APOLOGY, CRITO, PRAEDO, PHAEDRUS. H. N. Fowler. (*4th Imp.*)

PLATO: LACHES, PROTAGRAS, MENO, EUTHYDEMUS. W. R. M. Lamb.

PLATO: POLITICUS AND PHILEBUS. H. N. Fowler. ION. W. R. M. Lamb.

PLATO: THEAETETUS AND SOPHIST. H. N. Fowler. [to X.

PLUTARCH: THE PARALLEL LIVES. B. Perrin. 11 Vols. Vols. I

POLYBIUS. W. R. Paton. 6 Vols. Vols. I to IV.

PROCOPIUS: HISTORY OF THE WARS. H. B. Dewing. 7 Vols. Vols. I to IV.

QUINTUS SMYRNAEUS. A. S. Way.

SOPHOCLES. F. Storr. 2 Vols. (Vol. I, *4th Imp.* Vol. II, *3rd Imp.*)

ST. JOHN DAMASCENE: BARLAAM AND IOASAPH. Rev. G. R. Woodward and Harold Mattingly.

STRABO: GEOGRAPHY. Horace L. Jones. 8 Vols. Vols. I to III.

THEOPHRASTUS: ENQUIRY INTO PLANTS. Sir Arthur Hort,

THUCYDIDES. C. F. Smith. 4 Vols. [Bart. 2 Vols.

XENOPHON: CYROPAEDIA. Walter Miller. 2 Vols.

XENOPHON: HELLENICA, ANABASIS, APOLOGY, AND SYMPOSIUM. C. L. Brownson and O. J. Todd. 3 Vols.

XENOPHON: MEMORABILIA OECONOMICUS. E. C. Marchant.

XENOPHON: SCRIPTA MINORA. E. C. Marchant.

IN PREPARATION

Greek Authors.

ARISTOTLE, NICOMACHEAN ETHICS, H. Rackham.

ARISTOTLE, ORGANON, W. M. L. Hutchinson.

ARISTOTLE, PHYSICS, Rev. P. Wicksteed.

ARISTOTLE, POETICS AND LONGINUS, W. Hamilton Fyfe.

ARISTOTLE, POLITICS AND ATHENIAN CONSTITUTION, Edward Capps.

ARISTOTLE, RHETORIC, J. Freese.

ATHENAEUS, C. B. Gulick.

DEMOSTHENES, DE CORONA AND DE FALSA LEGATIONE, C. A. Vince and J. H. Vince.

DEMOSTHENES: OLYNTHIACS, PHILIPPICS, LEPTINES AND MINOR SPEECHES, J. H. Vince.

DEMOSTHENES, PRIVATE ORATIONS, G. M. Calhoun.

DIO CHRYSOSTOM, W. E. Waters.

DIOGENES, LAERTIUS, R. D. Hicks.

EPICTETUS, W. A. Oldfather.

EUSEBIUS, Kirsopp Lake.

GREEK IAMBIC AND ELEGIAC POETS. E. D. Perry.

ISAEUS, E. W. Forster.

ISOCRATES, G. Norlin.

Greek Authors.

(Continued.)

JOSEPHUS, H. St. J. Thackeray.
MANETHO, S. de Bicci.
PAPYRI, A. S. Hunt.
PHILOSTRATUS, IMAGINES, Arthur Fairbanks.
PLATO, CRATYLUS, PARMENIDES, HIPPIAS MAIOR, HIPPIAS MINOR, H. N. Fowler.
PLATO, LAWS, R. G. Bury
PLATO, LYSIS, SYMPOSIUM, GORGIAS, W. R. M. Lamb.
PLATO, MENEXENUS, ALCIBIADES I and II, ERASTAI, THEAGES, CHARMIDES, MINOS, EPINOMIS, W. R. M. Lamb.
PLATO, REPUBLIC, Paul Shorey.
PLUTARCH, MORALIA, F. C. Babbitt.
ST. BASIL, LETTERS, R. J. Deferrari.
SEXTUS EMPIRICUS, A. C Pearson.
THEOPHRASTUS, CHARACTERS, J. M. Edmonds; HERODAS; HIEROCLES PHILOGELOS; CHOLIAMBIC FRAGMENTS; CEREIDES NAUMACHIS; SOTADES, etc., A. D. Knox.

Latin Authors.

AULUS GELLIUS, J. C. Rolfe.
BEDE. ECCLESIASTICAL HISTORY, Rev. H. F. Stewart.
CICERO, AD FAMILIARES, W. Glyn Williams.
CICERO, IN CATILINAM, PRO MURENA, PRO FLACCO, PRO SULLA, B. L. Ullman.
CICERO, DE NATURA DEORUM, H. Rackham.
CICERO, DE ORATORE' ORATOR, BRUTUS, Charles Stuttaford.
CICERO, DE REPUBLICA AND DE LEGIBUS, Clinton Keyes.
CICERO, PHILIPPICS, W. C. Kerr.
CICERO, PRO CAECINA, PRO LEGE MANILIA, PRO CLUENTIO, PRO RABIRIO, H. Grose Hodge.
CICERO, TUSCULAN DISPUTATIONS, J. King.
CICERO, IN VERREM, L. H. G. Greenwood.
HORACE, EPISTLES AND SATIRES, H. R. Fairclough.
LUCAN, J. D. Duff.
OVID, FASTI, Sir J. G. Frazer.
PLINY, NATURAL HISTORY, W. H. S. Jones and L. F. Newman.
ST. AUGUSTINE, MINOR WORKS, Rev. P. Wicksteed.
SENECA, MORAL ESSAYS, J. W. Basore.
SIDONIUS, LETTERS, E. V. Arnold.
STATIUS, I. H. Mozley.
TACITUS, ANNALS, John Jackson.
TACITUS, HISTORIES, C. H. Moore.
VALERIUS FLACCUS, A. F. Scholfield.

DESCRIPTIVE PROSPECTUS ON APPLICATION

London - - WILLIAM HEINEMANN, LTD.
New York - - - - G. PUTNAM'S SONS